READ ALL ABOUT IT!

THE COLLECTED ADVENTURES OF A MAVERICK REPORTER

SIDNEY ZION

SUMMIT BOOKS
NEW YORK

Published by SUMMIT BOOKS
A Simon & Schuster Division of Gulf & Western Corporation
Simon & Schuster Building
Rockefeller Center
1230 Avenue of the Americas
New York, New York 10020

SUMMIT BOOKS and colophon are trademarks of Simon & Schuster
Designed by Irving Perkins Associates
Manufactured in the United States of America

10   9   8   7   6   5   4   3   2   1

FIRST EDITION

Library of Congress Cataloging in Publication Data
Zion, Sidney, date.
  Read all about it!

  I. Title.
PN4874.Z5A25   1982   814'.54   82-10819
ISBN 0-671-43458-6

Grateful acknowledgment is made to the following for permission to reprint the articles listed:

"The Suspect Confesses—But Who Believes Him?" May, 16, 1965; "Legal Rights in Inquest," September 3, 1969; "The Troubled World of Mike Burke," October 9, 1977; "A Decade of Constitutional Revision," November 11, 1979; "High Court vs. The Press," November 18, 1979; "Outlasting Rock," June 21, 1981; "Genesis, Rewritten," July 31, 1981 © 1965, 1969, 1977, 1979, 1981 by The New York Times Company. Reprinted by permission.

Continued on page 363

HATS OFF!

To my Alma Mater: Ben Hecht, Charles MacArthur, H. L. Mencken, Damon Runyon, Ring Lardner, Dorothy Parker, Red Smith, Jimmy Cannon, John McNulty, A. J. Liebling, Walter Winchell, Dan Parker, William O. Douglas, Hugo Black, Fred Rodell, Lorenz Hart, Johnny Mercer. All of them gone, but as John O'Hara said when Gershwin got away, I don't have to believe it if I don't want to.

The newspapermen, artists, gangsters, judges and lawyers who remain quick are acknowledged inside—occasionally with the back of my hand.

Alvin Davis, who gave me my first newspaper job, gets special mention here because he died shortly after the manuscript was delivered. I kick him around plenty, and I'm mad as hell that he won't get a chance to read all about it. This isn't entirely mean-spirited. I know Al, and he'd have enjoyed the raps.

A friend in need may indeed be a pain in the ass, but that's not how Victor Temkin looks at life. My stateliest bow to the best foul-weather friend in the world.

The families of newspaper people do not live like other civilians. For surviving the Life and making it cushy for me, love and kisses to Elsa and the kids—Libby, Adam, and Jed, in order of appearance.

Of course, none of this would have happened but for my grandma, who taught me never to feel sorry for anyone with more money than I have.

To Annie, my author, who always wants to see my name in the papers.

And in memory of the Doc, who slipped out of my arms in April 1982. Pushing 81.

CONTENTS

INTRODUCTION

WHEN I TRIED criminal cases as a kid lawyer in New Jersey, I noticed that my clients had certain things in common. All of them were broke, all of them were innocent, and when asked how come the cops put the grab on them, they all said: "I dunno, I wasn't doin' nothin'—I was just standin' around."

I give the same answer to people who wonder how I got to be a newspaperman.

Late on a December night in 1962, a phone call caught me at a party in Manhattan. It was Victor Navasky, an old pal from Yale Law School. Would I write a fast 750 words for a parody edition of the *New York Post* that Vic was about to deliver to the empty newsstands of the city?

New York was at the shank of what turned out to be the longest newspaper strike in its history. Navasky, always scheming for money to keep afloat *Monocle*, the political satire sheet he invented at Yale in the late 1950s, saw a way to score on the strike. The *New York Pest* was the ticket, he said, and I was the only guy to parody the great columnist Murray Kempton.

"You can do it in an hour," Victor said.

"When do you need it?"

"In two hours."

I hung up and went back to Johnnie Walker.

But Navasky, as unrelenting then as he is now as editor of *The Nation*, called again, and when I hung up he called again and then another time, until finally the hostess slipped an Olivetti in front of my drink and said do it or the party's over. I wrote it in half an hour, caroused some more, and dropped it off at the *Monocle* office right on deadline.

Had I known better, I'd have taken much longer to do a piece like that—or any other piece. But I had never written for a newspaper, and except for a couple of stories in the early *Monocles*, nothing at all for publication.

Even so, it never occurred to me to wonder why Navasky asked me to do Kempton. I was a newspaper buff, Navasky knew that, and

Kempton was one of my heroes and Navasky knew that too. What I didn't know was that Victor hadn't thought of any of this until he'd gone to half the reporters in town for the Kempton job. After they came up empty, he tapped the *Monocle* secretarial pool. Like all great editors, Navasky has the knack of making you feel that nobody else can deliver the goods, which is the knack of lying your ass off.

Anyhow, the Kempton parody was a great big hit, although I didn't know it for a month. What happened was I got married a couple of days after I wrote it and did a honeymoon in Mexico. When I got back to my office—at this point I was an assistant United States attorney in Newark—I found a stack of messages from Alvin Davis, the managing editor of the *New York Post.*

It scared me. What did Davis want and how did he know who I was? The piece didn't have my name on it, just a pseudonym. I must have rubbed somebody wrong at the *Post* and now I'd be in hot water with the Justice Department. Bobby Kennedy was my ultimate boss and he was close to Dolly Schiff, the *Post* publisher; what the hell had Navasky done to me?

"Davis wants to *hire* you," Navasky said. "He loves the piece, they all love it. Kempton says he's sure *he* wrote it. Jules Feiffer sent a note saying it was the best parody he ever read. You should call Al Davis right now, and then do it, take the job, it'll change your life."

I was too stunned to be flattered. Change my life? But I liked the way I was living. My ambition was to become a great trial lawyer, and after four years at the bar I thought I was on my way. Juries had been good to me; I was as comfortable in the courtroom as in my kitchen. I had tried scores of cases before hooking up with the government, and I figured in a year or so I'd go back to private practice, only this time my innocent clients would come in with plenty of whip-out. I'd be crazy to walk away for anything, much less an industry still on strike with bust-out written all over its future. Plus, I was twenty-nine years old, which in the newspaper game meant at best young veteran, surely not rookie.

Of course, I dismissed the idea. Of course, ten minutes later I called Al Davis. The secret Navasky spotted was that I wanted to be Ben Hecht long before I wanted to be Clarence Darrow.

The city room of the *Post* was a portrait in grime, its windows smoked up like a leftover speak-easy, its walls a backdrop for dustbins, the desks gouty as an old sailor. Right out of Ben Hecht's typewriter, and the typewriters out of the set of *The Front Page*. I fell in love with the joint straightaway.

Al Davis, however, was anything but Central Casting—unless you were casting *The Asphalt Jungle*. Balding, heavyset, hyper-eyed, Davis looked like a dress manufacturer in the off-season. His clippy delivery, supporting a street-smart argot, backed up this image, which didn't bother me at all. In fact I liked it. Davis reminded me of my cousins from Passaic, my hometown. Like them, he was in his late thirties, and like them he looked at least ten years older. They talked tough but smiled warm—and so did Al Davis.

After the strike, Davis said, the *Post* would be a different paper. It was going to establish a major investigative unit that would expose corruption top to bottom. "We'll break the town wide open," he said. The things everybody knew but nobody printed—mob-connected lawyers, legislators, and judges, Harlem numbers banks and Wall Street bankers—name the scam and the *New York Post* would nail the scammer.

I was the guy who could do it, Davis said. It was the perfect combination: I could write and I was a federal prosecutor. The *Post* would back me all the way—a big staff, an ample expense account, and not to worry, they'd groom me, Davis himself would teach me the ropes.

That was the pitch, only it didn't come as quickly as I make it sound. Davis probed like an internist, and I belched out one after another story about the mob-politico scene in Jersey. Most of it was hearsay, the stuff that came with mother's milk in the Garden State, but some was the McCoy, which I learned from hanging around FBI agents and other action factions. Davis was throwing back his inside dope as fast as I gave mine, and if you were a fly on the wall you wouldn't know who was interviewing whom. A pretty good double con job is what it amounted to, though I doubt that either of us thought of it that way.

Paul Sann joined us after a while, and he clearly knew what was happening. Sann was the executive editor, the boss, a wiry little guy with a sidesaddle manner, a perfect tintype of the tabloid newspaperman. He sat down with a bottle of bourbon, poured us each a paper cup's worth and listened laconically as Davis blueprinted the plans for the morrow.

"We've only been trying to get that stuff for thirty years," Sann said. "But maybe your boy here has the key." Then, looking at me for the first time, he said, "Being a lawyer, I don't have to tell you we don't have subpoena power in this business. Last I heard, you guys weren't putting the slam on too many judges and pols with your subpoenas and grand juries. But I'm always willing to learn."

Davis tried to laugh it away, but I said, "I don't have a key; I don't even know where the keyhole is."

Sann's response was midway between a grin and a grimace, which was about as good as I'd ever get from him. I don't remember what he said after that, only that he stuck around for about a half-hour, refilling the cups and acting as if he didn't give a shit.

When he walked away, bottle in hand, Davis said, "Don't worry about Paul, he likes to play the cynic. But he's behind everything I said."

I wasn't worried about Paul, I was worried about my bride. The night we met, she told me, "Thank God you're not a writer." She was a graduate of Bard College and so knew more than an elegant sufficiency of the genre. Now I was about to commit a consumer fraud on her.

I told Davis about this a week later, over dinner in a Little Italy mob joint. He laughed, thought it was cute, but I thought it was grounds for annulment. "Tell her you're only trying it out," he said. "And you won't be lying. Both of us have three months to decide— that's union rules. Get the Justice Department to give you a leave of absence. I wouldn't expect you to come here any other way. I'd feel too responsible."

Strangely, I hadn't thought of doing it like that. But obviously it was the perfect solution. If I could get a leave, I'd have nothing to lose, right? My wife couldn't complain about nothing to lose. But would they give me the leave?

Well they did, though they said I was nuts, and she didn't bitch, though I knew she thought I was nuts.

And that's how I got into the newspaper game. All it took was for every paper in New York to be shut down.

The Israelis have a story for American Jews who make *aliyah*, who move to the Promised Land for keeps. It's about a man who dies and is given his choice of heaven or hell. He looks around heaven and sees everyone sitting on clouds, picking on harps. The Devil escorts him downstairs and the joint is jumping—feasts, orgies, le jazz hot.

He goes to limbo to think it over, but it's no contest, he chooses hell. When he gets back down he's immediately tossed into the fires.

"What's going on?" he screams to the Devil. "You showed me wine, women, and song—what happened to all that?"

The Devil says, "Ah, but then you were a tourist."

I reported for work at the *New York Post* on a sunny April morning in 1963, got a nod and a grunt from Al Davis—and that's all I got, from him or anyone else. Nobody introduced me around, nobody gave me a desk; I stood there counting my fingers while copy boys whizzed by and reporters buzzed on the phones. At the lunch break I caught Davis' eye, but he ignored me and walked into a back room with a couple of editors. Go figure *this* out, I said to myself. Then, as now, when I say that to myself I find the nearest bar.

After a couple of martinis things looked brighter. It was, after all, a special day at the *Post.* For a month, the paper had owned the city; Dolly Schiff had broken with the Publishers' Association and made a separate deal with the unions, so the *Post* was on the streets by itself. Now, this very day, the *Times,* the *Daily News,* the *Herald Tribune,* the *World-Telegram & Sun,* the *Daily Mirror,* and the *Journal-American* were back for the first time. No wonder Al Davis had no time for me, of course.

I could have come to the paper in March, but I was committed to a trial. This wasn't Davis' fault, so said the Beefeater, and indeed he'd been terrific about it, so said the second Beefeater. I went back feeling guilty.

By five o'clock I was despondent. Davis hadn't said a word to me all afternoon; I was still standing around, feeling more like a dummy every hour-long minute. Finally he waved me over. "See you tomorrow," he said. And looked down at his work.

The next morning was more of the same. This time, however, the drinking lunch had a different impact. I went back determined to tell Davis to shove the joint, I didn't sign up for Chinese tortures. Whether he saw it in my eyes when I walked in, I don't know, but before I could reach his desk he was out of his seat with his arm around me.

"It's been crazy here," he said. "Tomorrow we'll send you over to the courthouse and the police shack and the next day you'll go to Brooklyn. I want you to see how things work outside. By next week we'll get you going. How are you, are you all right?"

I said, "Who do you have to fuck to get a desk around here?"

Innocent as a babe, Davis said, "You mean these dumb bastards had you standing around all the time? Why didn't you tell me?" He whistled up a copy boy and told him to set me up. "Give him whatever he wants. You want an aisle? Yeah, you're a big guy, you need an aisle. Give him a desk on the aisle, get moving." With that, Davis took me over to meet the editors. And then said, "We'll have a drink later."

I was nonplused. Could he not have noticed me standing there sucking my thumb? Or was this some rite of passage I hadn't heard about?

After work, Davis took me to a bar around the corner, where he gave me a glowing introduction to the reporters hanging out there and reiterated all the high hopes he had for me. I drove home to Jersey high as a kite, and not just on the booze.

The next morning there was a guy sitting at my aisle desk. I tapped him politely and told him he was in my seat. "Are you for real?" he said. "The only people with desks here came with the lease. I've been around five years and I don't have one. In this joint you take what's open."

When I told this to Davis, he said, "Where the hell do you think you are, in a goddam law office? Find a place and sit down, I got work to do." I walked away, thinking why the hell wasn't I in a goddam law office, but before I could get halfway to the door, Davis called me back.

"Anyway, you're not even supposed to be here now," he said. "You forgot—or I forgot—you're going to the criminal courthouse today. Call me at about five. And don't worry—smile. I'll take care of the desk business."

I didn't realize it, but Davis was teaching me a lesson in power bureaucracy. I came with assurances of a big staff and a high-rolling future and here I was negotiating for a desk!

Anyway, I spent a week in the criminal court press rooms and at the police shack, the reporters' headquarters across the street from Police Headquarters in Manhattan. These places are the central nervous system of city news, and yet editors traditionally populate them with a mix of cubs and washed-out reporters. So this side of the metropolis is the backwater of journalism—with results we see every day in the press: handout stories delivered to gaping or cynical reporters.

Following this stint, Davis assigned me to investigate the State Liquor Authority, then the hottest scandal in town. "I know it's a tough way to get your feet wet," he said, "but there's no pressure, we don't expect anything."

A couple of days and I scored a big beat—the inside story of the Playboy Club's payoff to politicians and lawyers for a New York liquor license. I nailed it down on a Friday in an exclusive interview with Hugh Hefner.

I called Davis and gave him a fast rundown.

"Good work," he said. "Come in Monday and we'll run it Tuesday on page one."

"You're kidding," I said. "This won't hold for Tuesday, the whole town's after it. I can be there in fifteen minutes. I'll write it now, we can run it tomorrow."

"Don't tell me when we'll run a story, I tell *you* that," he said. "You're off until Monday, so you come in Monday and write it."

"But Al," I pleaded, "what if somebody else breaks it?"

"We're not doing any overtime, forget it. And don't worry, it'll hold. It sounds like a great story. Relax, have a good weekend."

"I'm not worried about overtime," I said. "I'll do it for nothing, I don't care about the money, I want the story."

"I'm not here to explain union rules to you," he said. "You'll write it on Monday for Tuesday." And he hung up.

On Monday afternoon I was touching up the piece when Johnny Bott, the city editor, dropped a late edition of the *Journal-American* on my desk. "There goes your story," Bott said. And there the bastard was, nearly word for word. My first story—blown away to a rival paper. For overtime pay I didn't want.

I went fuming over to Davis and threw the *Journal* in front of him. "So much for how it'll 'hold,' Al."

"I read it," he said. "What are you so excited about? It's our wood for tomorrow, like I told you."

"What's 'wood'?"

"The front-page headline," he said. And laughed. "There you go," he said. "You've just learned something about the newspaper business."

The next morning, festooned under an exclusive banner, was the headline: "PLAYBOY'S PAYOFF—INSIDE STORY."

Such was my welcome to Dolly's Place, the penny-candy store of the New York newspaper world. To show I wasn't singled out for the budget pinching, here are some choice samples of what I saw and heard during my twenty-two-month stint at the paper.

Nora Ephron was on her way home from work one night when shots rang out on Times Square and she saw a man fall. Nora, then twenty-one, had been hired by Al Davis off her parody of Leonard Lyons for Navasky's *Pest*. She ran to a street phone and reported the shooting to Mort Schiffer, the night city editor.

"But you're off now," Schiffer said.

"I'm standing right here," Nora said. "A man just got shot and there's a crowd around him. Don't you want me to check it out?"

"You're off now," Schiffer repeated. "Go home, we'll pick it up from the wires."

The victim turned out to be a cop. When that came up on the wires, the *Post* sent half the night staff out to find a witness. They found nothing, but so what? Better than overtime—better anytime.

Joe Kahn, the legendary investigative reporter, told me about the time he got a call from a guy who said he was about to jump off the George Washington Bridge because his girl had dumped him, but first he wanted Joe to interview him. Kahn yelled this info over to the city desk where Mort Schiffer was just taking his seat. Schiffer looked up at the clock, noticed it was after five, and said, "Ask him if he can do it tomorrow on straight time." Joe said to the guy, "My editor wants to know if you can do it tomorrow, on straight time." The guy broke up laughing. "Forget it," he said. "I can't leave a world as crazy as this." Kahn checked the wires for days, but no jumpers.

I was having lunch with a couple of reporters when somebody came in and said Jack Kennedy was shot. We zipped back to the paper, where all was quiet. We went over to the city desk and asked Johnny Bott what the latest word was on the President.

"What are you talking about?" Bott said.

"We just heard that Kennedy was shot in Dallas, Johnny."

"Look," he said, "I'm trying to put out a paper, don't bother me."

One of us turned on Bott's radio, and Johnny, who wore a leg brace, jumped up and ran to the wire room like a wide receiver. The clerk Davis had installed in the wire room held a Ph.D. in philosophy, but he wasn't too quick on the trigger. He was standing there reading some "B" copy about the Saint Lawrence Seaway, and so he didn't notice that the "A" copy was running out the door.

The bells on the "A" wire were ringing like Notre Dame on

Christmas Eve, but when asked why this didn't alert him, the Ph.D. said, "The bells are always ringing." He was right, too; every urgent bulletin activated the bells, and to the wire services a cat caught in a tree was as urgent as a cat burglar caught at the Russian embassy.

Paul Sann screamed "Stop the press," and this stopped everybody in his or her tracks. Nobody ever heard these movie lines ring out live. Sann said later that he'd waited all his life to do it, though it's doubtful the dream included nearly getting scooped on the assassination of the President. And the *Post* would have been scooped; Sann caught it just in time.

The young doctor of philosophy was barred from the wire room, but he wasn't fired. He'd always been Davis' favorite joke butt and after this Hall of Fame performance, Al wasn't about to let him go. It didn't hurt, either, that if he had been cashiered, the union would have fought it, and Mrs. Schiff would have discovered what had happened.

After the *Post* discovered that Kennedy was shot, Dolly came down to the city room from her perch on the seventeenth floor and immediately went into the conference room with her brain trust. The New York press had chartered a plane for Dallas, but once it was announced that Kennedy was dead, the *Post* decided there was no point in sending a reporter down there. They could pick it up from the wires, what the hell.

When Jack Ruby killed Lee Harvey Oswald, there were second thoughts. And third, fourth, and fifth thoughts. The late Normand Poirier, one of the top reporters on the paper, was told to pack while they had sixth thoughts. Finally, they shipped Normand to Dallas— and he arrived there in time to catch everybody on the way back to New York.

Despite the Playboy Club fiasco, I was pretty well hooked by seeing my name in wood, and I got hooked harder a few days later when I broke out again on the front page with a State Liquor Authority story nobody could snatch. Two on One, right out of the gate, was heady stuff, and I remember thinking if I quit now I could retire undefeated.

But I wasn't going to quit; I was sure I'd never quit. I had taken some crap, but so what? Wherever you work there's crap; I had taken plenty in the U.S. attorney's office and before that from judges and clients. True, I didn't expect to find bureaucracy and careerism in the newsroom, but I put this off as naiveté. What made me think there'd be purity here—just the fact that nobody in his right mind would be in it for the money?

A press card, unlike a lawyer's license—or anything else—provided a front-row seat to the lively doings of the world; it was an entree to everything, including the shadows. And when you got the story, you didn't go home and tell your wife and friends, you printed it, right out there for all to read, under your own byline. What could be better than that?

Of course, I hadn't yet been exposed to the dirtiest secret of journalism: Self-Censorship. Soon I would be, soon enough.

I stayed with the liquor scandal for several weeks and broke some good stories, which pleased Davis so much he found me a desk and told me I'd "made it"; he was cutting short the three-month tryout period.

Joe Kahn said, "Kiddo, you're riding high, let's talk." Joe had been looking into the financing of Robert Moses' World's Fair, set to open the following spring, and he'd found enough hot stuff to keep me listening a good hour.

"How come I haven't read any of this in the paper?" I said.

Joe smiled and said, "I've been doing this on my own, kiddo. They don't want it from me anymore; I'm from the old regime. Davis and Sann are out to create their own heroes. That's why I'm talking to you. If you'd be in interested in working with me, they might let me ride your star."

Joe Kahn had won nearly every prize in the business. He'd picked up a slew of them a couple of years before when he (together with William Haddad) forced Robert Moses, the Great Builder, to resign a state job, something nobody had ever done before. But that happened while James Wechsler was the top editor at the *Post*. Wechsler had since been kicked up to the editorial page, and Joe Kahn was now shit-listed.

"You're supposed to ride *my* star?" I said. "That's crazy. I'm embarrassed to think about it, no less ask those guys to have you work with me."

"Don't let it worry you," Joe said. "I'm coming to you, remember that."

A couple of weeks later, when the liquor scandal petered out, Sann and Davis asked me what I wanted to do next. I said the World's Fair, with Joe Kahn. They said the idea was a good one but that

Kahn had a "hard-on" for Moses, and it was important to be "objective." I should think of another partner, they said, strongly implying that, in any event, Joe was over the hill. I told them that Kahn had already done a ton of great spade work, that it was his idea, that it wouldn't be right to do it without him. Finally, they said okay.

Joe was overjoyed; you'd think I'd given him the Hope diamond. I was to find out that the best reporters always react that way to the smell of a great story. The tony types want to cover big stories; the pure newspapermen and women want to uncover them. Joe Kahn was the purest reporter I ever met.

Shortly after we began digging, a hint of scandal surrounding the financing of one of the pavilions at the fair broke in one of the gossip columns. Joe and I found the key figure, a young man, at his hotel in Manhattan and kept him in his suite all afternoon. He told us a hair-raising story, complete with threats of blackmail and physical injury. He was involved as a kind of front for the pavilion, and, according to his account, some of the sleazoids who had used him wanted him out. One of them, he said, had hit him over the head with a candelabra.

Reporters from all the other papers kept calling his suite, so I wrote a noncommittal statement for him to read to them—which managed to keep them at bay. Meanwhile, since his tale was so sensational, I put it into affidavit form and had him sign it. Further, we insisted on witnesses, and he provided a couple. Then, with the affidavit, the witnesses, and the front man in hand, we all went down to the *Post.*

Joe Kahn stayed in the corridor with them while I bitched at Al Davis. As expected, Davis said he couldn't run a story like this without a sworn affidavit, at the least. I showed him the affidavit. Davis then said he'd have to meet the young man. I went out and brought him and the witnesses in. Davis cross-examined them all and then took Joe and me aside. "Come in tomorrow and write it," he said.

Late the next morning, I got a phone call from Bob Schwartz, a lawyer I'd recently met in connection with the liquor scandal. Schwartz was a wonderfully colorful character who always operated on the cutting edge of disbarment, not to say indictment. "Let me take you to lunch," he said. I told him I couldn't; I was working on a story for deadline.

Schwartz said, "You're working on the fair pavilion kid, you were with him at the hotel all yesterday. Come have lunch."

"How the hell do you know that?" I said.

"I know more," he said. "The story's been killed. Somebody talked to Paul Sann. Forget about it, don't waste your time, it ain't making the paper."

"Who talked to Sann, what the hell do you mean by that?"

"Meet me for lunch, I'll tell you," he said.

"Bobby," I said, "I'm going to finish this piece no matter what you say. And I think you're full of shit."

"The piece won't see daylight," he laughed, and I hung up.

Schwartz was the kind of guy who'd know such things, and I was plenty worried. I took Joe Kahn into a corner and told him about it. Joe said, "Don't let it trouble you, kiddo. I know Bob Schwartz, I know a million like him. He's got an angle, he always has an angle. Keep working, the story will run, nobody got to anybody around here."

I wrote it, Davis loved it, and it was passed by the *Post*'s lawyers. It would be wood tomorrow.

I walked into the office in the morning, picked up the paper, and it wasn't wood—it wasn't in the paper at all. Davis, seeing me turning the pages, called out: "I didn't kill it, Paul did."

I must have registered plenty of shock, because Davis immediately tried to back off. "It's not killed, I didn't mean killed," he said. "We're just going to hold it off—we want you to make it part of a series. If you get enough, we'll run it for two weeks."

"You mean it's too good to run alone, we'd be wasting it if we published now?"

"Now you got it, that's right." Davis smiled.

"Al, I had no idea you took me for *this* kind of schmuck," I said, and walked away. I could hear him yelling "Zion, you're wrong" as I left the city room.

Joe Kahn caught me at the elevator and said, "Now don't get excited, let's have coffee."

Joe said he knew how bad it looked, but I shouldn't jump to conclusions. I said I wasn't jumping to conclusions, I was jumping ship. No, no, Joe said—a series wasn't the worst thing in the world; we'd do it and we'd get it in the paper.

"You know how cheap they are," he said. "A series like this will cost them a fortune. We're not doing a welfare story, we're going to be taking people to all the best bars and restaurants. If they really wanted to kill us off they'd cancel us out, they're not ashamed. Believe me, kiddo, they wouldn't bother in a million years if they didn't mean to print it."

"How do you explain Bob Schwartz's call?"

"I said I knew it looked bad," he answered. "But even so I don't believe Schwartz. I think it was a coincidence—he threw a line out and got lucky. Anyway it doesn't matter, you just got a commitment from the managing editor that the piece will run later, in the series."

It was no more persuasive then than it sounds now, nearly twenty years later. But *Joey* was persuasive; there was something catching about his optimism. Then again, he was in the same boat—why would he want to break his ass on a series only to see it deep-sixed? It got down to whether he knew more about the paper than I did, and he'd only been there since the early forties. All right, you crazy bastard, let's try it, I said. You don't have to be Dr. Freud to figure out that I sure wasn't looking to go back to the U.S. attorney's office.

There is a serious disadvantage in doing an investigative report in one lump—as a prewritten series—rather than dropping the stories in the paper as you get them. If you run it when you have it you attract sources—they come out of the woodwork—simply because they know you're after the scoundrels. Do it the other way and you attract the apprehension of the scoundrels without getting anything in return. The word gets around inside within hours; what you don't have are the others, who may know plenty, only they didn't know you were after it. In an iceberg story like the World's Fair, the last thing a reporter needs are extra weights.

During the six weeks we worked on the fair story, Joe and I occasionally tried to convince our editors that we had something too hot to hold, in the hope that we could, by printing one story, draw on the woodwork. One time we were certain they wouldn't turn us down.

Robert Moses had been dodging us; he never took our calls and he wouldn't show up at press conferences or at parties hailing the various pavilions planned for the fair. But we had a hunch he'd turn up at the bash for the Spanish Pavilion. Would Moses miss out on anything connected with Francisco Franco?

Sure enough, there he was, and Joe Kahn cornered him.

"Joe, how are you, my boy?" Moses said.

"Not so good, Mr. Moses."

"What's the matter, my boy?"

"Just haven't been able to reach you, so I'm depressed."

"Can't reach *me?* I'm always available to you, Joe, anytime. Are you saying you tried to call me? I never knew that."

"I call every day, like clockwork."

"Those guys around me never told me. What can I do for you? Anything you want."

"I want to see your books."

"Oh, is that all you want," Moses said. "Well how about this?" He pulled his pants pockets out. "You want this too?"

"Just the books, Mr. Moses."

"Who's the kid?" Moses said, pointing to me. Joe introduced us and Moses said, "Maybe you want something too—what do you want?"

"I want to know whether you're really going to give the city all those millions out of the fair's profits for education." I said.

This had been the big promise of the fair; not only would it bring tremendous business into the city, it would recompense the government for its large expenditures many times over by turning most of the profits over to education. The line had been accepted without question by the newspapers.

Moses looked at me quizzically for a second and then said, "Kid, the only thing the city's going to get out of this is a park. My park, in Flushing Meadows. I'll build it and that's what they'll get. Nothing more."

Moses' flack tried to stop him. "What the commissioner means . . ." he said. But Moses interrupted. "Keep out of this," he said. "I don't need you to tell me what to say."

He turned back to me. "Did you get it straight?" he said. "Just a park, that's it. Now let's get a drink."

We got drinks and Moses kept talking; he was clearly having a ball.

"Not a nickel for education, that's all baloney," he said. "A park, *my* park, and that's that." Savoring it, he paused, and then added: "Now you go back and tell that old bitch you work for that Robert Moses says he's gonna give nothing to education. Tell her that and tell her to print it—I don't give a damn what she prints in that rag of hers. And tell her I said *that,* too. You got everything you want now?"

"How about the books, Mr. Moses?" Joe Kahn said.

"I thought you only wanted my pockets, Joe," Moses said, and walked away.

We rushed back to the paper and put everything Moses said into a memo. Al Davis read it and handed it back to us, without a word. We stood by his desk, looking at each other. Davis paid no attention, just shuffled copy. Finally, Joe said, "Well, what do you think, Al?"

"It's good. Put it in the series."

"But Al," Joe said, "lookit what he's done here. He's repudiated his promise to the city, and he's putting it right to the publisher. Don't you think we ought to go with it tonight?"

"Don't be an editor," Davis said. "We'll run it in the series."

The series was dynamite; we had the fair taped. It would be a financial and cultural disaster, we said, and we backed everything with the best documentation. The *Post* lawyers quickly cleared it for libel.

"You're home free," Davis told us. "I told you not to worry. It's terrific."

"When will it run, Al?" I asked.

"Soon. No more than two weeks."

Two weeks went by. And then three weeks. So?

"Soon," Davis said.

Meanwhile, Joe and I had no assignments; we were spending the days in bars. I said to Joey, "If we were smart enough to get the story, how come we can't find out why they're not using it?"

We slipped off our bar stools and into the advertising department. Where we found a huge layout headlined: "Come to the Fair."

The advertising director was at his usual haunt the next afternoon. I sidled up to him at the bar. I said nothing, I simply stared at him. He looked down at his martini. And said, "Sorry, kid, it's a hundred grand."

The World's Fair was a bust-out. Everything we predicted came true, and then some. Hundreds of millions were lost; the place became a synonym for bankruptcy. All of which had been missed or ignored by the press, whose boosterism contributed shamelessly to the debacle. Joe Kahn and I had the drop on it, but the spike won out.

I stayed at the *Post* for more than a year after the fair series was killed. I used to think it was stubbornness that kept me there, a refusal to concede defeat. Looking back through the not-so-dim corridors, however, I see now that the young man spinning his wheels in that old city room was in love, head over heels for the newspaper game. In such condition, every kick in the teeth was nothing but a chuck on the chin. The girl was for me—she just didn't know it yet.

Romantic? Of course romantic. *Romance*, for chrissake. How else explain why I took one after another studied slight, smiling all the time, coming back for more? I didn't need the job; to the contrary, hardly a week went by without an unsolicited offer from a law firm. I loved the law, sure, but as the songwriter wrote, oh you kid!

I built a dream on every kiss. Sent out to do a profile of Duke Ellington, I'd be juiced up enough to suffer a month of interviews with half-assed statesmen, vapid civic leaders, and two-dollar politicians. A good tough series on the loan sharks kept me cheery during the ensuing dull days talking to right-wing Bible-toters. The original promise of a major investigative unit was forgotten, of course, but in pursuit of the Goddess one is thankful for small favors.

The trouble was, the Goddess didn't live at the *Post*. She was an uptown lady. She was . . . *The New York Times*.

It happened one night while I was writing a jazz piece. A guy at the copy desk called me over and pointed to a small story in the *Times*, an announcement that Anthony Lewis was leaving the Supreme Court beat to take over the paper's London bureau. "Why don't you try to get his old job," the copy editor said.

The next morning I asked Joe Kahn what he thought, and Joe said, "It's where you belong. Let's see if we can find a good connection. You don't want to walk in there and talk to a personnel man." Joe got on the phone and within minutes he had the contact. Mort Yarmin, his wife's boss at the American Jewish Committee, was a good friend of Harrison Salisbury, one of the paper's top editors. Mort said he'd be happy to arrange for me to meet with Salisbury.

Harrison Salisbury looked more like an assistant secretary of state than an assistant managing editor. Tall and bony, his long nose set off by a bristling gray mustache, Salisbury had a patrician air that signaled trouble for me. I'm loose to a fault, and people who look like Salisbury generally disliked me on the spot. I hadn't been tense when I showed up at the *Times*, but I was now.

He was courteous, he asked serious questions, and we got along fairly well. He told me at the outset that the *Times* had hired someone to fill Tony Lewis' job. Would I be interested in something else, perhaps on the city side? I said sure. He smiled, took my clippings and said he'd be in touch. Leafing through the clips, he noticed *Post* library stamps on them. "What did you do, steal these from the morgue?" he said. "The *Post*'s copy machine is terrible," I said. His smile was sour. Fucked to open, I said to myself as I got into the elevator.

But a few days later I got a call from A. M. Rosenthal, the metropolitan editor. Salisbury had turned me over to him, he said, and if I'd like to come up we might explore some ideas.

Everybody has his own version of Abe Rosenthal. He's one of those people of whom it is said, "You either love him or hate him—in equal doses." I was always comfortable with him, even when we weren't talking.

When I met him for the first time, in the winter of 1964, he was in his early forties, a pudgy, chain-smoking energy plant with an owlish face that displayed an oddly sweet smile. We talked for an hour, but I don't remember what he said, except for the punch line: "How would you like to be the Anthony Lewis of New York?"

"I'm not sure what you mean," I said, "but I like the sound of it."

Abe said, "I'm not sure what I mean either. Why don't you think about it—why don't we both think about it—and talk next week."

We talked about it over a period of several weeks. I wrote an extensive memo setting out the sorts of legal stories the paper was missing and what I would do to fill the gaps, which were large indeed. To cite the most gaping example: The *Times* had no overview on the criminal justice system, which was then experiencing severe jolts owing to the ongoing procedural revolution forged by the Warren Court.

The memo became our working paper, and out of it Abe developed the idea of creating a new beat, which would combine hard reporting with in-depth analysis of the metropolitan legal scene, everything from the impact of an individual case to the spotting of trends. The metropolitan legal correspondent would not cover the courthouse or the district attorney's office or the police department—he'd be responsible for an overview of the system as a whole.

So far, so good, except I wasn't getting an offer. Everybody kept interviewing me, all the top editors and what seemed like half the subeditors. I was told this was par for the course, which was true to a degree, but this was going on so long it felt like the third degree. There were two reasons for it, as I was to discover. The *Times* didn't think much of the *Post*, and they didn't think much of my clips. I couldn't blame them either way.

The *Times* seldom hired anyone from the *Post*. Paul Sann tried to hook on during the newspaper strike and was turned down, although I didn't know this until much later. Nobody told me my clips were in trouble, either, but it didn't require genius to figure this out. My best stories had been killed or ruined by delays, and the heaviest pieces that made the paper were often double bylined since they were in week-long series, and the *Post* generally assigned two reporters to a series. My personality profiles showed I could write, but the *Times* wasn't hiring me for features.

I decided to do what I could about it. I talked Al Davis into letting me write a series on the United States Supreme Court. As usual, it kept getting postponed. So I delivered it to Abe Rosenthal in manuscript.

Whether that pushed me over the top I'll never know, since Abe doesn't remember it. But shortly after I gave it to him he told me to see Turner Catledge, the executive editor.

Catledge greeted me in his fine, southern gentlemanly style and said, "I just wanted to see the cut of your jib. Now go back downstairs and make sure the boys don't screw you too much on money."

I was on *The New York Times.* The goddam *New York Times!*

That night, Davis said the Supreme Court series would begin the following week. I waited to see the first article in the paper before telling him I was leaving. "I knew you'd fuck us some day," Davis said. Sann said, "They'll work your ass off there. You won't get away with the shit you pulled here. Good luck, pal, you'll need it."

I said goodbye to Mrs. Schiff, who was very gracious, who said she was glad the *Post* had helped me get my feet wet in journalism. I asked her why she killed the World's Fair series. Dolly said, "I never killed it; I never *saw* it. Why would I protect Bob Moses? That's silly, isn't it? Did they tell you downstairs that I killed it? You don't have to answer, they always say that to the reporters. But they didn't ask me. I only heard about it afterward."

I didn't believe her. Paul Sann used to say, used to *brag,* "My balls are in escrow to the seventeenth floor." That was Dolly's office, the seventeenth floor. I never imagined anyone would say a thing like that if it weren't true. On the other hand, who could believe Paul Sann? But now I didn't have to care anymore.

Sann cared enough about me to fire a final shot a couple of weeks after I joined the *Times.* At an Associated Press dinner, Sann cornered Arthur Gelb, then the deputy metropolitan editor, and told him: "Thanks for taking Zion off our backs. We'd have had the bastard on our payroll forever."

I was on tryout; I had three months to prove myself. Sann's remark upset Gelb sufficiently for him to call James Wechsler at the *Post*. Jimmy, whom I scarcely knew, told Gelb not to worry, that they had never used me properly in the city room. But nobody stopped worrying until I wrote a couple of exclusives. I made the paper in about a month, which was when I first heard what Sann had pulled. But what the hell, I had nothing to worry about now. The girl was mine; I had the right key all the time. I just killed two years working on the wrong keyhole.

Of course, without the *Post* I'd probably still be practicing law in New Jersey, whatever that may say about sine qua non. Anyway, one postscript on Paul Sann.

In the autumn of 1966, nearly two years after I had left the *Post*, I ran into Sann at the Lion's Head, my favorite Village saloon. He gave me a $500 hello. "You're going great, I'm proud of you," he said. I waited for the usual knife work. But no. He said, "There's something I never told you. I gave you a big send-off when Rosenthal and Gelb asked me about you. I told them you'd be a star. You're making me look like a fucking prophet. Keep up the good work."

I'm not one to hold my tongue, but something told me to shut up. Why waste it at a bar, just the two of us. I'd wait until another time when I could put it to him in front of newspaper people. I should have done it the usual way, because the moment never came. So Paul Sann still doesn't know that I know what he tried to do to me that night at the AP dinner.

I worked for *The New York Times* a shade under five years. An unexceptional statement if there ever was one, and yet having written it, I stop. Something's awry here, I say to myself; there's a flaw somewhere, but what? I worked for the *Times*. . . . What's wrong with saying that?

I sit and think about those years. Of how I whistled my way to the paper every morning. Of how the day started all over again when I got my good night from the editor. Of how I prowled the courtrooms and back rooms and barrooms of the city. Of how I got my New York from *The New York Times*. And now I know what's wrong. I never worked for the *Times*, I was a kid on a carousel. "You mean they pay you for this?" Babe Ruth said when he broke into pro ball. That's how I felt "working" for *The New York Times*.

There's a book in those merry years, but all I can hope to do here is send up the scent of roses. Jottings, I'll try it with jottings.

They're still an entry, Rosenthal and Gelb, only now they run the paper from the top. When I showed up at the Gray Lady they were colts, just beginning their second season at the metropolitan desk. Abe and Arthur, hungry and on the make—what a commotion it was. Like great coaches, they molded a team out of veterans, rookies, a free agent here, a sleeper there. Abe was Vince Lombardi to Arthur's John Madden. Together they drove, cajoled, drank with you, lunched with you, *lived* with you. They were there when they weren't there: All we reporters were able to talk about, whether boozing at Sardi's, supping at Elaine's, home with the family, out with the girls, were Abe and Arthur, Arthur and Abe.

I remember a night at Manuche's when somebody's lady wrote on a napkin: "Let's fly away/let's find a land that's warm and tropic/where Abe and Arthur ain't the topic/all the live long day." Cole Porter loved it, wherever he was, and it got us off the subject for a good ten minutes.

There was a method to it, you can be sure. Our Gold Dust Twins had inherited the dullest report in the paper, a congeries of City Hall handouts, Board of Education pap, crime statistics respectfully reported as fact, night life at the Legal Aid Ball, and so on, unto infinite blandness. Abe and Arthur were out to change this, to take the Gray out of the Lady while leaving it a lady still. To do it they needed our attention, and they needed it full-scale, day in, day out.

The New York Times does not take the smallest changes lightly—they soul-searched for years before they removed the period from the logo—so one can imagine the resentment when Rosenthal and Gelb hit the city room. Older *Times*men would tell me all the time how Abe and Arthur were "destroying the paper's capital" by "jazzing up" the writing and covering "fluff." This stuff did not come only from those reporters whom the new editors had discarded as "deadwood." It was a deeply held view of some of the most respected members of the staff. I thought then, and I think now, that these people were wrong, and I believe history has demonstrated they were wrong. But they were convinced, and it was no easy thing for Abe and Arthur to turn the cityside around.

Example. At the regular Wednesday-morning meeting of the metropolitan staff—not the whole staff, of course, but twenty to thirty people—Gelb said it was high time we did a story about political patronage. And was shot down by the political reporters, young and old, who scoffed at the notion on the grounds that patronage was a thing of the past, that it ended with the New Deal when "nobody needed turkeys from the bosses anymore." Incredible? Well only three people at that meeting said it wasn't crazy: Martin Arnold, Martin Tolchin, and me. Immediately afterward, Arthur took the three of us aside and asked us to get on the story. Arnold and I were tied up with projects so Marty Tolchin got the call. The result: a gangbuster series that Tolchin later turned into a distinguished book.

It was at a Wednesday meeting, early on, that I got the franchise to cover the Liberal party. John Lindsay in 1965 announced that he was running for mayor. Since Lindsay was a Republican, he needed the Liberals to stand a chance. But Robert Wagner was the mayor and his ties to the Liberal party were so tight as to appear socked in. I thought Wagner was through, that he'd quit in the corner à la Sonny Liston versus Cassius Clay. At the meeting, which in those days was held in the managing editor's (Clifton Daniel's) office, I brashly predicted this and added that Alex Rose and David Dubinsky—who completely ran the Liberals—would soon give Wagner the message that it wasn't his night.

Abe and Arthur told me to do a piece on the party. I jumped at it—even then, at the outset, I was uneasy with the idea of a law slot, no matter how broadly it was charted—and I turned in a colorful story that got plenty of word-of-mouth in and out of the paper. Afterward, whenever the Liberals played a crucial role, I got tapped. I never thought it was because of any particular insight into that pins-and-needles party—just that I was maybe the only guy who could talk Yiddish with David Dubinsky.

Homer Bigart, Peter Khiss, Gay Talese, Murray Schumach, J. Anthony Lucas, David Halberstam, Martin Arnold, Joseph Lelyveld, Phil Benjamin, Martin Tolchin, Sydney Schanberg, Richard Shepard, R. W. Apple, Jr.—these were the stars or mainstays or about-to-be stars of the *Times*, all working under Abe and Arthur when I joined the paper. I missed a few, I'm sure, but anybody who knows anything about the newspaper world has the picture. It is difficult to imagine a shinier collection of talent under one roof at one time.

In this pantheon, Homer Bigart was the consensus Irving Berlin. Homer was so good, so respected, that one scowl out of him jumped the editorial Richter scale seven points. And he scowled plenty. Journalism was a calling to Mr. Bigart, and his standards were as exacting as those of a Jesuit. Sitting at his desk in the front row, next to Peter Kihss—our Richard Rodgers, whose standards were as exacting as those of a Hasid—Homer would fix an eye on an editor, not five feet away, and that editor would spend the next week trying to think of what he done wrong. If he couldn't figure it out, Kihss would finally tell him. Homer didn't give advice, he just looked at you. Richard Reeves, who joined the *Times* after the *Herald Tribune* folded, sat in Homer's seat one day. Homer just looked at him. Poor Richard jumped out of there so fast he nearly broke his kneecaps.

The night before R. W. "Johnnie" Apple, Jr., was to leave for Vietnam, a few of us had a bon voyage drink with him at Sardi's bar. Bigart walked in with Abe Rosenthal, and, as always, Homer ordered one neat. Apple, probably thinking Homer was there to toast him, said: "Homer, I'm glad you're here. I want your advice. I need it. I'm off to Vietnam tomorrow, and of course nobody knows more about that country than you. Can we talk?"

Homer Bigart downed the neat and said: "Kid, I couldn't give less of a shit where you go and what you do." And walked out.

Johnnie Apple, the ever-boisterous, full of himself, gung-ho cheerleader—and a hell of a reporter—reacted like a child slapped for the first time by his father. "Abe," he said, clutching Rosenthal, "Abe, he hates me, Abe I told you he hates me, Abe . . ."

If you were lucky, it worked the other way with Homer. One afternoon, after I was on the paper about a year, I happened to be standing next to him. Without looking at me, he said in his funny stammer: "You're doing good." That's all, and that's all I needed.

I understood from the get-go how fortunate I was to be breaking in a new beat, particularly a law beat. In newspapers, as in sex, new is good. Once the top editors decide to go with something different, everybody wants to make it work. More important, I was an "expert," if for no other reason than by designation of Abe Rosenthal. In fact, I *was* an expert, I knew more about law and how to write about it than any of my editors. Unlike politics or sports or pop culture—where everybody thinks he knows as much as the other guy—the law is mystique to the unschooled, including the unschooled editor. Result: I was able to define what was important and get it in the paper the way I wrote it. If you think that's ordinary, you don't know the newspaper business. Only columnists had more autonomy than I had on *The New York Times*. Is it any wonder that I whistled myself to work every morning?

Well, it wasn't all butter beans, of course not. Happy as I was, I wanted more—I always want more. The *Times* was never a jail for me, but it is a bureaucracy, and I bridle at bureaucracy. Why can't I break a political story if I have it, why can't I cover jazz if I want, why can't I float, why can't I do everything?

Example. In 1969, Hugh Carey, then a congressman, is a candidate for mayor of New York City. Out on the town late one night, I'm told by a total insider that Carey has decided to drop out and run for city council president on a ticket led by former Mayor Robert Wagner. First thing in the morning, I tell this to Arthur Gelb, who has been metropolitan editor since 1967, when Abe Rosenthal moved up to assistant managing editor. Arthur says write it.

As I'm finishing the piece, which is scheduled for page one, Richard Reeves comes to my desk and says Carey has denied the story. Reeves was then the chief metropolitan political correspondent. I say, "Dick, how the hell could he deny a story that hasn't been printed?" Reeves says, "I saw you had it in the summary [the summary is a paragraph that tells the editors what's to come], and so I called Hughey and he denied it."

I liked Dick Reeves, but I didn't like him now. "What right do you have to cross-examine my story?" I say. "Who the hell are you to check me out? Of course Carey will deny it, he denied it to me! But it's true, I don't put my byline over bullshit. Where do you get off pulling this crap?"

Reeves is apologetic and leaves. I finish the story. A few minutes later, Gelb comes over and says, "Look, are you sure about this thing? I'm having terrible trouble with Reeves and Clay Knowles." (The late Clay Knowles was a political reporter who had covered Wagner's City Hall.)

I say, "Sure I'm sure, don't worry about those guys, this is gold." Arthur says, "Okay, I trust you."

To make sure nothing has changed, I call my source. Five minutes later he calls back and says it's all "go." I'm satisfied, ready to leave for the night, when I hear screaming in the middle of the city room. Clay Knowles is waving his hands at Gelb, and Reeves is standing there looking bemused. I go over. Knowles says, "Since when has this paper become a gossip rag?" He says it *at* me, not to me. I like Clay, but he goes too far. I say, "Clay, I never insulted you, don't do this to me." Clay says, "I don't know what's going on around here." And dials a number. Gelb leaves but I hang right in. Knowles has Bob Wagner on the phone.

"Bob," he says, "Bob I'm up against the wall here. Sid Zion has a story that Carey is dropping out and going on your ticket. I want the truth now, you owe it to me, Bob. I'm saying the story is phony."

I don't know what Wagner is saying, but I see Knowles waving Arthur over. Knowles says, "Bob, I want you to tell that to the metropolitan editor." He puts Arthur on the phone.

Gelb is upset—why shouldn't he be? He's not supposed to be involved in this kind of thing. He talks calmly, in a low voice. I make out this: "Are you saying it's not true, Mr. Mayor? We have this story, Mr. Mayor—are you absolutely telling me it's false? Well, thank you. All right."

It turns out that Wagner does not deny it, he fudges. But Knowles is adamant. Reeves says nothing. Gelb says, "We have to go with the story."

Ten minutes later, Gelb tells me, "Look, Clay Knowles and Dick Reeves are driving me crazy. Let's hold the piece for a day."

I say, "Do what you want. I think it's a disgrace."

Arthur says, "Don't get mad—we'll just hold it for a day."

I'm about to pack it in when I get a call from the top political boss in New York. I had put in a call for him earlier and now he's returning it. I ask him about Carey, and he says it's baloney. I say, "I need this one—don't fuck with me. I know it's true and I don't want the line, I want it straight." He pauses, and says, "That bad? You need it that bad?" Absolutely. He says, "Of course it's true, but we never had this conversation."

I tell Gelb to run it, that I just got complete confirmation. He wants to know from who, and I won't tell him. I say, "Arthur, just go with it." Gelb calls Reeves and Knowles to the desk. "Sid has it totally hard now," he says. "I think we have to run it." Reeves lays off, but Clay won't. "I'm telling you," Knowles says, "that it's a fake. Carey is not out, Wagner never lied to me."

The decision is to hold the story.

I go down to Sardi's. Clay Knowles is at the far end of the bar. I tell the barkeep to buy him a drink. When Clay gets it, he's so nervous he spills it. I send him another, and I walk over to him. He says, "Sid, it's nothing personal. You're a good guy, I just didn't want to see you get hurt." I say, "Clay, you made a major mistake. If I'm wrong, it's my ass. If I'm right, it's yours. And you didn't have a thing to do with it. Why did you put your face in? You think you'll get credit if you're right? It's crazy."

On the WNBC six o'clock news the next night, Gabe Pressman breaks the Carey story. We run it on page one. Terrific.

There were a few other incidents where just by getting a hot story I'd get into hot water because I was stepping on sensitive toes. And toward the end of my life at the *Times*, Scotty Reston, then executive editor, spiked one of my best investigative pieces under circumstances you can read all about later on here.

So not all butter beans, but so what? It was a lovely time, a gorgeous time, at *The New York Times*.

———

EVERY ONCE IN a while, Abe Rosenthal gives me a quizzical smile and says, "Why did you leave *The New York Times?*" I tell him *Scanlan's,* I left to start my magazine, *Scanlan's Monthly.* He doesn't seem to hear me. He says, "You could have done anything you wanted on the *Times.* What made you quit?" *Scanlan's,* I repeat. "You left just when I took over," Abe says. "There was no limit to where you could have gone on *The New York Times.* I don't understand it, why did you leave?"

I resigned from the *Times* on my thirty-sixth birthday, November 14, 1969. Since then, Abe and I have had this repartee two, three times a year, like a regular Japanese Noh play. Sometimes Arthur Gelb happens to be around, and he adds a singular thought. "You always wanted to cover the Supreme Court," he says. "If you stayed, Abe would have given it to you, but you didn't have patience."

The truth is, I quit to start *Scanlan's.* And why not? I had a shot to do something big, and even in retrospect, even though it went down, I can't imagine not taking the chance. Indeed, I did it with full awareness that it might not work, that the odds were higher than a cat's back that it wouldn't work.

On the other hand, Abe Rosenthal's skepticism—or whatever you might call it—is not without foundation. If I thought I had such a bright future on the paper, I might not have gone through the extraordinary effort of putting together a new magazine. Had I known at the outset that Abe was soon to get the top spot, maybe I wouldn't have started the whole thing. By the time he got it, however, I was irrevocably committed.

Arthur Gelb's view, that I wanted the Supreme Court beat, was also grounded in fact, but his sequence was off. I wanted the job, but only early in my life at the *Times*. By the time I left, I wouldn't have taken it, partly because I was more interested in political coverage, partly because I wouldn't have left New York. In 1965, when I joined the *Times*, Washington looked great to me. But in 1965 I had just moved to New York. By 1969, I was a native New Yorker. Washington could have been Providence, or vice versa.

I wouldn't lay the family jewels on it, but I think the idea of making a new magazine began to germinate at the Democratic convention in Chicago, the summer of 1968. Harrison Salisbury was in charge of convention coverage for the *Times*, and if I wasn't the last person he'd choose for the team it was only by a dirty nose. He plain didn't like me. No specific reason I can point to, no run-ins—I had virtually no contact with him on the paper or off. But I wasn't surprised, because all my life people like Salisbury have glanced me off as a natural enemy. I think these correct, formal types take my loose style for arrogance. Since I'm uncomfortable around them, I react with a slouchy nonchalance, which only proves how right they are. Salisbury didn't catch it immediately—remember, he was the first to interview me at the *Times*—because I was too much in awe of the Gray Lady to be in any way loosey-goosey. It didn't take him more than a few weeks to spot me, but by then I had made the paper. Well, I wasn't going to miss Chicago. For about a year, I'd been friendly with Warren Hinckle, the eye-patched, bad-boy editor of *Ramparts*. I met him in New York in the summer of 1967, shortly after the Six-Day War in the Middle East. The *Times Magazine* asked me to do a story about the reaction of the Left to the Israeli victory. *Ramparts*, then the leading left-wing journal—or at least the most spectacular foe of the CIA and the Vietnam War—had just published an editorial on the Middle East that was generally perceived as anti-Israel. Given the way things have developed against Israel in the news media, I suspect it would look like a Zionist tract today, but my Jews were riding high then, and *Ramparts* appeared to be leaning over backward toward the Arabs.

Hinckle was staying at the Algonquin, and when I arrived at his suite he was wearing a towel and working the phones. At first he was wary of me, not because I was from the *Times*—the paper had treated *Ramparts* well—but because of the issue. Hinckle had some big Jewish money behind him—notably from Martin Peretz, now publisher of *The New Republic*—and a large Jewish readership, so he was jumpy about what I might write.

After a couple of drinks there was no problem. We hit it off great; we clicked just like that. It was more a matter of style than substance, as it turned out, but the style was so similar that for years it served to cover our real differences.

Mainly, it was the bar scene we had in common. Hinckle and I love a great bar. It's our court. Ordinary drunks need bars for the booze; me and Hinckle need them for the life. And we have a way of taking over a joint without being obtrusive, or anyway not being pains in the ass. Maybe it's a small talent, though I don't believe that—I think it's a gift—but more than anything else it made us tight pals, no pun intended. That, plus the odd thing about our way of talking. We have the same delivery, the same cadence. Strangers took us for brothers, while our respective friends thought each was copying from the other.

In the event, I never wrote the piece about Israel and the American Left. But Hinckle was forever floating into New York from his San Francisco base and we hung together all the time. In December 1967, *Ramparts* ran a cover picturing some of its editors burning their draft cards. The U.S. attorney's office in Manhattan, under Robert Morgenthau, was hot after draft card burners and so dragged the *Ramparts* people before a grand jury. I saw this as a back-door attack on the First Amendment, and said as much in the *Times*. The piece made Morgenthau back off and of course cemented my friendship with Hinckle.

In the late spring of 1968, I wrote a story for *Ramparts* about Nelson Rockefeller, then a prospective candidate for the Republican presidential nomination. Called "Rocky the Cop," it was an all-out attack on the mass-media perception of Rockefeller as a good-hearted liberal, and on Rocky himself for his draconian positions on law and order. Rockefeller, who was attempting to placate the Republican Right, made reprints and had them delivered to every delegate at the convention—surely the only time that crowd saw *Ramparts*. He also ran an ad in the *Times*, saying "some people call me Rocky the Cop," and okay, I am and I'm proud of it.

All of which is prelude to why I covered the Democratic convention in Chicago for *Ramparts*, which in turn is prelude to *Scanlan's*. If Salisbury wouldn't send me, Hinckle sure would, and at my suggestion, he sent Sydney Schanberg too. Sydney, who now handles the New York column for the *Times*, wasn't considered for convention coverage either, but he wanted to go as much as I did. Our editors didn't like it, to say the least, only what could they do short of firing us and that was forget about it. So we took a week off and what a week it was.

Hinckle wanted to do a daily convention paper but he didn't have the money, so he decided on a daily wall poster, Chinese-style. To produce it, he brought in a staff as big as that of the *Times*, or damned close, and housed us all in a posh hotel. *Ramparts* was busted out, but the credit card companies didn't know it yet—I didn't know it, exactly, close as I was to Hinckle—so why not live in grace and splendor? Nobody spent other people's money like Warren, and we worked the convention from the Pump Room when we weren't entertaining visiting peaceniks in a welcoming suite as large and well-stocked as the Pennsylvania delegation's.

The antiwar crowd frowned at the opulence, but they drank the champagne what we gave 'em. At one time or another, everybody was up there doing R and R, from Tom Hayden to Hunter Thompson.

Schanberg and I got a hot tip that Lyndon Johnson had taken an entire floor in the Hilton, where he supposedly had everything and everybody wired, including Hubert Humphrey. We did a wall poster saying just that, and later I was told by a White House aide that the floor was dismantled as soon as we hit the walls with our scoop.

The next night, our source had something even better for us. Johnson, he said, had a contingency plan to take the nomination from Humphrey if HHH went for any kind of peace plank on Vietnam. The plan was in writing, and our guy could get it for us. And would deliver—if we could get him laid.

I told this to Hinckle at the Pump Room, and he instinctively looked at the women at our table. They didn't buy that one—a couple shrieked in horror—so I took Warren aside and said, "Let's get him a hooker—there must be a hooker on call in this joint."

It happened that I knew someone on the hotel's administrative staff. When I broached the proposition, he said, "Why didn't you ask me an hour ago—they just left the bar." I thought I could spot hookers at ten miles, but these ladies had to be something else; I didn't know there'd been any in the room.

I said, "Look, do me a favor. If I can get a guy here laid tonight, we got a Pulitzer going."

Fifteen minutes later, he had somebody. "It'll cost you a hundred, and you gotta use your own room," he said.

I told the source he was in, and when could we get the contingency plan? Suddenly he squirmed. "Well, I don't have it here, it's in Washington, it'll take a day or two, you know how it is—I don't have it *on* me for chrissake."

I grabbed Hinckle again.

"Obviously, the guy's either lying or he's scared shitless," I said.

"For sure, and maybe both," Warren said.

"But what have we got to lose?" I said. "We're putting the hundred on the bill, which you'll never pay anyway, and if he doesn't deliver, we can lunch on this one for twenty years."

"Done," said Hinckle.

A couple of hours later, our lover boy walked into the *Ramparts* suite looking the glum one if there ever was one. "Hey, baby, how was it?" Hinckle shouted out over the din of peaceniks boozing, smoking, munching. And the guy said, "I had better on the Albany–Schenectady line."

Well, we weren't going to get LBJ's "plan"—who'd hand you a Pulitzer for less than the Albany–Schenectady line, right?—so we needed a headliner for the next wall poster. The movement crowd didn't think it a problem; they thought we should do a piece on Tom Hayden, who had just been busted by the Chicago police. I didn't like the idea and neither did Warren, partly because everybody had that story and partly because it was too solemn. What to do?

"What about the tear gas in the Pump Room tonight?" I said.

"Tear gas? What tear gas?" somebody—everybody—said.

Hinckle didn't say anything for a few seconds, he just looked straight ahead, but I could see that gleam in his eye. And then he said, "That's it, it's brilliant. Tear gas hits the Pump Room. That's the headline, perfect, it's perfect."

We did it, too, that was the wall poster—we wrote a whole goddam essay under that head. Which scandalized the peace movement and demoralized the *Ramparts* staff. Most of the kids whose job it was to hang the posters around town either refused to hang this one or gave it sewer service. But we got a few hung and believe it or not a lot of people believed it. Anyway it was good for laughs, and there weren't many laughs in Chi that whole crazy week.

What does all this have to do with *Scanlan's?* Only that it was now crystal clear that *Ramparts* was just about tapped out. I had suspected as much, but Hinckle was always talking about money coming in from this, that, or another sucker. After watching him con his way out of the hotel with plastic that I thought would burn in his hands like a draft card, he couldn't use that line with me anymore. We started tossing around the idea of starting a new magazine.

It was all pretty vague for quite a while, especially the question of wherewithal, filthy lucre, but as time went on and *Ramparts* looked more dead than alive, we began to talk about it as if it were real. With Nixon in office, we even gave our unborn baby a name—*Barricades*, which we incorporated when we began raising seed money. *Barricades*, as in off the ramparts and to the barricades. Except that we had no intention of turning it into a more radical version of *Ramparts*, we wanted to do a muckracker that would eschew ideology. *Barricades* was a smart-ass name that had to go as a consumer fraud.

We raised about fifty grand in seed during the winter and early spring of 1969. I was still at the *Times*, and for part of the time Hinckle was diddling around with *Ramparts*. The editors of the *Times* had no idea what I was doing until the eleventh hour when I told them about it. Rather amazing, given that my *Scanlan's* secretary used to come up to the paper every afternoon to work the phones and take dictation.

They were no dummies, by no means; I got away with it because that summer my editors weren't looking my way. Why? I had spent six weeks doing an exposé of the alleged judicial bias of federal Judge Henry J. Friendly, which Arthur Gelb was touting everywhere as a Pulitzer. But James Reston, then executive editor, killed it, under circumstances I later described in *Scanlan's* as a preface to the spiked piece. Here is that preface:

After Abe Fortas was forced off the Supreme Court, *The New York Times* asked me to look for untouched scandals in the lower federal judiciary. The paper had been badly singed on the Fortas story, reduced almost daily to reprinting the scoops of other publications. This may not have been well known to the general public, but it was the raging snicker among newsmen last spring, and since papers are edited for other editors, the *Times* was more than a little embarrassed.

Because of this, I thought it possible that the paper would publish the story on the judicial bias of federal Judge Henry J. Friendly. But I was aware of a few problems.

For openers, Friendly is a lifelong chum of Louis Loeb, who for forty years has been the lawyer for the *Times*. Then too, James Reston, executive editor of the paper at the time I worked on this story in my capacity as metropolitan legal correspondent, had recently described Friendly in his column as "the most respected judge in the lower federal courts." Indeed, Henry Friendly was the crème de la crème of the Harvard Law School, the legal establishment and the judiciary.

The New York Times has never been accused of muckraking people with those credentials.

I told Arthur Gelb, metropolitan editor of the *Times*, and Abe Rosenthal, then associate managing editor and now managing editor, all I knew about Friendly's relations with the paper's hierarchy. The story was going to be difficult to document, I said, and I had no interest in pursuing it if in the end I was to be met with a "policy decision" against publication. They told me to stop worrying and start working.

By the end of June, I had finished the piece and by Henry Friendly's sixty-sixth birthday on July 3, I had rewritten it to the satisfaction of Arthur Gelb. "Let's give him a birthday party," I said charitably, but it turned out that some people hadn't read it yet.

It was summer, but I could feel the chill. I asked to see Scotty Reston, who seemed to be the slow reader. He quickly told me that he wasn't going to run the story. I argued, but to no avail. I asked Reston what we would do if Friendly were appointed to the High Court. "Print it, of course," he said. "Why then and not now?" I asked. "Because," Reston answered, "it would then be up to the Senate and it would become our responsibility to print it."

I didn't understand the difference, but Reston said it was academic, as he had been informed that Nixon would not appoint Friendly, but instead someone from California. He was told this, he said, by someone in the Department of Justice.

"Did you tell him that we had a story on Friendly?" I asked.

"Yes," he said.

I told Reston that I would have to free my source. "He might succeed in getting a congressman to do something about it," I said. "What then?"

"If there's a newsbreak, we'll run the whole thing," Scotty said. "I just don't think we should initiate the story."

A couple of weeks later, *The Village Voice* noted that the *Times* was sitting on a story about Judge Friendly. The *Voice* made its way to Texas, where the American Bar Association was meeting, and the rumors got so wild that Fred Graham, who covered the convention for the *Times*, called the New York office to report that the lawyers were connecting Friendly with the Mafia.

The *Times* immediately asked me if my story was ready to go. I laughed and said that I knew the day would come when we would have to print it in order to protect Friendly's reputation.

The next day, Representative John Conyers (D-Mich.) of the House Judiciary Committee, said that he was requesting an investigation, based on the facts made available to him by my original source, Randolph Phillips. I thought the story would now run, since the newsbreak Reston had insisted on was finally available. But Scotty said no dice.

Randy Phillips then took his portfolio and showed it to *The Wall Street Journal* and *Time* magazine. The *Journal* assigned Ronald Kessler, one of its best investigative reporters, to the story, and Kessler was full of beans over it. For the next few days I heard from him frequently as he confirmed the facts of the Friendly story. I gently told him not to be surprised if at the end his story was spiked too, but he said there was no chance of this. His editors were "hot for it," and the *Journal* was willing to take on anyone. I told him I'd buy him a drink when the piece was killed. A few days later, at Gallagher's bar, I consoled him with

Scotch and water. "I just don't understand it," he said. "They didn't tell me why, they just said the story wasn't running. They never did this before."

Time magazine decided to handle the matter as a press story since Haynsworth had been nominated by the time Phillips told them about it. The piece got into type, a photographer took at least one hundred shots of my profile, and in the end Henry Grunwald, the magazine's managing editor, decided, according to Time staffers, that he didn't want to hurt Scotty Reston, and spiked it.

So not only was the story suppressed, the story about the story was suppressed.

It is perforce speculative whether Friendly would have been appointed to the Court had the White House and the Justice Department been unaware of the Times story. It is certain that the President knew about it, whether, as rumor has it, from Reston, who was said to have told him that he would not print the story unless Friendly was nominated, or through normal sources.

—*Scanlan's Monthly*
May 1970

I used Sardi's bar as my *Scanlan's* office when I wasn't using the *Times*. One day the phones went kerflooey there and stayed kerflooey the next night. So I ran an ad on page one of the *Times*—one of those small-print things that cost a hundred bucks—that read: "Telephone Company! Please fix the phones at Sardi's bar. Signed, *Scanlan's Monthly.*"

The following morning at eight, a half dozen repairmen were in the joint—they woke up Vincent Sardi for this—and we were back in business. When Leonard Lyons showed up on his regular rounds during lunch that day, I told him about it, and he used it as the lead item in his *New York Post* column.

While raising seed money, we of course were on the lookout for real dough. One night I had a drink with Bob Arum, the lawyer and fight promoter, and Arum said, "Why don't you go public?" Go public, just like that, go public? Arum said, "Sure, it's the best time to do it, before they know what you've got, while they can dream."

The new issues market was still going strong, and Arum, a partner at Louis Nizer's firm, represented Charles Plohn, the undisputed king of that market. "I'll get Charley to do it—don't worry about it, you're in," Arum said.

It wasn't that easy. We had to get commitments for a good portion of the money by ourselves, which meant nights of hustling at meetings and cocktail parties. It dragged on for months, until the market was bear, and for a time we thought we were finished. We'd spent most of the seed money trying to launch the public issue, and if Plohn wouldn't or couldn't go we were worse than nowhere.

But Arum came through; we were, I think, Charley Plohn's last issue. With a whirl of publicity, the price went from $3 to $4.50 the first day out.

Plohn, a colorful character with a marvelously profane tongue, handed me a check for $675,000 on November 25, 1969. "Okay, schmuck, here it is," he said. "You'll never forgive me for this, that's for sure, you poor dumb bastard."

We printed a copy of the check on our first cover, dated March 1970, and promoted it on Wall Street with newsstand signs that said "Plohn's Folly." It sold out in a couple of hours.

We never thought we had to forgive Charley for anything, but this view wasn't universally shared. Our stock fell precipitously within a few months—this was some bear market—and it wasn't long before Plohn & Co. bellied up.

The destruction of the new issues market—and it stayed dead for ten years—should have made us cut way back on our ambitious plans. From the outset we had figured on a secondary issue of $1 million within a year of the public offering, a hardly unreasonable prognostication given the bullish nature of the market when Bob Arum first dreamed up the idea. By the time we came out, it was out of the question, which is probably why Charley Plohn called me schmuck. Nobody could keep a national magazine afloat on $675,-000, unless it were run on butcher paper and a close-to-the-vest budget. Well, we certainly didn't want a little essayists' journal—we hadn't done all this for *that*—we wanted a big, exciting book with plenty of four-color photojournalism and artwork. So butcher paper was out, and of course so was budgeteering. To expect Warren Hinckle to cut corners was like asking all those Barrymores put together to work without an audience. I have no taste for accounting, either, and I'm a pretty good spender myself. It wasn't all Hinckle.

We opened offices in New York and San Francisco, the latter because Warren loves his hometown. It was supposed to be a cubby-
hole, but Hinckle breaks through holes better than Tony Dorsett.
We had a full-scale operation out there, and what with Hinckle flying to New York and me to California, not to mention the phone
bills and transmission machines—well, budget shmudget. Furthermore, we insisted on paying writers far more than the going rate—we
were, after all, a "writers' magazine" not a publishers'—and we'd
send a reporter anywhere in the world for a story and always first
class.

On top of all this, we carried no advertising: indeed, we *paid* for
ads on the few occasions when we found them worthy. Our ad policy
was the brainchild of Howard Gossage, for my money the most in-
ventive advertising man in the world. Howard was chairman of the
board of *Scanlan's* until he died at fifty-two, a few months before we
opened, and we listed him on the masthead as chairman (The Late
Howard Gossage) in every issue. Howard's philosophy was make
lemonade. If you got a lemon, make lemonade—he'd say it all the
time. Our lemon was we couldn't get the big advertisers because we
were muckrakers, so why not tell them to go to hell in advance and
make our readers part of an independent, feisty rebellion against
Madison Avenue? We'd do it on circulation alone and by pitching it
thus; by making lemonade, we'd get the reader to pay full subscrip-
tion rates, no half-price deals, no freebies, no gifts.

It worked, or at least it was working. Our newsstand sales were
strong from the outset, and after a couple of months we began our
own advertising campaign, consisting mainly of full-page ads in *The
New York Times*. I came up with a slogan: "You Trust Your
Mother, but You Cut the Cards," and Dan Greenburg wrote brilliant copy under it that turned out to be a huge success. Inside of
three months, these ads drew thirty thousand subscriptions at ten
bucks a shot. Despite our spending habits, it looked as if we were
going to make it. Growth curves of that magnitude have a way of at-
tracting fresh money even in bad times, and we had reason for optimism. We needed a strong controller, and by late summer even
Hinckle seemed in agreement on this matter.

Then something extraordinary happened. Hard-hat elements in
the New York lithographers union refused to work on our special
issue on guerrilla war in the United States and bullied the printer

into breaking his contract with us. The lithographers claimed that the issue was "un-American," mainly because it "taught people how to make bombs."

We had been working on the project for months, almost from the outset of the magazine. It was Hinckle's baby, and the core idea was to document acts of sabotage and terrorism in the country going back to 1965. The results were astonishing: We filled thirty pages in agate type of terrorist acts ranging from bombings to the shooting of police officers to the stealing of dynamite. Nobody had ever put it all together, and when put together it spelled out an appalling guerrilla war from coast to coast. It was good journalism, important journalism, replete with facts and figures plus interviews with the various urban guerrillas. So far as teaching people how to make bombs— all we did, in a section titled "What Guerrillas Read," was to reprint a Molotov cocktail sketch from a Weathermen propaganda handbill.

The idea that a few lithographers could assert censorship rights over the contents of a magazine was of course incredible, not to say un-American. I held a hurry-up press conference and announced that we were filing suit against the union and the printer and that meanwhile we'd publish elsewhere. I was sure the news media would rally behind us—how could they not?—and that we'd be better for this incident, it'd be lemonade for certain.

Little did I know. The press ignored us en masse, and the reason was that the printer somehow persuaded a *New York Times* reporter that we didn't have any money, that he was willing to print the issue, but we were deadbeats. This was such an obvious ploy it never occurred to me anybody would bite for it, but the *Times* guy bought it—despite that I was able to show him a Triple-A Dun & Bradstreet rating and despite that the issue was ready to go to press when the lithographers revolted, with no complaint about money from the printer.

Even so, we weren't too concerned. The issue would come out late, but there'd be no trouble getting a printer. We immediately made a deal with a San Francisco plant, but the day before the presses were to roll, he sent us back a check we had given him as a down payment. He hadn't cashed it. He said he could no longer print the issue. He gave no reasons.

Subsequently, we were turned down by other large printers in Colorado and Missouri. Their reason: The lithographers union had "put the word out on *Scanlan's.*" We were then approached by a number of printer's brokers in New York who told us there was no problem—they'd get it done. Each came back nonplused. They couldn't get it done—the word was indeed out on *Scanlan's.*

Meanwhile the months were rolling by, and the word kept spreading that we were broke. So everybody put us on C.O.D., and in order to quell the rumors, we were compelled to keep our staff on payroll. Catch-22. What to do? We finally found a printer in Canada, but just as it looked as if we were about to roll, the bindery called to say the Canadian Mounted Police had seized the issue. I had visions of Nelson Eddy; what the hell were the Mounties doing in a bindery? It turned out that the bindery had turned us in to the Mounties, and it was no joke. We had no choice but to fight it out in the Canadian courts, and though we eventually won it was at great cost, and none greater than the loss of Izzy Schawarzberg. Some terrific judge up there insisted that we get releases from the Montreal newsdealers and so Izzy ran around in a snowstorm from stand to stand, and the next morning his heart gave out.

Still it wasn't over. The Montreal police stopped the trucks carrying the issue at the border, sirens screeching. CBC radio asked the chief of police of Montreal why. He said, "The United States Government asked us to stop it." Meantime we had already flown thousands of copies to San Francisco. When they got to the distributor, the Immigration Service made a seizure. Now *The New York Times* ran a story and this quickly backed off the immigration boys. In Canada, the *Montreal Star*—which, unlike the American press, had played the story big and supported us editorially—blasted the government, as did CBC radio, and at long last the issue was released. Dated January 1971, four months after the scheduled publication.

Because of the long delay, we had to do what we never wanted to do—except for the cover, we had to go with butcher paper. But that was the least of our never-ending troubles. Our national distributor had dropped us and refused to release some $35,000 it owed us. We were nearly tapped out, our credit gone, and we had to organize a makeshift distribution.

Somehow we managed to do it—we found distributors all over the country. Only to discover that the newsdealers in some of our biggest markets were refusing to stock the issue. Chicago, Detroit, Los Angeles, Philadelphia—about thirty cities in all, wouldn't touch us. Why not? We got a few confidential calls from anonymous dealers who said, "The government's come around and told us it wouldn't be good for the country, and for us, to sell *Scanlan's.*"

We couldn't survive that, just as Hinckle and I could no longer survive each other. The pressure destroyed our friendship, though neither of us would admit it was pressure; we said it was a difference of opinion. Except that where once we would have laughed off differences, now we were at each other's throats. Thus, the apparent break—I wrote an editorial attacking the terrorists and the notion of guerrilla war in the United States, and Hinckle wrote an Op-Ed defending them and attacking me—was really a symptom of the malaise that split us. In the old days, we'd have promoted the two editorials, made lemonade, but now we were barely talking.

Once we were wiped off the newsstands, it was obvious we were finished. Warren, however, wouldn't accept it; he kept spending money out on the coast and talked and acted as if we were merely in a temporarily embarrassed financial condition. He wanted to move the whole operation to San Francisco. "I've been in bigger trouble before," he'd say. "We can keep going, no trouble."

I thought he was crazy—I *knew* he was crazy—and he thought I was just a middle-class oaf trying to save my ass. But there was no ass to save, we were gone, and in the end the directors voted overwhelmingly for bankruptcy and that was that.

Five years later, John Dean came out with his book *Blind Ambition.* Dean wrote that his first job, on his first day as counsel to President Nixon, was to go after *Scanlan's.* By order of Nixon himself! The reason: We had published a memo from Vice-President Agnew that referred to Rand Corporation studies to cancel the 1972 national elections and repeal the Bill of Rights—plus an administration plan to set hard-hat labor groups on peace marchers and "longhairs" in "spontaneous" demonstrations in New York and other cities.

We published the memo—actually one page of a four-page memo, which was all we had—without comment, just an overline saying "This document recently came into the hands of the editors." We thought this was the most dramatic way to do it and the most responsible. We trusted our source, who had been reliable in the past, but there was no way to totally prove the authenticity of the memo without going to Agnew, who would obviously deny it. So we figured, let's drop it in and see what happens.

All hell broke loose. Agnew denounced the memo as "completely false" and "ridiculous." Attorney General John Mitchell, in a break-fast conference with the Washington press corps, accused us of em-ploying Hitler's "Big Lie" technique and announced a Justice De-partment investigation.

We came back with a full-page ad in the *Times*, saying that we were happy to place our credibility against Agnew's any time, any-where. "The Vice-President's denial," we said, "is as clumsy as it is fraudulent. The document came directly from Mr. Agnew's office and he knows it."

The ad drew a record number of subscriptions and newsstand cir-culation soared. This was our August issue, on the streets in late July. It was a time when the press was scared shitless of Nixon–Agnew, and perhaps more of Agnew, who had been the hit man in the ad-ministration's relentless attack on the news media. We had from the beginning relentlessly attacked the Nixon Gang, and in our June number we ran a cover of Nixon with a fist in his face under the headline "Impeach Nixon." Our editorial accused him of high crimes and misdemeanors ranging from his unconstitutional war against Cambodia to his "rape on the stock market, mayhem on the economy, and felonious assault on the Supreme Court."

We had the hang on him long ere Watergate rang on him, and we were virtually alone in the field. I'm convinced that this had more to do with our early success than anything else we did—and as we'll see, we did plenty of everything. The public was starving for criti-cism of the Nixon administration, and almost nobody was coming through with it, certainly not the establishment press.

We weren't worried about Agnew, we welcomed his attack, but we had to be concerned about Mitchell's threatened investigation, because under no circumstances would we give up our source. The Supreme Court had not yet forced journalists to surrender sources at the risk of contempt citations and jail, but no case had been brought to them. With Warren Burger in as chief justice, who knew what they would do?

In any event, nothing happened. Mitchell quickly dropped the idea, either because he discovered we were right or he simply didn't want to give us a forum. We thought we were out of the woods, and it wasn't until John Dean's book came out that we discovered we were on Nixon's mind over this one.

A few days after the Agnew memo appeared, I got a call from a law clerk in Manhattan Federal Court. He said he had read the memo in *Scanlan's*, particularly the part about the "spontaneous" hard-hat attacks on peaceniks. The memo was dated March 1970, and a month or so later there was a big beating up of peace marchers by construction workers in the Wall Street area. In May, Nixon threw a party for the construction union biggies in the White House, with page-one regalia—clearly he was feting them for their "pro-American" support of the Indochina War, that is, the assault on the peace people.

The law clerk asked if I knew that Sidney Glasser was at that White House shindig. I told him I didn't know who Glasser was. He said Glasser had only a month earlier been convicted of extortion, for ordering the men in the glaziers' union, which he ran, to spray corrosive chemicals on plate glass installed by nonunion companies. Judge Constance Baker Motley hit him with a $20,000 fine, a five-year suspended sentence, and two years probation.

This guy, said the law clerk—who wouldn't tell me his name—turned up at the White House, while on probation, to celebrate with Nixon. "You can check it out," he said.

It checked out exactly, and so I assigned a reporter to find out the records of the other people who showed at the White House that day. We turned up a half dozen, who I called in an editorial titled "Nixon and the Bums" the "most extraordinary bunch of bums, gougers and defrauders of the poor ever to gather under one roof."

We ran this as our leader in the September issue and made it a full-page ad in the *Times*, called "The Great White House Tea Party." This editorial, backed by the ad, really sparked the lithographers' revolt the following month—not the crap about Molotov cocktails and guerrilla war. I can't prove it, but I was always willing to bet the house.

Here is John Dean on the subject. After detailing his problems with the Agnew memo, Dean wrote: "*Scanlan's* came back to plague me again the following month. This time it was charging the White House with inviting some "labor racketeers" to the President's famous 'hardhat luncheon.' I was asked to have the FBI check into the magazine's charges and reported back that the labor leaders were indeed shady characters. Shortly after this report. *Scanlan's* went out of business, its editors unaware of how much trouble they stirred up at the White House."

We were plenty aware of the trouble the Nixon crowd was causing us, only we couldn't convince anybody in the news media; they thought we were broke, paranoiac, or both. Again, this was long before Watergate; who would believe that the President of the United States would bother to go after what John Dean called a "shit-ass magazine"?

A couple of years later, when Nixon's paranoia unraveled, it became clear that we were anything but "shit-ass" to him. In fact, he didn't have to be paranoiac to worry about us, if you think about it, since we were running those ads in the *Times* every month. Sure we were getting to him, we knew that, but what we didn't know, until Dean wrote it, was that he himself went so crazy as to force Dean to put the Internal Revenue Service on our backs.

Dean was so upset by this "request" that he sought counsel with the late Murray Chotiner, Nixon's old California hit man.

"If the President wants you to turn the IRS loose," Chotiner told Dean, "then you turn the IRS loose. . . . If you don't, he'll find someone who does."

This quote got international circulation, though nobody bothered to connect it with *Scanlan's.* Five years after our death, the press still refused to give us victim credit, I don't know why. So far as I know, only *The New York Times* ran a small piece on Dean's revelations concerning *Scanlan's.*

The IRS never bothered me—how could they, I was busted?—but according to Dean they went after the principal organizers and promoters of the magazine. I never asked any of them, just as I never brought a lawsuit against Nixon or Dean—though Dean confessed he had "crossed an ethical line" by setting the IRS on us. It was over and done with and the hell with it. Enough for me that Dean said Nixon was after us—at least now nobody could tell me I was some kind of nut. The Nixon Gang had put us away, a precursor to Watergate, and who can gainsay it?

A decade later, I read over the eight issues of *Scanlan's.* I'm pleased, hell I'm *proud*—we had a great thing going. We were Johnny-on-the-spot from Nixon to the war to ecology to dirty kitchens. Joe Kahn, my old mentor at the *New York Post,* had long wanted to expose the underside of the fancy New York restaurants, but due to perceived (or real) advertising pressure, he got no takers at the *Post.* We let him loose and the first thing he did was put the Colony out of business. We gave ratings of garbage pails on a scale of four to one for the dirtiest kitchens in town and charted them next to

Craig Claiborne's stars. This series resulted in new Health Department codes that continue to shut down restaurants in New York and throughout the country, for it spread quickly.

In our first issue, Gene Grove wrote a piece on a bizarre effort by CBS television, together with the CIA and FBI, to invade Haiti. Murray Kempton did a great number on Dean Acheson, Maxwell Geismar wrote on Mark Twain, and we published Ben Hecht's unfinished biography of Mickey Cohen. We brought Hunter S. Thompson to national prominence in that and later issues, together with the artist Ralph Steadman. We ran stuff by Jean Lacouture and Graham Greene, Hemingway's cub reporting, Russia's underground political pornography, and a revolutionary, oft-reprinted piece on the rock culture by Sol Stern called "Altamont: The Woodstock Nation's Pearl Harbor."

I could go on ad infinitum; the point is we were true to our dream. We combined muckraking with literature and laughs—always there were laughs. Which is how Hinckle and I started.

Scanlan's. We found the name in Ireland at the West County hotel. A bunch of old IRA guys were drinking to one John Scanlan—all night they toasted him. We figured he was a hero of the revolt. Ten days later, on our way back through the country, we stopped for a round at the West County. They were still drinking to Scanlan.

"Who's this Scanlan," we asked. "Is he an IRA hero?"

"Hero?" They laughed. "Scanlan was the worst man ever lived in Ireland. He had seven illegitimate children, none of whom he'd recognize or support. He was a pig farmer, and greedier than the hogs he raised. Ah, he was an awful man."

"So why do you keep drinking to him?"

"Ah, because it's the anniversary of his death, is why. We're so happy he's gone, we drink until we can't stand to hear his name anymore, and then we do the same the next year. A terrible man, Scanlan, the worst."

We had our name, and though the laughs ran out for Hinckle and me, I drink to us every year on the anniversary of our death. To *Scanlan's,* not to Warren, not to me, to *Scanlan's.*

FOR YEARS, MY friends and enemies were sure that I was stuck with Daniel Ellsberg for life plus whatever, that the head of my obit would read, "Sidney Zion, 'Fingered' Daniel Ellsberg in Pentagon Papers." Hearing this, and I heard it all the time, I would smile and shrug, as if to say who gives a damn. I don't know if the act worked, but if it did I belonged on Broadway or at least Hollywood. I gave a damn all right. The whole business was absurd from the outset, and the idea that it would follow me to the grave was outrageous, it was unacceptable. Still, there seemed to be nothing I could do except to keep writing and hope that between Father Time and Mother Nature the bastard would run its course.

It began as a lark, crazy as that might sound. Shortly after *Scanlan's* folded, I took an assignment to do a crime piece for the Sunday *Times Magazine*. On the afternoon of June 15, 1971, I went up to the *Times* city room to check out some clips for the story. A few minutes after I got there, the news flashed that federal Judge Murray Gurfein had issued a temporary order restraining the *Times* from continuing publication of the Pentagon Papers, which had begun two days earlier under the rubric "Vietnam Archive."

The room was buzzing and I hung around talking to reporters. They wanted to know what I thought about the legal situation, and I said the restraining order would never stand up, which was an easy call given that this was the first prior restraint in the history of the federal courts. I wanted to know who leaked the Papers to the paper. Nobody knew. Some of them thought Abe Rosenthal and the publisher knew the source; and one said not even *they* knew it, that only Neil Sheehan, who wrote the story, held the secret.

"That's crazy," I said. "Abe would never go with something this big without knowing the source. I thought Abe looked a little smug today and he should be smug. He knows something I don't know and I consider that an outrage, it's intolerable. I'll find out and I'll tell you all tomorrow."

Everybody laughed and I laughed with them.

I went off to do a guest shot on the Dick Cavett show, which that night was hosted by Germaine Greer. The show was taped early and when I left the studio I forgot all about my "promise" to the reporters. I was feeling great, I'd gone over big on TV and was asked to come back in three weeks when Cavett himself would interview me. I went to Gallagher's to celebrate.

The big circular bar was filled with the regulars, and as soon as I bellied up they surrounded me. They wanted to know who leaked the Papers to the *Times*. The paper had run a box saying that Neil Sheehan broke the story through "investigative reporting," but nobody took that seriously enough to mention it. Who leaked it, they asked me.

I said, "Thanks for reminding me. I promised the guys at the *Times* I'd get 'em the name tomorrow."

"They don't know who it is?" somebody said.

"I don't think they want to know," I said.

Of course, there were plenty of rumors. Clark Clifford, George Ball, Nick Katzenbach, Robert McNamara, and so on were names bandied about as probable sources, but I rejected them because they were household names, and household names didn't get where they got by being the kinds of people who would leak something of this magnitude to the press. Barring miracles, men don't change their skins, particularly big men. And in this instance it wasn't a question of their not wanting to take the chance of being revealed. In this case there was no chance whatever that the source would *not* be uncovered.

It followed, then, that the person who leaked the Pentagon Papers was not a big dog and was someone who expected and perhaps wanted to be revealed. My mission was to find out who he or she was before anyone else—for no other reason than to show the people at the *Times*, my old buddies, that I could do it. Hence, a lark.

After a couple of drinks I left Gallagher's and went to a few haunts where I figured to find some people who could give me what I wanted. I knew most of the people in the peace movement, though I was never part of it. I was always against the war—hell, I was against the Korean War—but I don't join movements, partly because I'm a newspaperman, mainly because I'm not the type. I can't be in marches, and I'm uncomfortable with the piety and lack of humor that inevitably characterizes these groups. Still, they knew where I stood, and those who didn't know it before knew for sure once I started *Scanlan's*.

Anyway, by the time I got home to watch myself on the Cavett show, I knew that the source was well known to the peace movement and that he would break his identity if nobody else did. While they wouldn't tell me his name, three people assured me they'd confirm it if I got it myself.

The next morning, a friend called from Washington, and in the course of conversation he mentioned that *The Washington Post* had a list of people who had access to the Pentagon Papers. Most of them were household names but a few weren't and I wrote them down. I called my confirmation men and wheeled the names. On the second call I said "Daniel Ellsberg" and it was pay dirt. I then called the third guy and he confirmed, and I went back to the first and *he* confirmed.

Now that I had it, I was a newspaperman again. The idea of simply telling it to the boys at the *Times* was out of the question. This was a hot story and I wanted it for myself. But I had no paper, what the hell was I going to do with it?

The phone rang. It was Albert Landau, president of Transworld Feature Syndicate and my brother-in-law. Al said, "If you know anything about the Pentagon Papers, I'd appreciate help. The English press is driving me crazy for a story."

I said, "Well, I just got the name of the guy who leaked it to the *Times*."

There was silence. Then Al said, "My God, you do? That's terrific. Write it immediately—I'll sell the story to the English."

"Don't do anything yet," I said. "Let me see if I can find out more about Ellsberg, I can't just drop the name."

"Of course, but hurry," he said.

I called the man who I knew was the best of my confirmation people and said I wanted to come over and talk to him about Ellsberg, that I was going to write a story. He said fine.

I spent a couple of hours with him, and he told me plenty and gave me some of Ellsberg's writing on Vietnam. "It's a great story," he said, "and I envy you. I wish I could write it myself, but I'm too close to him, it wouldn't look good."

I asked, "Will it hurt him?"

He said, "No, he wants it out, he's making witness. Don't worry about that. And the FBI's about to arrest him anyway."

I went over to Transworld's offices and wrote the story. Meantime I kept calling Ellsberg's home in Cambridge, Massachusetts, leaving messages with his answering service. I called so often I got friendly with the woman doing the answering and finally she said, "Mr. Zion, why is everybody calling Dr. Ellsberg?" I asked, "Who's calling?"

She said, "*Time, Newsweek, The Washington Post,* the *St. Louis Post-Dispatch, The New York Times,* everybody keeps calling."

"*The New York Times,* did you say the *Times?*"

"Sure, everybody," she said.

I couldn't believe the *Times,* but subsequently it came out and they did indeed call. The reporters were trying to discover who leaked to *them.* It was obvious the press was onto something, though I couldn't be sure they weren't just going through *The Washington Post* list of those who had access to the Papers. Whatever, there was no time to lose; this story could break any minute.

Suddenly, there was a clinker. Landau had sold my story to the London *Daily Express,* but now the *Express*'s lawyers wanted to know my sources. England has tough libel laws, they said, and without my sources they couldn't publish. England does indeed have tough libel laws, but I didn't see how the revealing of sources would help, and of course I wouldn't give them that information no matter what. I won't give it now, ten years later. There is no statute of limitations on confidentiality. Period and end of sentence.

The *Daily Express* has a New York office, and I ran over there to argue my case. The editors were all for me; they understood how big this story was, and they didn't want to blow it. I wrote out a telex message for them, giving all the legal answers to their attorneys, but to no avail. Without my sources, they wouldn't publish. I walked out in a rage. It was too late to publish anywhere else that night and it was clear to me that somebody else would have it by morning.

It was a hot night. I went home, took a shower, and stomped around my apartment. "This is the biggest story I've ever had," I said to the four walls, "and I've got nobody to tell it to."

My five-year-old daughter said, "Daddy, you can tell it to me."

I laughed, but I thought wow! I'm down to my kid now.

My wife said, "Why don't you call Barry Gray?"

Of course! Barry Gray had a late-evening radio talk show, and I used to go on it all the time. Barry could call the press in, and I'd beat everybody to the punch. Perfect.

I phoned Barry, but he wasn't in. It was ten o'clock and he was on at eleven. I got dressed anyway, knowing he'd love this one. He got back to me in twenty minutes. I told him I had the name of the person who leaked the Pentagon Papers. Barry said, "How fast can you get down here." Now, I said.

On the way over in a cab I got jitters. What if I'm wrong, suppose it's not the right guy? Could somebody be setting me up? If I'm wrong, I'm dead, finished in journalism. But my sources were genuine, they wouldn't set me up. Still, after what happened to *Scanlan's*, how could I be sure? Maybe my sources were set up. I knew too much to reject paranoia.

When I got to the station, WMCA, reporters were congregating; Gray had done the job, as I knew he would; I didn't have to remind him. A phone call was waiting for me, Arthur Gelb, metropolitan editor of the *Times*, my friend, my mentor.

Arthur said, "What are you going to do?"

"I'm going to name the guy who leaked to Neil Sheehan."

"Who is he?" Arthur asked.

"You kidding? You don't know?"

"I swear I don't know."

"What'll you do if I tell you?"

"I'll tell Abe," Gelb said.

"If I'm wrong, will you call right back so I don't make a schmuck out of myself?"

"I can't do that," Arthur said.

"Then listen to the radio," I said.

Gelb laughed and I hung up.

The WMCA studio in those days had a glass enclosure with telephones. Gray put the reporters there while I was in the pit doing my number. As soon as I mentioned Ellsberg's name, the newsmen picked up their phones to call their papers. I kept my eye on Murray Schumach of the *Times*. And Murray Schumach, after a couple of seconds on the phone, smiled. That smile sent a chill through me. I thought, if Schumach is smiling, I'm wrong, and if I'm wrong, I'm gone. But I had to keep talking until the station break, and there was no break for a good fifteen minutes.

When it finally came, Schumach led the other reporters into the studio. He came over to me and said, coldly, "Arthur Gelb asked me to tell you that you are never to enter *The New York Times* again."

I was elated, I was right, it was all okay. I threw my arms around Murray—whom I'd known as a friend for years—and said, "Thank God."

He stiffened and backed away; his eyes were shocked. I said, "Murray, what the hell's wrong?" He just shook his head—he was looking at a pariah.

"Oh," I said, "it's like that. Well you tell Gelb for me that I don't give a damn, so long as his writ doesn't run to Sardi's bar."

The next morning, the *New York Post* headlined me on the front page with a story that included the quote barring me from the *Times*, but not my line about Sardi's bar. This banishment plagued me for years, long after I was welcomed back on the *Times* floor and even in its pages. But I'm jumping ahead of the story, which began in earnest at seven the morning after, with a call from the FBI.

"What could my friendly FBI agent want this early?" I said, half-asleep. The agent chuckled and said he wanted to come to my apartment to talk to me.

"The FBI is always welcome in my home," I said, "but if you're interested in who my sources were you can save a trip, I'll never give it to you or anyone."

"We just want to come up and talk. Can we come over in an hour?"

"I said you're welcome but not this early, make it after eleven." He said fine.

A few minutes later the managing editor of the *St. Louis Post-Dispatch* called. "Congratulations," he said. "You beat us to the A-wire by twenty minutes. We had Ellsberg's picture on page one, but you scooped us and I take my hat off to you. Great story."

The phone rang again and without a hello a voice said: "You rat bastard, you're a criminal, I'll get you for this." For a second I didn't recognize the voice, but as the invective increased I realized it was my old friend Jack Newfield of *The Village Voice*. I laughed, I really thought he was kidding.

"C'mon Jack, cut the crap, it's too early for jokes."

With that, Newfield went into a complete tirade that ended with a slam of his receiver. I turned to my wife and said, "Well, it looks like I'm in for it." It was the first time I thought about trouble; I had dismissed Gelb's line as heat of the moment and something that would quickly pass. But Jack Newfield wasn't under pressure, he had no objective reason to be upset, and yet there he was blasting me, his friend, and his friend from the day he came to the *Post* for a tryout some seven years before. If Newfield was so outraged, I knew he had plenty of company. Within a few hours I began to learn just how much company he had.

The whole goddam news media rang the phone off the hook after Newfield's call—they wanted a press conference. I arranged one at my place for 10:30; I wanted them there before the FBI guys showed so that *when* they showed I could talk to them on television and so dispel any possible crap that I was "cooperating." It worked like a charm, that part did, because two FBI men walked into my besieged living room and marched directly over to me while I was being interviewed on network TV. "Can we go somewhere where we can talk quietly?" one said. I answered, right into the mike, "The FBI has now asked me to talk to them in private, and I want to repeat to them here what I said to them on the phone earlier this morning: I will not reveal my sources under any circumstance; and so I see no point in a private meeting."

The FBI guys turned around and left. The reporters scurried after them into the hallway but got no comment. When the reporters came back, Murray Schumach yelled out to me, "How do you know they were FBI men—they showed no identification." I laughed and said, "The crew cuts, the narrow ties and those St. John's night school suits were enough for me, how about you all?" Everybody laughed—it was the first and only time I got a laugh that day—except Schumach, who said, "Have you no shame?" I shot back, "I don't take moral lectures from you or *The New York Times*, Murray, so just try and stifle yourself."

That crack restored the tension level to ten. The newscasters and press had been at me from the start, and now they picked it up again. Over and over they asked, "Why did you do it? What was your motive?" At first, I didn't think they were serious—what the hell is a reporter doing asking another reporter why he broke one of the big stories of the time? And so I brushed them off by asking them what their motives were in asking me about my motives. Finally, it dawned on me that something else was cooking, and I wasn't crazy about the smell.

What bedeviled the press was the fact that I wasn't working for a paper or a TV station. I don't know how much of it was conscious, but the clear-cut feeling was that you don't go around breaking stories unless you've got a job. Certainly I would never have been attacked had I broken the story for *The Washington Post* or even the London *Daily Express*—hell, they'd have given me awards. Nobody said a word against the *St. Louis Post-Dispatch* reporter whose piece came out a few hours after mine—nobody mentioned his name.

Everybody inside the business was expected to go after the story. As an outsider—albeit temporarily between engagements—I was considered an immoral bastard. The implications were scary, because fundamentally my crime was that I had no Eichmann defense; I wasn't ordered to do it, therefore I had no right to do it. Obviously, nobody said it that way, but just as obviously that's what they were thinking, else why no outcry about the *Post-Dispatch* reporter or all the others who were breaking their humps trying to discover the source of the Pentagon Papers? And why wasn't anybody upset with Barry Gray, who gave me the forum?

While my lack of an Eichmann defense was the central reason for the attacks, ideology provided the underpinning. The man who leaked the Pentagon Papers was a hero to everyone opposed to the war and by 1971 this grouping included most of the news media, particularly in New York. That I considered Ellsberg a heroic figure, and said so on the Gray Show, was of as little consequence to them as the fact that I had been against the war from the outset—long before nearly all of them got the message and before Ellsberg got religion; indeed, while Ellsberg was whooping it up in Vietnam, regaling the troops to get the gooks.

In retrospect, I find it amazing that I never considered any of this. I was just scooping the world press, and my only worry was that I might be wrong. Eventually, virtually all of my critics saw it my way, but "eventually" turned out to be a long, long run.

The blacklist was imposed as soon as various editors woke up on the morning after my broadcast. During the news conference—read inquisition—at my apartment, Dick Cavett's people called and left a message that I was canceled. An hour later, the *Times Magazine* phoned to tell me that "under the circumstances" my crime story assignment was out. Meanwhile, John Leonard, editor of the Sunday *Times Book Review*, announced to his staff, "Zion will never write for us again."

Leonard deserves more than a passing reference. He began his big-time journalistic life at *The National Review* as an acolyte of William F. Buckley, Jr. But he had come all the way around and was now a leading literary and moral force against the war. We were never close but always friendly and we had drinks together on occasion. When *Scanlan's* folded, Leonard gave me a book to review, *The Grandees*, about the rich Sephardic Jews of America. The piece was a hit, it drew all kinds of great mail, and John said, "Our pages are open to you anytime you want." That was two months before Ellsberg.

Leonard's word was good to the last drop. His last word. As long as he was the editor, I never wrote for the *Book Review.*

After the camera crews left my house, I went to Sardi's. It was lunch time, and the place was filled with the usual combination of tourists, bar regulars, theater people and *Times* crowd. I stopped first at the little bar in front of the restaurant, and was cheered by my drinking buddies, who were vying with each other to buy me drinks in celebration of my scoop. They had no way of knowing there was trouble ahead, though when they found out it only made them stick with me more. I hung around for a couple of minutes and then worked the dining area, where I was cut dead by the *Times* people, who wouldn't look up as I came around to say hello.

Back at the bar, Gerry Walker, an editor at the *Times Magazine,* took me aside. "I now know what the Salem witch-hunt was about," he said. "The whole paper is going nuts over this, the elevators are buzzing. I've never seen such hysteria—they want to hang you. I'm sorry to tell you this, I think it's a disgrace, but I thought you ought to be forewarned."

I toured my haunts the rest of the day and night, and by the time I got back to Sardi's, I was feeling little pain, not just because of Johnnie Walker. Except for a couple of newspaper guys, everybody was clapping my back. At Elaine's, where the writers live, I even got a standing ovation. And walking into Sardi's for a nightcap, I caught Abe Rosenthal and Arthur Gelb on their way out. Abe looked down, but Arthur gave me a quick smile, and I thought everything would be fine.

Abe and Arthur meant more to me than all the news media put together. Were it not for them, I would have quit the newspaper game. The tawdry little candy store that was the *New York Post* had turned me into a near-cynic about the business. Rosenthal and Gelb, the best metropolitan editors ever, opened up a new world for me. They gave me freedom, taught me discipline, allowed me to grow— in a word, they restored my faith. And they were good friends.

When Arthur barred me from the paper, I assumed it came from Abe and thus didn't take it seriously. Abe is an emotional man; he gets mad on the spot, but he's ultimately reasonable and is possessed of a good and sweet character. That he cooled me at Sardi's was nothing much, given Artie's smile.

In the end, I was right but premature by many moons. Rosenthal was seething and it was going to be a long time before we talked.

I was in more hot water the morning after the apartment press conference, and it was my fault. In answer to one of the innumerable questions as to why I went after the story, I said, "To satisfy my ego." There was truth to it—if no ego, what's a byline for?—but I was stupid to say it. The *New York Post* picked right up on it and ran a quasi-profile of me headlined "Zion & His Ego-Tripping." I'm not in the habit of handing bullets to my enemies, but I schmucked into that one and paid the price. I looked like a scoundrel.

Still, by the beginning of the following week, I thought the worst was over. Except for the *Post* piece, nothing had appeared against me in print. Then, on Tuesday, June 22, Pete Hamill weighed in with a furious attack in his then popular column in the *Post*. Hamill accused me of setting "our secret police" on Ellsberg and predicted that "some Arnold Schuster, working out of innocence, will probably finger him, and if he is charged and convicted of violating national security, he could go away for a long time."

Hamill wrote, "Sidney apparently doesn't care. It doesn't matter to him that other brave men might be afraid to talk to newspapermen if another newspaperman might eventually turn them in."

He was settling a score, Hamill was, and he as much as said so in his column. About a year earlier, I wrote a piece in *Scanlan's* on Elia Kazan called "Hello, Informer," keyed to a fight night at Toots Shor's when I noticed Hamill browning up Kazan. Pete was writing movies and I couldn't resist asking him—in front of Kazan—what his old man would think of him talking to an informer. Hamill's father was in the Sinn Fein; Gadge Kazan in 1952 gave up everybody he could think of who shared with him a brief membership in the Communist Party during the 1930s.

Pete nervously avoided my question at Shor's, but a couple of days later dropped me a note, which said, in part: "I don't know very much about Kazan, although I'm reasonably familiar with the bullshit he committed in the 1950s. The thing is whether that kind of thing can forever damn a man, or whether a writer can afford not to learn something else about the guy's character."

No writer trying to hook to Kazan could afford the loss of this learning experience, so I thought I'd learn Pete something more about his man. I reprinted in *Scanlan's* the notorious ad Kazan published in *The New York Times* on April 12, 1952, the day his secret testimony to the House Un-American Activities Committee was made public. The ad was a mishmash of confessionado, rationalization, and a plea to other "liberals" to "speak out," presumably to rat.

In the piece accompanying the ad—and we sent Kazan a check for the ad, *Scanlan's* policy was to pay for ads—I quoted Pete's letter, which understandably pissed him off. He blamed my partner Warren Hinckle for it, but I told him it was me, and I apologized because it was a somewhat crummy thing to do. He said forget it, it was just one of those things, only of course he wasn't going to forget it. When *Scanlan's* began having trouble with the Nixon Gang, Hamill refused to say a word about it in his column, and I figured that was his way of getting even, and fair enough.

But I had overlooked something. In the planning stages of *Scanlan's*, Pete wrote us a long letter proposing himself as a roving columnist. John Leo, one of the three original editors of the magazine (together with me and Hinckle) was for it, but Warren and I were cool to the idea, mainly because we didn't want any permanent fixtures; we thought that was what was wrong with most magazines and newspapers—too many people with contracts. We turned him down, and it was for this perceived slight that he couldn't forgive us, particularly me, since he had to know that my vote was decisive. He knew Hinckle only casually, but I was his friend, and now he had the chance to stick it to me and he made the most of it.

He wrote that I was a "shyster lawyer," I was "scummy," that it was "all over" for me in New York, "because in the real world some things simply are not done." His column concluded with these words: "And now it's going to get pretty lonely too. I just hope Sidney has time to apologize to Kazan."

The column was libelous *per se*. I got calls from lawyers who told me that if I sued the *Post*, I'd end up on the masthead—that's how good I had them for this. I never considered it. I don't believe in the libel laws; I think they violate the First Amendment. That only Justices Black and Douglas took this position on the Supreme Court was pointed out to me by the lawyers, but the fact served to solidify my view; Black and Douglas were my heroes. Anyway, I don't like lawsuits—no good lawyer likes to start them; they end up consuming your life.

I did, however, call Paul Sann, still executive editor of the *Post*. I said, "Paul, I want space to answer Hamill—he murdered me in that column." Sann said, "Buy a fucking ad." That answer, I knew, would have given me punitive damages, but to hell with it, I let it go; the thing would pass.

That night, my father called. His voice was agitated. "Did you read Pete Hamill?" I said sure, but don't worry about it. "I'm plenty worried about it," he said. "I want to know what you're going to do about it." I told him nothing, I'd do nothing, everybody was crazy, it would go away by itself.

"Let's have a drink tomorrow," my father said.

"Daddy," I said, "I can't come to Passaic—I've got too much to do around here."

"I don't mean Passaic. I'll meet you in New York. Where do you hang out for lunch?"

Was this my old man talking? I never met him for drinks, in New York or anywhere. I chuckled, a little nervously, and said, "Okay, Gallagher's at noon."

He was all business, my father. People were trying to destroy me, and I was standing around, letting it happen. I had a reputation to protect, I had a family to protect. "You're laying down," he said. "Since when did you lay down?"

I said, "Daddy, I know what I'm doing. The bastards are after me now, but they have nothing, it's all madness. Soon it'll be tomorrow's headline, relax."

"You're the only one who'll be tomorrow's headline," he said. "They're going to leave you for dead. You've got a pen, use it. If you don't answer these guys now, you're finished."

"What do you want me to do?"

"I told you. Write a story, defend yourself."

My father. He'd never asked me to do anything, just let me fly, all my life. When my mother thought I should follow in his footsteps and become a dentist, he simply let me ruin the denture room one day, and that satisfied everybody that I had no hands. I can't remember him ever giving me advice, and I told him that at Gallagher's.

"You didn't need it before," he said.

"Okay, Papa, you got it, I'll write the piece."

The Village Voice was the natural place to publish my defense. I'd written for them on occasion while I was on the Times, I was friendly with everybody there, and on the very day I met with my father, Nat Hentoff ran a page-one story headlined "U.S. v. N.Y. Times v. Zion v. Earth." Hentoff, an old buddy, was generally critical of my role in the Pentagon Papers—"My initial reaction," he wrote, "was both anger and incomprehension"—but unlike Hamill he had called me first and gave my side of the story.

I talked to Ross Wetzsteon, an associate editor on the *Voice*, and told him I wanted to write my full position. Ross said the paper would welcome it. So I ran it off fast, sent it over—and waited. And waited. Finally, I called Wetzsteon. He said, "We've decided against using the piece; the feeling is that you've told your story on television and the radio."

The Village Voice, in the ordinary course of business, used to run a good six months on an issue, any pissant issue, and they still do it. Suddenly, I had had my say, they were telling me that! Now I really knew I was in trouble.

True, I did get a lot of time on the air, particularly television. As soon as Hamill's column came out, Ted Kavanau, the editor of channel 5 news, asked me to come over. Ted was a conservative, but he didn't like what was happening to me, however little he agreed with my views. He said, simply, "You should be up for prizes; instead, these liberal fascists are after your ass. I won't let it happen. I want you on this station—we'll stick with you as long as it takes to turn it around."

And he did. He set up a debate with Newfield and others; he had me on almost every night. When the *Voice* spiked my story, I called Ted and he put me on to tell about it. That night, Dan Wolf, the editor of the *Voice*, my friend for years, sat watching me beat hell out of the place for censoring me. He was a wreck over it. Imagine *The Village Voice*, that citadel of free speech, killing a story. But Wolf was the one who did the job, against his better judgment, I'm convinced. He listened to his writers, most of whom didn't want me to have my say, and for good reason. My piece was powerful, unanswerable, it laid bare the liberal hypocrisy. Once my daddy asked me to do it, I wasn't going to do it nice, I put the knife to the sons of bitches.

Still, what good was it if I couldn't get it printed? And if not in the *Voice*, where? I phoned Sterling Lord, one of the city's premier literary agents. He wasn't my agent—I had no agent at the time—but he agreed to meet with me immediately. Over drinks, I told him what had happened at the *Voice* and gave him a copy of my piece. He read it right there and said he'd get it placed. It was a marvelous gesture. The last guy Sterling Lord needed was me, and on top of that he hardly knew me. But he took me on and I'll never forget his kindness.

Sterling delivered the piece to *New York* magazine, then run by

Clay Felker. When Felker started *New York*, he asked me to come there, to leave the *Times*. "Join me and we'll wipe up the town," he said, and he repeated it every time he saw me. Surely he'd publish my story, it was up his alley.

It turned out that Clay was vacationing in Spain—or was it the south of France?—but Sterling said it would only mean a short delay, the managing editor would give him a summary on the phone. Sterling said it sounded good, the managing editor liked the piece, and it was only a question of clearing it with Felker. A couple of days later, Clay Felker rejected it. For the usual stated reason: "It's great, but it's not for us."

Not for *us*? Christ, *New York* lived on stories like this. The real reason was that Felker sniffed the prevailing wind and decided I was too unpopular for his trendy sheet. And now I was really worried, because, unlike the *Voice*, Felker's magazine was nonideological, which meant an across-the-board blacklist. Plus, where the hell was I going to get the story published? The monthlies were out because of long lead times, even assuming they'd be otherwise interested. And the dailies would never touch it. So where to go?

I went to Sardi's bar, where somebody said, "Why don't you try *Women's Wear Daily?*" Bingo! I knew it would work. *Women's Wear* was then a very hot paper edited by James Brady. They loved controversy. Amazing that it never occurred to me. I quick phoned Sterling, and he said "right." He immediately delivered the piece to Brady. Two hours later, Sterling called me at Sardi's and said, "Jim Brady wants the piece, but he'll only pay $300. Even so, I think you should take it."

Take it? I'd have paid a lot more than $300 to get it published. You betcha, baby.

A few minutes later, Jim Brady called to thank me for the piece and said it was running on page one. I said, "When?" He said, "Tomorrow morning." "What?" Brady laughed. "Hey, we're a newspaper, not a magazine." Jim apologized for the low fee, but he said he had something in mind and would be in touch in the next day or two.

On Thursday, July 1, 1971, there it was, on top of the front page, headlined "Why Zion Unmasked Ellsberg as Source." All it did was to save my ass. I didn't realize it for quite some time, but the piece began the long process of changing minds. It was reprinted across the country—*Women's Wear* had a terrific syndicate—and it appeared on the front pages of *The Washington Post, The Boston Globe*, the *Chicago Tribune*, and the *Los Angeles Times*, to name the most well-known papers.

I took a lot of shots at *The New York Times* in the piece, for example: "The *Times* has treated me to lectures on morals and ethics, which is like learning about love from Attila the Hun," and somebody there liked it enough to post it on the city room's bulletin board. All day, the staff gathered around to read it, barely hiding their chortles from the editors. As Izzy Schawarzberg would say, "You pulled their teeth, and now they could only gum you."

George Frazier, the great *Boston Globe* columnist, picked right up on it and wrote an orchid, devoting his entire "Lit'ry Life" column to me. I had never met Frazier and didn't get to meet him until after he did another full column a couple of weeks later, blasting my enemies. We got to be fast friends and stayed that way until he died at cocktail time on June 13, 1974. Ever elegant, George wouldn't get away at some dumb hour. I still keep his phone number in my Rolodex, and one of these days I'll find him in. I wrote his obit for *The Soho News*, and months later *The Boston Globe* reprinted it. But Frazier lives, don't worry about it.

The *WWD* piece had other immediate effects. I went on TV talk shows in Boston, Philadelphia, Washington, Chicago, and scored a few lecture dates. With these events came some good press, notably a warm column by Tom Fitzpatrick of the Chicago *Sun-Times*, which made my parents happy because it appeared in the Passaic *Herald-News*.

All of this was nice but I knew it didn't mean a hell of a lot, because there were no calls to write. Then Jim Brady gave me real hope. He asked me to do a weekly media column for *WWD*. The very next day, Brady was fired. No connection, but I was back to square one. Yesterday's newspaper, or so it looked.

One morning in early July I overheard my wife, working the phones like mad, telling people our address, and I asked what was going on. Elsa said, "We're having a party to celebrate the one-month anniversary of your Ellsberg story. I'm calling it the June 16th Movement."

"Where you gonna hold it, the telephone booth at Sardi's?"

"You'll be surprised—we're going to pack 'em in here," she said.

I asked her why she was giving out the address. We had a couple of big parties every year; our friends knew where we lived.

"My rule is that nobody gets invited unless they called here within forty-eight hours of the broadcast."

In that case, I said, Sardi's phone booth was too big.

"Watch and see," she said.

Eighty-six people showed up on the night of July 16. I knew them all, of course, but only a handful had been at my house before. I took Elsa aside. "Do you mean to say that all these casual acquaintances called in the first two days, and just these few of our friends?"

She smiled and said, "That's the way it went, baby. You were all around town, I was right here."

I can't describe a chill except to say a chill ran up and down my spine. I'd been doing something very wrong if this was the way it was—and obviously this was the way it was.

The following evening, I was telling the Sardi's bartender about the party, about how shaken I was by the lack of "friends." Sure it was great that so many others were there, but what happened to my old pals? I'd been running parties for ten years, with the same people. Where were they last night?

An elderly man tapped me on the shoulder. I recognized his face, but didn't know his name. He said, "Pardon me, young man, I couldn't help overhearing. I know who you are, of course—by the way, my name is Guy Repp, just an old actor. I want to tell you, sir, that you're a lucky man, a very lucky man. And please forgive me, but how old are you?"

I told him thirty-eight.

"Ah," he said. "Ah, how lucky."

"I'm sorry," I said, "but I don't get what you mean."

"Young man," he said, "you have discovered something that very few people discover. Usually only the widows find out at the graveside. But you know it now, how fortunate for you."

"I'm still in the dark," I said.

"No you're not. You know *everything* now. You know who your friends are not."

Around that time, *The East Village Other* ran a long interview with me. The cover pictured me holding two of my kids, and over it ran the headline "The Most Despised Man in the American Press." The interview was pretty terrific and so was the inside head: "Sid Zion Wipes Out the Scriveners." But who reads inside. The cover accurately described the situation.

And I was busted out, to boot. Not only broke but in debt. The bankruptcy of *Scanlan's* put me in a big hole. My answer was to go into heavy debt. I borrowed thirty grand from six rich guys, five apiece. I told them it might be a long time before they'd get it back, and I wouldn't pay interest, but eventually they'd have it.

"I'm going to live as if nothing happened," I said. "I don't want my family to suffer one iota. I'll be going to all the old familiar places, I'll be drinking Johnnie Black, the whole shmear. If you can't handle that, don't give me the dough."

A few turned me down, but I got it. I told nobody about this, not even my wife. I knew that if I stopped living well, I'd be buried—and no way I'd let them bury me.

The rumors started fast. I was on the CIA payroll, the FBI. How else could I go on this way—didn't everybody know I was tapped out, tapioca?

Very nice, indeed. Here I was, put out of business by the government, and the word was I was on the pad! I needed a cover. I could go back to Jersey and practice law, but what kind of cover was that? I'd simply be conceding defeat; they'd have driven me out of journalism. I signed a book contract, I was going to write a book about *The New York Times. Against The Times*—that was the title. A ten grand advance, but nobody knew that, nobody ever has to know how much—you can brag. I told people it was fifty Gs.

I was going to write the book, until Peter Bergson showed up from Tel Aviv. Bergson is about the smartest man I have ever met, not to say the most courageous and honorable. Raised in Palestine in the 1930s, he was in the high command of Irgun (and considered by the British their second Most Wanted man—Abraham Stern, of the Stern Gang, was first) when he came to New York in 1939 and established the Committee for a Jewish Army, the Emergency Committee to Save the Jews of Europe, the Hebrew Committee for National Liberation, and a few more such organizations. He brought hundreds of congressmen to the banner, and most of all he brought Ben Hecht, who became co-chairman and publicist on all his committees.

I told Peter about the book and he said no. Just like that—no. Why no?

"Look," he said. "You were walking down the street one day and you bumped into *The New York Times*. When Ben Hecht met us, he said he bumped into history. You bumped into the *Times*. Now they want to drive you out of journalism. But wait a while. They're smart people. Let the emotionalism wane, and it will be as if nothing ever happened. They'll understand that you bumped into them, there was no malice. And you'll be back. It will take time, but it will happen. If you write this book you're thinking about, if you go after them that way, they'll never forgive you. Then you'll be dead, then you'll have to go back to law or whatever you come up with. And you'll be unhappy the rest of your life."

Deep down, I knew he was right, but I pecked away petulantly at the book, on and off, for months. It's a good thing I never finished it, not only because I would have irretrievably lost the *Times*. The book would not have been good; it would have been full of half-truths. I was coming at it out of bitterness, a bitterness whose depth I didn't realize until I looked at what I had.

Within a year, Bergson's prediction began to come true. I was holding court at Sardi's upstairs bar one night. Abe Rosenthal and a group of his editors came in to drink at the other end of the bar. This in itself was an event; ever since Ellsberg, Abe would go downstairs if I was upstairs or vice versa. Now he stayed, and he caught my eye a few times, and I thought maybe something was happening. After a while, I needed the john, and as I passed by Abe took my arm.

"*Gnug,*" he said, which in Yiddish means "enough." "Have a drink." I said, "Well, Abe, on such an auspicious occasion do you mind if I pee first?" He laughed and said come right back.

The barman had my Johnnie Black ready and I reminded Abe about the first time we had a drink together at Sardi's, a few days after I joined the *Times*. Before we could order, the guy had my drink poured—in those days I drank Beefeater's—and Abe gave me a look that said "What kind of lush is this I just hired?" Here I was on tryout and this schmuck barkeep has the martini out there like I do it every day. Of course I did it every day, but this time I gave it the cold eye and said, "What's this? I didn't order this." The bartender understood immediately and apologized for his "mistake," but Abe wasn't fooled, and all that happened was I had to drink something else, a Virgin Mary or some damned thing.

Abe smiled at my recollection—I don't think he remembered it; why the hell should he?—and then clinked glasses, said "L'chaim," and before I could bring the drink to my lips, he said, "I forgive you."

I put the drink down. "I'll see you," I said and walked toward the stairs. Abe came after me. "What's wrong?" I said, "Abe, if you don't know, I can't teach you. Forget it, I'm leaving." He was distraught. "Tell me what I did."

I used Peter Bergson's line. I said, "One day I was walking down the street and I bumped into *The New York Times*. For which you tried to drive me out of journalism. Now you forgive *me?*"

Abe said, "Are you asking me to apologize?"

"I'm not asking you for anything. I just want to get out of here."

He wouldn't let me go. He said he understood how I felt but he didn't want any more of this—the whole thing was crazy. I had to come back to the bar; we couldn't let it go this way. Did I want an apology?

"No," I said. "But don't forgive me, I won't take that."

He put his arm around me. "Come, we'll drink. I want to talk to you."

It was good enough, I wasn't going to be a perfect asshole.

"You know," Abe said, "when I read your piece in *Women's Wear*, I knew you were right. First of all, that line about Attila the Hun, it broke me up, it was hilarious. But the important thing was when you said that if you'd written it for a paper nobody would have objected, they'd have given you prizes. As soon as I read that I said to myself, 'He's exactly right.' And ever since, I've wondered why I didn't understand that from the first, why I was so upset with you. You broke a great story, what could be wrong with that? You had every right to break it—you weren't working for us. But you put your finger on it. You weren't working for anyone. That should have made no difference, only it did. I never thought of it until you wrote it, but that was the real reason we all turned against you. It's remarkable."

I thought to myself, What took you so long to tell me this? But I stifled myself. It was time to leave well enough alone. What took me so long to get that?

Abe followed up by sending word to the Sunday department—the *Magazine, Book Review,* and *Week in Review*—assuring the editors that he had no objection to my writing for them and suggesting they give me assignments. Later such a note from Abe would have been fiat, but at the time he didn't control Sunday; it was still autonomous and under the aegis of Max Frankel. I hardly knew Max, but apparently he had no interest in me; nothing happened.

Still spinning my wheels, I decided in the spring of 1972 to go back to law. I could have gone to Jersey, where I had a multitude of offers, but that would have been too much of a break, and as I said before, a full-scale admission that I was out of journalism. If I could get into the New York Bar, maybe I could play the piano: try a few cases and still be available for writing.

I had one problem. To be admitted by motion in New York—that is, to get in without taking the bar exam, and I surely wasn't about to take the bar exam—one had to have practiced five years in another state. I was about six months under that number. But it wasn't hard and fast; there had been numerous exceptions, including President Nixon, who was admitted in New York though he practiced in California for only a year.

I went to see Bernard Botein, the former presiding justice of the appellate division in Manhattan, then the head of a law firm. Botein always liked me, and he offered to be my sponsor. He didn't think the six-month thing would matter. With him in my corner, how could it matter?

Did I say I had learned how to leave well enough alone? I went before the bar committee, and when somebody there pushed me about the six months, I right away threw Nixon at him. "You let Nixon in and he hardly practiced at all; I don't think he tried a case in California. I tried a hundred cases, I was an assistant U.S. attorney, I tried more cases than most litigating partners on Wall Street."

Bernie Botein called me. "What made you mention Nixon? You got their noses out of whack. I'll see what I can do, but that wasn't too clever, my friend."

To say the least. The committee turned me down, with leave to appeal to the New York Court of Appeals. Talk about stupid. Who else could have lost with Botein as sponsor?

In the event, the Court of Appeals sent it back with a recommendation that I get the license. In May 1972 I was sworn in as a member of the New York Bar. A month later, an old friend offered me a partnership in his newly founded law firm. "You'll make a hundred grand the first year," he said. Thanks, but no thanks. If I did that, I'd be in forever, and I wasn't going to be in forever. The idea was to make a few bucks until I could get back to the newspaper business.

A criminal lawyer who thought he could use my news connections—I couldn't get a story published, but he didn't know it—offered me free space in his office. I did nothing for him—I didn't *try* to do anything—and I did nothing for myself, either. Instead, I wrote a piece on Meyer Lansky for *Esquire*, covered the Democratic convention for *The Antioch Review*, and wrote a piece on gossip for *Harper's Bazaar*, whose new editor was Jim Brady.

Things were definitely looking better on the literary front. Nobody hissed anymore when I walked into a room, and I buried the hatchet with people like Jack Newfield. In March 1973, Pete Hamill wrote a full column apology—he even called it "Apology"—in the *Post*. I sent him a wire: "I assume this is the start of a series." Hamill's column ended with a plea that the blacklist stop.

Somehow it didn't stop, not to where I could make a living. I was down to scrounging for rent money and reached bottom one night when my best friend from kindergarten days turned me down for $750. Okay, I had to make a move. I put out the word that I was in the market for a criminal trial.

Very few lawyers know how to try cases before juries. Within a couple of days I had a narcotics case, five grand down, but I had no office. I'd left the guy who tried to hustle me, and you can't operate out of an apartment. Doug Ireland to the rescue. Dougie, my old Lion's Head drinking pal, introduced me to Saul Rudes, a successful real estate lawyer, and Saul gave me space, no strings attached, in his Wall Street office.

It was a rough trial. My client, a young Irish guy on the list of top junk pushers, was indicted for selling a pound of cocaine to an undercover cop. The trial was in Queens Narcotics Court, where nobody had ever been acquitted. I won it by effectively putting the cop on trial. The next day my phone rang off the hook. Everybody facing narcotics raps, it seemed, wanted my services. I begged off; I had my pin money and I wanted to stay loose. I was determined to get back into mainstream journalism.

But the only call I got was from Mike Goldstein, who had recently founded the *Soho Weekly News*. The paper ran twelve pages, and was a cut above a giveaway. Goldstein offered me a column. I could write anything I wanted, he said, and I'd have the best spot in the paper. He'd pay me twice as much as everybody else. How much? "Ten dollars," Goldstein said.

I *shenked* him his sawbuck—I didn't even believe he could pay that much—but I told him I'd do it for a piece of the action. After some bargaining, he gave me 5 percent of the paper. It turned out to be one of the best deals I ever made.

I wrote for *Soho* for four years, without editing. They didn't even have the right to correct typos. I always believed the eight hundred–word column was my métier, but I had never had the chance to prove it. Looking back over these columns—a small, representative sampling is included here—I think they're among the best stuff I ever wrote.

Soho grew in size though it never developed a large circulation. Eventually, however, it was read by all the editors and most of the writers in town. After a while, Sid Goldberg, head of the NANA syndicate, began to distribute my column to papers—mainly small ones—around the country. It hardly paid the bar bills, but it got me exposure. Most important, the *Soho* column helped me to hone my talent. And by providing me with a platform, it released my frustration.

It did not, however, serve to bring big-time editors to my doorstep. If anything, it proved to them that I was trouble—assuming they needed proof. The column was outspoken, hard hitting, iconoclastic—everything they didn't want in their pages.

It was only after I wrote the Mike Burke cover for the *Times Magazine* that I got a shot at mass circulation, in Rupert Murdoch's *New York Post*. Had it not been for *Soho*, however, I doubt Murdoch would have given me a column. So it paid off that way, and later, when Mike Goldstein sold the paper, I got $50,000 for my five points. And so was able to pay my old creditors and have a cushion after taxes.

One more word about filthy lucre. During my years at *Soho*, I survived financially by trying a couple more cases and doing visiting lecture stints at Antioch College and Seton Hall Law School. That, plus another book contract, and the help of a friend or two, allowed my family to live as if Daniel Ellsberg never happened.

In 1980, Harrison Salisbury's *Without Fear or Favor* was published by Times Books. Subtitled, a bit self-consciously, *An Uncompromising Look at The New York Times*, the book focused heavily on the Pentagon Papers. It revealed something startling: That Neil Sheehan and his wife, Susan, stole the Pentagon Papers from Dan Ellsberg's Cambridge, Massachusetts, apartment.

Ellsberg, of course, had allowed Sheehan to read the Papers and make notes, but he never gave him permission to make photocopies. He gave him the key to the apartment, since, as Salisbury wrote, "it would take Neil quite a while to make his way through the many volumes."

On the weekend beginning March 19, 1971, Sheehan and wife arrived in Cambridge, registered under a fake name in a Cambridge motel, went to Ellsberg's flat, carted out the Papers, and had them copied. This clandestine operation took, in Salisbury's words, "three nerve-racked days," at a cost of $1,500 in fees to all-night copying agencies. Ellsberg never knew about it, Salisbury said, and probably only found out when he read Harrison's book.

Why all this cloak-and-dagger business? It seems that Ellsberg was becoming an annoyance; he was making demands as to how the Papers would be published, he was talking about bringing them out through others. The *Times* decided to control the matter; Sheehan and wife were the instruments.

Ellsberg had reasons to be nervous. The *Times* was taking its own good time, and he probably suspected that the Gray Lady might never publish the Papers. If he thought that, he was on the nose: The decision to go was only made at the eleventh hour.

Once the final order to publish was given, Sheehan didn't tell Ellsberg. Dan found out about it a few hours before the presses rolled when Anthony Austin, a *Times* editor, called him in something of a panic. Austin had written a book about the Tonkin Gulf affair of 1964. When Tony heard from a colleague that the *Times* was to publish that very night something called the "McNamara papers," he feared his book was scooped. Since Tony had consulted Ellsberg, he called him to ask what Ellsberg knew about it.

According to Salisbury, Ellsberg tried to buck up Austin, and at the same time seemed "extraordinarily excited" about the publication of the McNamara papers.

"Are you sure?" he asked Austin. "Are they really publishing those papers Sunday?" Austin reiterated that the *Times* was going to press within hours.

Ellsberg immediately called Sheehan. But Sheehan never returned the call.

Well. Had Tony Austin not called Ellsberg, Dan would have discovered the story the next morning, on page one. Like everybody else in Cambridge, Mass. He would have thus been left naked, wide open to arrest and search of his apartment. The FBI knew he was the source of the Papers—during his trial it came out that they knew he copied the Papers at the Rand Corporation over a year before. And of course, Kissinger knew—the whole Nixon Gang knew who it was.

I mention it here with some relish, because of all the withering stares I caught in the days following my broadcast, none was as disdainful and pious as the one I got from Neil Sheehan. I thought it was fair enough; after all, I'd blown Sheehan as a great investigative reporter. It's clear after Salisbury that this was but a part of it. He knew what I didn't know. He knew he had screwed Dan Ellsberg, and what I was getting was guilt pouring over.

A few months ago, a friend was lunching with Mrs. Neil Sheehan, Susan Sheehan of *The New Yorker*. The friend mentioned me, and Susan Sheehan blasted away. "How could you talk to so vicious a bastard. Don't you know what he did to Daniel Ellsberg?"

The funny thing is, Ellsberg didn't think I did anything wrong. I know that because he told me so.

After his espionage indictment, Ellsberg told a mutual friend that he wanted to speak with me. I called him immediately. He said, "I hope you don't think I owe you anything." That was so odd that it stopped me for a second. "What could you owe me?" I said. Ellsberg answered, "Well, the press has been very rough on you; I thought you might have blamed me. But every time they ask me about you, I tell them you had every right to do what you did—I hold nothing against you. So far as I know, they've never printed that, I don't know why."

I thanked him and asked him what I could do for him. Ellsberg said, "I was hoping you could help me at the *Times*. They haven't been covering my pretrial motions—I can't get more than an inch in the paper."

How crazy can things get, Dan Ellsberg asking me to help him with the *Times*? Absurd is absurd, but this was *really* absurd. Years later, I was told that Ellsberg thought I was always part of the *Times*, even when I broke the story about him. There's always one more "really" after you think you've heard the very end.

In the end, Ellsberg beat the rap, and I beat the Ellsberg rap. Nobody asks me why I did it anymore. Nobody talks about Daniel Ellsberg anymore. The obit looks safe, but who wants obits?

WHAT DO RUPERT Murdoch, *The New York Times*, Son of Sam, Mike Burke, the *New York Post*, *New York* magazine and the State of Israel have in common? Me. Read all about it!

In 1978, a year after Murdoch, the Australian invader, took over the *Post* and *New York* magazine, he hired me to write a column for the *Post*. The reason: Rupert and his executive editor, Roger Wood, loved the cover story I did for *The New York Times Magazine* on Mike Burke. That story, reported further on, effectively wiped out Burke's great image, carefully cultivated over the years by Mike and his press pals. It also marked my reentry to the *Times Magazine*, after nearly a decade.

My return to the *Post*, after a decade and a half, was even more spectacular and almost as much fun. David Berkowitz, the self-proclaimed Son of Sam, who killed six women and held New York in terror throughout the summer of 1977, was scheduled to go on trial in the late fall or early winter of '77. There was great confusion in the press as to whether he was sane enough to stand trial and what might happen if he was or wasn't.

On Wednesday, October 26, 1977—the day after my first column appeared in the *Post*—I went over to the Brooklyn Supreme Court to interview Justice John Starkey, who had been assigned to preside over the trial. No reporter had tried to talk with Starkey on the apparent grounds that judges don't discuss pending cases with reporters. I knew plenty who did, and with nothing to lose but time I took a shot. And hit blackjack.

Judges who talk virtually always do it on condition of nonattribution. But not Starkey. All he wanted to know was when the piece would run. He found out on Friday morning, when the Murdochian headline shouted: "Sam Judge Talks." A few days later, "Sam Judge on Way Out." The appellate division, reportedly "astonished" at Starkey's "indiscretion" in discussing the case with me, forced the seventy-one-year-old jurist off the case. I can see why, of course, given the hypocrisy of the free-press, fair-trial syndrome, but only because of that.

In retrospect, I made a mistake getting this scoop; I raised the expectations of my editors, who were never entirely satisfied with "just columns" from me, though I signed on for columns. Every once in a while they'd ask me, "Why don't you do more reporting—that Son of Sam thing was great, that's the kind we want." To make matters worse, I had followed the Starkey story with an exclusive on President Carter's secret meeting with Moshe Dayan at the UN Plaza. That time I *knew* I was taking a chance—the first two out of three pieces exclusives—not columns, exclusives. But who could resist?

Anyhow, I did good stuff for the paper, and for a couple of months they were nice to me, playing my column in the centerfold. Then things got cold. I never knew why for sure, though as I say, I believe they wanted reporting.

In late January, I got a chance to give them reporting. Rabbi Joseph Ehrenkranz of Stamford, Connecticut, was invited by Anwar el-Sadat to visit Egypt with members of his congregation. Through a friend, I got an invitation to join the group—the rabbi called them "peace pilgrims"—and the next thing I knew I was in Sadat's villa outside of Cairo. I managed to buttonhole him for twenty minutes on the steps as he was bidding us farewell. He had really rolled out the old red carpet; he was making a big effort to rally American Jews against Israeli "intransigence," which naturally Menachem Begin didn't like and Mr. Begin let us know it by his cool reception when we reached Israel—and so I was able to file a number of exclusive stories.

When I got back home and looked at the clips, I knew I was in big trouble. The *Post*, which never hesitates to promote its reporters, had downplayed my stories, had put all but one inside the paper. Here they had their own columnist alone in Egypt, scooping the world press, and no headlines! I did better in the *Times*. Yes. The *Times* ran a picture on page one of our group standing with Sadat, and me smack dab in the middle. (Abe Rosenthal told me that one of his picture editors, upon spotting my kisser, came in to ask him if it was okay to run it; the guy thought I was still shit-listed, which was funny, since I got my *Post* column because of *The New York Times*.)

Well, the *Post* ran the same picture, but on page four, with no identification of yours truly, which again was not like them at all. So I knew it was a matter of time; I wouldn't be around much longer.

Meanwhile, I was anxious to do a full-scale piece on the Palestinians and the Kingdom of Jordan, a subject that had intrigued me for years. The received opinion that the Palestinians are a homeless, stateless people cannot stand against the historical fact that Jordan is 80 percent of Palestine. I had written columns on this for *Soho* and the *Post*, but now I wanted to do a longer treatment, because after spending time in Egypt I was more convinced than ever that it was fundamental to any legitimate analysis, not to say solution, of the Arab-Israeli problem.

I called my pal John Berendt, who was editing *New York* magazine under Joe Armstrong, whom Murdoch had brought in to run the show. I explained the piece to John and he said do it, write it, and I did. As it happened, the piece came out just as I was parting with the *Post*, which was fortunate for me since it made everything easy. I simply signed a contract to write a weekly column for *New York*, which meant moving from one Murdoch publication to another, thus sparing everybody embarrassment, especially me, since I didn't have to say I was fired.

The piece itself—titled "The Palestine Problem: It's All in a Name"—was a straightaway hit and was widely reprinted. I republish it here; of the scores of pieces I've written on the Middle East, I like this one best—I think it's the most important.

It was good writing for *New York* magazine—for about six months. Mainly I covered politics: national, international, state, and city. As long as the editors left me alone, I was happy. They don't leave you alone forever. For reasons I know not why, John Berendt began pushing me to do more local stuff. I was doing it when I saw fit—on Governor Hugh Carey, New York City Mayor Edward Koch, the city's controversial highway project Westway, the Convention Center, the transit fare—but Berendt wanted more. I was getting queasy, and it got worse after I went to Israel and filed a major story that got buried under somebody's dumb piece on the Surrogate's Court in New York. Maybe it was inevitable, but I didn't like it, and I let them know it.

In the fall of 1978, I teamed up with Uri Dan, the Israeli journalist, to do a behind-the-scenes book on the Camp David peace accords. We made a deal with The New York Times Book Company. It was an excellent arrangement, which included the publication of excerpts in *The New York Times Magazine*.

I kept writing my column for *New York* while working on the book. By December, we had completed some twenty thousand words, and the *Times Magazine* decided to run it as a two-part series. I hadn't said anything to John Berendt about it; I thought it might worry him and then he'd worry me, which I didn't need. I was juggling enough without that. The thing was, I had an exclusive contract with *New York* magazine, and I figured this would make Berendt nervous, coming out in the *Times*, though it was ridiculous—the book had no relevance to the magazine contract. I was doing this one with Uri Dan and under no conditions would *New York* consider publishing twenty thousand words on the Middle East.

I threw a party New Year's Eve—I'd been doing it for ten years, as a defensive gesture against having to go to boring parties with rock and disco—and Berendt was invited and came. And worked on me to go to Cleveland where Dennis "The Menace" Kucinich, the Kid Mayor, was running for reelection. The last thing I wanted to do was to go to Cleveland, but thinking I might have a hassle with John later over the book, I went, and on a sprained ankle, which I picked up doing the goddam hora at the party.

The Kid Mayor was interesting, which is more than anybody could say about Cleveland, particularly in January. I spent a few days in that ice bowl, and on getaway afternoon I got a call from Martin Arnold at the *Times*. He said he needed me in New York the following week as the magazine was going with part one on January 21. He said the cover was John McEnroe, but we'd get a slash across the top. I hit the ceiling but got nowhere; the cover was being shipped that very night.

While packing in my hotel, I thought about the date and quick called Marty. He wasn't at his desk, so I told his secretary to write down the following message and get it to him immediately. To this day, Arnold has the message pinned to his wall. It said: "A tennis cover on Jan. 21? Jan. 21 is the Super Bowl. Are you kidding?"

Fifteen minutes later, Marty called me back. He was breaking up, laughing so hard I had trouble getting what he was trying to say. What happened was, he ran the message right into Abe Rosenthal, and Abe put his hands on his forehead and said, "Oh, Jeezus, the Super Bowl! Kill the tennis, put the Israeli piece on the cover. Thank God Sid called, we'd be a laughingstock."

A couple of years before, while Max Frankel was in charge of the Sunday paper, the magazine ran a hockey cover on Super Sunday, and was ridiculed for it. Abe didn't need to repeat that.

So we wound up with the cover, and what a cover! Up against time, Arnold and Ed Klein pulled a dramatic line out of the text and ran it in large type on the outside. It said:

The story begins in July 1977, when Prime Minister Menachem Begin received a visit in his office from the men who run
Israeli intelligence. They came with a thick file on a startling
plot: The Libyan dictator, Colonel Qaddafi, had organized an
operation to assassinate the Egyptian President, Anwar el-
Sadat. Begin thumbed through the file. Without looking up, he
said, "Why don't you give this to the Egyptians?"

Underneath, the bold type read: UNTOLD STORY OF THE
MIDEAST TALKS by Sidney Zion and Uri Dan.

Editors like to say it doesn't matter if you're on the cover (of
course, when you're not on it). Doesn't matter my ass. This thing hit
so big—by dint of appearing on the cover—it made headlines all
over the world. And ultimately won us the Overseas Press Club
Award for the best magazine interpretation of foreign affairs.

The piece immediately got me fired from *New York* magazine. I
had told Berendt about it a week before, when I handed in my piece
on Dennis the Menace. John wasn't upset, he only wanted to know if
I would identify myself in the ID box as a *New York* magazine columnist. I had already done it, and he said great.

The day after the cover story appeared, and just as I was dressing to
go over to *New York* magazine to touch up my Cleveland piece for
closing, Berendt called me up.

"I'm shocked that you did a thing like this to us," he said. "It's an
outrage, it's a disgrace, I can't believe you pulled this."

I said, "John, are you being taped or something? What the hell are
you talking about? I told you it was running. You said fine, you said
great, for chrissake."

"You're in violation of your contract," he said coldly.

"C'mon, John, I know you ten years, stop this crap. I'm on my
way in to put a new end on the Cleveland piece, I'll talk to you when
I get there."

"The Cleveland piece is killed and you're terminated," Berendt
said.

Ten days later, he asked me to have a drink. We met at Costello's,
and he was nervous as hell. Berendt told me that his boss, Joe Armstrong, had ordered me fired, that Joe had been in Beverly Hills when
the piece appeared and had woken up that Sunday morning to find a
big story about it on page one of the *Los Angeles Times*. This sent

him up the wall—Berendt had never told him it was coming out—
and so he told John to get rid of me, John said.

"I hope you understand. I hope you're not going to do anything,"
Berendt said to me.

"I don't have my check yet, from two weeks ago. What did you
do, did you stop it?"

Berendt said, "Well, yes."

"How about the insurance, did you cancel that too?"

"Ah, ah, I, ah, think maybe we did, let me check."

He ran to the phone, but nobody was around at the office.

I said, "You better pray that nothing happens to me or my family
before you straighten this out. You crazy bastard, you stripped my insurance and didn't even tell me."

He said he'd work it out, and he just hoped I wouldn't do anything. Berendt knew me well, knew I got even, and he was showing it.

"I'll do whatever I have to do," I said. "But I doubt I'll have to do
anything to you. They'll get rid of you here, don't worry about it, you
and Armstrong. People that fire me get fired sooner or later."

And they did get fired, within a year. Anyway, I hold no grudges
against either of them; they're okay guys, they just panicked. I don't
know where Armstrong is, but I see John now and then and we never
talk about it. Done is done, and anyway my insurance was reinstated
and I got the back pay.

Eighty-sixed from *New York* magazine, I signed up to do pieces
for *The New York Times Magazine*. Out of which came the Supreme Court and Sinatra cover stories, reprinted herein. And to close
the circle with Israel, a piece appeared on the Op-Ed page of the
Times in July 1981, which for lagniappe made the *International Herald Tribune*. Read all about it!

I.

JEWS, CROOKS, AND HISTORY

MY JEWS,
AND MAYBE YOURS—
AN INTRODUCTION

I GREW UP among Jews who were witty, dull, angry, gentle, rich, poor—like all other nations, as it is said. The main thing they had in common was the knowledge that they were lucky to be Jewish. Until I reached college, I assumed all Jews felt that way. For this retardation I credit my hometown, Passaic, New Jersey.

If the Jews didn't run Passaic when I was a kid in the 1940s, it sure looked that way. The police commissioner was a Jew, most of the top lawyers, doctors, and businessmen were Jews, the best athletes were Jews—even the football players—and the finest students were Jews. The aristocracy was Dutch, but who thought about aristocrats in a bustling industrial town like good old Passaic? The only political competition we had were the Italians, and we got along great with the Italians.

Now and then, some innocent child would come out with an anti-Semitic remark. Our instructions, from older brothers or cousins, were to swing away, to "kiss first, talk later." Unless the kid was bigger *and* older. In which case we were to report back, and somebody capable would take care of the rat bastard. This was not without its danger. If it turned out that you could have handled the guy—in the unappealable opinion of the surrogate slugger—the older brother or cousin would belt *you*.

In such a milieu, the idea of being ashamed of one's Jewish heritage was beyond the pale. I didn't worry about Jews until I discovered that all around me there were Jews who worried about being

Jewish. And this didn't get going in earnest until I was in my mid-twenties, when I began spending my nights in Manhattan.

Across the years, I've become increasingly suspicious that my upbringing was unique. Philip Roth lived in Newark, a half-hour away from my house. Viewed through his writings, he could have been brought up in Shnipitzik. I never knew—then—his kind of Jew: self-conscious, self-deprecating, always worried about what the *goyim* might think. We didn't give a good goddam about what the *goyim* thought. We took care of the few who had the gall to bad-mouth us and assumed that the rest were our friends.

Obviously, Roth isn't the lone Jewish writer preoccupied by his place in the Gentile world. Most of them look at it with similar longings—whether from Chicago, Los Angeles, or New York. The same seems to go for the majority of Jews I've met since I've left home. The difference, I suppose, is that us kids from Passaic never thought we were living in a Gentile world.

I raise it here because so many people—mainly Jews—have expressed their disbelief, not to say shock, at my "cavalier" attitude toward *goyim*. I've been accused of arrogance, of chauvinism, particularly for my views on Israel and Jewish-American criminals. Some say I'm the flip side of Rothism.

The truth is, it never entered my mind. I rest my case on the people of Passaic. To Passaic, I'm another Jew from Passaic.

DEATH OF A JEWISH GODFATHER

DOC STACHER DIED in bed the other day at the Munich Sheraton next to a twenty-two-year-old blonde, a circumstance that surely would have brought forth memories of John Garfield, except that nobody seemed to note Doc's passing, much less the blonde. When Garfield called it a career under similar conditions some twenty-five years ago, the tabloids fell over their own headlines trying to top the story every day, until one exhausted editor suggested the banner "John Garfield Still Dead." And to think that two weeks after his demise I have to tell you who Doc Stacher was.

In the twenties, Stacher was one of the two largest importers of bootleg hooch in the United States, the other being his partner and boon companion, Longy Zwillman. Longy and Doc ran as an entry out of Newark, which they also ran, and while Zwillman was the more famous, Doc was known in underworld and police circles as the brainier, no mean comment since Longy had one of the finest noodles in the business.

"Longy went to night school while Doc went to nightclubs," Manny Manishor, the venerable Broadway oddsmaker, recalled at Gallagher's one cocktail hour last week. As usual, Manny was on the nose. Stacher was what the girls at the Board of Education would call a "functional illiterate," which is to say that he couldn't read a menu, but who needs menus when you can buy steak for the house? Dutch Goldberg, who invented the Combination at a convention assembled in Atlantic City in 1929, credited the Doc with the best legal mind in the country, and this was a country that had Justice Holmes, not to mention Bill Fallon, the Great Mouthpiece. But Goldberg knew exactly what the mob was doing against the statutes, and if Doc Stacher was house counsel we have only to look at how few of the big dogs went to the can to understand how little reading skills had to do with Blackstone.

After Repeal, Longy and Doc picked up substantial points in the legitimate liquor business and plenty of other legal entities, even as they sat in the top echelons of the Combination, which was rapidly growing into the Syndicate. It's a toss-up whether the Mafia mavens or the B'nai B'rith are more embarrassed by the names that dominated the rackets from the twenties through the fifties, but facts are facts and let the vowels fall where they may. So: Arnold Rothstein, Waxey Gordon, Dutch Schultz, Lepke Buchalter, Gurrah Shapiro, Meyer Lansky, Bugsy Siegel, Moe Dalitz, Nig Rosen, Boo Hoff, Tootsie Herbert, Isador (Kid Cann) Blumenfield, Hymie Siegel, the Detroit Purple Gang, Murder, Inc.—and of course Stacher, Zwillman, and the Godfather himself, Dutch Goldberg.

Alas, all but Dalitz, Nig, Kid Cann, and Meyer have gone to the Maker from this select Hit Parade, though this is by no means to imply that others of the brothers have no say-so in the Syndicate and is surely not to say that Lansky and the survivors are out to pasture. That, however, is another tale, and we have room only to praise poor Doc, still warm in his final resting place in Israel. To die in Munich and be buried in Israel—well, there must be a story goes with it, though just what Doc was doing in Germany is a mystery to me. There was always talk that he ran a string of whorehouses there, but the only thing I know for sure about him and the Nazis is that he and Longy used to like breaking their heads whenever they put on the brown shirts in those Bund rallies outside Newark. Lansky did the same in Yorkville, which is one reason I found it nice to shake hands with both of them one afternoon in Tel Aviv about five years ago.

Stacher, whose intimates called him "Gedalia," and whose Diaspora name was Joseph, went up to the homeland in 1964, though not entirely out of a spirit of *aliyah*. The Feds had him convicted on a tax rap and gave him the option of Israel or durance vile. The Israeli government welcomed him, or at least gave him no trouble, which is hardly the way they treated Meyer when he showed up in 1970. The U.S. wanted Meyer back as fervently as once they wanted Doc out, and in what became known in Israel as the "Phantoms for Lansky Detente," Meyer was booted back to Miami, where the government was unable to do a thing to him.

They were never able to do much to Doc, either, which is why, when I met them by chance in the lobby of the Tel Aviv Sheraton that day, I was caused to blurt: "Gentlemen, it's like meeting Ruth and Gehrig." Maybe Gedalia didn't live as good as the sluggers, but a lot longer and you have to admit he died better.

—*Soho Weekly News*
March 17, 1977

LANSKY IN ISRAEL

I stopped at Gallagher's on my way to Israel in the winter of '72, and in a flash a guy named Cuzzy sidled up to me at the bar and said, "When you see Meyer, tell him hello for me." Cuzzy was so named because he was the cousin of Joe Adonis, the Jersey mafia don who rode sidesaddle with Meyer Lansky during the halcyon days of the Combination. Lansky was battling to stay in Israel, away from the teeth of the Nixon Justice Department, which in the event turned out to be without gums. I had no thought of seeing Meyer, but of course this didn't occur to Cuzzy, who couldn't imagine any other reason for a guy like me to go to the Holy Land. I was going over for Esquire, on an open contract, which is to say they paid my expenses and took a chance that I'd come up with something terrific.

Cuzzy walked away after delivering his message and I announced, "Well, now I've got my assignment; I've got to see Meyer Lansky." One of the oddsmakers at the bar said, "No chance. Meyer never talks to newspapermen." That was for sure, but I didn't love the way he said it. "I think I'll talk to him," I said. Smelling a sucker, the bookie said, "For how much?" With a crowded bar listening I had no choice. "Make a price," I said. "It's four to one," he said.

It was an underlay, but I couldn't live with being four to one against talking to anybody. I bet him a hundred. "You got to get it published," he said, "otherwise no payoff." I said naturally. And then five more guys wanted action, all against me. I was down for $600 and not even at the airport.

Cuzzy grabbed me at the door.

"Don't let nobody tell you the Jews is nothin'," he said. "Meyer's smarter than all of us—with the possible exception of Joe A."

Joe Adonis was dead, which is how I felt about my bet. But by the time the plane passed over England, I was sure I'd interview Lansky; the alternative was too terrible.

On jet lag in a Tel Aviv pub I ran into an Israeli reporter who told me that Uri Dan knew Lansky well, that he'd written an exclusive series on him in the Hebrew press. I started counting my winnings. Uri Dan was my buddy, he'd even done some work for me while I had Scanlan's Monthly. I called him at home, told him what I wanted, and he said he'd see me for lunch. But he dampened my hopes. "Meyer has to be very careful. He talked to me, but he hasn't talked to any other reporters. All the American newspapers are after him, they follow him around, they stand at his doorstep, but he won't even say hello. I'll see what I can do, my friend, but I can't promise anything."

The next day Uri picked me at my hotel. Without saying a word about Lansky, he took me to a restaurant on Ben Yehuda Street. Where we had lunch with Meyer Lansky, his wife, and his poodle.

The piece that came out of that lunch follows, but a story goes with it.

Uri did not introduce me to Lansky as a newspaperman, only as a friend. Brash I may be, but I wasn't about to write an article on Meyer without his knowledge. Uri said it was okay, but I wouldn't touch it until he said better than okay. A few days later, he said it was clear, all clear. I didn't ask how and I didn't ask why. I called Esquire. They said fabulous.

Back in New York, I wrote the piece fast. Within forty-eight hours of delivery, Don Erickson, the executive editor of Esquire, called to tell me it was one of the best essays the magazine ever received. Did I have any pictures? I not only had pictures, I had Lansky praying at the Wailing Wall, I had him at his grandparents' graves in the Mount of Olives. Erickson was ecstatic. "Send them right over, I think we've got a cover," he said.

I could have walked on water that day. This was my first magazine piece since the Ellsberg incident. Imagine, less than a year after the blacklist, coming with an Esquire cover!

But ten days went by without a word. My agent, Sterling Lord, told me not to worry, it didn't mean a thing, magazines worked slowly. I tried to believe him; but I knew something about magazines, about the business. Only good news travels fast in publishing; everybody puts off the other kind. Didn't I get the word quickly when they loved the piece? And this had been the way it always worked.

The next afternoon, at one o'clock, Erickson called. There is no good news at one o'clock. Editors phone then only to be able to say they did; they're sure you're out to lunch. That day I wasn't.

"I hate to say what I'm about to say," Erickson opened. "We're paying you for the piece, but we can't run it. I've never been so ashamed, but I have no choice."

I said, "Forget the flowers, just tell me why you're killing it."

Erickson said, "John Smart feels it will hurt him with Israel."

Smart was the owner of Esquire. All I knew about him was that he gave plenty of money to Israel each year.

"What do you mean?" I said. "Are you trying to tell me that Golda Meir won't take his six figures?"

Erickson was nervous. "I really can't say anything more."

"Does John Smart say the piece is anti-Israel?" I said. "Because that would be a first for me. The only thing I've never been accused of is being anti-Israel."

"Look, this is terribly embarrassing for me," Erickson said. I cut him short. "You'll survive it," I said. "What I really want to know is why you sent the story up to Smart, since when does he edit the magazine—I thought he was just the sucker with the money. That piece Nora Ephron did on tits, did you send that up to him too?"

Erickson said, "Mr. Smart never told us what to do before, so far as I ever knew. Believe me, I didn't show him your piece."

"Well who did?"

"I don't know."

Well, I'd heard that before, the same old song and dance. No point in berating Don Erickson, he was just another editor carrying out orders. I told him to send everything over to Sterling Lord. He said, "You'll have no trouble getting the piece published, it's great."

I ran into Gay Talese that night at Frankie and Johnnie's Restaurant and told him about it. Gay was incensed. "Let's hold a press conference," he said. "I'll denounce them for this—it's raw, it's pure censorship." Gay was a contributing editor at Esquire and its most important writer. I always thought he was a stand-up guy but I never expected an offer like that.

It's virtually an iron law that reporters don't stick their necks out for other reporters caught in the vise of editorial censorship. This is not due to an inherent lack of character or an endemic failure of nerve. If anything, reporters begin their careers with feisty, fearless, independent spirits unknown to most vocations, professions, and callings. Soon enough, however, they discover they are living on a plantation. They may get fancy salaries, they may wear fancy hats and collars, but they work under a tyranny of editors and publishers. And there are mighty few editors and publishers in this country who believe that the First Amendment belongs to writers, when the writers' views come into conflict with their interests and even their whims. So while any reporters worth their salt would go to jail rather than submit to censorship by the government, they are routinely prey to censorship by their bosses. If your editor kills a story and you can't take it, you can quit. Otherwise you can only bitch, and if you bitch too much or too loudly you're likely to end up in the Staten Island police shack.

That's why no publication has ever been struck because it spiked a story. If a reporter can't afford to stick his neck out for himself, why should anybody else be in a better position? Of course, in union there is strength, but perhaps because writers consider themselves independent—or, more likely, because the plantation philosophy clucks in their bones—they don't organize around this issue. They walk picket lines for money and working conditions but never for freedom of the press.

Against this sad history, I was overwhelmed by Gay Talese's offer to hold a press conference on my behalf. But I turned it down. Why? Because I knew that if I did it, I'd really be finished. No editor in the country would go near me after a scene like that. And chances were that the papers wouldn't even carry our story. It might get an inch or two here or there, owing to Talese's fame, but no more, no way.

As it was, the Lansky piece had terrible difficulty finding a home. Sterling Lord sent it all over the place but it kept being rejected. I wasn't sure whether it was me or the fact that the piece was critical of the Israeli government for trying to throw Meyer out of the country. The journalism magazine [MORE] had run an item about the Esquire kill. I didn't leak it to them; I didn't want it to run—for the same reasons I didn't want the Talese press conference. But everybody assumed I leaked it, which was the same thing.

Finally, we submitted it to Harper's. It didn't seem like a natural for a piece on Lansky, but it occurred to me that Harper's didn't have many Jews at its top level—nor others who were foolish enough or "inside" enough to worry about an imagined slight to Jewish or

Israeli sensibilities. For a change I was right. Or maybe I wasn't right. Maybe Harper's just liked it, is that possible?

After it hit the newsstands, I saw Clay Felker, editor of New York, at Sardi's bar. Felker volunteered that he'd turned down the piece because it "glamorized a criminal." A couple of weeks earlier New York had run a portrait of Mario Puzo, author of The Godfather, on its cover. I mentioned this to Clay. He said, "What's that got to do with it?"

MEYER LANSKY, sitting with his wife and poodle in the Yiddish restaurant on Ben Yehuda Street, looks anything but "the man who runs the mob that runs America." When he stands to greet a couple of intruders, the short, compact body brings to mind the Sunday-morning frames of old handball players at the Passaic, New Jersey, YMHA. Lansky's eyes are sky-blue, and on this chilly day he is wearing a brown tweed sportcoat over a three-hole gray shirt buttoned to the throat.

I am with Uri Dan, one of Israel's top newspapermen. The night before, upon hearing that Dan had published a series of exclusive interviews with Lansky, I embarked on a casual hustle dedicated to having him introduce me to the great Jewish outlaw. Now, without a nod, with no time to contemplate the occasion, I am sitting next to Meyer Lansky and he is touting me off stuffed miltz.

"But my grandmother used to make stuffed miltz," I say.

"There is a place for stuffed miltz," Meyer Lansky says, "but here I advise kishke."

The kishke is delicious.

"Where are you from?" Lansky asks.

"New York."

"Do you get to the hockey games?"

"Just last week."

"I miss the hockey most of all."

Lansky moved to Israel in July 1970. The U.S. State Department canceled his passport a year later, presumably because he refused to return to Miami to answer two indictments arising out of alleged skimming of gambling receipts in Las Vegas. Although neither charge is extraditable under the United States–Israel extradition treaty, the Israeli government thereafter refused to renew Lansky's tourist visa and denied his application for citizenship under the Law of Return. This caused a small furor in Israel—among other events, hundreds of students and professors signed a petition supporting Lansky's bid—and when I met him he was sweating out an appeal pending before the Israeli Supreme Court.

The appeal is based on the fundamental tenet of Zionism, which holds that all persons born of Jewish mothers are ipso facto members of the Jewish nation, automatically entitled to live as full citizens in the homeland. Until a decade ago there would have been no question about Lansky's right to Israeli citizenship. In 1962, however, Dr. Robert Soblen fled to Israel from New York after the U.S. Supreme Court refused to review his conviction for conspiracy to commit espionage. Under pressure from our State Department and the American Jewish establishment, David Ben-Gurion booted Soblen out of the country without benefit of a court hearing. Israeli opinion was outraged for a time at this summary action, but the net result was an amendment to the Law of Return permitting Israel to deny citizenship to "undesirables," including persons with criminal pasts likely to endanger the "peace of the State."

In the abstract, this amendment creates philosophical problems Talmudic in scope. (It also reveals a fundamental ghetto mentality in the last place anyone would expect to find it.)

"It's enough to cross a rabbi's eyes," laughs Uri Dan, as Lansky toys with the coffee cup. "If every Jew is part of the Jewish nation, how do we have the right to deport a member of our nation? If Meyer was a sabra we couldn't throw him out if he raped Golda. But, we say, sabra-shmabra, every Jew is the same, except that most Jews are too stupid to come to this paradise to live. So Meyer comes here to live and now we want to kick him out. It's crazy."

Crazy-shmazy—Israel has been known to bend principle to satisfy American wishes. Even though Lansky's only conviction in his seventy years was for common gambling—for which he served three months in jail in 1953—the smart money in Tel Aviv says that the Israeli Supreme Court will find him a "threat to the peace of the State."

"Phantoms for Lansky—it's a perfect trade," says Uri Dan.

Still, Lansky appears optimistic.

"My lawyer tells me I have a good chance," he says. "But it's tense, it's got to my ulcer. Win or lose there'll be no bitterness about this country. I just don't want to let this Justice Department guy in Miami ride my name to a career."

(Lansky's ulcer led to his last arrest, in Miami in March 1970, for possession of drugs. The charge was dismissed when the drug turned out to be a mild sedative to relieve indigestion, perhaps brought on by some counterfeit kishke. Whether to escape the latter, or to avoid the increasing heat, Lansky went to Israel four months later. The indictments that underline his present difficulties came in March 1971. In June of this year, Lansky was again indicted by the federal government on tax charges arising out of money he allegedly made from the booking of gambling junkets to London.)

I suggest to Lansky that he has a perfect right to be bitter over the Israeli government's efforts to kick him out of the country.

"I understand you did plenty for Israel through the years, particularly in 1948 when they were up against it."

Lansky pauses, playing with his cup, his eyes down. He does not smile.

"Let's just say that the Jewish people have not suffered because I was one of them."

I am reminded of Benya Krik, the greatest of Isaac Babel's Jewish gangsters—Benya the King.

Benya says little, but what he says is tasty. He says little, and one would like him to say more.

(Lansky told Uri Dan of a visit by Israeli secret agents in 1948. The Israelis were concerned over large quantities of arms being smuggled to the Arabs through the port of New York. Lansky was slipped the name of the prime suspect, a man from Pittsburgh. "I dealt with the matter immediately," Lansky said. "There were no more complaints about Arab arms shipments.")

Where do the police begin, and where does Benya end? wailed Tartakovsky, the wealthiest Jew in Odessa, after Benya Krik made a spectacular raid on his riches. *The police end where Benya begins,* replied sensible folk.

Babel was one of the few authors in modern history to write about Jewish outlaws. Diaspora literature, from Sholom Aleichem's *Tevya* to Bellow's *Dangling Man* to Roth's dangling dingus, portrays the Jew as ChosenVictim, sainted fool, back-bent and nose-hooked into the noble needlework of the Great Plight. "The virtue of powerlessness, the power of helplessness, the company of the dispossessed, the sanctity of the insulted and the injured"—these are the "great themes" of the literature as celebrated by none other than Irving Howe.

Where, against the music of such fiddlers on the gallows, is there a tune left for the Jewish gangster?

Yet this was not Babel's Odessa at the turn of the century, just as it was not Meyer Lansky's Lower East Side circa 1917. Not altogether, anyway.

Forget for a while that you have spectacles on your nose and autumn in your heart, Reb Arye-Leib tells the young man who wonders why Benya Krik, alone among Odessa's outlaws, climbed to the top of the ladder.

"The first time I defended my honor as a Jew," says Lansky, "was when the Irish kids asked me to play basketball in a schoolyard game. In those days the Irishers would pull the beards of old Jews and open the flies of Jewish kids to check their origins. During the game one of them made an anti-Semitic remark. I slugged him, even though I was a shrimp. The other Irishers liked that; they told me that from now on they'd call me Mike. I said no thanks, the name is Meyer."

Throughout history Jews have found it necessary to forget the spectacles on their noses and the autumn in their hearts. But only for a while. One such a while came to New York in the middle thirties when the German-American Bund tossed verbal thunderbolts (and worse) at Jews from their brown-shirted enclave in Yorkville, the "Reich Valley."

Rabbi Stephen Wise, the exalted leader of Reform Jewry, became upset by these happenings, and in 1935 he sent word to Lansky that "something must be done" about the Nazi outrages. Lansky agreed to supply the necessary means and asked for only one consideration: that the Jewish press lay off him and the methods he might have to employ.

For the next couple of years the Nazi strut was increasingly tripped up by Jews tossing sticks and stones and bombs. Heads were smashed, bones broken, and the thud of fat German necks hitting sidewalks sounded a new kind of Jewish rumba. The bomb throwers and fist swingers were drawn from every level of Jewish life. Few were aware that Lansky was behind the operations.

"And who do you think came out against us?" Lansky says. "The Jewish press, of course. They called us Jewish gangsters, these fair souls who sat peacefully in their beautiful homes while we were on the lines defending Jewish honor. They kept up the pressure, they wanted us destroyed, we were 'shaming' Jewry by attacking Nazis. The heat got too much for Rabbi Wise, and he ordered us to put an end to our actions."

I told Lansky that Rabbi Wise had been less successful in his efforts to silence Ben Hecht some years later. As head of the Committee to Save the Jews of Europe, Hecht in 1943 wrote a pageant called "We Will Never Die." Rabbi Wise got hold of the script. He phoned Hecht and "ordered" him to stop work on the show and to be sure to consult him if in the future he wished to work for the Jewish cause. Hecht hung up on him.

Governor Thomas E. Dewey then agreed to proclaim a day of mourning for the murdered Jews of Europe in conjunction with the production of Hecht's pageant at Madison Square Garden. Rabbi Wise and a delegation of important Jews journeyed to Albany, asked Dewey not to issue the proclamation, and warned him that he would lose the Jewish vote if he didn't break with Hecht and his "dangerous and irresponsible racketeers who are bringing terrible disgrace to our already harassed people."

When Ben Hecht got word of this, he called Wise and let loose with a barrage of barracks-room language. As Ben's widow, Rose, recalled recently, "He started by telling this 'Chief Rabbi of the World' that he'd rip his balls off. After that it got unprintable."

Governor Dewey went ahead and proclaimed the day of mourning, and forty thousand people jammed the Garden for the two performances of "We Will Never Die."

Lansky nodded wisely at the recounting of this tale, but his eyes betrayed a touch of shock that anyone would dare talk that way to a rabbi. Lansky, the terrible mobster, obediently accepts "the word" from a rabbi; Ben Hecht, then the highest paid screenwriter in Hollywood, tells him to gazump himself.

Ben Hecht, like Babel, was one of those rare birds with enough serenity—and gaiety—to celebrate Jewish criminals. He wrote of them naturally, as though it never occurred to him that Jews were not allowed to have their outlaws. Imagine the futures book of the Anti-Defamation League if such thinking became contagious. Dore Schary on the panel shows—every night!—clucking his tongue, shaking his head, recounting for a deadly bored world the glorious passivity of Jewish culture.

To deny Lansky, it occurred to me while talking to him, is to betray a full-blown ghetto mentality. One need make no brief for his character to say this—quite the contrary. For what more abject kowtowing to the goyish world can be conjured up than to say that we will vomit out our gangsters to impress you with our goodness.

And that is what the argument is all about in State of Israel *v.* Meyer Lansky.

We are dealing with a farrago of ironies, from the absurd to the tragic.

The absurd first.

Not to break the hearts of Hadassah ladies, but the picture the West has of the Israelis as an upright, law-abiding, early-to-bed, hard-working citizen for the commonweal is a good many kilometers from nothing-but-the-truth. He is hardworking, to be sure. He had better work hard if he is to avoid the tentacles of the tax collector who will grab most of his wages if he is not constantly *au courant* with the latest cheating devices. He had better work hard if he is to turn the corner on a pervasive bureaucracy that has made *protectia*—influence—the coin of the realm. He had better work hard if he is to survive a runaway inflation that has small apartments in Jerusalem selling for $70,000, Volkswagens going for $8,000—an inflation bottomed on an economic system that has been aptly described as a combination of "nineteenth-century socialism and twenty-first-century capitalism."

Tax avoidance, *protectia*—these are the rules of the game in Israel, and he who lives by them will have the wherewithal to indulge all the ancient vices. A visitor to Israel, unless he is on a UJA tour, or is a correspondent for *The New York Times,* quickly discovers that just about everything is available in the Promised Land—from gambling to hookers to hashish.

"It is a well-known fact," Ephraim Kishon, the Israeli Art Buchwald, put it recently in his column in the afternoon paper *Maariv,* "that the life of the average citizen in our State is based on a system of laws whose ordinances outline in small print how they ought to be circumvented."

But these rules do not apply to Lansky, Kishon added.

"In Lansky's case," he wrote, "we ignore the rules of the game as well as the standards of due process. In his case we are all pillars of rectitude, all of us are as guileless as distilled water. Our features become solemn, our eyebrows shoot up and our nostrils quiver.

"Just imagine: A former member of the Mafia is sitting among us. Among us! Sitting!

"The experts of the fast buck are rolling their eyes heavenwards. The champions of Mediterranean bribery are wagging a warning finger, hashish fiends are shocked, the government is thundering—our conscience has woken, shouting hoarsely."

The surface hypocrisy of the Lansky case is obviously a banquet for satire. Yet the same can be said of any nation's selective evangelism. The difference here—aside from Israel's "vices" being generally unknown to the outside world—has to do with what the country is supposed to be about.

Which is to say that it is a sad spectacle to witness the founding fathers of Israel, who upon leaving their *shtetls* in Eastern Europe so assiduously attempted to shed all signs of ghetto mentality, acting out in the Lansky affair the classic ghetto syndrome: "How will it look for the goyim?"

But *is* that what's going on here?

There are Israelis who vehemently deny it, who insist that the deportation of Lansky is simply a practical accommodation to American pressure.

If they are right, it's bad enough. For as such it would serve as ammunition for Israel's enemies who have long claimed that the state is little more than a U.S. satellite.

But there is nothing to this "pressure" argument. Is it not preposterous to believe that the United States would permit its global policy to be affected by what the Israelis do with Meyer Lansky?

If the question does not thunderously answer itself in the affirmative, then Israel's dependence on the United States stands on a reed so thin as to make the angels tremble.

No, it is not what the United States will *do* to Israel if Meyer Lansky is permitted to live in the Holy Land; it is what the world will *think* now that America has spotlighted the case.

"How will it look for the goyim?"

Well, how will it look for the independence of the Israeli judiciary if the Supreme Court, which will decide the appeal shortly, rules against Lansky on the basis of hearsay evidence? Because for all everyone may "know" about Meyer Lansky—and we all grew up "knowing" plenty—his rap sheet still records only that conviction for common gambling. The rest of the "proof" against him consists of news stories, Kefauver Committee hearings, and "confidential" FBI reports.

As my cousin Maxie would say, thanks a lot.

Courts in other democratic nations have occasionally bailed out the honor of their governments. Can such a miracle be brought forth in Jerusalem?

And Benya Krik had his way, for he was passionate, and passion rules the universe.

Still, that was Odessa—before we were free.

—*Harper's Magazine*
August 1972

IZZY SCHAWARZBERG

*You are about to meet Israel Schawarzberg. I envy you. I won't
ruin the story by saying anything about him in advance. A couple of
acknowledgments, however, are in order.*

*I owe Al Davis for sending me to see Izzy shortly after I joined the
Post in 1963. Given the joy I got over the years from this introduction, I should forgive Al for everything. But of course, being Al
Davis, he managed to screw it up good. He never let me write a word
about Schawarzberg for the Post, probably because he had once
done a piece about Izzy for Esquire and so thought he owned the
perpetual copyright to this colorful, outrageous, lovely sonofabitch.*

*Later, on the Times, I did a bunch of stories about Izzy. What
follows here is a recollection, culled partly from the pieces in the
Times but mostly from memory. It appeared as a chapter in a book
called Super Crooks: A Rogue's Gallery of Famous Hustlers, Swindlers and Thieves, published by Playboy Press in 1973. And for this I
owe Victor Navasky, who suggested it to the editor.*

*Only Izzy Schawarzberg could bring me, Davis, the Times, and
Navasky together, while I was in my Ellsberg exile and Izzy was in
his grave.*

ISRAEL SCHAWARZBERG LIKED to say that with Israel Schawarzberg
you could start anywhere. He was forever imploring me to write his
biography, but something always came up. Once, out of guilt, I told
him that the trouble was I wouldn't know where to begin.

"Why, was there ever a dull moment?" he said.

"Maybe that's the trouble," I replied hopefully.

"Don't cayoodle me, I know you," he shot back. "Don't give me
you wouldn't know where to start. With me you could start any-

where. What's the matter if you start at the start? Didn't they cir-
cumcise me twice? You want anything better than that? But what's
the difference, start anywhere. Only do it, we'll get off the *shnide*,
we'll get rich, it'll be a movie, what are you talking about? Start with
whatever you like best, who cares?"

Izzy ran against the law for more than forty of his fifty-six years,
with as many lives as he had aliases. On police blotters from the precinct house to Interpol he was a/k/a Mizo, Irving Ace, Irving Ticket,
Fat Tiger and Mr. Israel. He would never qualify for the Mount
Rushmore of crime, but he was perhaps the last great single-o act in
the American underworld, an entrepreneur in a game gone soft with
corporate-style bureaucracy. "I am *of* the mob, not *with* the mob,"
he would say, and he proved it with every move in his bizarre and
colorful life.

He pioneered the college basketball fix, and in his spare time he
fixed horses, cops and witnesses. He swindled banks and shylocks
and Mafiosi. He made book and took off bookmakers. In his various
stints behind bars he developed into the most famous jailhouse lawyer of his time, boasting a record of twenty-nine wins for thirty-two
writs brought on behalf of fellow prisoners. "It's the same record as
Thurgood Marshall," he said, "and what kind of a press did *I* have?"
He performed these services almost entirely out of what he called his
"psychopathic vendetta" against law enforcement. But he was well
paid in the coin of the realm—ice cream, lemon drops and chocolate
bars. "In prison," he noted, "only an amateur or a bum would take
money. With me, drugs was always out of the question. But I needed
to eat and my clients needed a lawyer, so it was a perfect marriage."

On the outside he invoked an ancient statute to become certified—despite his prison record—as a law clerk by the New York
Court of Appeals, and he used his mob connections to build up a
flourishing practice that became the bane of federal and state prosecutors. This career lasted seven raucous years, ending only when the
feds pinned a rap on him and the lady lawyer he worked for, convict-
ing them of trying to fix a witness in a major narcotics trial. He represented himself and succeeded in gaining acquittal on all but one
charge of conspiracy.

His speech at sentencing was by common consent of the organized
bar the greatest in the history of jurisprudence. Alluding to his codefendant, the lady lawyer, who had just received two years, he said:
"Your honor, I'm shocked beyond recall that you could give this

poor woman a deuce, to throw her, a polio victim, in there with all them lesbians and deviates. After all, your honor, I'm innocent. But she's *really* innocent."

Probably because of this speech he himself got only a deuce, despite a record that would easily have justified the five-year maximum. He considered this bit in prison, which was to be his last, "Ping-Pong time," meaning short and light, and he did it, "without taking my shoes off."

He got out in 1968 and hooked up with *Ramparts* magazine, of all places, as an ombudsman dedicated to representing the interests of prisoners, past and present. He had grandiose plans to file a class-action suit to restore voting rights to convicted felons, but *Ramparts* ran out of money. When I started *Scanlan's* in 1969, I brought him over as office manager. He died in the service of our lovely little muckraking sheet and at about the same time it did, a few days before Christmas, 1970.

All of which is the sketchiest of sketches and misleading in the bargain. For one thing, it implies that he died on the straight if not the narrow. For another, it leaves out the violence, often submerged and always brilliantly camouflaged under a Runyonesque façade of jolly fat con merchant.

So it is not so easy to start, even if I start with what I liked best. I liked most things best about the life of my old friend, whose ghost beseeches me now to "write already, we'll be rich, it's thirty-nine weeks network TV, start *anywhere. . . .*"

It is a summer morning in 1965, so pretty that even the birds caught in the Bronx are tweeting. Israel Schawarzberg is reclining contentedly in his oversize bed in a ground-floor apartment hard by the Grand Concourse.

He is now 240 pounds, which he considers "chubette" after a comedown from better than 300. His hair is nearly all white and his sideburns are stylish. He is smiling, which makes him look like a garment manufacturer with a line of credit, rather than an ex-con with twelve years to the other side of the ledger.

The smile is not exactly for the newspapers, as Mr. Schawarzberg has not yet placed his dentures, but it is a sweet smile nonetheless—a *dayenu* smile, as he later recalled it. (*Dayenu* is a Hebrew prayer said on Passover, which goes: "If He only brought us forth from the Land of Egypt and did not open the Red Sea it would have been *dayenu*" —sufficient.)

"There I am in bed," Schawarzberg recounted for me later, "with my law office ten feet away in the same apartment, with the locks on the doors installed by the best cat burglar in New York, with alarms in the toilet because them amateur bums always need the john in the midst of a score, there I am in the middle of all this security, mental as well as physical, and I am saying to myself, *dayenu*. After all, I'm fifty-one, and the fact that I even make it to fifty, isn't that *dayenu*? How many guys from my old neighborhood on Rivington Street do you think made it to fifty, are you kidding? I don't believe in God or anybody like that, but after all I'm a Jew, and I figure that if I make it to fifty, even if I'm in durance vile on my birthday, it would be *dayenu*. After all I did they didn't catch me for, what are you talking about? You'd blush if I told you. Sometimes *I* blush.

"But I'm not in durance vile, I'm right here in my bed in my own office, practicing law, beating up my enemies *every day*. Not only am I alive and free, I'm in business. I got cash, I got wops kissing my ass for writs, I bet horses every track, I need a blow job I pick up the phone, what's wrong with that?

"I want a story in the paper I call editors—am I gonna bother with working stiffs?—I go to the top and it don't cost me, they're honest, believe it or not—can you believe that?

"I'm hungry I eat at Lou G. Siegel's or Shmulky Bernstein's or the Delancey Ratner, what else do I need, isn't that *dayenu*? I only wish my mother was alive to see it."

When the doorbell rang in the midst of these happy ponderings, Israel Schawarzberg had a premonition.

"I figured right away it's trouble, that I gave myself, God forbid, an *einhura*, the old Jewish whammy. And sure enough it's a cop, what are you talking about? Well naturally I don't come this far to let cops infiltrate my premises without a warrant so I tell him to get lost and what do you think the bum says? He wants to know if that Volvo across the street is mine. I take the Fifth, I tell nothing, what I should do—get out of practice?

"What do you think the bum does then? He says to me, nice and calm, 'Don't get smart, I'm just trying to help you. There happens to be a bomb under that car.'

"I'll tell you, only me and my laundryman knows how scared I was then."

The bomb was to set off a reaction that effectively ended Schawarzberg's legal career. It did not happen as a direct result of the bomb, but more as an aura that seemed to chase after him. Schawarzberg prided himself on being able to throw "psyche waves" at his adversaries, whether they be cops or prosecutors, judges or waiters. The "psyche waves" would make these adversaries lose their timing, run off their game just enough to allow Izzy the inch that gave the mile. The bomb turned out to be a psyche wave directed against him.

There was never an official determination of who placed the bomb under the Schawarzberg car, though a police investigation was conducted and the story hit all the papers and TV news shows. Izzy did not cooperate in the police probe, but he conducted his own lightning investigation and reported to me a few days later that there would be no more trouble "from the particular source."

According to Izzy, the genesis of the difficulty began some weeks earlier when a woman who was to be a government witness in a narcotics conspiracy case turned out to be missing. The woman had come to Izzy for legal advice and recounted to him the testimony she was about to give to a grand jury, testimony she had already gone over with the U.S. attorney's office. A couple of days later she was gone, never to be seen again, and according to her roommate the last person to talk to her was Israel Schawarzberg, who allegedly called and asked her to meet him on a street corner in the Bronx. She never returned from the meeting.

The woman happened to have been the girl friend of one Vincent Pacelli, who had recently been convicted of smuggling junk into the country. It was Schawarzberg's view that the federal narcotics boys told Pacelli that Izzy was responsible for making his sweetie disappear.

"Them bums are always looking to frame me up," he said, "and failing that, they try to have me totaled, what do you think of that?"

Ironically, the girl had been giving information against Pacelli himself, Izzy said.

"But how was he to know that when they were poisoning his mind against me?"

Now, of course, the question is pregnant as to whether Mr. Schawarzberg had anything to do with the mysterious disappearance of the lady. Suffice it to say that he always denied it, though I wondered sometimes about the winks, which he claimed were twitches, and anyway, "who told you to look?"

There are those in and out of law enforcement who assert that

Schawarzberg made a major score off the mob for setting up the woman, and I've even heard it said that he knocked her off himself. But nobody ever proved it—and then again, who told me to ask?

Vincent Pacelli was to turn up again in Izzy's life. He was made a codefendant in the case that ended the legal careers of Schawarzberg and his lady employer, the obstruction-of-justice case in which Izzy, the lady lawyer and Pacelli were said to have offered a government witness $25,000 if he refrained from testifying against Pacelli in the narcotics-smuggling case.

Schawarzberg moved to sever his case from Pacelli's on the grounds that Pacelli had tried to bomb him and therefore wasn't your usual friendly co-conspirator. It didn't work any better than the bomb itself. Nor any better than the bribe attempt that was the subject of the prosecution. For the witness in that case did testify, managing to convict Pacelli, just as he now was to sink Izzy and the lady lawyer.

Although, as I said, the bomb had no direct connection with the trial that finished Schawarzberg's lawyering days, I always believed that the bomb led him into strange moves that inexorably created the atmosphere for his indictment.

It also led him into a delicious move. On the evening of the day the bomb was discovered, Izzy decided to drive down to his old haunts on the Lower East Side to show his pals he was "standing pat." It was important for him to indicate no fear, but he wasn't about to start the car. He called the Automobile Association of America, claiming he couldn't get it moving.

"The AAA guy came down and naturally it turned right over. It's a good thing he didn't see me holding my ears across the street. After that I called them every day, why should I take chances, what did it cost me—a buck? But after a week they wouldn't come anymore, they figured I was crazy."

Even though Schawarzberg had by then received word that he was out of danger, he was not looking to take unnecessary risks. So he called on a fellow whom he had sprung on a writ from Dannemora some years before. "I knew he wasn't working, and he owed me one, so I asked him if he'd start my car every day, I'd give him a tenner each time. He knew about the bomb, but he didn't care; he said, certainly. He showed up every morning for three weeks, and I'd stand on the corner with my fingers in my ears, and he'd turn it over. Then one day what do you think the bum does? He quits on me."

Why would anybody quit a job like that?

"Catch why he quits," Izzy continued. "You won't believe it. He says to me, 'Izzy, you know how much I respect you and I know how much I owe you, I'd still be in college if not for you. But Izzy, please, I can't do this anymore. Every morning I get up early and take a subway from Brooklyn to the Bronx and I start your car, right? Now don't misunderstand, Izzy, I wouldn't mind, I'd do anything for you. But I come here every day now for three weeks and well . . . well . . . *nothing ever happens.*' "

Even though nothing ever happened, Schawarzberg decided to take a "long awaited" trip to Israel in the fall of 1965.

"It isn't that I'm afraid," he told me before leaving for the airport. "But it isn't that I'm copacetic either."

(If you're wondereing why we talked so much it was mainly because I was covering law and crime for *The New York Times*, and who could be better copy, are you kidding?)

Schawarzberg no sooner got to Israel than he began working up a currency swindle with a woman he met in Tel Aviv. But the Shin Bet, the Israeli secret service, caught on and quietly asked him to leave the country. He was mortified—"After all, ain't I a Jew?"—but he was generous in his praise of the Shin Bet.

"You can't even compare them to the FBI, what are you crazy?" he said. "The FBI is a glorified answering service, they know only what you tell them, and even then, they get the message wrong. But this Shin Bet is beautiful. I wasn't even on first base and they had me, not nailed exactly, but they knew what I was up to. I would have thought that broad set me up, but they kicked her out too. I never went against Jewish cops before, the ones I knew were always on my payroll when I made book in the garment center. Who ever figured Jews could be such cops, what is this?"

He traveled around the Continent for a few weeks, finally landing in London on the last leg of his journey. It was here that the "psyche waves" that began with the bomb started to really work up steam.

The British held him up at customs, claiming he was under investigation by the United States government. They gave him no details and would not officially bar him, but they wouldn't let him in either.

"That's when I got crazy," he said. "I kept going from one person to another, porters, anybody, telling them my name and asking if they knew why I was under investigation by the United States government. They thought I was nuts, and I *was*, what are you talking about? Then I started sending cables everywhere, to the embassy, to the narcotics bureau in Washington, to the U.S. attorney, to the Justice Department. I even sent one to Manny Celler, the head of the Judiciary Committee. I just stayed at the airport sending cables and bothering people. I must have been there for ten hours, I don't even know. Imagine how crazy I was that I didn't even get hungry."

He called at the *Times* when he got back to New York and he was even crazier. "I'm suing them, all of them, the bastards. I'm not letting them get away with this. Who are they to get me kicked out of England like some smallpox case?"

I told him to forget it, that it was just the U.S. attorney's way of harassing him.

"Don't I know what they're doing?" he said. "They got nothing on me—of course it's harassment—but why should I let them dogs get away with it on me? I'm going to drive them nuts, I'm filing papers, and you'll have them in the morning. It'll be a terrific story."

The papers were styled as a motion for a writ of prohibition, asking the federal court to enjoin the government from harassing, surveilling, bugging, tapping and "destroying the reputation" of Israel Schawarzberg. It was a brilliantly poisonous, scatter-shot document describing diabolical plots and stratagems that would have brought a blush to the Watergate 500. Reading the thirty-page affidavit attached to the motion, I could see Izzy growing more arrogant with every line. He was certain that the government had nothing on him—if they had anything, wouldn't he be arrested?—so he ended his motion by demanding that he either be indicted for whatever "frame-ups" they had in mind or else be allowed to live "in tranquillity."

He had delivered the papers to me at the *Times* and was standing over me in the city room as I read them. He was smiling and fully pleased with himself.

"Well," he said, "how do you like my perjury pen?"

"Don't file it," I said.

"Get away. I'm going to beat them up, who are they?"

"Izzy," I said, "you file this thing and I'll bet you a fat man you're indicted on the return date."

"They got nothin' on me, *bubkes*, are you crazy? Anyway it's filed already. Would I bring the *Times* a motion I didn't file? Don't I know the libel laws?"

On the return date of Izzy's motion, November 8, 1965, the government struck back. He, his lady employer and Pacelli were indicted on charges of obstructing justice. At best it was a case that had been long on the back burner, since it alleged a bribe attempt on a witness years earlier. It was the weakest sort of case, depending entirely on the testimony of an ex-convict with a long record, a frailty recognized in large part by the jury, which acquitted Izzy and the lawyer on all but a conspiracy count. That, of course, was sufficient to end both their legal careers.

I am all but certain that the government would not have bothered with the case had Izzy refrained from the direct challenge—a view supported by most of the lawyers I interviewed at the time. Schawarzberg, as might be expected, vehemently denied this, partly because he never admitted that law enforcement could outsmart him, partly because he felt guilty over the plight of his boss.

"Don't tell me that stuff," he said, "they were looking to frame us for years. Weren't we driving them nuts?"

The firm did have a way of driving prosecutors to distraction. They had a very good batting average, mainly because Izzy had correctly noted while in prison that the way to success was to avoid the trial stage and handle appeals and writs of habeas corpus.

"Who do you think my clients were in jail?" he would say. "Mostly fellows who had the best lawyers on the outside. So if these big lawyers put them inside and me with a junior high school education and one lousy law book was getting them out, what am I supposed to figure? That you don't stand a chance at the trial, they frame you up, they suppress evidence, they coerce confessions, they use faulty warrants, they go before judges who make errors wholesale to help them convict. So who needs to stand there and get killed like that? Later, with the record in one hand and my perjury pen in the other, I could get it reversed. Then I slander the trial lawyer, and before you know it I'm in business."

Schawarzberg had indeed hit upon a canny truth, and at precisely the right time. The early sixties was a propitious moment for criminal appeals, marking the advent of what came to be known as the Criminal Justice Revolution, forged by the Warren Court. One police and prosecutorial practice after another was held to violate the Bill of Rights, from search warrants to confessions to suppression of evidence. Izzy was one of the first to note this extraordinary development and, with the aid of what he called his "perjury pen," he rode its back to many a victory.

Of course, Israel Schawarzberg was not in business to give credit but to take it, and in his relations with clients he never so much as said a kind word about the Warren Court.

"Why should I?" he used to tell me. "If I lose do my clients blame Earl Warren? Forget about it! So when I win ain't I entitled?"

Even when they lost, Izzy and his lady managed to drive prosecutors up walls. One of Frank Hogan's most unflappable assistants got badly rattled at a hearing one day while Izzy floated notes to the lady lawyer. The assistant D.A. demanded that Schawarzberg be removed from the counsel table. "He has a long record and has no business sitting there advising an attorney," the prosecutor told the court. Izzy jumped up, showing the judge his law clerk's certification from the state's highest court, and was permitted to remain. "I don't know why the Court of Appeals certified you," His Honor said, "but I certainly can't overrule them." He insisted, however, that Izzy refrain from advising his employer. Izzy kept taking notes, occasionally giving head fakes toward his boss, sometimes moving a paper toward her and then pulling back. The district attorney couldn't take his eyes off all of this, and finally, when he caught Izzy actually passing a note to the lady, he stopped questioning a witness and demanded that the Court read the note. The lady lawyer at first refused but finally delivered the note to the bench under threat of contempt.

The judge's face flushed as he read the message, and the press table, always crowded for a Schawarzberg appearance, got ready to record an expulsion of the old con man.

"The People have demanded that I read this note, on the grounds that it may have violated my order to Mr. Schawarzberg," the judge said. "The note reads as follows: 'Fix your hair.'

"Now if the prosecutor will kindly conduct this hearing and stop the nonsense, we might get out of here today."

It was a prime example of the "psyche waves" Schawarzberg claimed he could waft over all opponents. He worked at it night and day, and I once watched him do such a number on a veteran waiter at Lou G. Siegel's Kosher that the poor fellow ended up pouring a Coke into a coffee cup. He began by simply demanding that the waiter write down our orders.

"Why should I write it," the waiter protested, "there's nobody here but you, do I look stupid or something?"

"Write it down, you'll do it wrong, you'll make mistakes, I'm telling you," Izzy said.

"I'm here thirty-five years, you think I'll forget two lousy orders in an empty house yet? Just tell me and don't worry."

Izzy ordered six baby meatballs "with nothing on it."

The waiter returned with six baby meatballs surrounded by lettuce and tomatoes.

"What did I ask for?" Izzy said.

"Six baby meatballs."

"And nothing on it?"

"Well, I thought I'd give you a little extra, so sue me."

"No *good*," Izzy said. "I don't want no garnishee, I don't want no lettuce, I don't want no tomatoes. Take it back, didn't I tell you you'd get it wrong?"

Things got terrible after that. His *macho* on the line, the waiter refused to write the orders, and when Izzy asked for mashed, he got baked potato, he wanted apple cake and he got apple cheese. The poor bastard even got *my* stuff screwed up.

When it all ended with Izzy's Coke being poured into my coffee cup, Schawarzberg looked like de Gaulle returning to Paris. On the way out he slipped the waiter a five spot. "Here," he said, "you'll use it for your retirement fund."

He reserved his best "psyche waves" for Robert Morgenthau's United States attorney's office. Nothing made him happier than to drive that office crazy. His biggest time came in the mid-sixties when he was brought before a federal grand jury on a well-publicized charge that he had violated the Mann Act by allegedly transporting a hooker to the Hudson County jail in Jersey to service a client.

The client turned out to be Harold "Kayo" Konigsberg, the Bayonne Bomber, known as the meanest mob enforcer, shylock and general bad boy extant. Years earlier Izzy had stayed up all night, gun in hand, waiting to kill Harold, whom he had invited over to collect a gambling debt from his older brother, Davey "The Mock." Kayo did not fall for the trap, however, and somehow, through the good offices of the "mustaches," things had been patched up and now Izzy was representing Konigsberg on an extortion rap. The grand jury wanted to know just how far representation went.

When Schawarzberg arrived at the U.S. courthouse at Foley Square the stairs were mobbed with reporters and television crews. He noticed a tiger tail in his car, the kind Esso used to give out with gas purchases. He grabbed it and moved smartly toward the cameras.

"Izzy, any comment on this thing?" the reporters shouted.

"Naturally," he said, with his most beatific smile.

He stood there like Tarzan, waving the tiger tail over his head. "With me," he said, "the government's got a tiger by the tail."

The scene made all the networks, and one commentator gave Israel Schawarzberg the last of his aliases: Fat Tiger.

Despite the provocations, Izzy was not indicted on Mann Act charges in the Konigsberg case, although I never met anyone who did not believe he was guilty. He took the Fifth Amendment before the grand jury—"Why, am I ashamed for my reputation?"—and apparently there was insufficient evidence to try him.

"I told you they're just an answering service," he said. "If you don't cooperate with them, they're dead, the bums."

Konigsberg did not fare so well. He was hit with forty years after a madcap trial during which he fired Izzy's lawyer-employer and conducted his own defense in the hope that an appellate court would find him too crazy to have been allowed to run his own case. It didn't work out, but Schawarzberg was philosophical. "I don't have to serve the time," he said. "And didn't I come out of it with a new a/k/a?"

(He picked up his first alias as a kid on the Lower East Side. Sammy Farber, the neighborhood boxing champ, asked him to carry his bag to Ridgewood Grove Arena in return for a ringside seat.

"Are you kidding me?" Izzy said. "What am I, some lobby guy or something?"

"Why you crummy little mizo," Faber replied. It was his way of saying "miserable" and the name stuck with Schawarzberg forever.)

Izzy was, he often said, "manufactured in the Russian-Polish Pale" but born on Rivington Street in 1914. It was years before he learned that his real name was Israel, since his parents, in the manner of immigrants, Americanized it to Irving when he started kindergarten.

His father, Jacob, still vigorous today at eighty-four, was a building superintendent while his children were growing up. "He operated like a floating crap game," Izzy told me. "As a super he'd get a four-month concession on the rent. So naturally every four months we'd move to another railroad flat where he'd be superintendent for a new landlord. He didn't pay rent in years. Why, weren't there enough landlords to go around?"

It was truly the "teeming" Lower East Side in the two decades following the Great War. Criminality flourished, with the area sliced into street mobs built on ethnic lines. By the twenties the Jewish gangs were in the clear ascendancy, their power stretching city-wide. Most of the names of the top Jewish hoods remain familiar today. Meyer Lansky Bugsy Siegel, Lepke Buchalter, Gurrah Shapiro, Longy Zwillman, Doc Stacher, Nig Rosen, Waxey Gordon, Pittsburgh Phil Straus, Tootsie and Neddie Herbert.

In later years, Schawarzberg would work for and with some of these people, but his early days showed a different promise, for he was a fine student. He played hooky, to be sure, but when the final returns were in, his name was embossed in gold letters on the honor roll of Mangin Junior High School.

(When he told me of his school days, shortly before his death, his language became oddly formal, as though he were back at Mangin trying to impress his teachers. He never talked the same way even in court.)

"Prior to graduation," he told me, "I pressed my homeroom teacher, Mrs. McDonald, and my Spanish teacher, Miss Peters, for information as to whether or not I would be graduated. They informed me that I had failed because of my absenteeism. Therefore, I did not attend the graduation exercises.

"It turned out that they were kidding me, but how was I to know? Much to their chagrin I failed to answer when the diplomas and medals were distributed. I had been awarded the Spanish medal and had scored top grades in all subjects.

"Both teachers hastily proceeded to my home, bearing the fruits of my scholarly efforts to my mother, who was shocked to learn that I was playing hooky. When I returned home and saw my teachers and learned the truth, I felt pleased and proud. That is, until they left and I felt the angry pinch on the back of my neck from my mother. It was a pinch only Sadie could *knipe*, may she rest in peace."

He enrolled in Seward Park High School but almost immediately dropped out and into a life of crime that he never really left. I occasionally asked him why and got the following answers:

"Good question! Why did I become a criminal, was I crazy? *Yes.* I'm a psychopath, I'm an egomaniac, what are you talking about?"

"You mean I shoulda gone straight? Go away! I need action. You want I should get up in the morning and go to work? My brother Chink once offered me, after the war, a third of his bialy business, he's known as the Bialy King. If I take it, I'm a rich man. But it's legit, are you kidding me?"

"Where I grew up on the Lower East Side you either became a judge or went to the electric chair. I'm the happy medium."

The happy medium was first arrested in a Delancey Street poolroom at age eighteen. It was a favor for some of the older guys in the neighborhood who had just pulled a holdup. They ran into the poolroom with the police in hot pursuit.

"I was a pool hustler then," Izzy said, "and it happened that I was the only one there that day without a record. So they imposed on me to hold the gun, they told me I'd get a short bit at worst, maybe probation. We didn't have much chance to negotiate, and before I knew it the cops were in there and the next stop was Rikers Island, where I drew an indeterminate sentence."

Rikers Island in the early thirties was a lot worse than it is now. Young Schawarzberg, having seen a few of the early prison movies, decided one dinner time to pull off a scene out of *The Big House*, or some such. He began tapping the saucers and when others followed he jumped on the table à la James Cagney and screamed that the food wasn't fit for pigs. A lovely riot ensued and of course Izzy got a taste of the hole, where the food was not improved.

"I could see that this indeterminate sentence was going to last a while as I was no model prisoner. So one day I'm perusing the books in the prison library when I come across Captain Dreyfus' letters from Devil's Island.

"Well I went crazy, these letters were great, even though I didn't understand half the words. So what, I had a dictionary. He wrote these terrific letters trying to get out of the can. 'I implore you, I beseech you,' one of them said.

"So what I did was this. I copied one of the letters, and where it said Devil's Island I wrote Rikers Island, where it said Dreyfus I put Schawarzberg. And I sent it off to the commissioner of corrections."

The result was a visit from Mickey Marcus, the assistant commissioner of corrections, the legendary Mickey Marcus who was to die in 1948 as chief of staff of the fledgling Israeli Army. "Marcus was impressed that a young Jewish kid from the Lower East Side could write like this," Izzy said. "For the first time in my life I tried to keep my mouth shut, figuring I'd give the game away. But when I saw he wanted to help me, I told him about a scandal going on in prison, whereby the guards were bringing in booze and dope and selling them to the prisoners."

Marcus investigated, a cleanup was instituted, and Schawarzberg was paroled. "I think he'd have gotten me out of there even without the whistle blowing," Izzy said, "because he really liked me and figured I was a victim of my environment. But I'll always squeal on hacks, why not? Nobody else, I never squealed on anyone else, but the hacks, what did I care, let 'em die, the rat bastards. You know what them sadists do when you leave the can? They stand there together, like the Andrews Sisters, and sing like this: 'Goodbye, Finnegan, you're out but you'll soon be in again.' Can you imagine that, after you just put on a suit for the first time in, maybe, years?"

Out of Rikers, Schawarzberg spent the balance of the thirties pulling stickups, committing forgeries and arranging small-scale swindles. It was not a period to be proud of in light of his later grandeur, but Izzy didn't mind talking about it.

"I did about a half dozen *shlom* jobs for Lepke and Gurrah," he said. "Shlom jobs were also called union specials, meaning that we would use sash weights and lead pipes on labor organizers and pickets in the garment center. They told us the labor guys were all Communists, but to tell you the truth I didn't need any justification. I *said* I'm a psychopath, what are you bothering me?"

In 1936, Schawarzberg and a few fellows from the old neighborhood decided to move into the big time. They would take Cartier's, the great Fifth Avenue jewelry store.

"We were making only small scores, so we figured why not one big one and get it over with. Imagine what greenhorns we were? We decide to hit the joint on a Saturday, the busiest day. We all wear white hats and blue suits and brown shoes. All we didn't have were numbers on our backs.

"I'm supposed to meet the fellows on Fifty-second Street and I'm holding four guns, handcuffs and mouth tapes. When I get there I see the other three guys, my co-conspirators, standing in front of Cartier's looking in the window. I don't even get to them when the Safe and Loft Squad swoops down on us, do they need a scorecard to figure it out? I deny everything, naturally, even though they find me loaded. But one of the fellows can't take the interrogation, which in them days consists of squeezing your balls and other quiet tortures. There was no *Miranda* decision [establishing suspects' rights] then, are you kidding? Well, one talks, the others do, and the result is I get my second bit, another twenty months in college, do I need that?"

He doesn't need me harping on the failures, either, and I can hear him now exhorting me to get on to the flush days.

In the late forties, Schawarzberg opened the Ace Ticket Agency in a subway arcade beneath Times Square. He had been doing a nice bookmaking business in the garment center during the war and now he needed a front. It was this front that led him to pioneer college basketball fixes, which scandalized the nation in the early 1950s. It also gave him a couple of new aliases, Irving Ace and Irving Ticket.

"Since it was the Ace Ticket Agency, I used to answer 'Irving . . . Ace' when the phone rang, and because I was able to get tickets to anything they began to call me Irving Ticket. But I didn't open to be a broker, that was just a living. I used it to make book and to bet with bookmakers."

But Irving Ace did not believe in paying off on such things as long shots, so the Ace Ticket Agency became the only literally collapsible corporation in town.

"I had counters that could fold up and shove at the drop of a hat, or a daily double. If I got stung I put up an out-of-business sign and in a couple of weeks I'd open up in another location. I must have had dozens of spots up and down Broadway. Naturally, this didn't make me popular with bettors or bookmakers, but am I supposed to make them fat?"

If swindling bookmakers sounds like dangerous business, Schawarzberg never seemed to worry about it. He was careful to avoid Mafia bookies, although on a couple of occasions he took them off as well.

"Once I hit a connected guy for twenty-five grand and the mob had a sit-down on me. But I beat the death penalty by conning them that I didn't know he was part of the outfit. That was just the cover to satisfy the voters. I had a fix in with the top *capo*, through a swindle I was working for him. So when he said he believed my story the others went along, not knowing about our private yakahoola. Divide and conquer was some guys' motto, but with me the fix was safer."

His chutzpah apparently had no limit. He took a top gambling casino in Las Vegas for $75,000 on forged *certified* checks and beat the rap by convincing them that *he* had been swindled. And a Mafioso once told me that Izzy talked his way out of an execution ordered by Willie Moretti, the late Jersey *capo*, by convincing him that a killing would serve to convince people that Moretti had been taken by a "two-bit Jewboy."

But his most sensational caper was the college basketball scandal, which he began engineering in 1948. During the next three years he fixed over twenty games in the East and Midwest by bribing players and referees.

It began one afternoon at the Ace Ticket Agency. One of Izzy's regular customers, a runner for a local bookmaker, came in and said: "Irving Ticket, would you be interested in obtaining the services of some basketball players from Manhattan College?" Schawarzberg was incredulous. Manhattan, after all, was a Catholic school, and to Izzy's way of thinking that made its players untouchable. "All day long they're taught by priests and nuns, how you gonna get to that?" he said.

The runner knew better. He was working a beat near the school and one of the players was betting horses with him. The player had introduced him to some of the other boys, and the runner had been softening them for the kill. With Izzy's bankroll he figured the fix could be accomplished. "They may not be ready for dumping yet," he told Schawarzberg, "but they'll go for point shaving."

Izzy met two of the Manhattan players that night, slipped them fifty bucks each to "think about it" and drove them home. "I told them they'd get five hundred for winning under the point spread [shaving] and fifteen hundred if they were willing to dump the game. They called the next day and said they would win *over* the points. I told 'em fine, I'd give 'em the five bills to go over four points. Little did they know what I had in mind."

Years later, Izzy told me that it always worked the same way with all the teams he fixed. The players would start by thinking they could collect for winning without even shaving points, which let them feel moral while talking money. Izzy would always play them along, pay them but never bet. The next time he'd tell them to shave, and still he wouldn't bet, because there was no way to assure a shave. After that, he said, the players would inevitably suggest a dump so that they could come in for the bigger money that went with losing.

"I swear on my mother's grave," he said, "that I never once told a kid to dump. They always figured it out for themselves."

Although Schawarzberg made many large scores during the two years he had Manhattan and various other schools on his pad, the fixing actually became so rampant that even a dump wouldn't guarantee a betting coup.

"Everybody got in on the act, and now and then you'd get caught in a double dump. I had one game in the Midwest where both teams were dumping so hard the score ended up thirteen-twelve. I had to laugh, even though it hurt, when I read *The New York Times* the next day. They said it was a great example of deliberate basketball. My trouble was that the other side had the whistle [the referee]."

Izzy claimed to have a number of "whistles" in his pocket, and when I doubted him once he showed me canceled checks endorsed by a Big Ten referee. "Why in hell did you pay him in checks?" I said.

"He was dumb enough to take it why shouldn't I give it to him? The canceled checks meant I owned him. After all, I didn't worry about my reputation and I didn't worry about doing a little Ping-Pong time. But *he* had to worry. And anyway, what good is doing it if you can never tell anybody? I'm a publicity fiend, don't I know that someday a guy like you will come along and doubt my word? Now, what do you say when you see the evidence?"

The extent of Schawarzberg's involvement in fixes—horse races as well as basketball—was brought home to me recently over dinner with a Hollywood producer. In his younger days, the movie mogul had been a heavy gambler, and for years he and Izzy worked together.

"We used to fix horses in Miami. I never saw a guy with bigger balls than Izzy Schawarzberg. He'd walk into a stall in the early morning—I'd lay chicky and believe me I was scared—and excuse the stable boy as if he were the owner. He'd hit the horse in the neck with a hypodermic and walk out as if nothing happened.

"Izzy knew from experience that you couldn't hype a horse to win, it would show in the spit box [postrace saliva test]. But if you hit the favorite with a drug to slow him down there was no problem, since they didn't do saliva tests on the losers. With the favorite out of the race, we'd have a big edge. I notice that the mob has been doing that lately, but Izzy was doing it when it was unheard of.

"As far as basketball was concerned, I was betting five to ten thousand a game in the early fifties never knowing the dumps were in. One day Izzy came to my hotel on Eighth Avenue—who'd squander money on rent?—and told me he had the Manhattan College team in the bag. I thought he was bluffing me and told him so. It never occurred to me you could get to good Catholic kids. 'Let me show you about them good Catholics,' he said.

"He took me to a hotel room near the Garden. We walked in and there were seven players from Manhattan. Seven! I took one look— they were standing there with the *M* on their sweaters—and walked out. I was in shock. It was unbelievable, unthinkable, but I had seen it. You know what? I never bet on a game again. Not just basketball—nothing, no games. So in a way, Izzy Schawarzberg cured me of my gambling habit."

Schawarzberg never claimed to have more than three Manhattan players in his pocket, but it would hardly be beyond him to arrange a party for seven, just for the icing effect. In any event, he was cured of his fixing habits in 1951. He didn't have that year's Manhattan team on his payroll, but in trying to hustle a button manufacturer who *thought* he did, Schawarzberg found it necessary to make a play for Junius Kellogg, the center and only black player on the team. He asked Henry Poppe, the previous year's co-captain, who had been on the pad, to offer Kellogg a bribe.

Unfortunately, Kellogg went to the district attorney. On the evening of January 16, 1951, after a game in which Kellogg was supposed to be in the bag, detectives visited Poppe's apartment. Poppe spilled on the spot, and that night Schawarzberg and a flock of others were arrested. It was the first break in the long-rumored college basketball scandals; before the year was out, some of the greatest players in the nation were exposed as dumpers. New York University, City College of New York and Long Island University had joined Manhattan College in the list of big-time schools whose names became synonymous with the fix.

What happened to Israel Schawarzberg, corrupter of youth? He pleaded guilty to a misdemeanor and got a one-year sentence, "a lousy little bullet," which he did in ten months on good old Rikers Island. It was an amazingly light touch, considering the gravity of the crime and the long sentences future fixers were to serve.

"They were looking to kill me, are you kidding?" Izzy explained. "But I beat them up. Here I am, the first guy they catch in the biggest scandal ever. I'm due for fifteen years at least, right? I don't have a record an arm long, I have a record two arms long. But I wiped them out."

He did it by announcing that he would defend himself and would bring out everything he knew about the fixes. "I let them know I could implicate other Catholic schools. Does Cardinal Spellman have some clout in this town? Beautiful. The minute I show them what I got they're ready to deal—forget about it! So I walk away with a slap on the wrist. I catch a meatball, is that bad?"

When I hired Izzy at *Scanlan's* years later, the Manhattan College fix came back with an ironic twist. A radical paper opposed to our political iconoclasm accused us of employing a man who had "corrupted black athletes in the 1950s." Little did they know that it was a black athlete he couldn't corrupt who blew the whistle on him.

I brought him to the magazine because I wanted him around me, although the business excuse was that the staff needed disciplining. It was one of the best moves I ever made. He was completely devoted to the journal—after all, weren't we "beating everybody up," from Nixon down?—and he worked harder and longer than most, including me. It was only after his death that I learned he was plotting a major bank robbery as his "swan song"—but that was on his own time, what the hell.

In the fall of 1970, the magazine was in desperate trouble. We couldn't get our September issue on guerrilla war in the United States printed. A "revolt" against the issue, sparked by hard hats in the lithographers union in New York, had spread nationwide. We suspected that it had nothing to do with the content of the guerrilla number but was a culmination of reaction to our unceasing attacks on the Nixon administration. Our August issue had featured an editorial called "Nixon and the Bums," which we made into full-page ads in the *Times*. The editorial exposed the fact that Nixon had invited labor thugs with serious criminal records to the White House to celebrate the hard-hat attacks on peace marchers in the Wall Street area. The combination of the hard-hat unions and the administration, we felt, was destroying our young muckraker in a kind of precursor to Watergate.

We were unable to get a printer for months, and soon our creditors got the idea we were in trouble and began to demand cash for everything. To prove we were solvent we made the payments and kept the staff intact.

Concurrent with this, my co-editor, Warren Hinckle, had imported some guys who turned out to be pro-Fatah Jewish Marxists to help put together the guerrilla war issue. "You're surrounded by assassins," Izzy told me one day, but I pooh-poohed him. He had something, however. The Fatahniks began attacking me as a "Zionist pig" and one day made veiled threats against my family. I called in Irving Ace. The next day they were gone.

"What did you do?" I asked him.

"Nothing, don't worry about it."

"C'mon, Mr. Israel, what did you do?"

"Nothing. I only told them that if they didn't get out of town they had one choice left. They could be buried dead or alive."

Unable to get a printer in the United States, we tried Canada. We got a printer, but the Royal Canadian Mounted Police stopped the trucks carrying the magazine at the border. The police chief of Montreal told Canadian radio that "the United States government asked us to stop it."

A major court fight ensued in Montreal, and when it seemed to be lagging interminably, I sent Izzy up to straighten things out. I would have done it earlier but was worried about his heart condition. He kept pressing and when I relented he said, "Good. Now you'll see action."

He ran around Montreal all weekend, at the demand of the court, getting releases from newsdealers. He called me on Sunday night, December 20, 1970.

"It's *good*, everything's okay, we'll win it, it's only because I got here and drove them crazy. Leave it to lawyers and you could forget about it. They needed me and my psyche waves. Anyway, sleep well, *bubele*, we're beating them up, leave it to Irving Ace. I'll see you tomorrow night."

The next morning the sonofabitch hauled off and died on me, are you kidding?

—*The Super Crooks: A Rogue's Gallery
of Famous Hustlers, Swindlers and Thieves*
Edited by Roger Williams, New York: Playboy Press, 1973

Alden Whitman, who invented the sophisticated obituary for The New York Times, was lunching with me at Sardi's when the word came that Izzy was dead. Alden loved Izzy and Izzy knew it. But Izzy also knew that if he ever died it might not make the "A" wire (while Whitman was working). He instructed me to call Alden first. "Forget about my wife, forget about my brothers, forget about my father," he said. "Just remember to call Whitman. Who knows if I'll go on straight time? So don't forget. I want an Alden Whitman obit, I want my picture to go with it, and I want it to be in the daily index. Otherwise, no good!"

With Alden sitting right there I didn't have to remember. He ran Izzy across the top of the obit page, a full column, picture with it, and of course the index. It was the premier obit of the day, reducing such minor leaguers as steel executives to short mentions.

The result was a packed house at Riverside Chapel in Manhattan. The S.R.O. crowd included reporters, TV crews, every Runyon figure who could walk, a sprinkling of literati, and the usual contingent of FBI men on the lookout for syndicated gentlemen who as usual did not appear. One rather nondescript fellow approached the immediate family and said, "I'm here to pay my respects on behalf of certain people, who Izzy will understand cannot attend."

The rabbi wanted a debriefing session on Izzy. I went in with his two brothers and his father.

"Tell me about the deceased," the rabbi said, in one of those sonorous, $50,000 voices.

When nobody answered, the rabbi repeated the question. It was obvious he hadn't read the obit, but with the mob scene out there he knew he was dealing with a major figure in the Jewish community.

"Did the deceased have any special interests?" the rabbi said.

Nobody answered.

"Did the deceased have children?"

Nobody answered. You'd think it was a grand jury the way the deceased's family shut up.

Perplexed, the rabbi tried again.

"Did the deceased belong to any organizations?"

"What?" Izzy's brother Chink said. The rabbi blinked.

I said, "Look rabbi, you don't have to worry about a thing. You just say the kaddish, that'll do it."

"Why is that, my son?" he said.

"I'm going to make the eulogy."

"That is somewhat odd, my son," he said. "May I inquire why?"

"Because the deceased asked me to do it."

After the opening prayer and a few brief remarks—"Be of good faith, the deceased is now gathered up with the Eternal"—the rabbi introduced me.

I told the congregants that Izzy had made certain requests for the occasion. He wanted an Alden Whitman obit in the Times, he wanted the obit indexed, and he wanted me to give his eulogy. He did not expect to die, or anything like that, but sometimes it happens, you can't be sure.

"As you all know," I said, "the first couple of items have been performed per his request. We got the Alden Whitman notice in the

Times, *we got it indexed and we got the lead piece to boot. Plus, I can now announce that* The Miami Herald *ran the Whitman obit on page one."*

The crowd cheered.

Izzy wanted me to do the eulogy, I said, because he didn't trust any rabbi to "tell the truth" about his life. "They'll make me look like some kind of schmuck who went to work every morning. No good, I don't want that. I want everything said, I want all the crimes told, no cleaning up after me."

The rabbi, who was standing next to me, began to move away.

"The only stuff I want you to leave out," Izzy said, "are those things on which the statute of limitations never runs." Of course, the only crime with no end, with no statute of limitations, is murder. But I didn't spell this out for the audience. All I said was that I asked Izzy why he would care about the statute at his funeral.

"Very good!" Izzy said. But minutes later he told me to leave it out anyway. I asked why. He said, "Suppose they don't accept me there, suppose they send me back? Do I need to walk into the hands of Frank Hogan with a confession on my back? All my life I took the Fifth, what am I gonna get stupid now that I'm dead? Forget about it!"

The joint cracked up. The rabbi was now close to the wall. By the time I finished laying out the no-longer indictable highlights of my friend's colorful life, the rabbi was looking for secret exits. But no good! He had to get back and say the final prayer for the deceased.

"Be of good faith," he said, his fifty-G voice now down to a sawbuck. "If he isn't bound up with the Eternal, he'll be safe elsewhere."

This rabbi had consigned Israel Schawarzberg to limbo! But there is no limbo according to Judaism.

I looked down at the open coffin and I saw Irving Ace smile. Better limbo than where he figured he was going. Without any other Jews there, imagine how easy it is to beat them up, to score all the time, to have everybody kissing his ass for writs. What else do you need in limbo but a lawyer?

BAR TALES

The upcoming story is the only fiction I ever wrote. I did it in an afternoon during the summer of 1971, shortly after the Daniel Ellsberg incident. Originally titled "Cagney Cohn," it was intended for publication in Esquire. I had met Gordon Lish, fiction editor of Esquire, through the good offices of my new friend and champion, George Frazier, who wrote regularly for Esky and persuaded Harold Hayes, the editor, to set me up with his top people to talk over what I might write for the magazine. At one such meeting, Gordon Lish encouraged me to try my hand at the short story.

Lish enjoyed a reputation as perhaps the finest fiction editor in the country. His rejection slip read: "It's a wonderful story and I loved reading it. But it won't be published in this epoch."

After I looked up "epoch" in the dictionary, I called Gordy and said, "It's your epoch, baby, you own the key. If you like it so much why do I have to wait for the next one?" He laughed and laughed, he said it was a great line. But I don't really think he knew what I meant; I don't think he knew what he meant. It's probably subconscious, but editors with power have a way of arranging their minds so that they convince themselves that what they do is somehow ordered by forces beyond them.

I've witnessed this phenomenon scores of time, often having nothing to do with my own work. I've watched the most powerful editors in the world read pieces in other papers or magazines with eye-popping admiration. And then heard them say: "I wish we could run a story like that." In every case they could have run it; it wasn't libelous, it wasn't in bad taste, it violated no journalistic ethics. But they "knew" they couldn't do it. Ask why not, as I always did, and the answer is a smile that says, "Ah, my boy, if only you understood."

In the case of "Cagney Cohn," my guess is that Lish really did like it—if he simply wanted to stroke me he could have said, as they generally say, "It's great but it's not for us"—but that it violated the "epoch," which dictated against realism in the short story. That he helped to create the epoch and thus could have changed it in a trice didn't occur to him because he couldn't allow it to occur to him.

Anyway, I mailed the story to Larry Grauman, the editor of The Antioch Review. Larry loved it but said he couldn't publish it as fiction, I'd need another "rubric." I couldn't figure that one out, since it was fiction. Larry said, "Aw, c'mon, Sid, I know you, you didn't make it up, nobody could make up a story like that."

This was some switch. Before I'd had trouble convincing editors that my stuff was true; now I couldn't convince one that it wasn't true. In the end, I thought up the rubric "Bar Tales," without which, I'm convinced the story would never have been published.

CAGNEY COHN is a guy whose very existence could turn you into an atheist, since if there is a God then why is there a Cagney Cohn. I like him, I don't bother to wonder why. I stopped doing that long ago about Jewish criminals. An old Hebrew terrorist once told Ben Hecht that whereas many people hated Jews without reason, he, Mr. Ben Hecht, loved Jews without reason. I love Jewish outlaws without reason.

Cagney Cohn taxed that indulgence, strained it, pushed it to where if they hadn't framed him at that moment, that instant, I would have had to ask myself certain moral questions about how I could *like*, forget about love, Cagney Cohn.

Even though ten years ago he did me a favor. I considered it a favor, although at that time I had not met him and the favor wasn't for me but for a friend and I had reason to believe that Cagney Cohn didn't know I existed or at least he didn't know I was responsible for the favor. Then again, you might not consider it a favor, Cagney Cohn's forbearance to kill my friend. But then again, I haven't mentioned how much pleasure he derived from murder, particularly when the murderee had swindled him.

I was an assistant county prosecutor in Paterson, New Jersey, in those days, a good one, perhaps "hotshot," though lacking that blue-eyed moral suasion so often the mark of Jewish D.A.'s.

I had reasons for rejecting the hard-nosed approach to prosecution, some of them conscious. First, it was unnecessary; I knew that from experience. Although I was only twenty-eight, I had tried scores of cases as a defense lawyer and now I had been on the other side of the table for a couple of years. It was crystal clear that once the clerk announced "State v. Jones" to the jury, the prosecution was rounding third and only a fool could kick it away.

Furthermore, I had no intention of remaining a prosecutor. I took the job in order to learn how better to defend criminals in the future. Breezing through one win after another, free, single, larky, convinced that by thirty-five I'd be Edward Bennett Williams or Jake Ehrlich or Percy Foreman—it never occurred to me to get evangelic about my future clientele.

Finally, my known ancestors came out of the Russian-Polish Pale, which meant that somewhere in the family herring barrel there lurked a horse thief, or better, and this effectively smothered my piety in onions.

On Passover of that fine year, right before the Seder, Lenny Rosen's mother called and broke down on the phone while wishing my mother a happy holiday. My mother couldn't make out the trouble, but when she mentioned it I decided I'd run over there after Seder. I knew Lenny was gambling heavily; and I had a feeling that some misplaced parlay was behind those mother's tears.

Lenny Rosen was my best friend until we got to be juniors in high school, when he decided I was snubbing him. He was right, though I wouldn't concede it to myself. I was lean and wavy-haired, the only guy in the class on the first-string basketball team, I had a column on the paper, I was a big man in my fraternity and I was dating eighteen-year-old girls from South Orange.

Lenny was in my fraternity, but only because I got him in, a fact I did not manage to conceal, in the pricky manner of old friends in such doings. His hair was already receding, he was getting fat, he worked in his father's butcher shop after school, and despite a crazy sense of humor he was afraid of girls.

We never officially split, he never accused me of the snub, and we put on an act sufficient to win the Best Friends sweepstakes in the senior class book. But from Friday afternoon until Monday morning, I spent no time with Lenny Rosen.

He tried premed at Rutgers, quickly dropped into accounting and then quit altogether when his father died after his sophomore year.

He ran the butcher shop, and got married a couple of years later to a girl named Sally. I hardly saw him after high school, and even now, though I was long since back in town, I seldom ran into him. He still had the butcher shop and a six-year-old son named Scott (for Sam, his father), and I assumed he was all right until I heard his name mentioned by a detective. I was eavesdropping, so I couldn't ask into it, but the detective was telling a cop that Lenny Rosen was in trouble with the shylocks. That happened a month or so before his mother called on the first Seder night.

Mrs. Rosen came into the house unexpectedly, just as we were starting the Passover service. A thin woman, unlike the rest of my mother's friends, she had one of those perennially sad faces that had made her look sixty-two when she was forty and curiously kept her looking sixty-two now that she was sixty. My grandmother had always called her Jenny Goldstein, after the Jewish tragedian of Second Avenue, and that was the only laugh anybody ever had over Hannah Rosen.

"Lenny's in the hospital, in Beth Israel, otherwise I wouldn't bother you, believe me," Mrs. Rosen said. "I don't know what's the matter, he don't talk to me about nothing, but he's in trouble, I know it. What can I do, my Lenny's a big twenty-eight years old and he's laying there with high blood pressure."

She cried now, and my mother tried to comfort her. I said I'd go to see him now.

"No, I wouldn't hear of it," Mrs. Rosen said, "this is terrible how I'm ruining your Seder—eat first, please—my God do you think it could be the heart?"

As I left I noticed my father eating the gefilte fish as though nothing had happened. I had to hold back a smile, realizing how delighted he must be with me leaving, as it meant no services, none of that *dovening*. He sat there oblivious to the hysteria, as usual when such things happened, and most particularly when he was hungry.

Lenny was in a private room, and on the elevator I thought how natural that was. Every Jew I know in Passaic, rich or poor, stayed in private rooms. Wards were out of the question; Jews did not stay in wards. I remembered my mother telling me how my grandfather and his friends would tour the hospital in the old days after shul on Saturday, and if they saw a Jew in a ward they'd have him transferred.

Sally Rosen, née Toplowitz, was standing outside room 304, alternately puffing a cigarette and biting her lower lip. She had pleasant, light brown eyes, dirty blond hair and an easy, soft, near-pretty face. She was a little thicker than when I had last seen her, about a year before, but not fat, nicely *zoftik*. She wore a plaid dress, slightly below the knees, no more than an $11.95 number, or less than Lenny bet on red lights, if my info was correct.

I was fifteen feet from Sally when she looked up. She ran over and threw her arms around me.

"Stretch, oh Stretch, old friends are the best, thanks for coming, Stretch."

I was vaguely annoyed by the intimacy. *Stretch.* Nobody called me that anymore, not since high school, and hardly then. I didn't think Sally even *knew* that name. Then I remembered that Lenny always liked it. And it occurred to me that Lenny talked about me a lot, he must have, and I felt the old guilt that hit me every weekend in high school while I dressed for a date and thought of Lenny hanging around with guys he didn't like because his old buddy was too big for him.

"Sal, honey, tell me what he's doing in that room."

"God, Si"—that was better—"how many times I wanted to call you, how many times I begged Lenny to go to you, but you know Lenny, he loves you so much. . . ."

"C'mon, kid," I cut in, "just tell me, if you know. Have they beaten him up?"

Before she could unregister the shock, I noticed two men getting off the elevator.

"I've got to talk to him alone, Sally, now don't argue, go down and have coffee and a cigarette and I'll be there in twenty minutes. Go, go."

Lenny looked forty-five years old in that bed. His face, which had added a couple of chins, was meat red, and though he smiled at me, his eyes were frightened. "Lenny," I said, "we'll know in a second if I'm right, but I think you're getting company. Let me handle it, don't get scared."

The men walked right by me and moved to the edge of the bed. One of them, a fat little greaser, stood directly over my friend. "What's gonna be Lenny, what's gonna be," he said.

"Leave me alone, chrissake, can't you see I'm lying here in bed—leave me alone, chrissake, I'm sick," Lenny said.

I stood there like a fool, handling nothing, mesmerized by the boldness of these two guineas.

"Listen Lenny and listen good," the little fat guy said. "That'll be your last fuckin' bed if you don't come up with it by Friday. Today's Wednesday, Lenny, so you got two days for the two tousan, that's a tousan a day, you should be able to do that, Lenny."

"How could I do that, I'm lying here with 200 high blood pressure, how could I do that, gimme a break willya?"

"We'll give ya a fuckin' broken back, Lenny, that's what we'll give ya. Now you listen, Lenny. You got money for them fuckin' hundred-dollar windows, you got the two big ones for Cag. That's how Cag figures and that's how you gotta figure, you got that Lenny?"

Finally, the taller one chimed in, with a low, gurgly laugh. "Cag says to wish you a happy Pesach," he said.

I think that's what woke me up, the perfect way this big wop pronounced the Hebrew word for Passover.

"You tell Cag the prosecutor's office has a little Kaddish planned for him if he touches this kid," I said, flashing my D.A.'s badge. "Now get your fucking, cocksucking guinea asses out of here before I pull you in." They ran out a lot quicker than my fingers could light the cigarette.

Lenny, who had been close to tears, all of a sudden began laughing. "A little Kaddish planned for Cag," he mimicked. "You tell Cag I got a little Kaddish planned for him." He was rolling over in bed with the laughter. It was contagious, or perhaps my nerves, but I started mimicking myself.

"Get your fucking, cocksucking guinea asses out of here," I swaggered. "Is this the end of Rico?"

"Stretch, you're still a Jew chauvinist, I know you," Lenny said, bringing the laugh down to a chuckle. "What bothered you was that Cagney Cohn hired *talianers* to do his work."

"Worse than that," I said. "I couldn't take that dago saying Pesach with the 'ch' so well, the black hand mother. That's really what got me, you degenerate Jew horseplayer, what the fuck have you got me into?"

I knew damn well what I was into, and I was beginning to chill at what I had gotten *him* into, but there was no point in troubling him. His eyes had some light again, and it seemed to me that he hadn't looked so alive since we had to fight our way out of the Russian People's Home in Garfield in '48 after we beat the Slovac club in basketball. We were fifteen years old and the Slavs had a couple of older ringers who didn't like these little Jew boys taking them. In the locker room after the game, a guy made a crack about how the Arabs would finish off Hitler's job in Palestine. Lenny went for him, kicked him in the balls, and we were lucky to get out with our pants. The only thing standing between us and a pogrom was a Polish councilman, who ran in and ushered us out.

"Lenny," I said, "how bad is it? If you owe Cagney Cohn two grand you must be in for another twenty to the ginzos."

"Another forty. Forty-two to be exact."

"On how much principal?"

"Fifteen, sixteen."

"And Cag was the last?"

"What do you think?"

"So you kited him. Schmuck, you had to kite Cagney Cohn. That's beautiful, Lenny, that's very intelligent."

What my pal Lenny Rosen had done was to get two thousand dollars from Cagney Cohn and pay it to some other shylock who was leaning on him. This is known as kiting. If Cagney Cohn discovers that he is being kited, his answer is to kill the kiter.

I had learned something of Cagney Cohn's modus operandi early in my legal career. I was defending a man who had been caught trying to hold up a liquor store. He was in his middle thirties, he had a college degree and no previous arrest record. Men seldom begin a crime career at that age, and I questioned him closely in an effort to discover his motive. He was quite evasive, but I kept at it. Finally he said: "I owed Cagney Cohn. Do you know what that means?"

I said I knew of Cohn's reputation as a mean shylock and a gangland executioner, but I didn't know that people had to resort to stickups to pay him off.

"Stickups? I'd do anything short of murder rather than face him without my payments. You have to go to his office every Monday night and pay him the interest, the vigorish they call it. He doesn't care about the principal, why should he, the vigorish is so high. The longer you owe the principal, the more you pay in vig; it's simple. Well I've been into him for months now, and on a couple of occasions I had no money. It's not pleasant. You might get a lead pipe in your belly, a kick in the nuts, loose teeth—depending on his whim. I had enough. I vowed after the last time, two weeks ago, that there'd be no more of it. I'd come with money, wherever I had to get it."

"Why did you go to him in the first place?" I said. "Or didn't you know what he was like?"

"I went to him for the same reason everybody goes to him. I was tapped out, broke, there was no place else to turn. I had taken all there was to take from my family and friends. My credit was gone with all the shylocks I knew. I'm a gambler, I bet baseball and basketball, all sports, no horses, it doesn't matter. What you asked is why I went to him. I went because I couldn't get a dime elsewhere. It's the only reason anyone goes to Cagney Cohn.

"Did I know what he was like? If I didn't know before I went to him, I learned immediately. He tells you, and he tells you very clearly. I guess when you become degenerate enough to walk in that door you don't care, you don't want to think of anything, you try not to believe him. But he tells you. I'll give him that."

I had to give it to him, too. The way he works.

"I went into his office," my client continued, "and he simply said 'how much.' I told him five thousand. He opened his drawer, counted the money, and threw it at me. He said nothing for a few seconds and I thought it meant that it was time to go, so I stood up.

" 'Where the fuck you goin',' he hollered. 'Where you goin', you degenerate cocksucker, you got a hot tip? Sit your ass down.'

"I didn't notice it, but Cohn has a big piece of wood sitting on his desk. Suddenly the wood split in two; he had whacked it with a mallet. While I looked at the wood lying on the desk, broken perfectly down the middle—wham!—I got the mallet across my leg, directly under the knee. I hadn't seen him move from the desk, but there I was holding my leg. He told me, very calmly, very politely, to roll up my pants leg. I was black and blue. Cohn pointed to my leg. 'That's your collateral. Those bones.'

"I was willing to accept that. Then he asked for my wallet. He took out the pictures of my wife and kids and put them in his drawer.

" 'That's the rest of your collateral,' he said.

"He stood up, he's very big, hulking, powerful, very imposing, and he roared at me.

" 'Now you listen, you degenerate fuck,' he said. 'You don't like the deal, give me the money back and get the fuck out of here. You got ten seconds. After that I own you, you miserable bastard.'

"I'll never know why I didn't leave; he seemed to be hoping I'd leave, as though he didn't want to see what I was about to become.

Then again I don't know, I don't want to romanticize him. Still it was a feeling I had. But I didn't leave.

" 'All right,' he said, kind of softly, 'that's it. Get out. But let me tell you, I hope you don't make the vig. I'd rather kill you than collect from you. You belong in a sewer. You just handed me your kids for a lousy bunch of green. Here's the pictures back. I won't touch them, or your wife. I pity them. Now get out. You don't deserve to live, you miserable cunt.'

"He was right," my client said, "but I'd love to choke him to death."

As I looked at Lenny in the hospital bed I wondered if he had gone through the same routine. More to the point, I was trying to figure out how I'd get us both out of this mess. By impulsively pulling the badge I had placed Lenny in imminent danger of a knock-off. By now, Cohn would have been told about the D.A. in the room and he would deduce that Lenny was informing. By tomorrow, every shylock in the area would get the word, and feeling vulnerable, the demand would be to get rid of Lenny and quick. For though an informer is usually safe after he testifies, since nobody can be helped by killing him then, and indeed only trouble can come out of it, he is wide open for a hit if they find out about him in advance.

I had two choices. I could tell Lenny about his new difficulties, convince him to become an informer and place him in protective custody until we could get Cohn and the other shylocks to trial. That would mean a year at least, but there were other reasons to reject the idea. First, I didn't want Lenny to be an informer. I don't like informers. I knew Lenny didn't like informers. Moreover, the publicity would be glaring, and this would send his mother into a coma, or into my mother's hair for the duration. Most important, I didn't trust the cops and I didn't trust my office to protect Lenny Rosen.

The only alternative was to get to somebody who could get to Cagney Cohn and straighten things out. This would be extremely delicate, since if it came out that I was arranging something with Cagney Cohn, avoiding my responsibilities as a prosecutor, etc., I'd be finished, perhaps disbarred. I needed a connection, a connection so first-rate that he could be relied on to keep it to himself—and by all means to keep Cagney Cohn from knowing my identity.

I needed time to think. I told Lenny to relax, that I'd handle everything, and I went down to the coffee shop to soothe Sally. After leaving her it occurred to me that Lenny needed protection at the hospital, immediately. I drove over to the American Legion Post, where I knew I'd find Stanley Polodny.

Polodny was a cop whose father used to work in my grandfather's produce market. His mother got TB when he was ten and she was sent away. My grandma practically brought him up, and when he got out of the army my grandfather pulled strings and got him appointed to the force.

Every Christmas, Stanley and his family came to our house bearing gifts and wine. The day went always to form. By dusk Stanley would be nicely loaded and would start talking about my grandparents and my mother would cry and Stanley would walk over to look at the pictures of my grandparents and he'd say a prayer in Polish and then he'd cry.

He was in his mid-forties now and still he came every Christmas. I knew he'd help, and without any questions.

I told Stanley what to look for. He finished his beer, told me not to worry and said he'd be there all night, outside the hospital room. The hell with it, he said, he'd call in sick in the morning. He'd say he spent the night in the hospital.

I had a few drinks at the Legion bar and remembered Thomas R. Culligan.

Culligan was the best trial lawyer I had ever seen, easily the best in the state. He was fifty-three, tall, lanky, with a thrust of red hair covering a balding pate. He had a capacious mind, a fresh wit and a style so adaptable that he could be, in the course of a single cross-examination, Adlai Stevenson and a Hoboken dockwalloper. He was Cagney Cohn's lawyer.

I had been in court with Thomas R. Culligan on a few occasions, the first time on the same side when we represented co-conspirators in a hijacking case, later as a prosecutor against him in two or three matters. He didn't get into Passaic County often, operating mainly in Newark, and I hadn't seen him for several months. He liked me, I knew that, and mainly I thought because he enjoyed the way I handled liquor. "Counselor," he'd say, "you're the only Jew I ever saw could hold the spirits."

Culligan always drank at 20 Green Street, a bar across from the federal courthouse in Newark, but when I called there the bartender said he left for a dinner appointment at Gallagher's Steak House in

New York. I phoned home and told my father to pray for me, I was about to break the Passover and would be home late. My old man said congratulations and asked if that meant we could do without the *dovening* at the second Seder tomorrow night. I said no chance and reminded him that he had taught me all I knew about hypocrisy, and he laughed and told me to get laid while I was at it. I said it was very nice for a father to talk like that, but if he would, I would.

It was after nine when I got to Gallagher's and I expected to find Culligan deep in conversation with a mafioso, but he was holding court at the bar with a couple of regulars. When he spotted me he called out, in his best brogue: "Counselor, and what the bejesus are you doin' here and it bein' the Seder night, have you no respect, m'boy for the religion of your ancestors? Ah, the hell you say, c'mere and down one with us heathens."

After a few drinks I dragged him to a table and told him the story, top to bottom. He never interrupted, which impressed me, because in his place I would have asked twenty questions. Culligan simply ordered more drinks, a couple of steaks, and excused himself. He stopped at the bar to talk to a man I hadn't seen earlier and I figured that this was the appointment he had. The man left and Culligan walked to the phone. When he was gone five minutes I brought his drink over but he shooed it away and me with it.

It was a good ten minutes more before he returned to the table.

"Great Culligan," I said, "I have just witnessed an historic event. I never saw you turn down a drink before."

"Never drink while I'm working, counselor, don't have that good Jewish stomach of yours, might get to saying foolish things."

"Like me in the hospital, huh? I hadn't even had the first glass of Seder wine, for your information."

"If you did that sober, there's no excuse, my young friend. But I'll not lecture. Tell me now, how well do you know Morris?"

Morris? I had forgotten his name was Morris. I never heard any-one use Cagney Cohn's real name, not in conversation. *The New York Times* said Morris (Cagney) Cohn, and his yellow sheet said Morris a/k/a Cagney, but nobody said it out loud. Typical of Culli-gan, I thought, to treat a whore like a lady.

"I don't know Morris at all," I said, "never met him. I know about him, that is I know him by reputation."

"And you have concluded from that reputation?"

"I have concluded that Cagney Cohn, I'm sorry, Mr. Morris Cohn, is a vicious rat bastard cunt cocksucker sonofabitch mother-fucker."

"He is most of those things, though quite heterosexual," Culligan chuckled. "Very vicious, very much so, he has been responsible for numberless requiem masses, not to mention Kaddishes and whatever the Protestants call it. But I may have phrased it wrong. Do you dis-like Morris Cohn, counselor?"

"I like all Jewish criminals. As long as they don't kill my friends."

"Wonderful, counselor, I knew I didn't read you wrong," he said, smiling. He was coming on like Claude Rains now, and having watched him cross-examine witnesses I sensed he was setting me up for something.

Clearly, Thomas R. Culligan could not have been entirely pleased with the fact that he had been responsible for keeping Cagney Cohn out on the streets all these years. Culligan was not an amoral man, quite the contrary. He was deeply involved in community affairs and civil rights and at least 50 percent of his practice was on the arm; he was forever representing indigents in and out of jail. I had heard law-yers asking him, only half-kiddingly, how he could represent a men-ace like Cohn, but Culligan would laugh them off. "Money," he would say, "filthy lucre," and then he'd buy another round of drinks.

Figuring that he was setting me up, I tried to throw him off bal-ance. "Great Culligan," I said, "I never asked you this, but tell me straight now. How could you keep a bum like Cohn on the streets? How could you keep getting him off the hook? And don't tell me the stuff about a lawyer's obligation; I know the Canons of Ethics."

He didn't like it. I had overstepped. His eyes darkened, he sipped more bourbon, and for a few terrible seconds he said nothing.

"We won't discuss me, counselor, we're not here for that. As I re-call it, you're here to ask me to help your friend, and you too, if I'm not mistaken." He paused a moment. "Now why do you think you could come here and ask me to bail you out of this very serious diffi-culty you've arranged for yourself?"

I was looking down at my hands, like a second-grader being lec-tured to by the principal. He startled me.

"You can look at me, counselor, it isn't going to hurt."

But he wasn't smiling.

"You were correct in thinking that I liked you enough to do you this favor you ask, you were very correct in thinking that. But I'm

surprised you don't know why I feel that way about you. What I'm
about to say has nothing to do with why I represent Morris Cohn—
that's my business. But it should have something to do with why you
think you like him, despite all the things you know about him by reputation.

"I remember many a night at 20 Green, listening to you go on
about the Hebrew Revolution, about the Irgun and the Stern Gang.
That's how I came to like you, counselor, not because you're a good
lawyer—I know a lot of good lawyers. Listening to you talk about the
Irgun was like hearing a record of my father, forty years ago, talking
about the IRA.

"I just assumed you knew about Morris Cohn's role in all of that.
Are you telling me now, counselor, that you're ignorant of that?"

"Never heard a word of it," I said.

"During those days, in 1946, 1947, when the Jews in Palestine
had their scrawny tailbones against the wall, fighting the English
with hand grenades and Bren guns, while the silky, respectable Jews
were sitting in their fancy temples wringing their hands over the
'terrible terrorists,' while you were little more than a Bar Mitzvah
boy—let me tell you what Morris Cohn was doing in those days,
when he was no more than twenty years old.

"Morris Cohn in 1947 stole a warehouse full of guns and ammunition, right under the noses of the FBI and the Treasury Department,
and he rode it out of here one night, from the Hoboken docks,
straight to the Jewish terrorists. Three hundred thousand dollars
worth of weapons, my boy, three hundred, when they were down to
matzo balls over there. And when I asked him, years later, whether
the Israelis had taken care of him for that, he belted me in the
mouth. 'You Irish cocksucker,' he said, 'you think I'd take money
from *us?*'

"Well, counselor, forgive the lecture. It should make it easier for
you to solve your Morris Cohn problem than it is for me to solve
mine. Anyway, I just talked to him. Your friend will be fine. Tell him
to be at Morris' office Monday at six. And don't worry. He doesn't
know you're involved. Tell Rosen he's supposed to be an old family
friend of mine."

Cagney Cohn did more for Lenny Rosen than merely keep him
alive. He called every shylock Lenny owed and made them cancel
the vigorish on all the debts, which cut the amount due to less than

one-half the current $42,000. And he worked out easy terms, as well.

"The guy's amazing," Lenny told me. "When the shys balked and wanted to know who Rosen is that we've got to be so good to him, Cag said it's me you worry about, not Rosen. 'I'm God,' he said, 'and I so order.' Honest, he really said it, the guy's crazy."

The only debt Cagney Cohn did not reduce was the two thousand Lenny owed him. But he moratoriumed the interest.

Two years later, Lenny Rosen's body was found jackknifed in the swamps of northern New Jersey. He had gone back to the horses and it could have been any of twenty people who did him in. No arrest was made, and though every shylock in the state, including Cagney Cohn, was called to the grand jury, nothing happened.

Cagney Cohn got bolder and seemingly more vicious through the sixties. He had diversified into labor unions and was used increasingly in mob executions. He was a superb killer, and because of his close relationships with the top Mafia dons he was able, on one notable occasion, to slip through extraordinary security to fulfill a contract on one of the most powerful *capos* in the nation.

He had what appeared to be complete immunity from the law during those years. But by the late sixties it was clear his number was about to pop. The papers were beginning to attribute every murder to him, and half the rackets, and that is the first telltale sign of heat, since crime reporters know only what the enforcement authorities want them to know.

In 1968 they brought him down. A federal task force obtained an indictment in Newark charging Cagney Cohn and thirteen other men with a conspiracy to sell narcotics. It was a palpable frame, Cohn never touched junk, and the testimony of the small-time canary that cooked him made even the prosecutor blush. Cag, finding himself at the defense table with a baker's dozen of Sicilians, never had a chance. He got ten years in Leavenworth, where he sits today.

I published a critique of the trial for the *New Jersey Law Journal* after the U.S. Supreme Court refused to hear the appeal. (I had long since been back in private practice, specializing in criminal law.) The day after the article appeared, Thomas R. Culligan called.

"Congratulations, counselor, very fine dissection of the law of conspiracy. I have delivered it in person to Morris, who was very pleased by it indeed. He asked why you didn't publish it before the Supreme

Court got the case. I explained that the law journal refuses to print commentary on any subject still in litigation. Was I right?"

"Absolutely right. The bastards are cockeyed. They think the Supreme Court's like a jury and shouldn't be overcome with press releases, or something like that. I wrote the damn thing two months ago."

"Don't fret on it, counselor, it was a superb job. And now I am pleased to inform you that Morris Cohn would like the pleasure of your company this evening at the West Street jail. He apologizes for the short notice, but he must leave for Leavenworth in the morning."

Cagney Cohn had lost sixty pounds since his arrest. For the first time in his forty-two years he looked his age, rather than fifteen years older. We met in the warden's office, which needless to say is not the usual living room for prisoners, and when I came in Cag told the warden to get out.

"How the hell'd you manage that," I laughed.

"Fuck him, everything costs me here."

"What about food, it looks like they're starving you."

"My choice," he said, "the doctors scared the hell out of me. I get salads sent over from Broadway Joe's. Anyway, forget that, I wanted you here to thank you personally for that article, I like guys who don't forget a favor."

I thought, that sonofabitch Culligan, he said he never mentioned me, the bastard. It was seven years ago, sure, but it was still no good. I happened to believe Cag was railroaded and my piece had nothing to do with Lenny Rosen.

Reading my mind, Cag said: "What's wrong, kid, you look upset. Relax. It wasn't Culligan told me. It was your friend, Lenny Rosen."

"Bullshit."

"Don't talk like that to me. Have respect, don't be a schmuck. I respect you, I expect the same. It was your pal Rosen, whose ass you saved. He told me."

"When did he tell you?"

"Two years later."

"He was back into you again?"

"They all come back. All fuckin' degenerates."

"How did it happen that he told you about me?"

"He swindled me again, same thing, kiting. I told him that out of respect for Tom Culligan I wouldn't touch him, but only if he told me the name of the prosecutor in the hospital that night. You understand, I never believed Culligan knew that kid; I figured the prosecutor from the hospital got to Culligan. See, if it was a legit prosecution bit I'd have had heat and plenty of it, if they had this Rosen singing. Of course I didn't say it to Culligan, out of respect. Now I had the kid where I figured he would tell me. It interested me, I wanted to know. So he told me."

"Did you beat it out of him?"

"Never laid a finger on him. He ratted on you, straight ratted."

"Why are you telling me this?"

"No special reason. But off the law journal article you're a good guy. I thought I'd let you know. I wouldn't want you saying Kaddish every Yom Kippur for a rat."

"Got any idea who killed him, Cag?"

"Coulda been anybody," he said.

—*The Antioch Review*
June 1973

THE WILD JEW BOY

IT WASN'T EXACTLY a contract, but I did tell Mickey Cohen I'd review his autobiography, and then this, that and the other thing came up and last week he was dead.

How many times, in his rip-roaring life, do you think Mickey Cohen heard the ancient lament, "woulda, coulda, shoulda."

He was in New York last fall to hustle his book—"Mickey Cohen: In My Own Words"—and we had lunch at Sardi's.

He was a has-been, of course, and had been a has-been since Bobby Kennedy sent him to Alcatraz in the early sixties on a tax rap. In the can, a crazed guy took a lead pipe to his head, leaving him a cripple, and he left prison in 1972 in a wheelchair.

But he pulled up to Sardi's in a limo, he managed to walk with a cane and I was pleased to see the captain treat him as if he were still Mickey Cohen of Sunset Strip.

I smiled too, when certain editors who hadn't seemed to care for years, suddenly exhibited an interest in my well-being; people came to the table in droves, and it was a lovely afternoon.

The first thing that struck me was his clothes. Mickey Cohen in tweeds, in a vest! In the late forties, if you said Mickey Cohen, the Rorschach would register as follows: silk, sharkskin, shantung, suede, double-breasted, white linen, camel's hair, cubavera, manicures, massages, 200 suits at $400 a clip. Not to mention horses, tommy guns, the Jewish Mafia.

"Times change, you change with them," Michael M. Cohen of West Los Angeles said.

But only sartorially, that's all he meant.

"Either you're born right or you're born wrong, there's no in between; that's my belief in life," he said. He thought he was born right and, given certain things I know about him, I think so too.

In 1947, while Cohen was riding high, striding the rackets in L.A., Ben Hecht enlisted him in the Hebrew Revolution.

(That term itself is likely to turn heads today—"What revolution? Didn't the U.N. create Israel?"—but between 1944 and 1948, the Irgun and Stern Gang fought and won a bloody street war against the British Empire.)

Hecht, Hollywood's top screenwriter, was the chief propagandist and money raiser for the Irgun. Since the Zionist Establishment, here and in Palestine, were collaborating with the English, and the fancy Jews of America were rooting for them in their Frank Lloyd Wright temples, Hecht and his cohorts depended for help on the average guy, and for extraordinary help on Jewish gangsters.

Mickey Cohen, excited by Hecht's account of the Hebrew terrorists—"these guys actually fight like racket guys would, they didn't ask for a quarter and they didn't give no quarter"—called on his connections around the country, "the Italians, the Jews, the Irish," to "set up whatever positions there were to be helpful to the Israeli cause."

And though he was busy dodging mob bullets, he fixed up a party at Slapsie Maxie's Cafe. A thousand people came—judges, politicans and, of course, the top drawer of the underworld.

Ben Hecht made a fiery speech, after which everybody put up the cash he was told in advance to put up.

"Make another speech and hit 'em again," Cohen told Hecht. But Ben, just out of serious surgery, begged off.

So Mickey pushed one of his henchmen toward the stage. "You tell 'em," he ordered. "Tell 'em they're a lot of cheap crumbs and they gotta give double."

Pointing to Hecht, Mickey, his eyes filmed over, said: "You heard him. It's for the Jews ready to knock hell out of all the bums in the world who don't like them."

One by one the boys doubled the ante. The take was $230,000 and no welshers.

I have been charged, ad nauseum, with being soft on mobsters. Mickey Cohen was a hustler, a racketeer, a killer.

But the Wild Jew Boy has my Kaddish—my memorial prayer. He helped his people when they were up against it, and, as he eloquently put it in another context, "I don't call a man a son of a bitch who's in a walk of life that calls for him to be a son of a bitch."

Olav ha sholem—Peace be unto him.

—*Soho Weekly News*
August 5, 1976

II.

LEFT, RIGHT, AND MIDDLE EAST

FORWARD TO ZION

I'VE ALWAYS HAD Zion on my mind, but until the Six-Day War of 1967, all I ever did was read about it, gab about it, argue about it, and once in a while fight about it. I never wrote about Israel, never went there, and had no real desire to see the Land of our Fathers. A contradiction to be sure, and curious: I was always curious about why I was spending so much time thinking about a place that I obviously didn't care enough about to see or write. And I'm curious still.

The Six-Day War changed all that. Now all I wanted to do was run right over there and start writing. The trouble was, all my credentials were in my head. Nobody, certainly not the *Times*, was about to give me an assignment to cover the biggest story going simply because I wanted it. So I didn't bother to ask. I went there on my own, on vacation time in August 1967.

I've been back a dozen times and written scores of pieces. The three that follow are those I like best.

BACKWARD TO BEGIN

"And the Hebrews learn it backwards, which is absolutely frightening."

—Prof. Henry Higgins

Leave it to my Jews. They make a revolution and twenty-nine years later the leader of the revolution comes to power. First the collaborators, *then* the revolutionaries. The Hebrews don't just learn it backwards, they do it backwards. In that spirit, I celebrate Menachem Begin for what he was, before raising questions about what he seems now to be.

Begin took command of the underground army, Irgun Zvai Leumi, in 1943. At the time, this "army" consisted of a couple of hundred people, mainly young men, all utterly frustrated by events beyond their control. The British, in charge of Palestine under a League of Nations mandate since the end of World War I, had completely abrogated the mandate in 1939 by closing off Jewish immigration to the Holy Land. This infamous act, known as the White Paper, locked the Jews of Europe in with their killers. Since England was at war with Germany, the Irgun—which, unlike the Zionist Establishment, had long opposed British rule—was effectively locked into an alliance with the English against the Nazis, it being deemed impossible to conduct a campaign of liberation on the enemies of the Third Reich.

When the dimensions of the Final Solution came into sharp focus, and the British shoulder nonetheless remained cold, the Irgun high command, in Palestine and the United States, decided to end the truce and deal with the mandatory government as the enemy it was. On February 1, 1944, Mr. Begin issued a Proclamation of Revolt, promising a "war to the end" with the British regime "which hands our brothers over to Hitler." The proclamation demanded that the British immediately transfer power in Palestine to a provisional Hebrew government. "There will be no retreat. Freedom—or death."

The British shrugged it off. Ben-Gurion's Jewish Agency, convinced that England would give them a nice piece of Palestine after the war, denounced it as "madness." But the revolt was on for fair, and true to the proclamation, it did not end until the British were kicked out of the country in 1948.

It was a classic revolution, perhaps the most extraordinary in history. The Irgun, never more than ten thousand strong, blew up British installations, copped British arms, liberated British prisons, flogged and hanged—in retaliation—British soldiers. Condemned in the world press as "terrorists," informed against, kidnapped, tortured by order of the Jewish Agency, it fought on, but, by order of Menachem Begin, it only fought against the British and the Arabs. Whatever provocation, Irgun soldiers were not permitted to raise arms against fellow Jews. Ben-Gurion, Golda Meir, and their cohorts, took full advantage: Hundreds of Irgunists were delivered to the English, most ending up in African prison camps. But the edict held—no civil war.

They got no thanks for any of it; they turned out to be the shooting agency for the Jewish Agency. Ben-Gurion had the population in thrall; the long years of lies and vilification, the egregious slander that Begin and his followers were "fascists," succeeded. In the first Israeli election in 1949, Begin's Herut party got 10 percent of the seats in Parliament. "I will have a Government," B-G announced, "without the Communists and without Herut." Israel gained the distinction of being the only country in history in which the collaborators took power and the revolutionaries were reviled.

And now the irony. After his election in May, Begin received his opponent, Shimon Peres, who said, "You are doing exactly as Ben-Gurion did—you have a government without the Communists and without Herut." It's true, there's not a single member of his old party in the Begin cabinet. Instead, the top spots went to B-G's favorite generals: Moshe Dayan, Arik Sharon, Ezer Weizman.

This would hardly surprise Ben-Gurion, who lived to see Begin propose him, shortly before the 1967 war, as head of a National Unity Government. It cannot, however, be easy for some of Begin's old soldiers to swallow, particularly those of them who were not so much his soldiers as his equals. Which is one reason, among many, why so few of them are there to share the spotlight. Like B-G, Begin did not easily suffer equals. That he still must suffer libels, in the name of Ben-Gurion, even as he more and more resembles Ben-Gurion, is probably the inevitable price of doing it backwards.

Similarly, when a revolutionary has to wait twenty-nine years for power, he is not very likely to be a revolutionary on the day it comes. The crowning irony is that Begin is perceived as such, and "blamed" for his heroic past in the bargain. If that's not absolutely frightening, I'm Henry Higgins.

—*Soho Weekly News*
July 14, 1977

THE PALESTINE PROBLEM: IT'S ALL IN A NAME

THE ONLY THING about the Middle East that goes without argument and even without saying is that the Palestinian Arabs are a stateless, homeless people.

You can't pick a fight on that anywhere in the world, including Tel Aviv. The fact that four wars have been fought for the ostensible purpose of resolving the plight of the Palestinians has solidified this consensus. Everyone believes it.

And today, the Sadat peace initiative lies in near ruin over the inability of Israel and Egypt to agree on a formulation of principles concerning the right—or lack thereof—of the Palestinians to determine their own future on the West Bank of the river Jordan, the area universally regarded as the historic, political, geographic, and demographic landmass of Palestine.

But even as the arguments rage over whether or how this should or can be accomplished—a state, a homeland, an entity?—*everybody* agrees that there is not now and never has been a Palestinian nation.

The problem with this notion is that it is not true. There is and *has been* a Palestinian nation since May 14, 1946—only two years to the day before there was an Israeli nation.

Originally called the Kingdom of Transjordan, that nation is now the Kingdom of Jordan. It lives on the East Bank of the Jordan River and comprises 80 percent of the historic, political, geographic, and demographic landmass of Palestine. It has a population of 2 million people, virtually all of whom were either born there or arrived there from the other 20 percent of Palestine—Israel plus the "occupied territories" known as the "West Bank."

Palestine, then, includes *both* sides of the Jordan River, bounded on the west by the Mediterranean, on the east by Saudi Arabia and Iraq, on the south by Egypt, on the north by Syria and Lebanon.

These boundries were universally acknowledged from the end of World War I until 1946, when Great Britain created by fiat the independent Kingdom of Transjordan—thus lopping off four fifths of Palestine and handing it to the Arabs, in direct violation of the mandate over the territory granted to Great Britain by the League of Nations.

In the years since, Jordan has been recognized as a nation separate and apart from Palestine, its only connection being its role as the principal "host country" for Palestinian refugees displaced by the creation of Israel.

While Israel won its independence through revolution against the British mandatory, it is viewed as a creature of the United Nations, owing its existence to a world guilt-ridden over the Holocaust. Since its victory in the Six-Day War of 1967, Israel—it is said—now controls the whole of Palestine. Its refusal to cede the territory occupied after that war—from East Jerusalem to the Jordan River, plus the Gaza Strip—is therefore considered the bar to national rights or "self-determination" of the Palestinian Arabs.

Because the Palestinian question lies at the heart of the Arab-Israeli conflict, Israel's flat objection to self-determination is considered a major stumbling block to peace, on a par with the determination of important elements of the Palestine Liberation Organization to destroy the Jewish state.

So goes the conventional wisdom of much of the world, and, because it is so widely believed, it is naturally thought to be fair and objective. No matter that it is based on an incredible distortion of history, politics, geography, and demography. Yet, unless this distortion is corrected, there is little hope for anything close to an enduring Middle East peace. A brief look at relatively recent events puts the problem in perspective.

Before World War I, the word "Palestine" had no clear-cut geographical denotation and represented no political identity. In 1920, however, the Allied powers conferred on Great Britain a "mandate" over the territory formerly occupied by Turkey. It was called the Palestine Mandate and included the land on both sides of the Jordan

River. This mandate was confirmed by the League of Nations in 1922 and remained unchanged during the League's lifetime.

The mandate incorporated the Balfour Declaration, the famous 1917 proclamation by which Great Britain committed itself to provide a homeland in Palestine for the Jewish people; it did not provide a homeland for the Arabs living there, but it did protect their "civil and religious," although not their political, rights.

However, two months after the League of Nations approved the mandate, Winston Churchill, then Britain's colonial secretary, changed the rules of the game. "One afternoon in Cairo," as Churchill later boasted, he simply took all the land east of the Jordan River and inserted the Hashemite Abdullah—the grandfather of King Hussein—as its emir. But he did not free it from the mandate, and the people living on the East Bank were in all respects Palestinians. The people living there traveled under Palestinian passports, as did the Jews and Arabs living on the West Bank. But the whole country was effectively ruled by Britain.

Why did Churchill do it? Because Abdullah was bitterly disappointed that he hadn't been chosen by the British as king-designate of Iraq—a post that went to his brother. Churchill wanted to stroke Abdullah's ego and at the same time serve the empire.

But, according to Britain's East Bank representative, Sir Alec Kirkbride, this land, constituting 80 percent of the mandate, was "intended to serve as a reserve of land for use in the resettlement of Arabs once the National Home for the Jews in Palestine, which they were pledged to support, became an accomplished fact. There was no intention at that stage of forming the territory east of the river Jordan into an independent Arab state."

Indeed, Churchill persuaded the Zionists to go along with suspension of Jewish immigration to the East Bank on the grounds that this would mollify the indigenous Arab population on the West Bank—then 200,000 strong—and thus make possible a Jewish homeland west of the Jordan.

Of course, it did no such thing; instead, it whetted Arab appetites for the whole of Palestine, an objective which was nearly achieved several times: the Palestinian Arab uprising against the Jews in 1936; the British White Paper of 1939, which cut off Jewish immigration to the Holy Land, locking European Jews in with Hitler; and the united Arab war against the newly proclaimed state of Israel in 1948.

Until 1946, however, Transjordan remained under the British Palestine Mandate. The English declared Transjordan an independent entity without a soupçon of international authority.

As a result, what began in 1920 as a mandate to turn Palestine into a Jewish homeland turned into a reverse Balfour Declaration, creating an Arab nation in four fifths of Palestine and leaving the Jews to fight for statehood against the Arabs on the West Bank.

The upshot: Jordan is now considered an immutable entity, as distinct from Palestine as are Egypt, Saudi Arabia, Syria, Lebanon, and Iraq.

But a country whose population is virtually all Palestinian can hardly be considered as something less than a Palestinian nation.

Still, the notion that Jordan has nothing to do with Palestine is so deeply embedded that it came as no real surprise when *The New York Times* treated it as a world apart. In a three-part series on the Palestinians, the *Times* drew historical maps cutting Transjordan out of the British mandate—and repeated the fiction that Israel occupies the whole of Palestine.

While the *Times* was breast-beating over the "stateless" Palestinians, I. F. Stone was complaining in a story in *The New York Review of Books* that Jewish dissidents, like himself, could not get a word in edgewise in behalf of Palestinian nationhood.

Stone knows all about the two banks of the Jordan, as his piece indicated. It seems, however, that it didn't register with him; he suggested neither that the Palestinians already have a state nor that the one thing the American press never reports is the fact that Jordan *is* Palestine.

On the other hand, the Israeli government doesn't say it either, and a story goes with that fact.

When the Zionists agreed in 1922 to suspend immigration to the East Bank, in accordance with Churchill's request, Vladimir Jabotinsky signed on.

But Jabotinsky, the elegant, fiery Zionist leader who later became the father of the terrorist Irgun Zvai Leumi and the "eagle" of its commander, Menachem Begin, changed his mind about the deal a year later after it became clear that the Jews had traded away most of the mandate for nothing.

The Establishment Zionists, however, stuck with the British ever after. "There are no Palestinians, there are only Jordanians," said Golda Meir again and again.

Of course, she was wrong. In fact, there are no Jordanians, only Palestinians. One reason why Golda insisted on the opposite—as everyone with a passing knowledge of Zionist politics understands—was that her political enemy Jabotinsky was on the other side.

Meir and her Mapai party, which ruled Israel until Begin took over, hated Jabotinsky and his followers, considering them all "fascists."

The Jabotinsky vision held that both sides of the Jordan belonged to Israel; he wrote a song about it: "The West Bank is ours, and the East Bank is ours."

Menachem Begin marched to this tune most of his life. For domestic political reasons he dropped it some years ago, but now that he is prime minister, it's surprising, to say the least, that he does not even allude to it.

This is not to suggest that Begin make a play to conquer the East Bank. But, by reciting the history of Palestine, he could clear up the confusion and make a contribution toward peace.

Thus, if the world were to understand that Israel now occupies only 20 percent of Palestine rather than 100 percent, would it not make a difference?

If it becomes clear that the Arab refugees and their children who crossed over to Jordan in 1948 did not enter a "host country" but rather the Arab part of their own country, would it not make a difference?

Would it not make a difference to the prestige and future of King Hussein, perceived by the PLO as an interloper only a cut above the Israelis, to point out that he succeeded in maintaining Arab hegemony over four-fifths of Palestine?

Of course it would make a difference.

Israel is being robbed of its political, historic, and geographic legitimacy while seeming to rob the Palestinians of a nation it already has.

"If there is a Palestine, there can also be an Israel," says Peter Bergson, who led the Hebrew Liberation Movement in the 1940s. "But if we paint Jordan as if it's just another Arab nation, as if it's Saudi Arabia, then the fight is on for the extinction of Israel in stages.

"Because," Bergson adds, "if we insist that the whole of Palestine is the West Bank, anything we return is simply the fruit of a crime.

But if we tell the truth, if we point out that 80 percent of the land is already in the hands of the Palestinian Arabs, everyone—here and around the world—will see this dispute for what it is.

"And what is it but an argument over boundaries? We are two nations sharing one country, and we're talking about a strip of land that amounts to 4 or 5 percent of the whole. Every boundary disagreement in history has been settled by drawing new lines. But you can't settle it if someone thinks his nationhood has been ripped off."

If all this sounds theoretical, impractical, unpragmatic, it's the opposite.

No neighboring Arab nation wants a separate state on the West Bank—not Egypt, Jordan, Saudi Arabia, Syria, Lebanon. Some of them say they want it, but whosoever accepts rhetoric in the Middle East belongs in the U.S. State Department. Or *The New York Review of Books.*

—*New York* magazine
March 13, 1978

GENESIS, REWRITTEN

In July 1981, the Israelis destroyed the Iraqi nuclear reactor and bombed Beirut. The American press, which for at least five years had turned sour on Israel, now went into overkill. None were more critical of the Jewish state than the editorial and Op-Ed pages of The New York Times.

Charlotte Curtis, then the editor of Op-Ed, published numerous attacks on the Israeli military actions from outside contributors. Meanwhile, Times columnists Anthony Lewis and Flora Lewis were weighing in with their blasts on the same page. Together with Max Frankel's editorials, it was a media carpet bombing.

I was determined to do something, but the roadblocks were awesome. I couldn't go to Abe Rosenthal because Op-Ed and the editorials were outside his control. Charlotte Curtis, an old friend, had long since made it clear to me she was not interested in opening her page to my views on the Middle East. Charlotte had fallen for the Palestinian line, it was plain for all to see. She was running what I called the Fatah page of the Times.

I decided to set her up, old friend or not. What she was doing now was beyond obscenity and a violation of the fundamental purpose of Op-Ed, that is, to provide a forum for differing views. So I'd write a column without calling her to ask if she wanted it. I was sure she'd turn it down, and my plan was to then take it to the publisher. Punch Sulzberger is a fair man and I thought he'd be convinced of her prejudice when he saw her spike my piece on the Middle East. I had more than enough credentials on the subject, most particularly with the Times, where my pieces on the Israeli–Egyptian peace talks—written with Uri Dan for the Sunday Magazine—had won the Overseas Press Club Award for 1979.

*Well, the best laid plans. When I delivered the column, Charlotte
Curtis was in Europe!*

*A couple of days later, her assistant editors, Phil Drysdale and
Howard Goldberg, called to say the column was accepted. I almost
blurted out "Aw, shit!" but held my tongue. I really wanted to put
her away, I thought that would serve truth and Israel far better than
any piece. In the event, I had it both ways. The piece ran and nine
months later Charlotte Curtis was deposed, busted to a column on
the news pages.*

*The piece that follows was reprinted around the world, most im-
portantly on the Op-Ed page of the* International Herald Tribune.
*The Israeli press ignored it, which, if anybody needs more proof,
ought to answer why the State of Israel has such fabulous public relations.*

THE MIDDLE EAST memory bank is empty again. Just read the
papers, watch the television. The new Book of Genesis begins with
the raid on the Iraqi reactor and climaxes with the bombs over
Beirut. The world is outraged and the world will not forget. The
world has forgotten everything else, and if the American news media
is representative, the world does not want any reminders. It is angry
with Menachem Begin, it is impatient, it is at wit's end. And so history becomes intolerable. Still, history has its claims, does it not?
And a memory bank is the only bank in history that needs a run on it
to get back in business. So here are a few facts.

Lebanon. Israel never touched Lebanon until the Palestine Liberation Organization moved in after King Hussein drove it out of Jordan
in September 1970. Prime Minister Golda Meir warned the Leba-
nese government that Israel would not countenance a new sanctuary
for terrorists. Still, Lebanon gave the inch to the PLO and the rest is
what we see, the destruction of a nation. The PLO, with leftist Leba-
nese forces, sacked and pillaged Christian cities until Syria, fearing a
radical takeover, came in and began slaughtering the Palestinians
and their cohorts. After the Syrian "peacekeeping" mission had succeeded in putting the PLO under its control, Syria and the PLO
turned their guns on the Christian minority. There are 32,000 Syrian
troops in Lebanon and at least three times that many Arabs have
died in that land in the last decade thanks to these peacemakers and
their Palestinian allies.

During this period, successive Israeli governments have bombed Palestinian enclaves in Lebanon. Sum up all these Israeli strikes, including the invasion of Lebanon in 1978, including the bombing of Beirut, and still the casualties inflicted by Israel are minuscule next to what the "Arab nation" has done to its own people. The world hardly took note. When more than 90,000 Arabs die by Arab guns and bombs, it's just one of those crazy things. When 300 Arabs die by Israeli fire, it's a Holocaust committed by a Jewish Mad Bomber. Begin. It begins with Begin. Read the papers, watch the television.

Jordan. In September 1970, Hussein killed 10,000 Palestinians and drove the PLO out of Jordan. From that moment on, the Jordanian border has been virtually without incident. No PLO, no trouble. There is balm in Gilead, but nobody notices. Indeed, President Reagan is asked to press his "client state" Israel to establish a Palestinian entity next door. But not a word is said about leaning on Jordan—a client state if there ever was one—to recognize Israel and join the Camp David Accords.

When it comes to Jordan, the memory bank was closed before it opened. I know people who think it's two thousand years old. But Jordan was only the name of a river until 1922, when Winston Churchill, then colonial secretary, turned its East Bank into the Emirate of Transjordan—created an emirate out of the British Mandatory territory of Palestine. Transjordan was 80 percent of the land mass of Palestine. Transjordan *is* Palestine. In 1946, by British fiat, Hussein's grandfather, Abdullah, became King of Transjordan. In 1948, Abdullah changed the name of his country to the Hashemite Kingdom of Jordan. Presto! The Ancient Hashemite Kingdom of Jordan. So what? So everything. What was in every respect Palestine became a refugee camp for Palestinian Arabs, a host country for those "driven out" by the Jews. And so it is viewed today. The Hussein family, brought out of Arabia by Churchill, are the only truly non-Palestinians living in Jordan today. Yet the world sees Palestine as wherever the Jews live.

Hussein, who took over in 1953, is considered a benign, embattled monarch. Yet from 1948 until 1967, Jordan not only occupied but annexed the West Bank. Without a scintilla of international authority, without the consent of the West Bank population. And without a whimper from the world.

Egypt. A consensus as big as the Pyramids holds that Israel gave nothing for peace with Egypt. By turning over the Sinai oil fields, which it discovered and developed, Israel merely gave up its economic security. The future will tell whether it surrendered its physical security as well. And for little more than Anwar el-Sadat's word of honor.

Israel did not, however, agree to turn over the West Bank and Gaza to the PLO. For this it is accused of intransigence. But why do it, at least until those who want the territories recognize Israel, not to say sue for peace? Have we forgotten that Hussein lost the West Bank because he went to war against Israel in 1967?

Have we forgotten that only yesterday the Arab world condemned—and still condemns—Sadat for Camp David? If not, why are we continually advised that Begin is the obstacle to peace, that he has isolated Sadat from the Arabs? Does anyone really believe that the Arab world wants a Palestinian state? Israel's neighbors, if they want peace, have a track to follow. They need only walk in Sadat's footsteps.

History is often intolerable—just ask the Jews. It also instructs—just tell the Arabs.

—*The New York Times*
July 31, 1981

III.

DON'T TALK TO ME ABOUT JUSTICE

A DECADE OF
CONSTITUTIONAL
REVISION

It's been a dozen years since I worked for the daily New York Times, and still I run into people who tell me they wish I were still covering the United States Supreme Court for the paper. I never face down a compliment, but the truth is I didn't cover the Supreme Court for the Times. So why do so many—and mainly lawyers, at that—think I did? What they call educated guesses are in line.

When I started up the metropolitan legal beat in 1965, the Warren Court was making its revolution in criminal procedure. The Court was both expanding the rights of suspects and nationalizing the Bill of Rights by requiring the states to honor them. Most states fought back and bitterly—through the police, prosecutors, legislators and the judiciary. None resisted with more vigor than New York, whose powerful law enforcement establishment had the strong support of the state court system, particularly the highest court, the New York Court of Appeals.

In covering this war between the federal and state systems I wrote extensively on the Warren Court, in news stories and in interpretive columns. For example, when New York or New Jersey or Connecticut (the metropolitan span) interpreted the Warren Court's rulings on confessions, searches, or right to counsel in a niggardly manner, inevitably I'd concentrate on what the Warren Court had said. So in this way it's understandable why people thought I was covering the Court itself.

There was another reason. Jack Desmond, editor of the Sunday Week in Review, liked my stuff and often asked me to write for his section. More times than not, these pieces were about the Supreme Court. It wasn't my territory, but how would the reader know that? Fred Graham, who covered the Court for the paper, inherited a weekly column in the Review from Anthony Lewis. Tony, whether you agree with him or not—and I seldom do—broke the mold on Supreme Court journalism, establishing the Court, and the Law, as a coequal with the other branches for newspapers and magazines. I don't think it's too much to say that until Lewis came along, few editors took the Supreme Court seriously, and for this all of us who followed—not to say the public itself—owe him a permanent debt.

Fred Graham had essentially the same views as Tony—judicial "self-restraint" out of the soul of Felix Frankfurter. I thought, and still think, that "self-restraint" is just a fancy way of justifying the status quo. So did a majority of the Warren Court. The result, so far as Fred and I were concerned, was that he was in rather constant philosophical disagreement with the Court while I was with the majority for the first and only time in my life.

If Tony were still covering the Court, I wouldn't have gotten a word in edgewise. But Jack Desmond kept slipping me in, not to the exclusion of Fred but as a contrast. This did not sit well with the Washington bureau, and of course it sat worse when Desmond occasionally jettisoned a Graham column for mine. Jack got a kick out of the bureaucratic hassling, and he stuck with me unless he couldn't. There were times when he couldn't, but those times seldom had to do with the Supreme Court.

Once, for example, Desmond asked me to do a column on the proposed New York State Constitution. The Times was editorially opposed to the constitution because it substituted the words of the First Amendment, on church and state, for the Blaine Amendment. The Blaine Amendment was specific in its disallowance of any state aid to religion. In fact, however, New York was providing plenty of money to parochial schools, through school lunches, and so on, and one day at Sardi's bar I mentioned this to Desmond. "Do a piece," he said, and I wrote a blast for him against those, i.e., the Times editorial board, who had turned a virtual nonissue into the only issue on which voters should judge passage of the constitution.

A couple of days later, the Times ran a lead editorial attacking those "crystal ball gazers" who were assuring people that the U.S. Supreme Court would never permit direct aid to parochial schools, such as salaries for teachers and school construction. The crystal ball *was mine alone and so far it's turned out true, but the* Times *managed to gut what would have been a great constitution over nothing at all. John Oakes, then the editor of the editorial page, wrote a nine-page memo to Desmond about my piece. It began, "I see Zion has done it again." Desmond had to lay me off for six months after that. As always, however, he got me back in again.*

A few years ago, after he retired, Jack Desmond called me at noon and asked me to meet him for lunch. I had other plans, but his voice told me this was special. I knew he'd been ill, and though I didn't want to think about it, I suspected the worst. After a couple of drinks he told me he had three to six months to live. "If I take chemo I may have a year," he said. Guys like Desmond don't bargain that way. "What are you gonna do instead?" I said. "Travel," he said. Six months later he "got away" as the Irish say. A lovely man, a gracious man, a great editor.

What follows appeared in the Times Magazine *in two installments in November 1979, the first as a cover with a picture of Chief Justice Burger, titled "The Supreme Court: A Decade of Constitutional Revision." I include it here—as against many other pieces I've written on the Supreme Court—because it's timely and says just about everything I want to say about the Court.*

The genesis of the piece was this: Martin Arnold called in the late summer of '79 and said Abe Rosenthal wanted me to do a definitive article on the Burger Court. Abe had been thinking about it for some time, and now was exactly right because The Brethren, *the heralded inside story about the Court, was set for publication sometime in the fall. The piece would not try to compete with the book, Marty said, since there'd be no way to outdo it in courthouse gossip, but we had to come out before the book lest it look as if we were riding it.*

I didn't jump at the idea because I'd been away from Court-watching for a few years and it looked like a ton of work for August. Still I wanted to write about this Court; it was frustrating reading the apologias in the press to the effect that the Burger majority hadn't really changed the direction of the Warren Court. And naturally I liked the idea of stealing a march on The Brethren, *writing a substantive analysis that I thought would stand up against the book very well indeed. I decided to call Professor Yale Kamisar at the Michigan Law School. If Yale could update me in a hurry, I'd do it.*

Kamisar was my number one source from the outset of my career at the daily Times. *Nobody knows more about criminal law, and no-*

body is more articulate, than Yale. Most important, he's intellectually honest, which is more than I can say about most legal academicians. I spent four hours with him on the phone one Sunday, and I
knew I could do the piece—I knew just what I wanted to say. But I
wanted to talk to Abe Rosenthal first, I wanted everything clear from
the outset. What I really wanted was his okay, because I knew my
approach wouldn't go down with Ed Klein, the Times Magazine
editor-in-chief.

We set up a meeting in Abe's office with Marty Arnold and Klein,
but at the last minute Klein couldn't make it. I gave Abe a rundown
on what the Burger Court had done and was continuing to do to the
Constitution. I told him that the Court had to be taken head-on,
that I would not do a reporting job—opinions from professors on
one side and the other—but an essay based on the Court's work. I
knew Abe was upset about the way the Court was stomping on the
First Amendment, but I said freedom of the press was not the only
issue, that the Burger majority was violating wholesale the rest of the
Bill of Rights. It would be mistaken to isolate the First, it would
smell of special pleading. Abe said, "Okay, write it." He doesn't fool
around, he's always been that way. You give him your best shot and
if he likes it he says write it; if not, he'll tell you why.

Ed Klein asked me to have lunch the next day—he wanted to
know what went down with Abe. I told him, "You're going to hate
it, Ed, but Abe likes it so you might as well sit back and enjoy the
rape." Ed said, "If Abe likes it, I love it." Not this time," I said.
"This time it's going to go right to your kishkes, you'll hate everything about it." I then outlined the piece for him, and he said "no
problem." I knew there was no problem because I had Abe; without
Abe my kishkes would go.

I had a serious problem writing it at first and it took a while to
know what was wrong. Marty Arnold had come up with a solid
idea—that I support everything with detailed case analysis. The
trouble was space; I couldn't do it in one piece, it'd have to be a
two-parter. Once again, Arnold came to my aid. "I'll talk to Ed," he
said, and Ed agreed.

Everything ran smoothly after that, until the day before part one
was ready to be locked up. Klein called me, Marty and Glenn Collins
(the line editor) into his office and announced that he didn't like the
lead, we'd need a new lead. Of course, the entire piece was connected to the lead; a new lead meant a new piece. I told Klein,

calmly, that it was out of the question. He was steaming and finally he blew. "The piece is a disgrace," he said. "It's one-sided, it's unfair, it will bring the entire legal world down on us." He had the piece on his desk for three weeks and this was the first time he read it, that was obvious. It was also obvious that he couldn't do a thing about it. I warned him he'd hate it, didn't I warn him?

The night before the magazine hit the stands, Klein had my wife and me to dinner. "I just reread the piece and it's great," he said. By then, Abe had read the piece, and so maybe Ed's wise first reaction—"If Abe likes it, I love it"—was back to work again.

IT SEEMS SAFE to say that, until fairly recently, most Americans believed they possessed certain rights that were so fundamental no governmental authority would dare challenge them, much less take them away. They went without saying, these beliefs—they were the "givens" of our American heritage:

- That all people who were accused of crimes were entitled to trials by juries of twelve; that in every case the trial judge was required to instruct the jury that the accused was presumed innocent until proved guilty; and that no jury could convict an accused person unless its verdict was unanimous.
- That the courts belonged to the people, and that the public and the press alike had the constitutional right to enter the halls of justice of our cities, our counties, our states and our nation.
- That indigent defendants who were charged with nonpetty crimes had the right to free legal counsel.
- That bank and telephone records were private, and could not be seized by government agents without a person's knowledge and consent.
- That the police could not legally ransack newsrooms, and that reporters could not be jailed for protecting their confidential sources of information.
- That a person's good name and reputation were sacred, and were secured by the Constitution against wrongful assaults by public officials.

But in every instance these beliefs, these "givens" of our heritage, were wrong. We do not have the rights we thought we had. Indeed, we are told we did not have them in the first place. And we are told this by the men with the power to make their opinions prevail: the justices of the United States Supreme Court.

A decade ago, the Supreme Court would have been the last place where these rights were called into question. Under Chief Justice Earl Warren, the Court protected and expanded civil liberties to a degree that had never before been approached. "The essential scheme of our Bill of Rights was to take the Government off the backs of people," Justice William O. Douglas wrote in 1972. In large measure, the Warren Court enforced that purpose.

But the Court that Earl Warren left ten years ago last June was markedly different from the one that his successor, Chief Justice Warren E. Burger, called to order on the opening of its new term last month. Gone, along with Justice Warren, were Justices Douglas, Hugo Black, John Harlan and Abe Fortas. In their place were four men appointed by President Nixon: Justices Burger, Harry A. Blackmun, Lewis F. Powell, Jr., William H. Rehnquist; and one Justice, John Paul Stevens, appointed by President Gerald Ford. Remaining from the Warren Court are Justices William J. Brennan, Jr., Thurgood Marshall, Potter Stewart and Byron R. White. Of the latter, only Justices Brennan and Marshall were consistently part of the libertarian march that characterized the Warren era. That march has been largely turned back by the Burger Court. The broad-scale revision may be summarized this way:

- The criminal justice revolution forged by the Warren Court has been virtually dismantled through a series of decisions that have sharply limited the rights of suspects—in the streets, in interrogation rooms, in police lineups and in the courts. This has been accomplished by narrow interpretations of the Warren Court's landmark rulings, rather than by outright reversals.
- Conflicts between an individual and the government have been resolved mainly against the individual. For a Court that was heralded as "conservative," as a counterbalance against the power of government, this is ironic. So, too, is the fact that the Burger Court has proved to be as "activist" as the Warren Court.

- Conflicts between an individual and the press have been resolved mainly against the press. This includes conflicts between the criminally accused (even the criminally convicted) and the press. Thus, an apparent paradox: The Burger Court, far less concerned about the rights of suspects than the Warren Court was, has been far more concerned about their rights when the press has been on the other side.
- In response to all of this, a small but important trend has been emerging in the state courts, where—instead of relying on the Supreme Court—judges are looking to their state constitutions to protect individual rights.

Despite this wide-scale revision, the Burger Court has been pictured by many in recent years as nonideological and unpredictable. This was not the case in the earlier years of the Burger Court, when it was generally viewed as a "conservative" bench bent on substantially altering the constitutional jurisprudence of the Warren Court. As we shall see, the Burger Court has changed little from its early days; its stance has been essentially consistent. But the perception of it by some of those in the news media has changed considerably.

Chief Justice Burger has probably had much to do with this development. In a rare news conference three years ago, Justice Burger astonished civil libertarians by stating that there had been "no significant changes in the Court's attitude toward the rights of criminal defendants." In the ensuing years, Chief Justice Burger—who declined to be interviewed for this article—has repeated this theme, and more and more it has been picked up by various law professors around the country. These professors have found a receptive audience, largely because none of the Warren Court's landmark rulings have actually been overruled by the Burger Court. However, legal scholars know that a case may be as effectively undermined by interpretation as by reversal. That some of them choose not to point this out is not so surprising as it may seem. Few law professors make a habit of criticizing the Supreme Court in the mass media. They need the Court for various reasons: They wish to have their articles cited by the Court, they vie to place clerks with the justices, and some even argue cases before the Court.

Moreover, the professors generally resent what they consider to be "simplistic" reporting of legal matters. By nature they prefer complexity and the examination of small distinctions to anything resembling a sweeping overview of the work of the Supreme Court. Indeed, some of them deny that there is even such a thing as the Burger Court.

These legal scholars point to cases where, for example, President Nixon's appointees have not voted as a bloc. How, they ask, could there be a "Burger Court" when sometimes Justice Blackmun, or sometimes Justice Powell, do not go along with Justices Burger and Rehnquist, even in criminal cases, even in press cases? It is altogether too complex to be labeled, they say.

But this analysis is in itself simplistic. As legal scholars know, Justices White and Stewart had dissented from most of the Warren Court's criminal justice decisions, and they vote with the majority in most of the Burger Court criminal justice rulings. Thus, it makes no difference that, occasionally, one or another appointee of Mr. Nixon breaks away from the majority—so long as, in the end, there is a majority to eviscerate the Warren Court holdings.

Those who say that there is really no such thing as a "Burger Court" are hard pressed to explain why Justice Brennan, a bulwark of the Warren Court, and Justice Marshall, a late Warren Court arrival who upheld the traditions of that Court, now nearly always find themselves dissenters in civil liberties cases.

In the few instances when they are in the majority, the Court is almost invariably involved in striking down police procedures that are so flagrant—like the random stopping and searching of automobiles—that they probably would not have been attempted by the police, and surely not defended by prosecutors, without the earlier encouragement of the Burger Court. It is mainly in these kinds of cases that the justices appointed by President Nixon split; that is, where Justices Burger and Rehnquist take pro-police positions that are considered too extreme for Justices Blackmun and/or Powell, not to mention Justices White, Stewart and Stevens.

Still, the Burger Court is looked upon as a "moderate" one by many, and in some quarters even as a "progressive" force.

Meanwhile, the libertarian critics of the Court have generally been relegated to the law reviews or to the small journals of opinion. Criminal suspects have never had much of a constituency. The media, which obviously has a voice, more often than not refuses to challenge the Court's press rulings on the grounds that to do so would be "self-serving."

＊　＊　＊

But there is a Burger Court, and nobody knows this better than the prosecutors and the police. They feel they have a friend in the Burger Court, no ambiguity about it, and they express their appreciation in the most eloquent, effective way they can: by never blaming the Supreme Court for fostering crime.

In the sixties, hardly a day went by that some police chief or district attorney did not blast the Warren Court for "coddling criminals" and encouraging "crime waves." Decisions that many believed breathed life into the Fourth Amendment's proscriptions against unreasonable searches and seizures, the Fifth Amendment's protection against self-incrimination and double jeopardy, the Sixth Amendment's pledge of assistance of counsel and trial by jury, and the Eighth Amendment's prohibition against cruel and unusual punishment, were often bitterly denounced by law enforcement people. More often than not, these attacks were joined in by some of the press and the public, which provided a kind of rhythm section to an omnipresent chorus of police officers and prosecutors.

Although the Burger Court has not stemmed the rate of crime, its rulings have served to keep the police and the people off the backs of the justices. This is as it should be. Whatever one may say about the Burger Court, one may not say that it is responsible for the rising crime rate.

Nor was it fair to pin that responsibility on the Warren Court, a point underscored, albeit inadvertently, by the record of the Burger Court. For if that record teaches anything, it teaches that the Supreme Court can have no appreciable effect on crime.

Yet the Burger Court has continued to eviscerate the holdings of the Warren majority, as if to vindicate Mr. Nixon's 1968 campaign oratory that the Warren Court had "tended to weaken the peace forces as against the criminal forces in this country."

On the other hand, the Burger Court has continued to press for school desegregation and has attempted, most legal scholars believe, to strike a fair balance in the so-called affirmative action, reverse discrimination cases. This article does not study the affirmative action cases, or the sex discrimination cases, because in these areas the Burger Court was writing on a relatively clean slate, and there was little question of revising the Warren Court rulings.

This piece surveys the two landmark areas that span both the Warren and Burger Courts—criminal justice and freedom of the press, which are at the core of the civil liberties guaranteed by the Bill of Rights.

Professor Yale Kamisar of the University of Michigan Law School, one of the preeminent scholars in the field of criminal procedure, observed recently: "Reading the criminal law decisions of the Burger Court is like watching an old movie run backward." Here are some of those movies—involving the Burger Court's interpretations of the Fourth, Fifth and Sixth Amendments—run forward.

THE 5TH AND 6TH AMENDMENTS: CONFESSIONS

The Warren Court delivered its landmark ruling on confessions in 1966, in *Miranda* v. *Arizona.* The Court held that when police have a suspect in custody, they may not interrogate him without first warning him of a number of things: that he has a right to remain silent, that anything he says can be used against him in a court of law, that he has the right to the presence of an attorney, and that if he cannot afford an attorney, one will be appointed for him prior to any questioning if he so desires.

The purpose of the ruling was to secure for suspects, in a meaningful way, the Fifth Amendment's protection against self-incrimination and the Sixth Amendment's guarantee of assistance of counsel—both of which, previously, had been held by the Warren Court to apply to the states through the Fourteenth Amendment (". . . nor shall any State deprive any person of life, liberty or property, without due process of law").

Before the *Miranda* decision, no admonitions to a suspect were necessary. Confessions, or other statements damaging to a defendant, were admitted into evidence at the trial if they were found to be "voluntary." And the courts had held that the determination of voluntariness depended on the "totality of the circumstances" surrounding the taking of the statement.

Under this standard, however, statements elicited by virtually every method short of the third degree were held to be "voluntary."

The effect was the establishment of a double standard: one for the interrogation room of the police station, where the defendant's rights were often honored in the breach; another for the courtroom, where his rights were scrupulously honored. However, once a case got to court it no longer really mattered, because once a person confessed, it made little difference how properly he was treated in court, for the confession sealed his fate.

In the *Miranda* case, the Warren Court sought to narrow, if not entirely abolish, this double standard. A suspect could still be questioned, without the presence of a lawyer, but only if he waived his rights, "voluntarily, knowingly and intelligently."

The decision created an uproar among law enforcement officials, in judicial circles and in much of the press. High-ranking police officials across the country, arguing that some 75 percent of reported crimes were solved by confessions, threw up their hands en masse.

But various studies, including one by the Los Angeles district attorney's office, showed that the importance of confessions had been grossly exaggerated. (Most cases are not solved at all; but the vast majority of the cases that *are* solved employ means other than confessions—by catching the culprit red-handed, by relying on information from eyewitnesses, or by employing ordinary detective work.) Although confessions "cement" a case, they proved necessary in less than 10 percent of the cases studied by the district attorney's office.

That the *Miranda* warnings themselves have had a minimal impact on police effectiveness is perhaps best indicated by the fact that the police outrage over the decision had largely died down by the time the Burger Court first considered the implications of the case in 1971.

That year, in *Harris* v. *New York*, the Burger Court ruled that if statements have been obtained from a suspect in violation of the *Miranda* safeguards, those statements can be used to "impeach his credibility" when the suspect testifies at trial. Thus, if the defendant takes the stand and says anything that contradicts what he told the police, the prosecution can bring to the attention of a jury an otherwise inadmissible statement.

Of course, if he does not testify, the statement cannot be used. But as every lawyer knows, a defendant who does not take the stand in his own behalf is far more likely to be convicted than one who is willing to explain his alleged actions. By offering this Hobson's choice to a person who has been unconstitutionally questioned by the police, the Burger Court has undercut the fundamental purpose of *Miranda.* Or, as Justice Brennan wrote in dissent in the *Harris* case: "The Court today tells the police that they may freely interrogate an accused [person] incommunicado and without counsel, and know that although any statement they obtain in violation of

Miranda cannot be used on the State's direct case, it may be introduced if the defendant has the temerity to testify in his own defense."

The Court was also telling something to state and federal judges. As Professor Kamisar wrote at the time: "After [the] *Harris* [case], a lower court judge unhappy with *Miranda* has cause to believe that almost no emasculating interpretation of *Miranda* may be too outrageous."

Before the Burger Court decided the *Harris* case, twenty-three courts faced the precise issue of "impeachment," and twenty of them held that statements obtained by the police in violation of the *Miranda* rules could *not* be used against a defendant who took the stand in his own defense. The main reason the courts cited: The Warren Court, in the *Miranda* case itself, had specifically said that such statements could not be used for impeachment purposes. Therefore, the argument that *Miranda* could be so easily circumvented was considered too outrageous, no matter what the judges might think of the *Miranda* decision.

It was not too outrageous for Chief Justice Burger. Writing for a 5–4 majority in the *Harris* case, he said that *Miranda*'s discussion of the issue "was not at all necessary to the Court's holding, and cannot be regarded as controlling." That is to say, according to Chief Justice Burger, *Miranda* could have been written without reference to the possible use of a statement for impeachment purposes.

Generally speaking, the same thing could be said of all precedents—since, technically, all that is "necessary" to a decision is what was directly before the Court. But *Miranda* was specifically structured to canvass a wide range of problems that were not directly raised by the case, in order to "give concrete constitutional guidelines for law enforcement agencies and courts to follow."

In any event, the Burger Court has never held a single item of evidence inadmissible on the authority of the *Miranda* case. Furthermore, Geoffrey R. Stone, associate professor of law at the University of Chicago, pointed out in a definitive article in the *Supreme Court Review*:

"Despite the relative frequency and complexity of these decisions, neither Justices White or Stewart, both of whom dissented in *Miranda*, nor any of the four justices appointed by Richard Nixon, has found it necessary to cast even a single vote to exclude evidence because of a violation of *Miranda*."

The Burger Court's decisions in the dozen-plus cases it has taken up—not to say the scores of lower-court rulings it has left standing—indicate a desire to discount the *Miranda* holding and return to the old "voluntariness" test for confessions.

Indeed, five years ago in *Michigan* v. *Tucker*, the Court appeared to have done just that. Speaking for the majority, Justice Rehnquist took the position that the *Miranda* warnings were not themselves "rights protected by the Constitution," but were merely "prophylactic rules" designed to "provide practical reinforcement" for the constitutional privilege against compelled self-incrimination.

Therefore, Justice Rehnquist said, the failure of police to give the full *Miranda* warnings does not violate the Fifth Amendment's self-incrimination clause; in order for such a violation to occur, the ensuing admissions must be involuntary, "as that term has been defined in the decisions of this Court."

As Professor Stone has observed, Justice Rehnquist's reading of *Miranda* is an "outright rejection" of its core premises. *Miranda* was anchored squarely in the Fifth Amendment. Had it not been, the Supreme Court would have been powerless to reverse *Miranda*'s conviction. The High Court has no supervisory powers over state police practices; it can only strike down procedures that violate some federal constitutional guarantee.

Justice Rehnquist would strip *Miranda* of its constitutional basis, and leave the case in an analytical vacuum. Had he stopped there, *Miranda* would have been interred. But, for whatever reason, Justice Rehnquist ultimately found a narrower ground to hold against the defendant without overruling *Miranda*.

Since then, the Court has continued to dismantle the case in a piecemeal way, and most observers believe the Court will always stop short of a direct reversal. In any event, the case has already been so confined by the Court to its basic facts that, some have said, now only Ernesto Miranda himself could take advantage of it. And Ernesto Miranda himself is dead.

THE 4TH AMENDMENT: SEARCHES AND SEIZURES

What of the individual's protection against the unreasonable incursions of government? Before the *Miranda* case came along, the Warren Court's most controversial criminal-procedure ruling was

Mapp v. *Ohio*, decided in 1961. There, the Court required state judges to bar from trials any evidence that had been seized in violation of the Fourth Amendment's proscriptions against unreasonable searches and seizures. Previously—in 1914—the Court had applied this sanction, known as the "exclusionary rule," to federal courts. Now, through the Due Process Clause of the Fourteenth Amendment, the exclusionary rule was made applicable to the states.

The reasons for this were clear and simple. If a court could not sanction a search or seizure before the event—because, for example, the police lacked sufficient cause to make the search, or were unable to describe the items they sought with the particularity required by the Fourth Amendment—then a court could not, or at least should not, affirm or sanction the search or seizure after the event. To do otherwise—to permit into evidence items unconstitutionally seized by the police—would violate the imperative of judicial integrity by making the courts partners in police lawlessness. The Court quoted the famous remark of Justice Louis Brandeis:

"Our Government is the potent, the omnipresent teacher. For good or ill, it teaches the whole people by its example. If the Government becomes a lawbreaker, it breeds contempt for law; it invites every man to become a law unto himself; it invites anarchy."

Without the exclusionary rule, the Warren majority concluded, the Fourth Amendment would "remain an empty promise," for the privacy rights protected by it would be "revocable at the whim of any police officer who, in the name of law enforcement itself, chooses to suspend its enjoyment."

The *Mapp* case was met by a firestorm of protest comparable to the one that later greeted *Miranda*. Enforcement officials—ignoring the fact that the Federal Bureau of Investigation had operated effectively throughout its existence under the dictates of the exclusionary rule, and that twenty-six states had imposed the rule on themselves—cried out that they could not protect the citizenry with the new handcuffs that had been clamped on them by the Warren Court. Paraphrasing a line out of an old New York Court of Appeals opinion by Benjamin Cardozo, the police asked rhetorically: "Should the criminal go free because the constable has blundered?"

It was hardly a matter of "blundering," however. The police systematically ignored the Fourth Amendment in those states that had no exclusionary rule, a point implicitly conceded in the outraged reactions of the police, as well as in the broad-scale efforts undertaken after *Mapp* to "retrain" officers in their understanding of the law of search and seizure. Sometimes the concession that the Fourth Amendment had been ignored was explicit. At a post-*Mapp* training session in New York City, Leonard Reisman, then the deputy police commissioner in charge of legal matters, said, "The *Mapp* case was a shock to us. We had to reorganize our thinking, frankly. Before this, nobody bothered to take out search warrants. Although the Constitution requires [search] warrants in most cases, the Supreme Court had ruled that evidence obtained without a warrant—illegally, if you will—was admissible in state courts. So the feeling was: Why bother?"

Mapp was the Warren Court's answer. But its effort to rescue the Fourth Amendment from its steerage-class status has been gutted by the Burger Court—despite the lack of evidence that *Mapp* has substantially curbed the efforts of the police, and against the clear knowledge that state-court judges seldom grant motions to suppress evidence that has been gathered in alleged violation of the Fourth Amendment.

Last spring, in response to a request by the Senate Judiciary Committee, the comptroller general of the United States produced a study showing that evidence was suppressed on Fourth Amendment grounds only in about 1 percent of federal cases; motions to suppress were made in only 10.5 percent of the cases studied. Nonetheless, many legal experts predict that the Burger Court will soon emasculate the exclusionary rule by requiring defendants to prove that police officers did not act in "good faith" when conducting otherwise unconstitutional searches and seizures.

In the meantime, the Burger Court has conducted a substantial watering down of the Fourth Amendment itself; and so, it has often managed to get around the exclusionary rule without purging it of all significance.

This has been accomplished by sharp limitations on the meaning of "probable cause," the constitutional standard upon which arrests, searches and seizures are permitted; by a dramatic expansion of the concept of "consent searches," wherein suspects "voluntarily" consent to searches that would otherwise be illegal; by narrowing the scope of the exclusionary rule through holding that it does not protect grand jury witnesses; by depriving defendants of the right to test the legality of searches in federal habeas corpus proceedings once the state courts have ruled against them, and by holding that some things are outside the purview of the Fourth Amendment—that they may be seized by Government agents without a warrant, without probable cause and without the knowledge and consent of the individual.

Here are examples of some of the above; the last concept will be dealt with first, because of its potential for "Big Brother" abuse:

Outside the Fourth Amendment: In 1976, the Burger Court ruled that the government can subpoena from banks a person's checks, deposit slips and financial statements without regard to the Fourth Amendment. The reason: A depositor has no "legitimate expectation of privacy" in his accounts because, by dealing through a bank employee, he has "revealed his affairs to another" and thus has "assumed the risk" that they "will be conveyed by that person to the Government." And "even if the information is revealed on the assumption that it will be used only for a limited purpose, and [that] the confidence placed in the third party will not be betrayed."

Since it is next to impossible to survive in today's world without having a bank account, the Court leaves a person with no choice but to "waive" his privacy—unless he decides to deal only in cash, and to keep his money under the pillow.

Moreover, as Justice Douglas once observed: "In a sense, a person is defined by the checks he writes. By examining them, the agents get to know his doctors, lawyers, creditors, political allies, social connections, religious affiliation, the papers and magazines he reads, and so on ad infinitum."

If bank records do not provide the government with all it needs to know about a citizen, the names of the people he calls on the telephone may help to bridge the gap. Last term, the Burger Court held that a phone company's installation and use, at police request, of a "pen register" to record the numbers dialed from a telephone at a suspect's home did not constitute a "search" within the meaning of the Fourth Amendment. (The "pen register" is a device that records the numbers dialed from a particular phone; the original instruments, now obsolete, used a pen to mark coded dots on tickertape paper.) This, the Court said, was because the pen register device does not record conversations, but only makes a record of the numbers dialed from a given phone, and a record of the time the number was dialed.

As in the bank-record case, the Court ruled that a person has no "legitimate expectation of privacy" in the numbers he or she dials, for the person has "voluntarily conveyed to the [phone company some] information that it had facilities for recording, and that it was free to record." Thus, the person "assumed the risk that the company would reveal to police the numbers he dialed."

The dissenters argued—there were two dissenting opinions, one by Justice Stewart (joined by Justice Brennan), the other by Justice Marshall (also joined by Justice Brennan)—that it could not be said that the defendant voluntarily turned over any information to "third parties." As a practical matter, a person had no alternative if he or she wanted to use the phone. Wrote Justice Marshall: "Unless a person is prepared to forgo use of what for many has become a personal or professional necessity, he cannot help but accept the risk of surveillance." The majority's "assumption of risk" analysis, Justice Marshall said, is therefore out of place. The question instead should be: What risks should a person "be forced to assume in a free and open society."

Journalists must assume the risk of government surveillance when using telephones quite as much as those persons engaged in criminal activity. In 1974, the Reporters Committee for Freedom of the Press sued the American Telephone and Telegraph Company, contending that both the First and Fourth Amendments require the phone company to give journalists prior notice before turning over their long-distance telephone billing records to law enforcement officials. This modest demand was rejected by the Circuit Court, and, in 1979, the Burger Court refused to review the ruling.

While such a refusal—known as a denial of certiorari—does not put the Supreme Court's imprimatur on a decision, there is little reason to believe that the Court will, in the future, put a stop to this kind of surveillance, given its reasoning in the pen register case, and its general view that the press stands in no better position than any other citizen, the First Amendment notwithstanding.

The implications for freedom of the press are serious, to say the least. By checking long-distance numbers—and in the "pen register" case the Court rejected any distinction between long-distance and local calls, so both can be seized—government agents are in a good position to discover confidential sources of information. The Burger Court, as we'll see in Part II of this article, has effectively held that the First Amendment does not give reporters a privilege to protect these sources. So the seizure of phone records provides another—and less politically sensitive—route for government to uncover "leaks" and to otherwise induce a chilling effect on a robust, investigatory press. It also allows a kind of end run around the state "shield laws" that are designed to protect sources; it does this by permitting agents to search out the leakers without giving notice to the reporter, thus preventing the reporter from protecting the sources with the shield law.

Consent Searches: The easiest, most propitious way for the police to avoid the myriad problems presented by the Fourth Amendment is to obtain the consent of a suspect to a search of his person or his premises. Once consent is given, the search is legal, and any contraband it turns up will be admitted into evidence, even if there was no probable cause to make the search. This is because the suspect (or any other person on the suspect's property who can give consent for the suspect, in what is known as "third-party consent") is deemed to have waived his right to privacy.

But the question the courts must decide in such cases is whether the alleged consent was that of a free and intelligent choice, or whether it was coerced; or, to put it in nicer words, whether it was a "true consent" or a "peaceful submission to authority."

In 1973, the Burger Court dealt a crippling blow to the nature of consent. In *Schneckloth* v. *Bustamonte*, the Court ruled 6–3 that a person can consent to an otherwise unconstitutional search—even though he didn't know, or wasn't told, he had the right to refuse the search.

The facts were simple. A police officer stopped a car in Sunnyvale, California, because one headlight and the license plate light were burned out. There were six men in the car, and they were asked to get out. As soon as they did, two other policemen appeared on the scene. The officer who stopped the car asked one of the men if he could search it. The answer: "Sure, go ahead." The search produced three checks that had been stolen from a car wash; they were wadded up under the left rear seat. The admission of these checks into evidence resulted in Bustamonte's conviction. Although he was in the car at the time, he was not the man who "consented" to the search. This was a "third-party consent," but it is not what makes the case important.

The crucial point was the Court's holding that the police need not tell a person that he has the right to say "no," when that person is asked to consent to a search that would otherwise violate his Fourth Amendment rights. Consent, the Court majority said, "cannot be taken literally to mean a 'knowing choice.' " It is enough that the consent was "voluntary," that is, free of coercion. The prosecution therefore need not show that the person made an "intelligent waiver" of his rights, only that the police didn't force him to waive them.

In dissent, Justice Brennan declared: "It wholly escapes me how our citizens can meaningfully be said to have waived something as precious as a constitutional guarantee without ever being aware of its existence."

But the majority opinion makes it clear that the Burger Court does not consider the Fourth Amendment a "precious" guarantee. The opinion agrees that to establish the waiver of a constitutional guarantee—according to the dictates of a forty-one-year-old Supreme Court decision—the state must prove "an intentional relinquishment or abandonment of a known right or privilege." But the majority said that this doctrine was only meant to protect a defendant's right to a fair trial:

"There is a vast difference," the Court said, "between those rights that protect a fair criminal trial and the rights guaranteed under the Fourth Amendment."

Like the old movie running backward, the Burger Court thus went a long way toward again demoting the Fourth Amendment to its steerage-class status.

"The holding today," Justice Marshall wrote in separate dissent, "confines the protection of the Fourth Amendment against searches conducted without probable cause to the sophisticated, the knowledgeable, and, I might add, the few.

"In the final analysis, the Court now sanctions a game of blind-man's bluff, in which the police always have the upper hand, for the sake of nothing more than the convenience of the police."

Ironically, the *Bustamonte* case might not even have reached the Supreme Court today, for Bustamonte's bid—to suppress the evidence the police had found against him—had been denied by the California state courts. His conviction was subsequently reversed by the Federal Court of Appeals on a writ of habeas corpus, a judicial procedure for testing the legality of a person's detention. The Burger Court reinstated the conviction, but, three years later, it barred federal habeas corpus relief for prisoners who had previously been afforded an opportunity for "full and fair litigation" of their Fourth Amendment claims in state courts. The practical impact appears to be that prisoners can no longer rely on lower federal courts to overturn their convictions on Fourth Amendment grounds.

This habeas corpus ruling was a startling decision even for the Burger Court, for it orphaned the Fourth Amendment, making it the only provision of the Bill of Rights (so far) which may not be vindicated by habeas corpus—the Great Writ, so-called because it is considered to be the single most important safeguard of personal liberty known to Anglo-American law.

"This denigration of constitutional guarantees and constitutionally mandated procedures," Justice Brennan wrote in a long, bitter dissent, "must appall citizens taught to expect judicial respect and support for their constitutional rights."

What was the Court's reason for this "denigration"? The same reason for its antipathy to the Fourth Amendment and to the exclusionary rule that enforces it and keeps it from being an "empty promise." When police make an illegal search and find stolen goods or guns or drugs, they nearly always have the guilty party. Shall the criminal go free because the constable has blundered—or even *plundered*—his rights?

But the fundamental purpose of the Fourth Amendment—of the Bill of Rights, in general—was to protect the guilty as well as the innocent.

As Justice Brennan added in his dissent: "Even if [the] punishment of the 'guilty' were society's highest value (and procedural safeguards [were] denigrated to this end) in a Constitution that a majority of the Members of this Court would prefer, that is not the ordering of priorities under the Constitution forged by the Framers, and this Court's sworn duty is to uphold that Constitution and not to frame its own."

THE 6TH AMENDMENT: THE RIGHT TO COUNSEL

The Burger Court has emphasized, in Fourth Amendment cases, the "vast difference" between (1) a person's rights that are protected by the prohibition against unreasonable searches and seizures and (2) "those rights that protect a fair criminal trial." One would think, then, that when the very question of guilt or innocence is involved, the Court would be especially concerned with a person's right to a fair trial. It might be expected that the Court would lend a sympathetic ear to a defendant's allegation that the police nabbed, and the jury convicted, the "wrong man."

It hasn't turned out that way, even in the area that legal experts universally deem the most suspect of all: eyewitness identification. In 1967, the Warren Court, noting that "the annals of criminal law are rife with instances of mistaken identification," ruled in *United States* v. *Wade* that an arrested suspect has a constitutional right to have his lawyer present when he is paraded in a police lineup before possible eyewitnesses. The major reason: to protect him from the suggestive techniques that are often employed by police and federal agents (for example, when the accused may be the only black person, or the only tall or short person, in the lineup). Such suggestion, once accomplished, may be irretrievably devastating.

"It is a matter of common experience," the Court said, "that once a witness has picked out the accused at the lineup, he is not likely to go back on his word later on, so that in practice the issue of identity may . . . for all practical purposes be determined there and then, before the trial."

Unless the lawyer for the suspect is present at the lineup, he can neither guard against improper suggestion, nor even know what really happened there. At a trial, this, in turn, deprives the accused of "that right of cross-examination which is an essential safeguard to his right to confront the witnesses against him." The lawyer must conduct the cross-examination in the dark, so to speak, making the assistance of counsel, guaranteed by the Sixth Amendment, an empty right.

In 1972, the Burger Court, in *Kirby* v. *Illinois,* had its first opportunity to interpret the Warren Court's *Wade* case. In the *Kirby* case, the lineup took place before the defendant was indicted. In *Wade,* the lineup took place *after* the indictment. The Burger Court chose to make the fact of the indictment the controlling distinction—the fact that determined the court's decision—and therefore ruled that Kirby was not entitled to counsel at his lineup.

Justice Brennan was in a peculiarly good position to say whether Wade's indictment had anything to do with the decision in that case, since he wrote the opinion for the Warren Court. He said the fact of the indictment was "completely irrelevant," and that "even a cursory perusal" of the *Wade* decision "reveals that nothing at all turned upon that particular circumstance." But now, in 1972, Justice Brennan was writing in dissent.

It is instructive to compare the Burger Court's use of distinctions—those facts that are crucial to a ruling—in the *Kirby* case with its treatment of the *Miranda* case. In the Burger Court's *Harris* v. *New York* decision, statements taken illegally from a suspect were allowed in to "impeach his credibility" when he took the witness stand. The Burger Court said that while the *Miranda* decision had barred the use of such statements, it was not a "controlling" precedent because "it was not at all necessary to the Court's holding."

Whatever one may say of that viewpoint, one can only wonder at a Court that would, one year later, create a constitutional distinction out of a mere description of a defendant's status—that is, whether he was in a lineup before or after his indictment. And one wonders at a Court that, in creating such a constitutional distinction, has signaled the police that there is an easy way to circumvent *Wade*: by holding lineups before filing formal charges.

In subsequent eyewitness identification cases, the Burger Court has moved step by step toward what Justice Brennan calls "the complete evisceration of the fundamental constitutional principles established . . . in *United States* v. *Wade*."

This development, says Professor Kamisar, is "in some ways more depressing than anything else the Burger Court has done in the criminal-procedure area." Why? "Because unlike *Mapp* and *Miranda*, which furthered societal values not usually—certainly not always—related to guilt or innocence, the Warren Court's 1967 lineup cases were explicitly designed to protect the innocent from wrongful conviction. What is more important than that? And where is the countervailing balance? The defense lawyer's presence in the interrogation room may well cut off police questioning altogether, but the defense lawyer's presence at a lineup will not—and cannot—eliminate lineups, only discourage the holding of *unfair* ones. How does that harm effective law enforcement? In fact, it helps it; if the wrong person is convicted, the system has failed and the real culprit is still at large. Even if one is convinced that the Warren Court substantially weakened the 'peace forces'—I'm not, but some justices evidently are—the Burger Court's retreat from the 1967 lineup cases is not responsive to that need."

* * *

In the lineup cases, as in some of the confession cases and the search-and-seizure cases, the Burger Court has reached out to reverse the actions of lower courts that have read the Bill of Rights more liberally than is to the High Court's liking.

This is the opposite of the situation that prevailed during the halcyon days of the Warren Court, when that Court continually patrolled the state and federal courts, which not only gave niggardly interpretations to its rulings, but often fought the Court in the press.

During the past few years, however, a trend has developed. In response to the Burger Court's reluctance to afford what they consider proper protections to the criminally accused, a number of state courts have dusted off long-ignored state bills of rights. Since the United States Supreme Court may only set minimum standards of justice, the states are free to grant their citizens more extensive rights. In cases in which they wish to afford such rights, in order to foreclose reversal by the Burger Court, the state courts need only say that they have based their rulings on state law, rather than on the federal Bill of Rights.

This development, which has reportedly annoyed and occasionally frustrated the Burger majority, is an event in the law. The trend is in its infancy, and has been taken up by only a handful of state courts—most notably those in California, Michigan and Pennsylvania. In the large majority of states, the judges seem only too happy to go along with the Burger Court and to accept its "signals," and go even further. But the new movement the other way is not without significance, and it has been encouraged by Justices Brennan and Marshall, dissenters in the tradition of Justices Holmes and Brandeis, and of Justices Black and Douglas.

In 1977, Justice Brennan published an article in the *Harvard Law Review* "saluting" those state courts that chose to use their own bills of rights to vindicate liberties no longer recognized by his Supreme Court brethren.

At age sixty, John McNulty, the great Irish-American journalist and author, wrote to his old boon companion, James Thurber: "Dear Jimmy, I think that maybe threescore years and 10 is subject to change without notice."

It turned out that way for Mr. McNulty, who died a few days later. In the law, it is supposed to go the other way: The older the precedent, the less subject it is to change without notice. But in the matter of the Burger Court, this comfortable maxim has not held true.

President Nixon's appointees to the Court were heralded by him as apostles of "judicial restraint," men who would adhere to precedent, "strict constructionists" who would not allow their political, social and economic views to influence their decisions. These themes dominated the Senate confirmation hearings, at which each of the four swore his dedication to such principles.

Here, though, are a few examples of how these principles have been practiced:

The Presumption of Innocence: In 1895, the Supreme Court, tracing the venerable history of the presumption of innocence from Deuteronomy through Roman law, English common law, and the common law of the United States, wrote: "The principle that there is a presumption of innocence in favor of the accused is the undoubted law, axiomatic and elementary, and its enforcement lies at the foundation of the administration of our criminal law."

On May 14, 1979, the Burger Court said that the presumption of innocence has "no application to a determination of the rights of a pretrial detainee during confinement before his trial has even begun." In so holding, the Court reversed two lower federal courts in New York, which had granted relief to inmates awaiting trial while housed at the Metropolitan Correctional Center. The inmates complained that they had been treated as convicts rather than as persons presumed innocent until proved guilty. They were subjected to body cavity searches following visits from friends and relatives; they were forced to "double-bunk" in rooms built for single occupancy; they were prohibited from receiving books unless the books were mailed by the publishers or by book clubs or bookstores; they were forbidden to receive food and personal items from outside the institution.

The lower courts enjoined these practices as unconstitutional. They relied primarily on the presumption of innocence as the source of an inmate's right to be free from these sorts of conditions. In a lengthy opinion by Justice Rehnquist, the Supreme Court lifted the injunctions of the lower courts, stating, among other things, that the presumption of innocence provides "no support" for the relief that was granted to the prisoners by the lower courts.

"Without question," Justice Rehnquist wrote, "the presumption of innocence plays an important role in our criminal justice system." But that role, he said, is confined to the trial itself.

One week later, on May 21, 1979, the Burger Court held that, at the trial itself, a judge could refuse a defendant's request to instruct a jury that he was presumed to be innocent until proved guilty beyond a reasonable doubt. So, now a jury need not be told that a defendant starts a trial with a clean slate, a right that was considered fundamental even in Biblical days.

"No principle is more firmly established in our system of criminal justice than the presumption of innocence that is accorded to the defendant in every criminal trial," wrote Justice Stewart. But now, this principle was relegated to a dissent, and Justice Stewart was joined by only Justices Marshall and Brennan.

Trial by Jury: In 1952, Justice Felix Frankfurter, in delineating for the Court those provisions of the Bill of Rights that have a "rigid meaning," as opposed to those without a "fixed technical content," wrote: "No changes or chances can alter the content of the verbal symbol of 'jury'—a body of 12 men who must reach a unanimous conclusion if the verdict is to go against the defendant."

By 1970, the Burger Court, saying it was unable "to divine precisely what the word 'jury' imported to the Framers," ruled that six-person juries were constitutional in criminal cases. Two years later, the Court held that a twelve-man jury need not reach a unanimous verdict to convict a defendant, upholding votes of 11–1, 10–2 and 9–3.

Indigent Defendants: Last term, the Burger Court ruled that an indigent defendant charged with a crime carrying a possible one-year prison sentence was not entitled to free legal counsel as long as the judge did not sentence him to jail.

This was a real surprise to the dissenters who had assumed—as did most lawyers and even most states—that at least when a person had a right to a jury trial he had a right to free counsel. Since the Supreme Court had already held that any crime punishable by more than six months in prison carried with it a right to trial by jury, it was natural to expect that it also required a lawyer—especially in view of the Court's earlier holding that the right to counsel occupies a higher constitutional status than the jury-trial right.

But Justice Rehnquist, writing for a five-man majority, said no, arguing in part that such a rule would economically burden the states.

In dissent, Justice Brennan termed the ruling "intolerable," noting that the crime that was involved—theft—carried a "moral stigma" indicating "moral depravity" and was therefore by no means petty, whether or not a prison sentence was applied. As to the economic burden argument of the majority, Brennan pointed out that thirty-three states provided for counsel in such cases and that, in any event, the argument was "both irrelevant and speculative."

Judicial Immunity: This is the one area in which the Burger Court has managed to divine an absolute right for a class of people—namely judges—despite the fact that the Constitution nowhere makes any provisions about judicial immunity.

In 1978, the Court ruled on a case involving a judge who signed an order to sterilize a fifteen-year-old girl—without a hearing, and merely at the request of the girl's mother, who said she was "somewhat retarded" and had been staying out overnight with "older youth or young men." The Court held that the judge was immune from a subsequent lawsuit by the girl—who was now a young woman—and her husband.

The girl was attending a public school at the time of the sterilization—despite the "retarded" appellation—and was told that she was going to the hospital to have her appendix removed. Instead, the doctors, acting in accord with the judicial order, performed a tubal ligation.

Two years later, the girl was married. Her inability to become pregnant led her to discover that she had been sterilized. She and her husband sued the judge. The Federal District Court in Indiana dismissed the action on grounds of judicial immunity, but the Circuit Court reversed, holding that the judge had forfeited his immunity due to "his failure to comply with elementary principles of procedural due process." The Burger Court reversed, by a 5–3 vote (Justice Brennan took no part).

Citing an 1872 ruling by the Supreme Court, the Burger majority held: "A judge will not be deprived of immunity because the action he took was in error, was done maliciously, or was in excess of his authority; rather, he will be subject to liability only when he has acted in the 'clear absence of all jurisdiction.' " The Court found jurisdiction in the sweeping language of the Indiana judicial code, which conferred jurisdiction "at all cases at law or in equity."

In sharp dissent, Justice Stewart (joined by Justices Marshall and Powell) wrote: "A judge is not free, like a loose cannon, to inflict indiscriminate damage whenever he announces that he is acting in his judicial capacity."

What gave a judge this freedom, according to the Burger majority, was the doctrine of judicial immunity. Where did that come from? From the Supreme Court itself, surely not from the Constitution.

It is quite remarkable, to say the least, that the same justices who disparage the exclusionary rule of the Fourth Amendment as "merely judge-made," think differently when judges are defendants in civil law suits. But as it is said: "Where you stand often depends on where you sit."

—*The New York Times Magazine*
November 11, 1979

HIGH COURT
VS. THE PRESS

THE TEN YEARS that Chief Justice Warren E. Burger has led the Supreme Court have been a decade of profound constitutional revision. Conservative court-watchers greeted the resignation of Mr. Burger's predecessor, Earl Warren, with a sigh of relief. The activist days of the Warren Court seemed to be over, and the expectation was that the new chief justice—supported by the other Court appointments that President Nixon was expected to make—would preside over a period of consolidation and judicial calm.

If there was to be activism by the Burger Court, conservatives hoped it would be in pursuit of a general retrenchment, particularly in the area of criminal justice, where the Warren Court had greatly expanded the rights of suspects.

Now, at the end of Chief Justice Burger's first decade—as last week's installment of this two-part series demonstrated—it is clear that the Court has indeed sharply cut back on the Warren Court's criminal justice revolution. And it is at least as activist as that Court had been, though in a different direction.

In this process, the Burger Court upset many of the most cherished notions of justice held by Americans. Most people believed, for instance, that those accused of crimes were entitled to trials by juries of twelve; that no jury could convict a defendant unless the verdict was unanimous; and that, in every case, the trial judge was required to instruct a jury that the accused was presumed innocent until proved guilty. By the end of the decade, the Burger Court had ruled that juries in state courts could have six instead of twelve members; that state court juries did not have to reach unanimous verdicts in criminal cases, and that judges did not have to instruct jurors that defendants were presumed innocent until they were found guilty.

The Court reshaped the Bill of Rights in other ways. It ruled that the public and press had no constitutional right to attend trials; that indigent defendants did not always have the right to free counsel; that bank and telephone records were not private, and could be seized, without notice, by government agents; that the police could ransack newsrooms, and that reporters could be jailed for protecting confidential sources.

But the constitutional revision of the decade did not stop with criminal law rulings. Crucial, too, was the handling of other types of conflicts between individuals and the government. Most profound were the Burger Court's interpretations of the First Amendment, which led to the greatest constitutional confrontation of the 1970s—that between the news media and the courts—which is the focus of this week's article.

Thomas Reed Powell, one of the great constitutional-law scholars of this century, was an acerbic man with a keen eye for the foibles of his fellow lawyers. During his distinguished career at the Harvard Law School, from 1925 to 1950, Professor Powell titillated generations of students with his observation about the "legal mind": "If you can think about something that is related to something else, without thinking about the thing to which it is related—then you have the legal mind."

A long row of cases over the years testifies to the fact that the "legal mind" is alive and flourishing inside the Burger Court. The result is often a double standard; this happens when two things that are related are separated by the legal mind. The following cases illuminate several types of "double standards" that have been employed by the Burger Court.

One case involves the Court's treatment of an individual when his reputation is damaged by police officials; a contrasting case shows the thinking of the Burger Court when the alleged defamation of an individual is by the press. As we shall see, the Court's sympathies seem to shift in ways that are not so much dependent on legal principles, as on the identity of the defendant.

THE INDIVIDUAL VS. THE STATE

Justice William H. Rehnquist, the most conservative member of the Court, writing in 1976 for a five-man majority, held that a person's good name and reputation are not protected by the Constitution.

In that case, Edward Charles Davis 3d was arrested for shoplifting by a private security guard in a store in Louisville, Kentucky. Mr. Davis, a photographer for the Louisville *Courier-Journal & Times*, pleaded not guilty; the charge was "filed away with leave to reinstate," meaning that the police never really intended to prosecute. Seventeen months later, the police chiefs of Louisville and Jefferson County, Kentucky, sent out a flier to area merchants; it contained mug shots and names of "active shoplifters." Mr. Davis' picture and name appeared in the flier, though he had not been tried on the charge, and had never been convicted of a crime.

Six days after the flier was distributed, the shoplifting charge against him was dismissed in court. The next day, Mr. Davis filed suit in federal court against both police chiefs. He sought damages, an injunction against further dissemination of the flier, and an order that the chiefs retrieve the fliers and instruct the merchants who received them that he was not a shoplifter.

Mr. Davis based his action on a congressional statute providing redress to persons whose constitutional rights are violated by those acting under "color of law"—that is, acting under the authority of one's office. The chiefs conceded that their conduct was intentional and was undertaken in their official capacities. The issue facing the Court was whether Mr. Davis had been deprived of "liberty" or "property" without due process of law.

"We hold," wrote Justice Rehnquist, "that the interest in reputation asserted . . . is neither 'liberty' nor 'property' guaranteed against state deprivation. . . ." Therefore, "however seriously" the flier may have harmed Mr. Davis' reputation, he had no recourse under the statute because reputation itself was not a protected constitutional right.

It is interesting to compare this reasoning—which Justice William J. Brennan, perhaps the most liberal member of the Court, termed in dissent "frightening for a free people"—with Justice Rehnquist's opinion for the Court last June in *Wolston* v. *Reader's Digest Association, Inc.*

THE INDIVIDUAL VS. THE PRESS

In 1958, Ilya Wolston pleaded guilty to criminal contempt for failure to respond to a subpoena directing him to appear before a federal grand jury in New York. The grand jury was then conducting a major investigation into the activities of Soviet intelligence agents in the United States. Mr. Wolston received a one-year suspended sentence and was placed on probation for three years; a condition of the probation was that he would cooperate with the grand jury in any further inquiries regarding Soviet espionage.

In 1974, the Reader's Digest company published a book entitled *KGB: The Secret Work of Soviet Secret Agents*. The book contained a passage that identified numerous Soviet agents operating in the United States after World War II. Mr. Wolston's name appeared in this passage, which explained that those listed were ". . . Soviet agents who were convicted of espionage or falsifying information or perjury and/or contempt charges following espionage indictments. . . ."

Mr. Wolston sued for libel. The Federal District Court in Washington, D.C., threw out the complaint on the ground that Mr. Wolston was a "public figure" and so had to prove "actual malice" to recover. While agreeing that the book appeared to state falsely that Wolston had been indicted for espionage—his contempt conviction did not follow an indictment, as the challenged passage stated—the court held that the First Amendment precluded recovery of damages because it was clear that the falsehood was not made with "reckless disregard of whether it was false or not"—that is, "actual malice."

This was the test devised by the Warren Court in 1964 in *New York Times Company* v. *Sullivan*. The purpose of the test was to protect the press against the "chilling effect" on free speech that was likely to be caused by libel suits brought by public officials. Later, the "actual malice" rule was held to cover public figures—that is, those who are not holding public office but who are nevertheless in the limelight.

The Circuit Court of Appeals, agreeing with the District Court, ruled against Mr. Wolston. But the Supreme Court reversed, in an opinion by Justice Rehnquist. Perhaps more than anyone else on the Burger Court, Justice Rehnquist has been noted for his "hard-line" positions on law and order. Yet reading his opinion in the Wolston case, one who had never heard of the justice might well think he was at least as sympathetic to his or her rights as the most liberal members of the Warren Court.

In his opinion, Justice Rehnquist allowed that Mr. Wolston's conduct was "newsworthy"—it had been the subject of fifteen stories in the New York and Washington press—and that Mr. Wolston had later been identified as a Soviet agent in two publications (including a report prepared by the Federal Bureau of Investigation). But the opinion said that Mr. Wolston had never become a "public figure." The reason: Mr. Wolston had not "voluntarily thrust" himself into the public controversy surrounding the investigation of Soviet espionage, but was "dragged unwilling" into it by the government.

Characterizing Mr. Wolston's conviction as a "mere citation for contempt," followed by passive acceptance of punishment, Justice Rehnquist wrote, for a six-man majority of the Court:

"We find no basis whatsoever for concluding that Wolston relinquished, to any degree, his interest in the protection of his own name.

"This reasoning," Justice Rehnquist added, "leads us to reject the further contention that any person who engages in criminal conduct automatically becomes a public figure for purposes of comment on a limited range of issues relating to his conviction.

"To hold otherwise," Justice Rehnquist concluded, "would create an 'open season' for all who sought to defame persons convicted of a crime."

Whatever one may think of Justice Rehnquist's sensitivity to the rights of criminals, or its implications regarding the First Amendment, it requires "the legal mind" to think of either without thinking of Edward Charles Davis 3d of Louisville.

Mr. Davis, an innocent man who was branded a criminal by police officers who admitted that they knew better, is precluded by the Supreme Court from seeking damages for harm that, the Court majority conceded, was done to his good name. Mr. Wolston, who pleaded guilty, is entitled to collect from a publisher and an author who, at most, negligently overstated the grounds of his conviction.

Taken together, then, the two cases stand for the proposition that, so far as the Constitution is concerned, the press may not, in good faith, defame criminal convicts, while government officials may, in bad faith, defame the innocent.

This result would be inexplicable were it not consistent with the record of the Burger Court, whose sympathy for the rights of individuals—whether convicts, suspects, or plaintiffs in civil suits—seems to surface only when the press is on the other side. Nor are these two decisions isolated incidents; they are representative of a pattern of judicial behavior displayed by the Burger Court over the years.

FALSE IMPRISONMENT

The Burger Court's view of a person's right to be compensated for false imprisonment reveals yet another aspect of the Court's penchant for establishing double standards. On the same day that the Wolston case was decided, the Court—with Justice Rehnquist again writing the majority opinion—ruled that a person who is falsely imprisoned is not deprived of a right that is "secured by the Constitution."

Linnie Carl McCollan was stopped for jumping a red light in Dallas; he was then held in jail eight days for jumping bail on a narcotics charge in Amarillo. Despite his protests that he was a victim in a case of mistaken identity, Mr. McCollan was not released until eight days later, when the authorities finally looked at the file; it showed, immediately and conclusively—by the evidence of fingerprints and photographs—that he was indeed the "wrong man." The culprit was Mr. McCollan's brother, Leonard, who had masqueraded as Linnie when he was arrested on the narcotics rap.

Linnie sued under the same statute that Edward Charles Davis 3d had employed against the Kentucky police chiefs—with the same result. The Burger Court ruled that Linnie had failed to satisfy the "threshold requirement" of the statute because he had not been deprived of "liberty" as the Court defined the constitutional meaning of the term.

In dissent, Justice John Paul Stevens—jointly with Justices Marshall and Brennan—noted that, under the theory of those in the Court's majority, Linnie would not have been entitled to be released through a writ of habeas corpus "since his detention is not a violation of his constitutional rights." Of course, a newspaper would have been subject to punitive damages if, under similar circumstances, it had accused the wrong man of a crime.

Likewise, had Mr. Davis—the Kentucky newspaper photographer—been called an "active shoplifter," or even a "former shoplifter" by the press—or for that matter, by an ordinary citizen—he would have had a right to money damages that could have reached astronomical figures if the defamation was intentional, and therefore "malicious."

False imprisonment and official stigmatization are surely more harmful than news-media defamation, and they are obviously far worse than slander by a private person. Yet the Court held that one's interest in his freedom and reputation are not protected by the Constitution—but are, nonetheless, sufficient to overcome the First Amendment's prohibition against any abridgment of freedom of speech or of the press.

THE GOOD FAITH OF POLICE OFFICERS

A case involving illegal searches and seizures would seem to have nothing to do with another case involving the freedom of the press. Yet, as the following two cases demonstrate, the Burger Court's actions point to the existence of another "double standard": that one set of rules is applied to the police, and another is applied to reporters.

On June 25, 1979—the day before the Wolston and Linnie McCollan rulings—the Court decided *Michigan* v. *DeFillippo*. In that one, Detroit police officers who were on duty in a patrol car received a radio call to investigate two persons who were reportedly drunk in an alley. When they arrived at the alley, they found Gary DeFillippo and a young woman.

Although Mr. DeFillippo did not appear to be intoxicated, the police asked him for identification. When he gave inconsistent and evasive answers, he was arrested and searched. The search turned up marijuana and another controlled drug, phencyclidine. He was charged with possession.

The arrest, search and seizure were made in accordance with a city ordinance—a so-called "stop and identify" law—permitting police officers to stop and question an individual when the officer has reasonable cause to believe that the individual's behavior "warrants further investigation for criminal activity." The ordinance makes it unlawful for a person to refuse to identify himself and to produce evidence of his identity.

Mr. DeFillippo's lawyer moved to suppress the drug evidence on the ground that the ordinance itself violated his rights under the United States Constitution, and that, therefore, the arrest and search were invalid. The Michigan Court of Appeals agreed, and quashed the charge.

The Supreme Court overruled the appellate court, 6–3. In an opinion by Chief Justice Burger, the Court held that an arrest that was made in "good-faith reliance" on an ordinance—which at the time had not been declared unconstitutional—was valid, regardless of a subsequent judicial determination of its unconstitutionality. Since a search that follows a valid arrest is valid, the evidence should not have been suppressed.

"Police are charged to enforce laws until and unless they are declared unconstitutional," Chief Justice Burger wrote. "Society would be ill served if its police officers took it upon themselves to determine which laws are, and which are not, constitutionally entitled to enforcement."

In his dissent, Justice Brennan called the ordinance "a sheer piece of legislative legerdemain not to be countenanced." It was a "transparent" effort to circumvent the Constitution, by permitting police to accost a person on "mere suspicion"—rather than "probable cause," as required by the Fourth Amendment—and to arrest him and search him if he chooses to remain silent, which is his right under the Fifth Amendment.

"The ordinance," Justice Brennan wrote, "therefore commands that which the Constitution denies the State power to command, and makes a crime out of what, under the Constitution, cannot be a crime."

Justice Brennan chided the majority for "focusing on the good faith of the arresting officers." The dispute, he said, is not between the arresting officers and Mr. DeFillippo; it is between Mr. DeFillippo and the State of Michigan. "The ultimate issue is whether the State gathered evidence against [the defendant] through unconstitutional means." Thus, Justice Brennan said, ". . . if it is unfair to penalize a police officer for actions undertaken pursuant to a good-faith, though mistaken, interpretation of the Constitution, then surely it is unfair to penalize [the defendant] for actions undertaken pursuant to a good-faith and *correct* interpretation of the Constitution."

THE GOOD FAITH OF THE PRESS

It is interesting to compare the DeFillippo case with last year's celebrated case of *The State of New Jersey and Dr. Mario Jascalevich v. Myron Farber and The New York Times Company.* Here, the good-faith standards that apply to the police seemingly do not apply to the press.

Mr. Farber and the *Times* were convicted of criminal and civil contempt for refusing to turn over confidential files to a New Jersey judge. Mr. Farber had used the files as the basis for a series of articles published in the *Times* concerning Dr. Jascalevich. The articles were instrumental in leading to the indictment of Dr. Jascalevich for multiple murders that were allegedly committed a decade earlier involving the use of the drug curare on hospital patients.

Mr. Farber was sentenced to six months for criminal contempt, and actually served forty days in jail for civil contempt. The *Times* was fined $285,000. Neither Mr. Farber nor the newspaper was afforded a hearing, despite repeated requests, before conviction and sentence were passed.

Dr. Jascalevich's attorney had subpoenaed the files. Mr. Farber and the newspaper opposed the subpoena principally on the ground that the state of New Jersey's shield law, by its explicit terms, afforded a journalist "a privilege to refuse to disclose, in any legal . . . proceeding" or to "any court" the "source . . . from or through whom any information was procured . . . and . . . any news or information obtained in the course of pursuing his professional activities, whether or not it is disseminated."

It is difficult to imagine how a legislature could write a more clear-cut, absolute statute. Yet the trial judge demanded to review the files in camera, privately, before deciding whether Mr. Farber and the *Times* could assert the privilege afforded by the shield law. When Mr. Farber and the paper refused, the contempt convictions followed.

The New Jersey Supreme Court upheld the convictions by a vote of 5–2. The essential reason: The Sixth Amendment and its New

Jersey counterpart guarantee the accused the right to have "compulsory process for obtaining witnesses in his favor."

The court acknowledged that the compulsory-process clause of the Sixth Amendment had "never been elaborately explicated by the Supreme Court," and that its New Jersey counterpart had "rarely been mentioned in our reported decisions." Still, where Constitution and statute collide, the New Jersey Supreme Court said that it is "unassailable" that the statute must yield. Although recognizing that other testimonial privileges—presumably those of lawyer and client, of doctor and patient, and the like—"seem to conflict" with this reading, the court confined its ruling to the shield law.

What, one may ask, has all this to do with *Michigan* v. *DeFillippo?*

Well, in petitioning the United States Supreme Court to review the case, the first point made by Mr. Farber and the *Times* was that they had relied in "good faith" on the "clear and precise words of the shield law." They argued that by retroactively revising the meaning of the statute, the New Jersey Supreme Court had indulged in ex post facto construction that deprived the petitioners of due process of law as required by the Fourteenth Amendment to the United States Constitution.

Mr. Farber, it was argued, had every right to assure his sources of confidentiality. As the brief put it, ". . . At least prior to the opinion at issue here, petitioners were, at the very least, justified in their belief that they were shielded by the statute against forced disclosure to the court of confidential sources and information." Furthermore, the United States Supreme Court had virtually invited the states to pass shield laws when, in 1972, it ruled, for the first time, that the First Amendment did not protect a journalist from divulging his confidential sources and information. The Court observed that Congress and the state legislatures were free to fashion such a privilege "as narrow or broad as deemed necessary."

Such encouragement, coming from the High Court, led to the passage of shield laws in a score of states. Was this not, in and of itself, sufficient to justify "good faith" reliance on the part of journalists, at least to the extent of protecting them from contempt convictions?

But the Supreme Court refused to hear the appeal, thus leaving the contempt convictions standing.

Ultimately, Dr. Jascalevich was acquitted without having had access to the files, and a New Jersey judge suspended Mr. Farber's criminal contempt sentence. But Mr. DeFillippo, on the other hand, was ordered to stand trial—because the police relied in "good faith" on an unconstitutional statute.

THE FIRST AMENDMENT UNDER SIEGE

The speech and press clause of the First Amendment has often been under siege, although its command is unequivocal—"Congress shall make no law . . . abridging the freedom of speech or of the press"—and although it is, in exact form, applicable to the states through the Fourteenth Amendment. Invariably, the heaviest assaults on the clause have come in the wake of national hysteria.

Now, in this relatively tranquil time, the press has been subjected to a judicial battering that has been more serious, and more fundamental, than the assaults that were mounted in more parlous days.

Perhaps nothing tells the story so strikingly as the fact that there is, today, a weekly publication called *Media Law Reporter*, filled with court decisions that affect the press. We have gone from a state of "no law" to the creation of a cottage industry.

This development reached its stride just when journalism was basking, as never before, in the glow of applause from much of the citizenry—due mainly to the uncovering of the Watergate scandal. Suddenly, the reporter was on the best-seller lists and was even depicted as a hero in the movies.

Almost as suddenly, the reporter was being tossed into jail for refusing to disclose his or her confidential sources to grand juries and defense lawyers. And his newsroom was being held to be fair game for ransacking by police officers. The reporter's inner thoughts and his discussions with editors and colleagues were being opened for discovery by plaintiffs in libel suits. The reporter's telephone records were allowed to be secretly subpoenaed by law enforcement officials who were out to find who his sources were. His publishers were being sharply restricted in defending against libel actions. Finally, the reporter's right to cover trials was held to be nonexistent—for neither the reporter, nor the public, had constitutional access to the courtrooms in America.

It is clear that the serious incursions on the First Amendment—

not to mention the rest of the Bill of Rights—would not have happened under the Warren Court. Indeed, had only Justices Hugo L. Black and William O. Douglas—both of them liberal stalwarts of the Court's previous decades—been together on the Court during the Burger years, the press would have won virtually every case it has lost before the High Court.

In any event, the press cases at issue during the Burger years surely would not have been resolved in the manner they were without the presence of President Nixon's appointees—Justices Blackmun, Lewis F. Powell, Jr., Rehnquist and Burger. Moreover, had the full panoply of the Burger Court's press decisions been in play, it is quite possible that the Watergate scandal might not have been uncovered. For example, the whole thing might have been cut off at the pass by closing the original bail hearing to the press. That way, reporters Bob Woodward and Carl Bernstein could hardly have noticed that high-priced lawyers were representing "third-rate burglars."

Ironically, however, the Burger Court provided the *coup de grâce* to President Nixon by forcing him to turn over his tapes to the Special Prosecutor. This, in turn, was to be a source of great difficulty for reporter Myron Farber and for *The New York Times.*

How, it was asked—by judges, lawyers, the public, and even by some in the press—could it be that a President must reveal confidential information, while a reporter need not?

This rhetorical question served to suppress relevant comparisons. Why, for example, is there a universally recognized lawyer-client privilege in the United States? The "search for truth" is vastly more hampered by this privilege than by a reporter's right to keep his confidential sources sacred. But if a lawyer were forced to disclose what his client said to him in private, the Sixth Amendment's right to counsel would be virtually worthless. Perhaps, in implicit recognition of this, nobody asks why—if a President must reveal the contents of his tapes—a lawyer need not reveal his client's secrets. Imagine what would happen if one defendant in a conspiracy case asked that the lawyer for another defendant be placed in the witness stand, on the grounds that the lawyer had information from his client that might exonerate the defendant. The mere suggestion of such a procedure would be met with judicial incredulity, to say the least. Yet reporter Myron Farber was jailed for refusing to reveal confidential information because it was said that without this information an innocent man might be found guilty. Is there a difference?

The Sixth Amendment no more explicitly grants a lawyer-client privilege than the First Amendment grants a newsman's privilege. Why should a privilege be said to flow naturally out of the Sixth Amendment, and not out of the First? And while it might be said that the lawyer-client privilege is covered by statute and rooted in the common law, Mr. Farber was also protected by a statute, the shield law, and to the extent that reporters were in the past rarely subpoenaed, his confidential privilege was implicitly covered by the common law as well.

Is the need for a reporter's privilege comparable to the necessity for such things as the lawyer-client, doctor-patient and priest-penitent privileges? Perhaps the answer was most eloquently stated by Justice Douglas in his dissent in *Branzburg* v. *Hayes*, the 1972 case in which the newsman's privilege was first denied by the Supreme Court:

"A reporter is no better than his source of information. Unless he has a privilege to withhold the identity of his source, he will be the victim of governmental intrigue or aggression. If he can be summoned to testify in secret before a grand jury, his sources will dry up, and the attempted exposure, the effort to enlighten the public, will be ended. If what the Court sanctions today becomes settled law, then the reporter's main function in American society will be to pass on to the public the press releases which the various departments of government issue."

The Court split 5–4 in the Branzburg case. The decisive vote was cast by Justice Powell, who wrote a concurring opinion that was sufficiently enigmatic so as to raise a reasonable amount of doubt about the clear meaning of the ruling. For example, Justice Powell wrote: ". . . If the newsman is called upon to give information bearing only a remote and tenuous relationship to the subject of the investigation, or if he has some other reason to believe that his testimony implicates confidential source relationships without a legitimate need of law enforcement, he will have access to the Court on a motion to quash and an appropriate protective order may be entered. . . ."

Buoyed by these words, press lawyers tried to put the best possible face on the Branzburg ruling, and they sometimes succeeded in persuading lower courts to protect reporters' confidential sources and information.

Nonetheless, Justice Powell's concurrence did not really disturb the core ruling of *Branzburg*, that there was no such thing as a reporter-source privilege. And in 1978, the Burger Court reiterated the point in *Zurcher* v. *Stanford Daily*.

In that case, the Court upheld the power of police, who were armed only with a warrant, to invade the offices of the Stanford University student newspaper and to rummage through files and wastebaskets in search of photographs that, the police said, they needed to solve a case. One of the positions the paper took was that such searches were likely to turn up confidential information. In response, the Court, citing the Branzburg ruling, said that such information was not privileged.

Because search warrants are by nature granted by magistrates without an adversary hearing, the lawyers for the student newspaper argued that at the least the prosecution should be required to subpoena the requested evidence. That is because at a subpoena hearing the press would be afforded the opportunity to raise the types of defenses that are suggested by Justice Powell in his Branzburg concurrence. The press would, as well, have the chance to employ state shield laws to protect confidentiality.

But the Court said that the press was not entitled to such special procedures, even where, as in the Stanford case, the press was not suspected of committing a crime, and despite the First Amendment. Indeed, Justice Byron R. White, who wrote the majority opinion, noted that a subpoena, by allowing the press to raise the questions mentioned above, might "seriously impede" criminal investigations.

In dissent, Justice Potter Stewart cited Powell's concurring opinion in *Branzburg* for the proposition that a hearing was required in order to permit the press to make its defenses. But Justice Powell, who joined the Court's opinion, wrote another concurrence, saying that he did not mean this at all.

While press lawyers continue to rely on Justice Powell's opinion in *Branzburg*, its limited language appears now to have even less force and effect than it did before the *Stanford Daily* case.

Shortly after the *Stanford Daily* case, Mr. Farber and the *Times* were convicted of contempt in New Jersey. Relying on the Branzburg case, the New Jersey Supreme Court rejected the idea that reporters had a First Amendment right to protect their confidential sources and information. As to the argument that Justice Powell's concurring opinion in *Branzburg* had left open the First Amendment door, the New Jersey court wrote: "... The argument is without merit."

While Mr. Farber and the paper were widely accused of "arrogance" for thinking that they had a greater claim to confidentiality than the President of the United States, it was largely unnoticed that, in the Nixon tape case, the Supreme Court held for the first time that there was a "presumptive" constitutionally based executive privilege—despite the absence of an explicit reference to such a privilege in the Constitution.

"The importance of confidentiality is too plain to require further discussion," the Court said.

President Nixon had to surrender his tapes because the "presumption of confidentiality" was overcome by the Special Prosecutor's lengthy and detailed argument showing the government's need for the tapes, and their relevance to the case. No such presumption was discovered for the press, despite the existence of the First Amendment; as we have seen in the Zurcher and Branzburg cases, the Court held that there was no privilege. By refusing to review the Farber case, the Court in effect reaffirmed it.

Of course, the Nixon and Farber cases were poles apart. Mr. Farber was investigating possible crimes; President Nixon was possibly committing crimes. Mr. Farber was talking to sources; President Nixon was taping himself talking to alleged conspirators.

FREE PRESS VS. FAIR TRIAL

It is often said that the First and Sixth Amendments are on a "collision course." That is, the unfettered press presupposed by the framers in the First Amendment of the Constitution must inevitably collide with the right to a fair trial that is protected by the Sixth Amendment. The Farber case was widely viewed as the classic example of this "collision course," for here the press was accused of "holding out" information that might have freed an innocent man. But against the background of the Burger Court's long row of decisions on defendants' rights, the jailing of a reporter for refusing to provide "aid" to an accused person is irony at its height. Had such a jailing been accomplished under the aegis of the Warren Court— however unlikely, given that Court's respect for the First Amendment—it might have been understandable, considering the Warren

Court's regard for the rights of the accused. In any event, the free-press versus fair-trial issue would have been approached in a principled manner by a Court that was concerned with both.

The record shows that the Burger Court can hardly be said to be concerned with either. That the news media have missed this crucial distinction in the never-ending national debate over the alleged "collision course" between the First and Sixth Amendments indicates that the "legal mind" is not confined to those who are lawyers.

Can it be seriously argued that the Burger Court is so anxious to achieve pristine trials for defendants that it is forced to abridge the freedom of the press? Yet the free-press versus fair-trial dialogue *assumes* this. As a result, the libertarians split, and even the press splits within itself, while the Burger Court has it both ways: It neither grants to the defendant that which is his under the Sixth Amendment, nor grants to the press that which is its under the First Amendment. And all the while, the victims fight each other.

By failing to recognize that the press is engaged in a war with men who are determined to clip its wings for reasons that often appear to have nothing to do with the rights of the accused, much of the press has legitimatized the Burger Court.

Yet, as prosecutors and defense lawyers understand, and as the Burger Court has said, "the instances in which pretrial publicity alone, even pervasive and adverse publicity, actually deprives a defendant of the ability to obtain a fair trial [are] quite rare."

What deprives a defendant of a fair trial—and in the vast number of cases deprives him or her of the opportunity to go to trial at all—are the kinds of decisions that have been described in this article's review of the Burger Court's history: decisions eviscerating the defendant's rights in the street, in the police station and in the courts.

Considering the effect on defendants' rights of the Burger Court's rulings in search and seizure cases, in confession cases, in right-to-counsel cases—not to mention its antipathy to the presumption of innocence itself—the damage that is done by the press to impair fair trials is *de minimis*.

CLOSING THE COURTS

The most effective way to insulate a defendant from adverse publicity is simply to close the courts to the press. In the Gannett case last July, the Burger Court did just that. In order to protect a defendant's right to a fair trial, it ruled, the courts may be closed to the press and the public—who, the Burger Court said, had no constitutional right to be there in the first place.

The Gannett case involved a "preliminary," or suppression, hearing that tested the admissibility of confessions in a murder case in Seneca County in upstate New York. The term preliminary is placed in quotation marks advisedly; in 1976, the year the confessions were processed, every felony prosecution in Seneca County was terminated without a trial. This statistic is characteristic of the functioning of the criminal justice system across the country, where some 90 percent of all charges are disposed of by guilty pleas or by dismissal before trial; about 85 percent involve guilty pleas.

The suppression hearing, therefore, is the only judicial proceeding of substantial importance in nearly all criminal prosecutions; and, in nearly all suppression hearings, the defendant loses. Since these hearings invariably involve the constitutionality of confessions and searches and seizures, the results could be said to prove that the police scrupulously honor the rights of criminals. What else are the courts implying when they deny, wholesale, defense motions to suppress evidence?

Obviously, this is not the way things are; the notion that the police are upholding the rights of the accused with extreme delicacy is light-years from reality. But so long as the courts continue to rule as if the police were indeed doing that, why should it matter to a defendant if his hearing is broadcast on network television? The contest is generally over for a defendant once the search or the confession is held to be admissible in evidence; the defendant has no effective choice but to plead guilty. On the other hand, in those rare instances where a court throws out the evidence, the prosecution has little choice but to dismiss the charges. Thus, in either event, the chance that the case will be heard by a jury is minuscule.

It is in the context of the possible suppression of illegally obtained evidence that much of the talk about the First and Sixth Amendments being on a "collision course" takes place. If the news media publicize information harmful to a defendant, and that information is later suppressed by a judge, then prospective jurors—the argument goes—will in the meantime have had their minds poisoned, and so the defendant will be deprived of a fair trial.

Since the aforementioned type of case almost never gets to trial, it is difficult to understand what all the fuss is about.

On this hypothetical platform, however, the Burger Court in *Gannett* closed the courtrooms of the country to the public: as if to say that it must promptly seal off the slightest possible crack in the great wall of protection it has erected for the criminally accused. It is hard to remain sanguine in the face of such a double standard—indeed, many of the Court's apologists, including those in the press who supported the jailing of Mr. Farber, were so nonplused by the Gannett case that they could find no alternative but to criticize the decision.

Of course, the majority in the Gannett case did not say they were closing the courts; they said the courts were not, and never had been, constitutionally open to the public.

"We hold," concluded the Court, "that members of the public have no constitutional right under the Sixth and Fourteenth Amendments to attend criminal trials."

The Sixth Amendment, applicable to the states through the due-process clause of the Fourteenth Amendment, provides, in relevant part:

"In all criminal prosecutions, the accused shall enjoy the right to a speedy and public trial, by an impartial jury."

Focusing on the word "accused," the Court said that the right to a public trial, like the right to a jury trial and to a speedy trial, was created for the benefit of the defendant. "The Constitution," Justice Stewart wrote for the majority, "nowhere mentions any right of access to a criminal trial on the part of the public; its guarantee, like the others enumerated [in the Sixth Amendment] is personal to the accused."

Viewed solely as a "strict construction" of the Sixth Amendment, this argument could not lightly be dismissed. But the Burger majority had a problem here: Fourteen years ago, the Warren Court unanimously ruled that, despite the words of the Sixth Amendment, a defendant could not waive a jury trial unless he had the consent of the prosecutor and the approval of the trial judge.

If Sixth Amendment rights are "personal to the accused," why should a prosecutor and judge have a veto power over the defendant's choice to waive his right to a jury? And if they have the veto in jury cases—later extended to the "speedy trial" provision of the

Sixth Amendment—why shouldn't the press and general public have the same veto when the accused wishes to waive his right to a public trial?

In answer to the first question, Justice Stewart wrote: "Because of the great public interest in jury trials as the preferred mode of fact-finding in criminal cases, a defendant cannot waive a jury trial without the consent of the prosecutor and judge."

But this, he said, is a "far cry " from the "creation" of a constitutional right of access to the courts on the part of the public. "In an adversary system of criminal justice, the public interest in the administration of justice is protected by the participants in the litigation."

Thus, the answer to the second question: The public does not need a veto because the prosecutor and judge are there to protect the public interest. Since, in the Gannett case, the prosecutor and judge had agreed to the closure of the court, there was no problem.

THE PROSECUTOR AS PROTECTOR

To support the proposition that prosecutors are defenders of the public interest, Justice Stewart cited *Berger* v. *United States,* a 1935 Supreme Court decision. There the Court said that a prosecutor "is the representative not of an ordinary party to a controversy, but of a sovereignty whose obligation to govern impartially is as compelling as its obligation to govern at all; and whose interest, therefore, in a criminal prosecution is not that it shall win a case, but that justice shall be done. As such, he is in a particular and very definite sense the servant of the law. . . ."

What Justice Stewart neglected to say was that these words were used by the Court not as a description of reality, but as an admonition to a prosecutor who, in his zeal to "win a case," had run roughshod over the defendant's constitutional rights. Preceding the lofty language cited by Justice Stewart, the Court listed a series of instances of prosecutorial misconduct, including "bullying" witnesses, "misstating facts," and generally acting in a "thoroughly indecorous and improper manner."

If it is dissembling to cite the Berger case for the proposition that prosecutors protect defendants' rights, it seems rather egregious to add, as Justice Stewart did, that "the responsibility of the prosecutor as representative of the public surely encompasses a duty to protect the societal interest in an open trial."

As Justice Harry A. Blackmun wrote in dissent: "Unlike the other provisions of the Sixth Amendment, the public-trial interest cannot adequately be protected by the prosecutor and judge in conjunction, or connivance, with the defendant. The specter of a trial or suppression hearing, where a defendant of the same political party as the prosecutor and the judge—both of whom are elected officials, perhaps beholden to the very defendant they try—obtains closure of the proceeding without any consideration for the substantial public interest at stake is sufficiently real to cause me to reject the Court's suggestion that the parties be given complete discretion to dispose of the public's interest as they see fit."

Justice Blackmun's dissent traced the history of open trials back to the time of the Star Chamber itself. The Star Chamber has long been synonymous with secret court proceedings; but even here, Justice Blackmun found evidence that such hearings were public. In any event, in the quotation that appears in the previous paragraph, Justice Blackmun pinpoints the seldom-discussed problem that lies at the heart of the free-press–fair-trial debate: ". . . to dispose of the public's interest as they see fit."

The notion that the administration of justice is their "table," their "game," not to be disturbed by the layman and by the journalist, is the glue that binds liberal and conservative lawyers and jurists together against the press.

It is hardly a conscious thing; they do not sit down and "plot" ways and means to "get" the press out of their hair. If it were, it would be easier to deal with, for, as all lawyers know, conspiracies can almost always be broken. What is at work here is a phenomenon that is as old as human history and as current as the legal mind: a combination of tribalism and of the resistance to clear-cut connections. How else can one explain why so many "conservative" lawyers and judges, otherwise insensitive to the rights of the accused, insist upon complete vindication of these rights only when the press is on the other side? Conversely, how can it be explained why "liberal" lawyers and judges, ever ready to go to the wall in defense of the First Amendment, think the news media are reacting "hysterically" to the rulings of the Burger Court?

In any event, the Gannett ruling has created great confusion, both in the public mind and in the legal mind. Pragmatically, defense lawyers have little choice but to move to close the courts whenever the possibility of prejudicial publicity exists—for if they do not, they are likely to lose the issue on appeal; and, if their clients lose the case at trial, the lawyers risk censure from bar associations. Convicted criminals, urged on by jailhouse lawyers, do not hesitate to complain to bar association grievance committees and to upper courts about their counsels' alleged lack of effectiveness and concern for their rights. A lawyer who fails to make a closure motion therefore leaves himself open to attack as a "publicity hound" who cares more about his career than his client.

The result has been to cause a virtual flood tide of motions to close the courts, both to pretrial suppression hearings and to jury trials themselves. Although the Gannett case involved only a pretrial hearing, the Court's majority opinion appeared in some of its wording to cover the entire trial process. Last month, the Court accepted for review a case in which a jury trial was closed to the public, so it seems that this issue, anyway, will soon be resolved.

In the meantime, five members of the Burger Court, in an unusual effort to clarify the decision, have publicly commented upon it. These comments have created even more confusion. Whether the Gannett case will survive in its present form is therefore problematical. Indeed, according to well-placed sources, Justice Stewart's opinion was originally the dissent, and Justice Blackmun's was the majority conclusion. A switch by Justice Powell at the eleventh hour turned the picture upside down, these sources say.

Whatever happened, one thing is certain. Only Justice Powell said that the closing of courts had First Amendment implications. And Justice Powell voted to uphold the closure. The other eight justices saw no freedom-of-the-press issue, or, at best, they "reserved" it, and did not address it.

It amounts to this: The Burger Court, out of sympathy for the rights of criminal defendants, closes the courts to the press, which, in the event, has no First Amendment right—at this juncture at least—to so much as contest the closure.

"The trial is always public," wrote Justice Joseph Story for the Supreme Court in 1833. As Justice Blackmun noted in his Gannett dissent, this has ever been true. Moreover, he said, the "Court today cites no case where the public has been totally excluded from all of a trial or all of a pretrial suppression hearing."

It is excluded now. That this has been accomplished by judges who claim blood allegiance to "judicial restraint" is but a minor irony in an altogether dim period for the great freedoms envisioned by the Framers and writ by them, supposedly forever, in the Bill of Rights.

The immediate future does not look bright for those who oppose the Burger Court's direction. Justice Brennan will probably retire in June, and Justice Marshall has been in ill health. Whether any future court appointees will be liberal or conservative depends largely on who the President is; and, of course, Presidents have been surprised before in their appointments to the Court.

But the Supreme Court has had a resilient history. Perhaps the day will yet come when the Court returns to the spirit set forth by Justice Joseph P. Bradley in 1885, when he wrote, for a unanimous Supreme Court: ". . . Constitutional provisions for the security of person and property should be liberally construed. A close and literal construction deprives them of half their efficacy, and leads to gradual depreciation of the right, as if it consisted more in sound than in substance. It is the duty of courts to be watchful for the constitutional rights of the citizen, and against any stealthy encroachments thereon."

—*The New York Times Magazine*
November 18, 1979

Contrary to Ed Klein's forebodings, the legal world did not attack the piece. This stunned Yale Kamisar, who was sure the professors would come after me, not only because I took off after them but because my entire thrust went directly against what most of them were saying day in, day out. I wasn't surprised that they shut up their mouths. I knew they had no courage to take on the Times, and if by chance one of the number did have it, he'd have to write a piece, not a letter, to begin to score. Of course, I didn't think anybody could score, I was sure of my ground.

The magazine only printed a couple of letters, one a kudo from Henry Steele Commager, another an attack by Henry Abraham, a political science professor at the University of Virginia. Dr. Abraham "charged" that the Constitution did not explicitly bar the use of illegally seized evidence in criminal trials and did not explicitly require that a twelve-member jury agree unanimously for conviction. Since I never implied that the Constitution contained such verbiage, I an-

swered Abraham with a brushoff, which is all a straw man deserves.

This answer so infuriated Anthony Lewis that he submitted a letter for publication which denounced me for "brusquely" dismissing Abraham's "challenge" and accused me of "grossly misleading" the public.

What I done wrong? Well, wrote Lewis, when I cited Felix Frankfurter for the proposition that the word "jury" stood unchangingly for twelve members and unanimity in criminal cases, I "well knew" but "did not tell the readers" that Frankfurter was talking about federal trials only. There was a footnote to the very sentence I quoted from Frankfurter's opinion, said Lewis, and that footnote read: "This is the Federal jury required constitutionally although both in England and in at least half of the States a jury may be composed of less than twelve or a verdict may be less than unanimous. . . ."

If Lewis was correct about the footnote, I would have been properly disgraced; not only would it have been "grossly misleading" but with malice aforethought. To protect me against this embarrassment, Ed Klein wrote to Lewis and told him I had a contract with the magazine and he wouldn't print the letter. I had no idea about this at the time—I didn't know about Tony's letter or Ed's response—but it was a nice gesture on Ed's part, and obviously he meant well. Indeed, he has always meant well toward me and if I say harsh things about him in this book, it's never personal because on that level we have gotten on famously from the get-go. Our differences have been strictly professional with no carry-over beyond the playing field.

This time, however, I'd have been better off if Ed didn't like me so much. Because Lewis was wrong about the footnote, incredibly and absolutely wrong. The ellipses, those three dots with which he ended the footnote, contained these words: "in some civil cases." Only in some civil cases, at the time Frankfurter wrote, could there be a jury of less than twelve or a nonunanimous verdict. And Tony Lewis left that out.

But Lewis was so sure of himself that he wrote a follow-up letter to Klein urging him to check with "journalists, lawyers, professors, whomever," so that my "disingenuous" response to Abraham would not go unanswered. Lewis wrote: "It is not my business to edit the Magazine. But I cannot escape caring about The New York Times. I have worked for the paper for thirty years. A significant part of the time and effort has related to the Supreme Court, and it hurts me when I see the Times publish sensational, misleading material on the Court."

As soon as I heard about all of this I told Klein to publish Tony's letter and I'd answer it with a short shot to the head he might never recover from. But no soap, Klein wouldn't go for it. So I wrote Lewis a murderous letter, accusing him of bobtailing the Frankfurter footnote. "Lucky for you," I ended, "the Times saved you from embarrassment. Once again, your paper came to your aid—which is more than you ever did for your paper." Copies to Abe Rosenthal and Klein.

Lewis' apology arrived promptly. It turned out that he had looked up the case in an old Harvard Law casebook, and there the footnote had been incomplete. "I have never before known of such a change," he wrote. He was not "conspiring" and "not so silly as to doctor a quote," but he was "wrong" and "chagrined."

I accepted that he didn't purposely fix the footnote, but he couldn't have made the mistake had my piece not sent him off on an emotional lost weekend. That is, if Felix Frankfurter had decided for a majority of the Court in 1952 that the twelve-member unanimous jury was required only in federal cases, why would the Burger Court be arguing the same points in the 1970s? And why wouldn't the Burger majority have cited Frankfurter in its decision? Normally Tony Lewis would have understood immediately. But the ghost of Felix Frankfurter—Lewis's mentor, the man who got the Times to hire him—lives in his heart and mind. When I cited FF to support a proposition of my own—me, who Tony knows loved Frankfurter's enemy Bill Douglas—Lewis simply went temporarily AWOL from reality.

Meanwhile, the Burger Court continues to gut the Bill of Rights. With little protest from the press, which appears to have been satisfied that the Court modified the Gannett court-closing case in the term following my piece. The article that appears next was written for The National Law Journal, and it says my say on that big deal.

HOW THE COURT
PARRIED THE
GANNETT DECISION

IN LAW, AS in love, the surest way to know how far you've fallen is to see what picks you up. Consider the coos, sighs and hosannas that greeted the U.S. Supreme Court's ruling that judges may not simply toss reporters and the general public out of courtrooms in criminal trials.

The media and other First Amendment freedom fighters are beside themselves in joy and tribute: Terms like "bench mark," "landmark" and "watershed" have been run about like clichés trailing shibboleths. To die in Rochester (*Gannett*)* and to be born again in Richmond (*Richmond Newspapers* v. *Virginia*);† ahh, the apple trees.

Yet consider the alternative. Imagine that the court had upheld the trial judge in *Richmond*, who summarily kicked the press and public out of court at the start of a murder case. Well, the point is that nobody would have imagined it were it not for *Gannett*, and who would have imagined *Gannett* were it not for *Gannett*? Bad enough to be thankful for small favors; to celebrate yesterday's foregone conclusion is to play the lickspittle.

The case should have been reversed out of hand, without argument. The Warren Court would have dumped it in a trice, assuming that any judge during the Warren Era would have had the chutzpah to bar press and public from a trial. Indeed, it's difficult to conceive

---

* *Gannett Co.* v. *Depasquale*, 443 U.S. 368.
† *Richmond Newspapers* v. *Virginia*, 79-243.

of any judge doing it in any time in our history, including colonial days. "The trial is always public," Justice Joseph Story wrote in 1833, and it was a truism then.

Why then were there seven opinions in the *Richmond* case? The answer is obvious: *Gannett*. In that one, the Court announced the novel proposition that the public and the press had no constitutional "right of access" to American courtrooms. The 5–4 decision was met with revulsion from virtually all quarters, including the lawyers. The best excuse that even the smarmiest apologists could give for Justice Potter Stewart's primary opinion was that it had originally been a dissent, converted into the law of the land by the alleged eleventh-hour switch of Justice Lewis F. Powell, Jr. The idea was that Justice Stewart had no time to polish it up, so it came out sloppy, as dissents sometimes will.

Sloppy it was, to say the least, though sloppiness was the least of its troubles. The idea that the Burger Court was so concerned for the rights of criminal defendants as to uphold the closure of a preliminary hearing on the admissibility of confessions was more than ironic; it was close to a sick joke. And of course, the notion that the Sixth Amendment provided no courtroom access to the public came across as the alien idea it surely was.

Although *Gannett* involved a pretrial suppression motion, Justice Stewart said—no less than twelve times—that the closure ruling applied to the trial itself. And this became one of many sources of confusion emanating from the case.

In an effort to clear things up, five justices publicly commented on *Gannett*, and this, of course, created more confusion. Last October, amidst a flood tide of closure motions around the country, the court accepted the *Richmond* case for review. At least it would settle the question of *Gannett's* applicability to trials.

Interestingly, the closure in *Richmond* predated *Gannett* by nearly a year, coming in September 1978. (*Gannett* was decided in July 1979). But a majority of the Burger Court had long since made its antipathy toward the press a matter of notoriety.

In *Branzburg* v. *Hayes*, 408 U.S. 665 (1972), the court held that reporters had no right to protect confidential sources and information, and would thus have to choose between turning informer and going to jail if a judge ordered disclosure. In the spring of 1978 this position was reiterated in *Zurcher* v. *Stanford Daily*, 436 U.S. 547, where the court upheld a blunderbuss police search of the Stanford

University student newspaper office. A few months later, on the eve of the lower court's closure order in *Richmond*, the Supreme Court refused to review the imprisonment of *New York Times* reporter Myron Farber, who thus languished in a New Jersey jail for forty days for refusing to turn over confidential information. By then, many reporters had done time rather than relinquish sources.

In such a milieu, it is understandable that a judge—without the "benefit" of *Gannett*—would be brazen enough to close a trial to the press. After *Gannett*, closure orders became a rather ordinary thing.

On the last day of the term this year, *Richmond* finally came down, with, as noted, seven different opinions. Perhaps the most interesting thing about it all—other than that nearly everyone chose to write—was Chief Justice Warren E. Burger's opinion, joined in by Justices Byron R. White and John Paul Stevens.

The chief justice based his reversal largely on the First Amendment. But if one were to substitute the Sixth Amendment, his opinion reads very much like Justice Harry A. Blackmun's erudite dissent in *Gannett*, in its reliance on legal history.

This was not lost on Justice Blackmun, who wrote a stinging concurrence clearly directed at the chief. The decision, Justice Blackmun wrote, was "gratifying" for two reasons. First, because the court was now "looking to and relying upon legal history in determining the fundamental public character of the criminal trial.

"The court's return to history is a welcome change in direction," he concluded.

"It is gratifying, second," Justice Blackmun continued, "to see the court wash away at least some of the graffiti that marred the prevailing opinions in *Gannett*." And here he took even more direct aim at Justice Burger. In the *Gannett* case, the chief had written a concurrence that appeared to limit the holding to pretrial hearings. But, as Justice Blackmun noted, Mr. Burger had joined the court's opinion—which applied the closure to the trial itself.

What makes this of special interest, of course, is that Justices Burger and Blackmun are the old Minnesota Twins. The chief had recommended Mr. Blackmun to President Nixon, and for years Justice Blackmun seldom strayed from Mr. Burger's views. Eventually, according to the usually informed sources, Mr. Blackmun began to rankle under what he considered to be Mr. Burger's patronizing attitude.

One particularly reliable tale has it that the breakup began in earnest a couple of years ago when the chief chided Mr. Blackmun for being late with his work, telling him that he was keeping the Brethren from summer vacation. When Mr. Blackmun, in turn, scolded his clerks, one of the clerks, who was friendly with a Burger clerk, informed Justice Blackmun that Mr. Burger wasn't finished with *his* caseload.

Whatever, they can no longer be classed as Twins, though they often take similarly conservative positions on criminal law.

That Mr. Burger chose to rely on the First Amendment is in itself noteworthy, since he has never been known as a Hugo Black devotee. The probability is that he took that route because he—and a majority of the court—had committed themselves against the use of the Sixth Amendment in *Gannett.*

But the chief was careful to distinguish *Gannett,* repeating again his view that *Gannett* applied only to preliminary suppression hearings. But the word "only" must not be taken lightly. Better than 90 percent of criminal cases never go beyond the preliminary hearing stage.

This does not necessarily mean that *Gannett* still stands as good law regarding the pretrial hearings. The First Amendment did not figure in that case, except in the concurring opinion of Justice Powell, who did not sit in *Richmond.*

The probable best bet is that the court, stung over the harsh reaction to *Gannett,* will modify it in the future.

But that is a long way from nirvana. And from a general opening up of public access to governmental establishments, such as prisons, or governmental information banks. Such was the implication of Justice Stevens' concurrence. But only he called this a "watershed case."

That the press rode with this line goes to show what happens when expectations are reduced to ground zero.

—*The National Law Journal*
August 4, 1980

BURGER'S WAR

After my magaziner on the Burger Court, I was a natural to review
The Brethren by Bob Woodward and Scott Armstrong. But the only
paper that asked me was The Village Voice, and that wasn't a natu-
ral. The Voice's founder, Dan Wolf, had refused to print my defense
in the Ellsberg incident, and had kept me blacklisted ever since.
When Clay Felker bought the paper from Wolf, I knew I'd never
appear there, but when Rupert Murdoch took it over I expected
things to change. Only nothing changed until early 1980, when my
old friend from the Times, Eliot Fremont-Smith, the book editor of
the Voice, called to say he wanted me to do this one. I told Eliot to
check it out with David Schneiderman, the editor-in-chief; he did,
and to my surprise the word was go. Herein, my return to the Voice.

THE HISTORY OF the Burger Court is fundamentally a history of a
statist majority at war with the Bill of Rights. In the best of times
this could hardly be a fair fight. Charles Evans Hughes knew what he
was talking about: "We are under a Constitution, but the Constitution is what the judges say it is." The Pope's armies are a nuclear
strike force next to what the Great Charter has going for it once the
Supreme Court decides to march. In the best of times.

Comes recently Bob Woodward and Scott Armstrong—respec-
tively the half-father and stepson of Watergate—to lift the red curtain, to penetrate the chambers, the very war rooms of the judicial
generals. Could the republic ask for better Davids? What Woodward
and Bernstein did to Nixon's presidency, Woodward and Armstrong
would do to the reputation of Nixon's Court. That was the Word. Two

years later we have the Book. And the question is: Will the Word survive the Book?

Everything Richard Nixon touched turned to irony, but perhaps nothing more than this: At Watergate, he announced a third-rate burglary and Woodstein discovered a war; in Burger & Co., he declared war and Woodstrong cannot even find petty larceny. Indeed, no fingerprints. It is not Nixon's Court, it is not Burger's Court, they write. Whose Court is it? Let's go to the videotape.

It's Tuesday, July 6, 1976—the last day of the last term covered by the authors. As it happens, it is also the first working day after the Bicentennial. The Supreme Court pays homage to the event by undercutting, in five separate cases, the Fourth Amendment's proscriptions against illegal searches and seizures. There will be worse days ahead, but this one is sufficiently egregious to cause the law clerks— those ubiquitous youngsters who served Woodstrong as much as they seem to believe they served their bosses—to call it "black Tuesday."

Typically, Woodward and Armstrong take no substantive position; like the Constitution, they are colorblind. They write: "But if it was 'black,' and ran contrary to (the clerks') liberal views, this turning away from the Warren Court was orchestrated and controlled not by Warren Burger, but by Stewart and White, who had served on the Warren Court, (by) Powell, the most moderate of the four Nixon appointees, and by Stevens, the new moderate."

The conclusion—and this is the last sentence in *The Brethren:* "The center was in control."

Well. Much has been asked of the mysterious ways and means by which the authors got so much inside information about the doings and peccadilloes of the High Court. What I want to know is how they managed to construct a controlling center out of a Court that has systematically eviscerated the Bill of Rights?

Let me tell you something. If Warren Burger had a sense of humor, he would laugh to beat the band. He is portrayed in this book not only as vain, supercilious, intellectually dishonest, and stupid; he is made out to be a loser!

In 1969, Burger set out to dismantle the civil liberties revolution forged by the Warren Court. Were he to die tomorrow, he could rest assured that his will was done, and where not quite done, in the doing. He has presided over a decade of retrograde revisionism of the

Constitution that is probably unparalleled in our history. I detailed much of this in a two-part series in *The New York Times Magazine* (November 11 and 18, 1979). Suffice it here that since the advent of Warren Burger, the First, Fourth, Fifth, Sixth, and Eighth Amendments ain't what they used to be. He got what he wanted, as did his sponsor, Richard Nixon. That he often got it with the help of Stewart and White is beside the point, for they were dissenters in the bulk of the Warren Court's libertarian rulings. The point is that *they* could not have done it without Burger—and the other Nixon appointees.

Does it matter? Is it important that Woodstrong constructs a "center" composed of "moderates"? On the primitive level of the meaning of words it surely matters; can words mean anything if a "center" is in charge of a wholesale glutting of the Constitution? Center, moderate—the words are not literally synonymous with "responsible," but they are perceived that way. If the center is in control we are in good hands, it goes without saying. And it goes in the long run, despite the hard-porno stories that lie at the skimming edge of *The Brethren.*

But it is more important than words. Woodward and Armstrong are not writing in a vacuum. In recent years, we have been subjected to a pervasive media blitz, which has instructed us that the Supreme Court is centrist, nonideological, unpredictable, individualistic, has not reflected Nixonian principles, is the Burger Court in "name only."

This astonishing notion got its start by Burger, who in 1976 said there had been "no significant changes in the Court's attitude toward the rights of criminal defendants." The theme, repeated on various occasions by the chief justice, was picked up by an influential clique of law professors and channeled to the public by the journalists who cover the Court. The latest example appeared in the January 6 *New York Times,* in a report by Linda Greenhouse, the paper's Supreme Court correspondent, on the proceedings in Phoenix of the Association of American Law Schools. Greenhouse's lead, as unquestioning as the rest of her coverage, states the party line:

"Constitutional scholars, meeting here to analyze the recent work of the Supreme Court, have generally concluded that the Court under Chief Justice Warren E. Burger has confounded expectations that it would retreat from either the activism or the principles espoused by the Court under Earl Warren."

Except for the word "activism"—the Burger Court is activist as hell in pursuit of denigrating the Constitution—it is difficult to conceive of a more outrageous lie than this one floated by the "scholars." Still, it is the consensus as expressed by "legal experts," and as such must be taken seriously, for this is war.

Woodward and Armstrong, who apparently do notice the "turning back" from the Warren Court, nevertheless play directly—with their "centrist" line—into the hands of the Burger Court's statist majority and its acolytes and sycophants. Fortunately for the republic, those hands have been so busy straightening out the robes of the justices after Woodstrong's peekaboos that they have generally overlooked the point. But they are gradually waking up to it.

Thus, in the current issue of *The New York Review of Books*, Anthony Lewis notes that while the book has generally been taken as a devastating attack on the Court, "a sensational exposé of the unworthy," a full reading "offers reassurance about the judicial process."

"On the whole," Lewis writes, "the justices appear as serious, committed men—imperfect, inevitably unequal to their extraordinary legal-political function, but struggling, careful, never cynical."

Ironically—and again fortunately—Lewis does not say this until he has used up considerable space attacking the book's credibility; and once having said it, he returns to the attack. But his point, while overstated, is well taken. Stripped of its gossipy giblets—which amount to relatively few pages spread thin across a lengthy volume—*The Brethren* often does make these justices out to be serious, struggling, committed, and, if not "never cynical," at least seldom so. Lewis views this as a saving grace and despairs that it has not come across. "The publicity accompanying the book has . . . distorted its contents by emphasizing the personal attacks," he writes.

But the redeeming social value of *The Brethren* lies in its pornography. That is to say, the very thing that has driven it to the top of the best-seller lists—the demystification of the Court, the uplifting of the robes—is its real worth, perhaps its only worth. To be sure, some of it is tasteless, irrelevant, scatological, and unlikely. Even so, it is hardly much of a price to pay if the payoff is a public revulsion to Nixon's Revenge. Those who control the Court, and therefore our majestic Constitution, are indeed "struggling and careful," but only in pursuit of hiding their cynicism.

With the aid of Lewis and the law professors, they have hidden it well, and they managed to hide it from Woodward and Armstrong. Only they couldn't hide from the media hype. I never thought false advertising could serve the commonweal, but in this case it has. Who said there's nothing new under the sun?

Will the Word survive the Book, that is the question. Since the answer depends on whether people who buy books read them, the question should answer itself. The rule of thumb is that publishers can't read, editors won't read, and the public don't read. Let us pray! And I never thought I'd say that, either.

A word about the law clerks, by way of addendum. Everywhere people ask me what I think of them. They were the principal sources of *The Brethren*. Obviously they betrayed confidences wholesale, and always anonymously. Just as obviously, the authors can't be faulted for taking it where they could get it. That goes every time in journalism and in spades with the Supreme Court, an iceberg institution if there ever was one.

In that sense, law clerks as informants are no different from Mafiosi as rats: You need them, you use them, but you don't have to like them. The difference is that we could have respected the clerks if they did the deed in defense of the Constitution. Maybe some did, but if you want anonymity you can't have it both ways. So if Woodward and Armstrong do not recognize that they are chronicling a war, if they can't tell the difference between Bill Douglas' bowel problems and Warren Burger's paranoia, if it's any giblet in a storm, much of the blame goes to the clerks. The authors, after all, are not lawyers; just as they looked to the clerks for inside stories, they had a right to expect from them some sort of overview.

It comes down to character. And the clerks come up short. No wonder. Most of them—probably all of them—were editors of law reviews at the top schools in the country. As character builders, law reviews rank a cut above high-class bordellos. Take the cream, put them in the Supreme Court, and you end up with elitists who are not only impressed with their own importance but quite anxious to impress the important with the inferiority of their employers.

One of the good things that might come out of *The Brethren* is an end to the clerkship system as we have known it. Permanent clerks, civil service clerks, would do as good a technical job, if not better.

Anyway, a lot of young lives would not be corrupted. Learned Hand quit the *Harvard Law Review* on the grounds that he came to Cambridge to get a legal education. Add ethics and pass Go.

—*The Village Voice*
February 4, 1980

THE SUSPECT CONFESSES—BUT WHO BELIEVES HIM?

George Whitmore, Jr., got nothing out of it, but he launched or flowered the careers of many in show biz and journalism, including mine. A couple of months after joining the Times, I covered the posttrial hearings that led eventually to Whitmore's exoneration. My stories caught the eyes of the editors of the Sunday Magazine, and I jumped at the chance to do a piece on the case, partly because I wanted to say more about confessions than the daily could handle, but mainly because I wanted to get into the Magazine.

I had never done a magaziner, and I knew you had to do them to get above the crowd. Once you were on the Times, it wasn't enough to just be on the Times. It surprised me then, it surprises me still, how few Times reporters understand this truism. Anyway, I was delighted to get the call and the result follows.

AT 7:30 A.M. on April 24, 1964, George Whitmore, Jr., a slow-witted nineteen-year-old Negro drifter with no previous arrest record, was ushered into the back room of a Brooklyn police station. Within twenty-two hours, he had confessed to one attempted rape and three murders—that of Mrs. Minnie Edmonds, a Brooklyn charwoman, and the double killing of career girls Janice Wylie and Emily Hoffert, New York's most sensational crime in recent years.

Now, after two trials, a reversed conviction (in the attempted-rape case), a hung jury (in the Edmonds murder) and, most recently, a dismissed indictment (in the Wylie–Hoffert case), the Whitmore affair has become a *cause célèbre*.

Already it has seriously undermined the credibility of the New York Police Department and stained the reputations of the Manhattan and Brooklyn district attorneys' offices. And for the future it promises to have an important impact on the revolution in criminal law now being forged by the Supreme Court of the United States.

That revolution reached its present high point last June—two months after Whitmore's arrest—when the Court issued a devastating, if limited, attack on the use of the confession, which has been the backbone of law enforcement in the United States. The justices were concerned with a Chicagoan named Danny Escobedo, who had been convicted in 1960 of murdering his brother-in-law. They reversed the conviction on the grounds that his confession, while voluntary, had been made after he had been denied permission to see his lawyer.

The ruling sent shock waves through the nation's prosecutors. From public platforms and in private interviews, they charged that the Court was "coddling the criminal element" and "swinging the pendulum too far" in favor of defendants' rights as against the public's safety. And then George Whitmore, Jr., came along and rained on their parade.

In a long harangue directed at a reporter, one of the top assistants of Manhattan District Attorney Frank S. Hogan explained the connection between the Escobedo and Whitmore cases. "Let me give you the perfect example of the importance of confessions in law enforcement," he said, leaning across his desk. "This, more than anything else, will prove how unrealistic and naive the Court is."

His finger punched the air. "Whitmore! The Whitmore case. Do you know that we had every top detective in town working on the Wylie–Hoffert murders and they couldn't find a clue. Not a clue!

"I tell you, if that kid hadn't confessed, we never would have caught the killer!"

Yet, last January, six months after this passionate statement, District Attorney Hogan dropped the charges against Whitmore for the Wylie–Hoffert murders (though the indictment was not quashed until May). In an affidavit filed in State Supreme Court he declared that Whitmore's confession had, upon investigation, been discredited. Shortly thereafter, another man, a drug addict named Richard

Robles, was indicted for the murders. It will be a long time before the public can accept a confession without thinking of George Whitmore, Jr.

The Whitmore case began shortly after midnight on April 23, 1964. Frank Isola, a young patrolman, was walking his beat in the Brownsville section of Brooklyn, a neighborhood with a long history of criminal activity, when he heard a scream from an alleyway. The beam of his flashlight picked out a Negro who appeared to be molesting a heavyset Spanish woman. He fired a shot, and the man ran.

After a fruitless four-block chase, Isola returned to interview the victim, Mrs. Elba Borrero. Isola has sworn that she gave him a detailed description of her assailant at that time.

Six hours later, Isola saw George Whitmore, Jr., standing in the doorway of a laundromat. Whitmore asked what the shooting earlier had been about.

"Why?" asked Isola. "What do you know about it!"

"I heard the shots and then I saw a guy running down the street. He almost ran into me and he told me the cops were after him and could I hide him," Whitmore said.

Isola took Whitmore's name and walked away.

Twenty-four hours later, Patrolman Isola and Detective Richard Aidala found Whitmore in front of the same laundromat, where he was in the habit of meeting his brother before going to look for work. Whitmore was unemployed at the time. The officers asked him to accompany them to headquarters "to answer a few questions" as a possible witness in the case.

Whitmore agreed. "I figured I had to go if they asked me," he said. But when they got to the station house there were no questions. Instead, Whitmore was searched and placed behind a peephole door, and Mrs. Borrero was brought in to identify him, which she did.

Here the first note of mystery enters. Isola testified in court that by the time he first saw Whitmore, six hours after the attack, he had obtained from Mrs. Borrero a detailed description of the assailant: a 5-foot 9-inch, 165-pound Negro with pockmarked face, wearing a tan raincoat with the lapel button missing (Mrs. Borrero had pulled it off), black pants and a green hat.

Patrolman Isola said that when he talked to Whitmore that night he noticed that he had a pockmarked face, was wearing a tan raincoat with the lapel button missing and had on a green hat and black pants. Then why did he not arrest Whitmore at the time?

Because, he said, "I didn't think he was the man."

There are three possible explanations for this. First, Isola may have been put off because Whitmore is shorter (5 feet 5 inches) and thinner (140 pounds) than the description. But the officer did not offer this explanation, perhaps because the prosecution was not anxious to stress the height and weight discrepancies.

Second, Isola may not have had the description he said he had. This seems most probable, since his own notes and the police reports do not reflect the details he testified to.

Finally, the patrolman may have been just incredibly negligent. This is the most logical explanation if we assume his testimony was truthful.

Regardless of which explanation one chooses to accept—with the possible exception of the last one—the fact that the arrest was not made the first night buttresses the defense contention that Whitmore was the victim of a frame-up.

In any event, soon after Whitmore was identified by Mrs. Borrero—and it should be noted here that a peephole identification is notoriously suspect—he confessed, and in November 1964, he was convicted of attempted rape. The evidence against him was powerful: his confession and the button that Mrs. Borrero had ripped from the coat of her attacker.

In his summation, Brooklyn Assistant District Attorney Sidney A. Lichtman thrust the button and Whitmore's coat before the jury and said: "We have nailed George Whitmore on the button, so to speak."

What Mr. Lichtman did not say was that he had an FBI laboratory report which in no way connected the button to the coat Whitmore was wearing when arrested. While the report did not negate the possibility that the button could have come from the coat, it said that the remaining buttons were "different in size, design and construction" from the one Mrs. Borrero had pulled off the coat of her assailant. Moreover, Whitmore had maintained throughout that on the night Mrs. Borrero was attacked he was wearing his brother's raincoat, and not the one that he wore on the morning of his arrest.

Last February, the conviction was reversed with the consent of

Brooklyn District Attorney Aaron E. Koota. In granting a new trial, the judge ruled that the prosecution had suppressed the FBI report and that the jury was prejudiced. One juror testified that ugly racial slurs were made during deliberations and many jurors told the court that they had read about Whitmore's confessions to the three murders.

The story of those confessions begins back at the Brooklyn police station on April 24, 1964, the day of Whitmore's arrest. By 10:30 that morning, he had confessed to the Borrero rape attempt. By noon, he had admitted the April 14 knife-slaying of Mrs. Edmonds. Then, at dusk, all the top brass of the New York City Police Department began to file into the 73rd Precinct in Brooklyn. The word had gone out: In this station house sat the perpetrator of one of the city's most sensational killings, the double murder of career girls Janice Wylie and Emily Hoffert.

That brutal crime had stunned a town thought to be shockproof. On the morning of August 28, 1963, Janice Wylie, the twenty-three-year-old daughter of advertising executive Max Wylie and niece of author Philip Wylie, and her schoolteacher roommate, Emily Hoffert, were found slashed to death in their East 88th Street apartment in Manhattan. Parents whose daughters were living on their own in the city were abruptly reminded that no neighborhood, however fashionable, was immune to violence, and the case touched off an unusual, if understandable, amount of hysteria.

Now, after eight months in which police had questioned a thousand people, George Whitmore, Jr., had confessed to the murders. At 4 A.M. on April 25, Chief of Detectives (now Chief Inspector) Lawrence J. McKearney announced to the press: "We've got the right guy; no question about it."

But Philip Wylie, far off in Honolulu, said skeptically: "It sounds to me like a guy who got scared into a confession . . ."

And at his arraignment, Whitmore recanted all three confessions and charged that they had resulted from police brutality.

"That's ridiculous!" said a deputy inspector. But it is a story that Whitmore has clung to ever since.

According to Whitmore's account, as soon as Mrs. Borrero identified him as her attacker, Detective Aidala and Patrolman Isola took him into a room and beat him "until I told 'em anything to get 'em off my back." He claims that everything he said after the beating— which he says was not repeated—resulted from the beating and from the fear of further beatings.

Aidala and Isola have denied the brutality charge. No one will ever know the truth. Policemen never admit to beating a man. To do so would mean instant expulsion from the department. Yet on many occasions appeals courts have thrown out confessions on the ground that they resulted from physical brutality. (For reasons they alone know, trial judges seldom rule out confessions.)

Whether or not Whitmore was beaten, the detectives who questioned him fit the tradition of interrogators to a fare-thee-well. The cliché calls for a "heavy" and a "buddy." The heavy fills the suspect with fear and the buddy puts him at ease—indeed, "saves" him from the heavy.

Detective Aidala is a big, burly man with hamlike hands and a tendency to lose his temper, as he occasionally did on the witness stand. Detective Joseph DiPrima, who entered the case at 8 A.M. on April 24, or, according to Whitmore, immediately after he was beaten, is calm, soft-spoken, fatherly. It was DiPrima who developed a "rapport" with Whitmore—and took all three confessions.

"The boy told me," DiPrima said during a hearing into the voluntariness of Whitmore's confession to the Edmonds murder, "that I was nicer to him than his father ever was." Detective Aidala never made that claim.

From the point of view of district attorneys in general, the Whitmore case could not have come at a worse time—hard on the heels of the Escobedo decision. Although the Supreme Court was careful to limit its ruling to the particular circumstances—Escobedo's lawyer was actually at the police station, asking to see him, at the time of his confession—Justice Arthur J. Goldberg, writing for a five-man majority, went on to launch a blistering attack against confessions in general.

"A law enforcement system that depends on the confession," he wrote, "is in the long run less reliable and more subject to abuses than a system which depends on extrinsic evidence independently secured through skillful investigation."

Does this mean that in the future the Court may rule that *all* sus-

pects have a right to see a lawyer before the police can talk to them,
whether they request counsel or not and whether they can afford one
or not? No one can be sure but the question itself is enough to turn
district attorneys gray. If that should ever happen, most lawyers
agree, confessions would disappear, because any lawyer worth his salt
would advise his client to remain silent.

"No system worth preserving," answered Justice Goldberg,
"should have to *fear* that if an accused is permitted to consult with a
lawyer he will become aware of, and exercise, his constitutional
rights."

But, contend the prosecutors, 75 to 80 percent of all crimes are
solved because of confessions. In murder cases the percentage is even
higher, they claim, because there are seldom any witnesses to murder. One district attorney told a reporter recently that if the Escobedo case is extended to provide counsel for all suspects, "we may as
well close up our homicide bureau." Others have echoed this view.

But prosecutors have cried wolf so often in the past few years that
it is sometimes difficult to take them seriously. In 1961, for example,
when the Supreme Court ruled that all evidence seized illegally
would be inadmissible in state court trials, district attorneys, almost
to a man, predicted they would have to shut down their narcotics
and gambling bureaus. At last glance, they were still doing business—in some cases more than ever.

The fact is that district attorneys have no statistics to back up their
claim that most murderers and rapists would walk out of the police
stations, thumb to nose, if confessions were banned. And while it is
true that a great many cases today are based on confessions, this does
not prove that convictions could not be obtained without them.

Recently, a New York State Supreme Court justice, who was a
prosecutor for many years before ascending the bench and is not
known for being "soft" on defendants, told a reporter that cases in
which the only evidence is a confession and a dead body are "extraordinarily rare." In most cases, he said (and New York Police Department statistics for 1964 bear him out), murder occurs after an alter-
cation between people who know each other. Such cases can usually
be put together through good police work even if there are no
eyewitnesses.

Whatever the validity of the prosecutors' contentions, the fact is
that they panicked over the implications of the Escobedo decision
and launched a counterattack to swing public opinion against it.

Then, in the midst of their campaign, at the height of the rhetoric, came the case of George Whitmore, Jr.

"How could it happen to Frank?"

There were three hundred prosecutors at the recent meeting of the National District Attorneys' Association in Houston. Most of them asked this question, in one form or another, whenever the Whitmore case was mentioned—and the Whitmore case was mentioned as often as the Escobedo case, which means every five minutes.

To other district attorneys, Frank Hogan is a little like Pope Paul to a parish priest. He runs the showcase office in the country, full of career people, many of whom have been there all their professional lives. They are very competent.

There are, to be sure, a few embarrassments, such as overzealous aides (one former assistant apparently considered it his mission to save the city from Lenny Bruce; another top aide, still with Hogan, has been the scourge of local gypsies), but embarrassments can happen in any good family. The office is clearly above politics and is generally considered one of the best. As far as many district attorneys are concerned, the proof of Hogan's superiority lies in the fact that he has been in office since 1942. No one ever runs against him.

But now one of Frank Hogan's assistants had taken a sixty-one-page confession—sixty-one pages, which is really unheard-of—full of incredible details, intricate drawings and amazing nuances, and this confession, in one of the biggest cases to hit New York in years, had turned out to be a phony.

"Here we are, with Goldberg teeing off on us on Escobedo, saying that confessions are untrustworthy—here we are trying our best to fight what we know in our hearts is a rear-guard action," said one district attorney, "and then Hogan—of all people, Hogan, the best of all of us—has to come up with a stink bomb like this.

"Do you know what it's like? It's like you're defending Stalingrad and they take away the snow."

Well, then, how did it happen to Frank? How could one of his experienced assistants take a confession for more than two hours and not realize that it had been spoon-fed?

One of Mr. Hogan's former assistants cast some light on the mystery recently:

"You have to understand the way the system works," he said. "As far as I know, it works the same way in every borough in New York City. There's an assistant district attorney on duty twenty-four hours a day in the Homicide Bureau. When a murder suspect is picked up by the police, the assistant is notified. But he isn't asked to come into the station house until the police are 'ready' for him.

"Translated, this means he doesn't enter the picture until the accused has given a statement to the detectives—or worse, as in Whitmore's case, until the detectives have given a statement to *him*.

"In short, it's 'see no evil, hear no evil.' Which not only puts the suspect at the mercy of the police but inevitably puts the district attorney there with him. And so, on occasion, you must expect a Whitmore case.

"Now I don't know why the assistant who took Whitmore's Q. and A. didn't smell a rat. [A Q. and A. is the stenographic record of a suspect's answers to questions posed by the district attorney.] But look at it his way. The Wylie–Hoffert case is the hottest thing in years. All the police brass are involved. Everybody is looking for glory. Their ship is in. Under these conditions not many assistant district attorneys are going to look for trouble. They themselves want to believe it's true.

"And then again it is possible that the detectives had the kid so primed that you just couldn't know there was something wrong.

"But the point is that this policy of not moving in early lends itself to innuendo and heartache."

It should be noted that many district attorneys do not move in at all during the interrogation stages. The first time they see a defendant is in court at the arraignment. At the other extreme, the Philadelphia district attorney has a representative at the police station as soon as possible after a murder suspect is apprehended.

"It works very well," an assistant from that office said recently. "With us there, the cops don't dare mess a guy up. As a result, we have very few defendants attack a confession on the grounds of duress."

But if Mr. Hogan must share the blame with the police for the Wylie–Hoffert debacle, he deserves praise for running down and finally exposing the flaws in Whitmore's confession. It is rare for a prosecutor to investigate his own case once a confession has been obtained.

*   *   *

But this fine gesture was not without imperfections. When Mr. Hogan, last January, discredited the confession and charged another man with the Wylie–Hoffert murders, he did not at the same time move to dismiss the indictment against Whitmore. Instead, Whitmore was merely "discharged on his own recognizance."

This technicality was carefully exploited in Whitmore's trial in Brooklyn earlier this month for the Edmonds murder, when the prosecutor pointed out to the jury that Whitmore could still be tried for the Wylie–Hoffert slayings. One result was to confuse the jurors. After thirty-four hours of deliberation, they reported themselves deadlocked, and the judge ordered a mistrial.

Three days later, the Wylie–Hoffert indictment against Whitmore was dismissed with the consent of Mr. Hogan's office. Why had it not been dismissed before the Edmonds trial? The New York Civil Liberties Union charged that Mr. Hogan had delayed the dismissal in order to help his Brooklyn colleague win a conviction.

Mr. Hogan's office denied the charge and said Whitmore could have had the dismissal earlier if he had requested it. Whitmore's chief counsel, Stanley J. Reiben, in turn, implied that the Hogan office had told him it would oppose a dismissal motion before the Edmonds trial—and the publicity surrounding such opposition could only have damaged Whitmore's cause.

It is a mystery that will probably never be solved, but a minor one compared to some others: Did Whitmore commit *any* crime? Was he intentionally framed in the Wylie–Hoffert case?

Someday a jury will likely answer the first. Whitmore may be tried again for the Edmonds murder and will surely be retried on the Borrero charge. Whatever the verdict, doubts will remain in many minds. In fact, the police officers who took the Wylie–Hoffert confession still believe, almost to a man, that Whitmore is guilty, as do many people in the Brooklyn district attorney's office.

In a way, this answers the second question. How can anyone say there was an intentional frame-up when those involved believe they have done no wrong? That, more than anything else in this strange case, is what puts a chill in the bones.

—*The New York Times Magazine*
May 16, 1965

WHITMORE: RAILROADED AND FORGOTTEN

THE CASE IS now titled *George Whitmore* v. *The City of New York,* but thirteen years after he was railroaded by a powerful combination of police and prosecutors, it is still New York on top. Whitmore may not appreciate it, but he has delivered the city up from venality to shamelessness.

Thus, having all but destroyed his life through its criminal justice branch, New York's civil arm has so far succeeded in denying him a penny for the trouble.

It's hard to believe that a new generation has come to maturity since that night in the spring of 1964 when Whitmore was dragged into the headlines.

He was a slight, light-skinned Negro kid of nineteen from Wildwood, New Jersey, who happened to be walking the streets of Brooklyn after visiting his girl, when a guy ran frantically by him. A cop followed, whistle blowing, and stopped to ask George if he saw anyone running.

Early the next morning, Whitmore came upon another cop and asked him if they had caught the fellow. The cop said no, but brought him to headquarters as a potential witness.

Twenty-four hours later, Whitmore was taken in handcuffs before the assembled press and TV cameras of New York, and charged with the attempted rape of one Elba Borrero, the murder of one Minnie Edmonds—and the double sex-murder of Janice Wylie and Emily Hoffert.

Wylie–Hoffert was the ticket that attracted the press, for these were the "career girl" killings on Manhattan's fashionable East Side that had scandalized the city—and the country—a year earlier.

Now, however, the chief of police was able to announce that Whitmore was the man—"no doubt about it"—and that he had given a sixty-one-page confession full of details that "only the killer could know."

To make a long story short—three books were written about the case and a TV movie was produced from which the "Kojak" series was a spinoff—Whitmore was cleared of all charges. But not before he served four years in prison for the attempted rape of Mrs. Borrero, and not before plenty of other things happened to him—and to the law.

For example, the Manhattan District Attorney's office established that he had nothing to do with the Wylie–Hoffert murders, but did not make this public, owing to an apparent arrangement with the Brooklyn D.A., who went ahead and convicted Whitmore for the attempted rape of Mrs. Borrero.

It turned out that the jury was prejudiced by the publicity regarding Wylie–Hoffert—and it also turned out that the Brooklyn D.A. had suppressed important evidence that would have exonerated Whitmore. Nonetheless—and despite the fact that another man was arrested (and later convicted) for the Wylie–Hoffert slayings—Whitmore was tried twice more on the Borrero indictment and was not cleared until 1973.

In the meantime, New York abolished capital punishment, and the assemblyman who introduced the bill based his case on Whitmore, who in the ordinary course of events might well have been executed for crimes he never committed.

Last month, State Supreme Court Justice Arthur S. Hirsch ruled that the city is not responsible for the malicious acts of its prosecutors, because while it pays them it does not "control them."

Since the state is not responsible for D.A.s—on the grounds that they are a "local office"—and the D.A.s are themselves immune, owing to a U.S. Supreme Court decision, Whitmore is now caught in a "revolving door," noted his lawyers, Myron Beldock and Arthur Miller.

To which, replied Assistant Corporation Counsel Elliot J. Mermelstein, "Is the City of New York to be the whipping boy for every grievance that cannot be laid elsewhere?"

George Whitmore sat in his lawyers' office the other day, an old man of thirty-three, on welfare because nobody wants to hire a guy who "killed" the career girls, and said he didn't understand the city.

"Is it right," he asked, "for them to send a person up the river for years and make him out to be a murderer, and then tell him 'see you later'?"

Well, what does he know about whipping boys?

—*New York Post*
November 18, 1977

There is no billboard quite like The New York Times Magazine, *and if I didn't know it before the Whitmore piece appeared, I knew it from that moment on. Publishers called with book offers, magazine editors with ideas for articles, radio talk show hosts wanted me on the air, the Sunday Magazine asked for more stuff, and Abe Rosenthal and Arthur Gelb looked at me with different eyes. All of which was gratifying, but in the long view not nearly so important as the response from the legal community.*

Liberal judges and law professors suddenly found a kindred soul on the Times *and so began to send me their articles and ideas. The moment was propitious—the Supreme Court had decided* Escobedo *and in the next term would decide* Miranda. *It was a furious war, and for the most part the news media sided with the law enforcement establishment. Though I think it simplistic to say that the Court follows the newspapers—or even, in the cliché, the election returns—on the delicate issue of confessions, the papers, particularly the* Times, *might well have a serious impact.*

It was clear that Justice William J. Brennan was the key man, the swing vote, and while few said so, the drumbeating on both sides was directed toward him. Ordinarily, Brennan would have been counted as a near-automatic liberal vote, but his father had been chief of police in Newark, and it was known that he was concerned about what any extension of Escobedo *would do to law enforcement.*

At the time, virtually everybody believed that the confession was the backbone of the system, accounting for the solution of 75 to 80 percent of all crimes. I used to think so; indeed, until I reread the Whitmore piece I was sure I thought it then. I'm glad to see I raised questions about the validity of the police claim, but I was tentative; I had no proof they were lying.

Six months later, Brooklyn Supreme Court Justice Nathan Sobel produced statistics showing that no more than 10 percent of the felony indictments in his county were based on confessions. Sobel's piece appeared in The New York Law Journal, and I grabbed it and got it on page one of the Times. The next day, Frank Hogan blasted Sobel's statistics in a formal address before the Grand Jury Association and he made page one. The game was afoot, and before it was over I had numbers from Los Angeles, Detroit, and other cities—from D.A.s and police chiefs—that not only backed up Judge Sobel but proved he was something of an alarmist, that far less than 10 percent of the cases required confessions.

These statistics convinced Justice Brennan, who provided the fifth vote in the Miranda case—which held that suspects must be warned of their rights and offered free counsel if needed. I wish I could say who told me this, but there's no statute of limitations on off-the-record comments.

As for Whitmore, his lawyers are still battling in the courts—and he's still looking for work, looking for a life.

ON PATTY HEARST
AND THE EVIL
OF BANALITY

IT WAS PATTY Hearst's good luck to have one champion who kept eyes and mind on the only incontestable fact in the case.

"If they had never kidnapped her," said Mary Nieman, "she would never have been in that bank." Mary, of course, was an alternate juror, and so did not get the chance to hang the jury, as she says she surely would have. When the dice are rolling, as they have been for Patty Hearst since that long-ago night when she was dragged out of her home by two hit men for the Symbionese Liberation Army, it was inevitable that the one chance she had would get no chance to help her.

The critical question is why Mary Nieman stood alone; why the jury appeared to have so little difficulty in hurdling the one issue that made this case unique in the annals of American jurisprudence? The prosecution, after all, never suggested that Patty Hearst was in any way involved in her own kidnap, and thus the "but for" suggested by Mrs. Nieman's statement should have been as powerful in the deliberation room as it seemed at the outset of the trial. Had Patty Hearst not been kidnapped, she'd still be living in Berkeley, perhaps even with Steven Weed. That much we know, and that, I submit, is all we can know for certain about this case, or at least all we can know "beyond a reasonable doubt." But in that wondrous old common law phrase lies, I suspect, the key to why she was convicted.

The judicial system is incapable of fairly determining guilt or innocence in so unparalleled a case, and to say this is not necessarily to attack the jury, the judge or even the system itself. It is simply to note that some happenings are beyond the capacity of litigation, and, if any are, this one surely is the shining example. The criminal trial, in the final analysis, is a forum for reconstruction of events that took place in the past.

Nearly every trial is thus an imperfect rendering of old facts, since there are seldom eyewitnesses, and even when there are we know too much about their accuracy to be sanguine about the certainty of guilt in all but the rare case. Still, the system generally seems to work out fairly enough, and in any event nobody has devised a better one. I believe it was Chesterton who said about juries, "I'd rather be judged by twelve fools than by one fool."

But how could twelve *wise* men and women know beyond a reasonable doubt that Patty Hearst had the required criminal intent to rob that bank that day? Medical science is still in its infancy regarding the impact of torture on the human mind. All we do know is that the most strong-willed have been broken in prisoner-of-war camps, have turned in friends and given away secrets to the enemy. It is happening now in Northern Ireland just as it happened in Korea, Vietnam and Dachau. The psychiatrists continue to study the results of torture, of "brainwashing," and these results may well be long-lasting and fundamental. That the doctors disagree—as they did in the Hearst trial—only goes to show what difficult, virgin territory we deal with here.

Against these complexities—and they include, of course, the well-documented business of people becoming emotionally dependent on their captors, even falling in love with them—the judicial apparatus appears capable of little more than the banal response. Thus Judge Carter gave the jury an ordinary textbook charge on "willfulness," as if this were an everyday bank heist. Though no one can directly examine a person's thoughts, he said, the jury was entitled to infer intent from conduct. That is the way it must be in the usual case, else there could hardly be trials at all. But how is this the usual case?

Yet, in the charge, the trial judge made it all sound very much like the daily traffic in felony court. The kidnapping could not exonerate the defendant, he said, unless the jury found that on the day of the robbery she remained in fear of her captors or was otherwise influenced by them to such an extent that she couldn't form the necessary "willfulness." How was the jury to determine this? By the medical testimony if they so chose, but if they didn't so choose, by "common sense," that is, "you may infer intent from conduct." So, one juror said, the psychiatric testimony was "one man's opinion, that's all it was." That may be all it is, but what has the "common sense" of an ordinary layman to do with so unprecedented a case?

Lee Bailey is already being second-guessed enough for me not to join the pack. I wasn't there, and I don't know what his real options were. I do know that he is a top-notch lawyer, and while it might have gone better had he produced kidnap victims or former POWs, it may be that he was unable to get them. But I think all this speculation is largely beside the point.

Patty Hearst was cooked because the jurisprudential system itself dictated that she be tried as if there were a way to determine with "moral certainty" whether she voluntarily robbed a bank. If there is such a way it surely could not be done within the prevailing rules of evidence and perhaps not within the adversary system. That system turned the trial—as it had to—into the case of Patty Hearst *v.* Tania and in such a swearing contest the real defendant could hardly be found, much less found to be innocent.

But what should have been done? My answer is nothing. She never should have been tried. Ridiculous? Well, consider that for a ten-grand bank heist all the participants but Patty Hearst are in their graves. That ought to be sufficient justice without tossing a kid—who, had she not been snatched, would be playing golf at a country club—into the deep with her killers.

Of course, had she not been brought to trial, we'd have been told that the power structure runs the country. But we were told that when Randy Hearst hired F. Lee Bailey. Maybe the Harrises ought to be allowed time to indoctrinate Patty again in how money talks in America.

—*Soho Weekly News*
March 25, 1976

ALLAN BAKKE:
THE SKIN GAME

FOURTEENTH IN DANGER

In his blind-dating period during the early 1950s, Joseph Kates of Sunnyside, Queens, would open his telephone pitch to the hopefuls as follows: "My name is Joseph Kates, I live in the borough of Queens, and I'm an accounting major at the City College of New York. *But don't hang up;* I have something to say."

This one is about the Bakke case, but don't hang up. . . .

So, while press coverage of the decision has achieved overkill, the most extraordinary point about it has been ignored: Only one justice on the Supreme Court found unconstitutional the racial-quota system employed by the regents of the University of California in their admissions policy at Davis Medical School.

This was not merely unpredictable. It was off the boards. The Davis program was so blatantly a case of reverse discrimination that civil rights leaders did not want it to go to the high court.

When the regents went anyway, a conspiracy theory developed among those leaders that the whole thing was a setup, that the regents were appealing only to destroy affirmative action.

It was no madcap notion, even in retrospect. Davis had no history of discrimination, and unlike other schools around the country, it made no effort to cover its quota with talk of "student diversity."

Furthermore, Allan Bakke was the worst kind of test case for the principle of affirmative action. An electrical engineer, a fine student, a Vietnam veteran who had developed a zeal to heal, Bakke's qualifications and character could not be faulted. He was rejected because he was white, in favor of far-less-qualified candidates.

Is it any wonder that many people in the civil rights establishment believed they were being betrayed by a board of regents who insisted on taking this one to the Supreme Court?

Yet four justices—Brennan, Marshall, White, and Blackmun—voted to bar Allan Bakke from a medical college that had barred him strictly because of his color. The equal-protection clause, they said, was no impediment to such skin games; indeed, they implied that the overriding purpose of the Fourteenth Amendment was to encourage any scheme that might help right the wrongs done to blacks in America.

That this view came within one vote of becoming the law of the land is astonishing. We seemed, after all, to have reached a consensus in the country, including the South, that the Constitution was colorblind, that no governmentally supported institution could exclude a person because of race.

This was and is an unrealized goal, to be sure, but nonetheless a noble one, mandated by the equal-protection clause. In *Bakke*, however, five justices agreed that the Constitution is not colorblind. To support this, they cited the internment during World War II of Japanese-Americans living on the West Coast, one of the most disgraceful episodes in American history. If that isn't the same as saying two wrongs make a right, what is it?

While this position did not result in the court's upholding the Davis quota system, it came so close that Justice Brennan, writing for the four who would have upheld it, said that, in effect, the majority also held the view. According to Brennan, Justice Powell, the swing man in the case, supported this reading of the equal-protection clause so long as a university did the deed covertly, rather than the way Davis did it.

Since Powell, the only justice who found the Davis program unconstitutional—four others rejected it as in violation of the Civil Rights Act of 1964 and thus did not reach the constitutional point—pointed to the Harvard plan as a legitimate method of taking race into account, Brennan could be close to the mark.

In any event he is not far off it—Harvard seems to have achieved something of a minority quota by indirection. And this, of course, makes some of the reaction to the Bakke decision incredible. The day after the ruling, for example, something new called the National Committee to Overturn the Bakke Decision held a rally at Foley Square. "Now we've got to use other means like force—and we mean strong," shouted the leader. Whereupon the crowd attempted to storm City Hall and then managed to tie up traffic on the Brooklyn Bridge. Hysteria, to say the least, but not markedly different from the exhortations of those expected to know better.

So Ramsey Clark, outraged that the court did not uphold Davis' quotas, writes in *The Nation:* "Bakke cannot stand. Bakke will not stand."

If it stood for what Clark wants, it wouldn't stand for long. Had the court excluded Bakke from medical school, Congress would have moved swiftly to amend the Civil Rights Act to make crystal clear that quota systems are illegal—certainly in cases where there is no proof of discrimination.

You don't have to be Dr. Gallup to know that the country is overwhelmingly opposed to reverse discrimination.

The amazing thing is that four justices were willing to endanger the Constitution for so quixotic a goal as affirmative-action doctors. That they did not quite succeed is reverse irony.

—*New York* magazine
July 17, 1978

IV.

TRUST YOUR MOTHER, BUT CUT THE CARDS

McGOVERN AND THE BOSSES: FRAUD IN MIAMI BEACH

*A summer night in 1972. I'm at the Lion's Head in the Village,
hanging the bar and scratching. My back is itching—it's been itching all the way downtown—it won't let up. A girl laughs. "You've
come a long way, buster," she says. "Now you even have to scratch
your back yourself." Just like that she lays Larry Hart on me. "And
order Johnnie Black for one," I say. It never entered my mind, but
now it does. I know why I'm itching, I know why I'm blue. Everybody's in Miami Beach covering the Democratic convention. What
am I doing in New York?*

*Of course, I understood quite well what I was doing in New York.
It was just over a year after the Ellsberg thing, and though my piece
on Meyer Lansky had come out in Harper's, the blacklist was
healthy, no editor was about to send me to Convention City. On the
other hand, the combination of an itch and a pretty girl's laugh sent
me straight to the pay phone.*

*I called Larry Grauman, the editor of The Antioch Review. In
Yellow Springs, Ohio. Collect. To understand how crazy that was
you need only know that a collect call from New York was enough to
soak up The Antioch Review's budget for the week. After Larry
caught his breath, I said, "I'm going to Miami to cover the convention for you—cable me the airfare." Larry said, "Well, now, wait a
minute Sid. . . ." I jumped him. "C'mon, c'mon, it's nothin', it's
bubkes, just send it, I'm doin' you a favor for chrissake. I'm payin' all*

248   Sidney Zion

my other expenses, you're getting this for nothin'. Don't be a schmuck, Grauman."

Larry's such a good guy. He sighed. He laughed. He said, "I suppose you're going to tell me you have no credentials and you expect The Antioch Review *to provide them." I said, "Who the hell needs credentials?" Larry sighed deeper. "Who the hell needs credentials?" he repeated. "Just go to Miami for* The Antioch Review, *no credentials, who needs it? That's outrageous!"*

I said, "Larry, only jerks bother to go on the floor—the story is never on the floor. I'll get you a great story, there'll be nothin' like it anywhere, that's guaranteed."

Grauman said, "That's what I'm afraid of."

"What's the deadline," I said.

"You'll have to do it as soon as you get back."

Now I laughed. The Antioch Review's *deadlines were something like the Apocalypse.*

"Awwright, Sid, awwright," Grauman said. "I'll never be able to justify this, but awwright."

It wasn't all right yet. I still had to cover the other expenses. I called John Berendt, who at that time had just become editor of a new magazine, Lifestyle. I told John I'd come up with something hot for him—all I needed was airfare. He said terrific, he said he'd do better: He'd give me the plane ticket plus a grand for the piece. My back didn't itch no more.

I called home to tell my wife I'd be off to Miami the next day, and she told me Mary Kaplan was trying to reach me. Mary had invested $30,000 in Scanlan's and never bitched when it blew away. An altogether right broad, old Mary, and beautiful and smart. I rang her straightaway.

Mary said she was leaving for Miami tomorrow and was I going? I told her sure, and she asked would I be her escort at a fat-cat dinner for George McGovern at the Doral Hotel? It was a small party, she said, only people who gave $25,000 or more. No press allowed, but they couldn't keep her date out, she said. You betcha, I said, and you betcha they wouldn't dare say no to Mary, whose father is J. M. Kaplan, the man who originated Welch's grape juice. Anyway, the chances were those big dogs wouldn't know who the hell I was.

It came off perfectly. Not only didn't they know my byline, they didn't know I was Mary's guest; they just figured I was one of them. Well now. What I did was I played Jimmy Stewart. "Are we all a little batty?" I'd say to any millionaire standing next to me with a drink. "What are we doing giving our money to a prairie populist who keeps on promising to take it away?" I didn't say "shucks," but otherwise I was all innocence. I got back knowing smiles and inevitably they'd talk about the Wall Street Journal ad.

"Didn't you see the Journal ad?"

Of course I had seen it, but I didn't let on. During the primaries, McGovern ran an ad assuring the business community that it was up to Congress to initiate tax and fiscal legislation. Since McGovern was on record for congressional seniority, which assured Bourbon control of the key money committees, his message was clear, at least to the moguls at the Doral: The populist talk was just talk, rhetoric, not to worry.

I was sure McGovern was a fake—that's what I knew I was going to write for Antioch—but I'd never heard it direct from the rich. Until this dinner party I hadn't much considered his monetary policy. Now I had a new angle, and now I had a piece for Lifestyle.

Otherwise, I covered the convention from the watering holes and back rooms, which is the best way. The only surprise was that so many reporters were impressed that I was working for The Antioch Review. I never figured on that.

I wrote both pieces in feverish time when I got back to New York. The money was from Lifestyle, but the best work went to Antioch. As so often it goes, and so the only thing that goes here is the one that went to Larry Grauman.

A CONSENSUS as big as the Fontainebleau holds that the Democratic party has been restructured, reformed and overwhelmed by a mild-mannered but tenacious prairie populist. What we witnessed in Miami Beach, we are told, was nothing less than a revolution, a smashing of the old order in which Senator George McGovern led a grass-roots insurgency of the disaffected, disillusioned and disenfranchised to victory over the party oligarchy—that is, the big-city bosses, the county and state leaders, the top elected officials, the ruling clique in the Congress. The weapon with which McGovern dislodged the entrenched powers is said to have been a set of reforms which he himself shepherded through the party, reforms that opened the National Convention to his army of women, youth, poor people, blue-collars, blacks, Chicanos, liberals, radicals and intellectuals. While all acknowledge that his nomination left in its wake eddies of resentment among the survivors of the former power structure, it is almost universally held that the party has been fundamentally changed, that come what may it will never be the same again.

There is only one trouble with this consensus. It is a farrago of lies, distortions and misunderstandings which, if allowed to go unchallenged, will seriously damage the country.

To begin where no one seems to have begun, why did the Democratic party oligarchy do nothing to stop McGovern? Reason and history prove that the bosses will go to any length to protect their power from the threat of destruction by an insurgency movement, as Eugene McCarthy can well attest. Yet they did less than nothing to cut down George McGovern.

It has been conveniently forgotten that the same oligarchy that ruthlessly destroyed the 1968 McCarthy insurgency handed the Reform Commission portfolio to George McGovern. Since the Democratic bosses have never been known for their suicidal tendencies, it must be assumed that they knew their man. He did not disappoint them.

McGovern in 1968 was a rather obscure senator with a moderately liberal voting record. When he announced for the presidency two weeks before the convention, he was dismissed as a stalking horse for Edward Kennedy. When Kennedy showed no interest in the nomination, McGovern's motives passed unquestioned. Whatever the motives, his candidacy served the interests of the oligarchy. By skimming off some 150 votes pledged to the late Robert F. Kennedy, McGovern split the left-liberal vote and added a needed element of confusion to the trashing of Eugene McCarthy. Having performed that service, McGovern rushed to the podium and embraced Hubert Humphrey. Shortly after the election, the party leaders rewarded him with the reform portfolio.*

---

* Inevitably, I will be accused by some of advancing a conspiracy theory. I do not imply that McGovern was in a conspiracy with the party bosses, only that he did them a major favor in the hope they would return it—and they did. There is nothing conspiratorial about people acting together in their common interest. When party leaders act together to do something that is considered laudable, no one calls it a conspiracy, for example, the nomination of Adlai Stevenson at the Stockyards Inn, Chicago, 1952. But when a political analyst points out that leaders sometimes act to-

Apart from his deeds at the 1968 convention, McGovern's career in the House and Senate gave every evidence that he was a man who could be trusted by the party oligarchy. He was a regular who showed no inclination to challenge the party power structure. Although he spoke out early and eloquently against our Vietnam involvement in a September 1963 Senate speech, he was curiously restrained for a long time thereafter (what could JFK or RFK have said to him?) and he did not become a serious spokesman for peace until 1967. And in that year, prepping for his reelection campaign, McGovern voted against permitting draft registrants to be represented by counsel at draft board hearings and against granting draft deferments for Peace Corps and Vista volunteers. In 1968 he voted to disqualify from government employment for five years anyone convicted of a felony committed during a riot. He could be counted on to vote against gun control. McGovern was a "good old boy" who could be trusted with "reforming" the party. (His regularity has remained constant. In 1970 he voted to retain the seniority system behind which the Democrats have long rationalized congressional inaction. This little-known vote assumes deeper significance in view of McGovern's famous advertisement in *The Wall Street Journal* during the primaries. There he assured the business community that, whatever his campaign rhetoric, it was up to Congress to initiate tax and fiscal legislation. Since McGovern favors seniority, which guarantees Bourbon control of the key money committees, his message should have chilled his "populist" followers, but there is little evidence that it even troubled them.)

Mayor Daley was apparently long aware of McGovern's party loyalty. According to Robert Sam Anson, McGovern's biographer, the South Dakotan met secretly with Daley in Chicago after Humphrey's nomination. "Daley, even if metaphorically, could hardly have been more explicit," writes Anson. " 'My dear mother, God rest her soul,' Daley said, 'always told me—Richard, as one door closes another door opens.' From Dick Daley such words did

---

gether to produce a reprehensible result—the nomination of a fake independent—he is said to have fallen victim to conspiratorial paranoia. What those who make these accusations are saying, in effect, is that party bosses cannot or will not commit malevolent acts and that anyone who thinks otherwise is crazy. As for those who claim that the conspiratorial paranoia lies in the "insane" belief that there *are* party bosses, I put it to them to explain who nominated Hubert Humphrey in 1968.

not come lightly and McGovern did not take them so. Now all he could do was wait and plan and most of all hope that history would come again."

Daley was more explicit after the 1968 election, according to McGovern. In an interview published in *Life* shortly before the 1972 convention, McGovern related that Daley told him at a Chicago dinner: "Well, you know the candidate in '72 is probably going to be either young Kennedy or you."

Having been appointed by the bosses to "reform" the convention rules, McGovern justified their faith in him. His commission— which did dispatch some gross practices, such as selecting delegates years before the convention, often behind locked doors—had as its centerpiece a quota system, by which delegates were to be chosen on the basis of sex, race and age. It was this reform, labeled "near revolutionary" by *The New York Times*, which was credited with producing McGovern's nomination and transforming the convention and the party.

It is an outrageous fake, undemocratic on its face, counterinsurgent in practice. It is a fake because it groups people in categories that have no relevance to reform, as though to say that women, or blacks, or Chicanos, or people under thirty were born with reform genes. It is counterinsurgent because it is difficult enough to mount an insurgency without complicating matters by insisting on quotas. A true insurgency lives off the land, gathering support where it can. If McGovern was generally able to produce slates that conformed to the quotas it was because he was not an insurgent candidate. Insurgents by definition seek to overthrow the bosses; they seek power. But as McGovern's political director, Frank Mankiewicz, explained in a postconvention interview: "Our people are not interested in power, they're interested in ideas."

This remark* explains much about the McGovern Phenomenon. It is the very definition of fake reform, and as will be demonstrated, it reveals why the bosses encouraged such activity.† It suffices for now to note that the remark explains how McGovern was able to fill his

---

* *Life*, July 21, 1972.
† In Ernst Lubitsch's film *The Merry Widow*, the king's adviser informs him that there is unrest in the country. The shepherds are talking, the rumor goes. The king is worried. "Influential shepherds?" he asks. The adviser shrugs: "East Side shepherds." "Intellectuals!" says the king. "Let them talk."

slates with "quota people" who surprised everybody in Miami (but the McGovern high command) with their good manners and pervasive pliancy. Real insurgents are rare birds, generally crusty and independent; it is against their nature to perform as a drill team. And because they are rare, it is nearly impossible to find them in proper proportions as to sex, age and race. The party bosses, on the other hand, have no difficulty filling slates with women (aldermen's wives, ladies' auxiliaries), ward-heeling blacks or young hustlers under thirty. That is why the party regulars were not heard to complain about the quota guidelines. Indeed, Mayor Daley announced initially that he would conform to them. Had he done so, of course, even the press might have seen the quotas as frauds. What sort of "near revolutionary" reform could be accommodated by the Daley machine? That Daley chose to ignore the guidelines indicates nothing so much as that he wanted an excuse *not* to attend the convention, the better to dump the top of the ticket in November, if called for. If Daley were dedicated to stopping McGovern, no one could have kept him out of Miami. (If this scenario sounds contradictory, it is important to note that nominations and elections are entirely different matters—that party bosses for their own reasons have in the past encouraged or allowed the nominations of candidates only to abandon them in general elections.)

CONCLUSION

The inescapable conclusion is that the McGovern reforms—with few exceptions—were in the interest of the party oligarchy. They were in McGovern's own interest mainly because the Commission itself provided him with a nationwide reputation as a reformer. (That this was in the party's interest, in fact was the intention of the bosses, will be explained *infra.*)

Having created McGovern as the "antiboss" candidate, and having cooperated with him in that role, what did his deadly enemies, the party oligarchs, do to stop him in the primary and nonprimary states? Again nothing.

A curious thing happened after Senator Muskie, the apparent morning-line favorite of the bosses, faltered in New Hampshire. Instead of rushing to his aid (as they did for Adlai Stevenson in 1956 when Estes Kefauver, an insurgent, beat him in a number of early primaries) the party leaders seemed to encourage Muskie's opposition. Thus, Hubert Humphrey and Henry Jackson had no trouble raising "war chests." Humphrey and Jackson ran ahead of Muskie in Florida. Later, in Pennsylvania, Humphrey beat Muskie head on and it was this defeat that effectively finished off the uncertain man from Maine.

While Muskie from the outset had been crowded by an abundance of candidates to his right (Humphrey, Jackson, Yorty, Hartke), McGovern had the left of center to himself. Since the party professionals are quite proficient at splitting the constituencies of their implacable foes, it needs to be asked why they left McGovern alone. Indeed, when John Lindsay entered with the stated intention of competing with McGovern for the left, he received no support from the oligarchy.

And when it became clear after Pennsylvania that only Humphrey could stop McGovern, why did the former Vice-President suddenly discover that his sources of cash and support had dried up? Where were his old friends in the labor movement? Why did they help him when he entered the race, only to abandon him when he alone stood between George McGovern and the nomination? The Michigan Democratic party, the only one in the country run by the unions, refused to distribute Humphrey's campaign posters and allowed him to suffer a humiliating loss to George Wallace. In New Jersey, a strong labor state, Humphrey received only $11,000 and was routed by a well-financed McGovern effort. And in the critical California primary Humphrey had to make do with $500,000 against McGovern's two million.

Interesting questions abound. Why, for example, was McGovern's voting record kept a secret until it was too late to hurt him with liberal voters? Why did the AFL-CIO wait until the convention to disseminate his supposed antiunion history? Why was his vulnerable position on Israel not made known until a desperate and isolated Hubert Humphrey broke it in California? Why, after Humphrey's surprisingly strong showing in California, did the major New York City bosses advise him to stay out of the state? Why, indeed, did the New York bosses—Meade Esposito, Patrick Cunningham, Matthew Troy—endorse McGovern if we are to believe that he only meant to destroy boss rule? (Those who remain convinced, despite these questions, that McGovern's nomination was inevitable should consider the following: What would have happened had Governor Wallace won every primary that George McGovern won? Is it believable that he would have been nominated? If not, how serious are the McGovern reforms?)

It adds up to this: McGovern was groomed by the oligarchy to be their "antiboss" candidate and was permitted to run a campaign unfettered by opposition and uncluttered by issues that would embarrass him. He was trusted to leave the bosses alone and he has left them alone.

A consideration of what happened—or rather what didn't happen—in the thousands of districts tramped through by the McGovern forces will adduce the clearest proof of this. The grass-roots movement bent hardly a blade. McGovern went through state after state without damaging the bosses. They were left standing pat, their district leaders virtually untouched, their candidates safely renominated. In short, their power was left intact at its foundation, at home, where they live and breathe. It requires an affirmative, tight-fisted effort to accomplish this in a popular national campaign that is advertised as an insurgency. Money had to be kept from local antiboss candidates, who in turn had to be kept away from McGovern; it was no accident that insurgents seldom appeared on McGovern delegate slates.

The contrast between McCarthy's 1968 campaign in New York and McGovern's 1972 race in the same state provides an excellent example of the difference between real and ersatz insurgency. McCarthy campaigned with every antiboss candidate—he avoided *only* bosses—and money flowed into his alliance. As a result, numerous insurgents were nominated for office, including a candidate for the Senate (Paul O'Dwyer), the New Democratic Coalition was formed, and the fever of reform rose everywhere.

McGovern, on the other hand, did not support Allard Lowenstein (who in 1968 had unsuccessfully tried to get McGovern to run against Lyndon Johnson, before turning to McCarthy) in his fight to unseat the egregious Representative John Rooney; he would not be seen with Elizabeth Holtzman, who on her own upset Emanuel Celler; he avoided the Brooklyn and Bronx reformers and kept such a tight fist around the money that it became a commonplace that McGovern had more accountants than Price Waterhouse.

It can be argued that this was "smart politics," that it will help McGovern against Nixon. But it cannot be said in the next breath that George McGovern overthrew the Democratic machines.

COLLISION

The obvious question is: Why did the bosses sustain such an elaborate charade over a four-year period to establish a fake reform candidate? For the answer we must look to 1968.

Eugene McCarthy's presidential campaign in 1968 traumatized the Democratic party. McCarthy performed the impossible feat of knocking a President out of the White House. He did it by galvanizing the peace movement, then at its apex, and moving it off the streets and into the precinct clubs. Dangerous as that was, McCarthy still might have been acceptable to the oligarchs had he been a man they could trust—a Robert Kennedy, for example, whose career, like his brother's, had passed every litmus test of party solidarity. But McCarthy was a different cut. He could not be trusted, though not for the reasons usually given—his philosophic tendencies, his idiosyncratic if not perverse nature, his poetry. What mattered to the hierarchy was that McCarthy insisted party power was the crucial problem in the country. He compared the two parties to the great dynasties—he kept referring to them as the Hapsburgs and the Hohenzollerns—and then he mobilized his troops. Such a direct attack on the vital organs of party power had to be answered at any price. Thus Chicago, 1968.

The convention exposed the party as a machine, ripped the "Party of the People" hedge out by the roots. Gone was the illusion of a happy commune of intellectuals, labor leaders, city pols, workers— the old Roosevelt Coalition living together, if pluralistically, within the comforting shadow of the Great Donkey.

Gone, too, was the cultivated "intransigence" of the southern Bourbons; one after another Dixie chairman stood with an HHH boater atop his head and cast all the votes for the man who drove half the South out of the party in 1948. Nor had the southern delegations been transformed willy-nilly into New York liberals, any more than Humphrey had become a "nigger baiter." Nor even could it be said that McCarthy was the "greater evil" on the race question; indeed, he had been accused often by the Kennedys of having no "gut" feeling for blacks.

What common interest then brought the South together with the contemptible North, the West with the East, the middle of the nation together with the rest, all together to provide Hubert Humphrey with an easy victory?

Was it that the party bosses simply believed that Humphrey could beat Nixon while McCarthy could not? But McCarthy held a solid five-point lead over Nixon in the polls while Humphrey was trailing by five to ten points. McCarthy had won substantial primary victories while Humphrey had refused to enter a single primary. More important, Humphrey came to the convention sorely damaged. Four years under Lyndon Johnson had made him appear to many as a sycophant, a man who had sold out the peace movement he had once championed. He seemed to the young as attractive as a tuna fish dipped in mercury.

But the party bosses did not come to Chicago to pick a winner. They came to kill off an antimachine candidate. To accomplish this they were willing to take the iron fist out of the glove, to toss delegates out of the hall, to pull plugs out of microphones, to use truncheons and tear gas, to spit obscenities, to embrace carefully cultivated "enemies"—and they were willing to do all of this on television.

Why? Because party power was at stake. To protect it the oligarchs made the ultimate sacrifice: They showed the country that it existed—that they, the bosses, kept the keys to the most powerful office in the world.

It is in the absolute interest of the parties never to expose the existence of this power, for it is power they have usurped from the people. A public that truly understood it had been robbed of its constitutional warranty of representative government—not by "special interests" or "pluralism" or the "corporate state" or "capitalism"—but by party leaders, might swiftly contrive to recover it.

We are, of course, never told about this—not by the news media, not by the academicians—though a few of us are eager to dismiss it as common knowledge. Party power remains the ultimate secret in American life, the unmentionable, the Holy of Holies. Parties are seen as mere instruments, agents, servants and translators of popular will, the "handmaidens of democracy," in Clinton Rossiter's phrase.

And although they are said to operate "at the center of the power struggle," they themselves have no power.*

The basis of this doctrine is the assumption that the men who run the two great political parties in the United States have in common an all-consuming singular motive—to win elections. They are portrayed as nonideological pursuers of the best bet, hard-bitten "pros" seeking only to discover the most popular issues so as to exploit them with the most attractive candidates. It follows that when they lose they have made an honest mistake, failing either to "tap the pulse" of the electorate on the issues, or leading with a candidate who lacked "charisma." A victory, on the other hand, is invariably viewed as a brilliant display of giving the people what they wanted.

Such is the prevailing wisdom. The best that can be said for it is that you can't read better fiction anywhere, including the racing form. The only interest this fantasy serves is the interest of the parties in obfuscating their *real* interests. If the public is convinced that the election returns mirror their views, the public will blame itself for whatever goes wrong.

Consider how they have massacred reality, our learned mentors of the press and the academy. They have managed even to take politics out of politics. There is nothing to do in the presence of so imposing a fabrication but to go back to first principles.

CONTROL

Did we not know once, before our minds were improved, that American politics was party politics, that party organizations monopolized political power, controlled the nominations of candidates, stood behind the ruling cliques in Congress and the state legislatures,

---

* An excellent example of the deeply imbedded belief that the parties, if they ever had power, have long since lost it, may be found in William Shannon's interesting article on George McGovern, *The New York Times Magazine*, July 2, 1972. "In most states," Shannon writes, "political machines fueled by patronage have been on the scrap heap for decades." One wonders what Mr. Shannon's response would have been had a copy editor asked him to name the states he had in mind. Surely not New York, New Jersey, Pennsylvania, Connecticut, Rhode Island, Delaware, Maine, New Hampshire, Vermont, Ohio, Illinois, Indiana, Michigan, Missouri, Kansas, Texas, Oklahoma, Nebraska, Arizona, New Mexico, Nevada, Utah, Montana—and the one-party oligarchies in the South, to name but a few. It is a rare state that is not dominated by machine politics, with one or the other party in ascendancy.

controlled most of the money that entered political campaigns, and
guarded the important avenues to public renown?*

Were we not fully aware that the issues brought before us as voters
were the issues raised by party leaders—that issues not raised by
them evaporated, as if they never existed?

To hold on to this extraordinary power is the First Command-
ment of party politics. All other considerations are subservient to
that end, *including the winning of elections.* If a victory at the polls
threatens to diminish the power of the party hierarchy, the party will
simply dump the election.

Dumping elections to avoid the loss of organizational control is as
natural to party leaders as snow falling. The reason was enunciated
with appealing candor by Senator Boies Penrose, the old Republican
boss of Pennsylvania, when he was accused of "ruining" the party by
putting up reactionary candidates in the face of a rank-and-file reform insurgency. "Yes," said Penrose, "but I'll preside over the
ruins."

A similar point was made in the musical *Fiorello!* There the Republican boss keeps interrupting the clubhouse poker game, be-
seeching the faithful to concentrate on finding a candidate for Congress "who's willing to lose." When La Guardia gets the nod and
proceeds to amaze the organization by actually campaigning, and
then to confound it by winning, the bosses sing the lament "The

---

* All of this is as true for the Republican party as for the Democrats. The major difference in the structure of the two parties is that big-city bosses dominate the Democratic state parties while suburban and rural bosses dominate the Republican party.
This is of course because the cities remain Democratic bastions while the Republicans generally win beyond urban limits. The Deep South is an obvious exception; in
virtually all of the region the Democrats hold one-party hegemony over the state governments.

Since Mr. Nixon's ascendance, little has been heard about the Republican state
bosses. The reason is elemental: There have been few, if any, insurgencies in Republican ranks since Nixon became President. Where there are no challenges, the bosses
can happily remain unseen. Their power, of course, endures.

The GOP has never been as unified as it is today, a condition stemming directly
from the 1964 presidential election. Senator Goldwater, it will be recalled, was said
to have captured the Republican party by combining brilliant political strategy with
a grass-roots movement. In retrospect, it is clear that the Republican oligarchy placed
no serious obstacles in his way *until* he was nominated, when suddenly Republicans-
for-Johnson clubs sprouted with the vernal inevitability of crab grass across the land.
After Goldwater's disastrous defeat, the Republican right ceased to be trouble to the
party, which is now virtually rid of its old ideological headaches. There are apparent
analogies here to the McGovern "insurgency," which do not augur well for the Democratic left in the event of a Nixon landslide in November.

Bum Won." In the background a mini-Greek chorus cries out the *true* lament: "God forbid, inde*pen*dent."

The apocalyptic vision of every political boss is the election of a candidate he can't trust to a position of great power. A governor who is indifferent or antagonistic to party needs and interests is worse than worthless to the hierarchy—he is a distinct threat. Allow him to dispense his considerable patronage, develop his own issues, impose his personality on the electorate, and you allow him to cut his umbilical cord to the party: his need to turn to the leadership for renomination.*

It is self-evident that party power lies at right angles to representative government. By definition, representative government means that elected officials are accountable to the public. But the party system is based on the proposition that elected officials are accountable first to the party leadership. In order to make them accountable the leadership must control nominations; to keep them accountable they must control renominations. There would be no party organizations, as we know them in this country, if the leaders could not reward the faithful and punish the dissidents.†

But if that is simple in theory, it is a hard day's night to execute. Socialist dogma may have it that Mayor Daley is "inevitable" under capitalism (on the grounds that the "dominant economic power" is corrupt and thus breeds corruption in its "puppets"). Mayor Daley knows better than to close his eyes if he is to maintain this "inevitable" power.

---

* If an independent governor could seriously damage a state party organization, an independent President could destroy the party oligarchy nationwide. He could do this in a variety of ways—by encouraging insurgents, withholding patronage, raising issues that would excite citizen interest, or by publicly exposing the oligarchy. The President of the United States holds the most powerful office in the world, which is precisely why the oligarchs must guard with their lives the door to the Oval Room.
† If this seems obvious, it is well to consider how few commentators perceive it to have national implications. Boss rule, to the extent it is acknowledged, is invariably held to be a local phenomenon. The moment a politician sets foot in Congress, he is thought to be free of organizational control from home, as though the leaders spend their lives filtering and X-raying candidates only to turn them loose once they achieve prominence. But, in Ben Hecht's lovely insight, "A married man in another woman's bed isn't freedom, it's the prisoner in the exercise yard." To explain why these emancipated representatives and senators "never do nothing and never do much" (Dorothy Parker), James MacGregor Burns devised a "Congressional Party," a kind of Tammany Hall for grown-ups, full of its own constraints but far removed from the grubby "locals." Pulitzers, I am told, have been awarded for less.

Party organizations are always in danger of falling apart, of becoming a congeries of independent, ambitious citizens intent on running for office, putting up candidates, pressing issues important to them. Both parties understand this completely, which is why the leaders work ceaselessly to keep serious issues out of politics, to fatigue protest movements, to make citizen participation appear hopeless, to impress on the public the bipartisan line that you can't fight City Hall.

Much if not all of this is lost on the nation's political commentators. Since they assume that parties, as mere agents of popular will, want only to win elections, they must perforce invent reasons why the parties refuse to exploit popular issues and refuse to run the most attractive candidates. If the "pros" are not acting like winners, it is assumed that something or somebody is stopping them. One of the customary reasons offered is the power of the "special interests," which are often said to control political decisions.

But if "special interests" had such power there would long since have been anarchy in the land, for invariably what benefits one interest harms another, or two or three or four. For example, the much-debated oil import quotas help the oil industry but hurt the petro-chemical industry. Thus, Dow Chemical, Du Pont and Olin Mathieson opposed the quotas and yet were helpless to upset them. But that is typical: Whenever a reform would benefit the commonweal *and* the special interests, the interests seem to be without power; yet let the two parties get together and pass legislation inimical to the public and immediately the apologists of the press will work up a froth of ink, blaming it on the "special interests." The interests thus are seen as having the power to veto what is good for the country but not the power to secure what is good for both them *and* the country.

A variation of the "special interest" thesis, but to the same point, is the theory of "pluralism." According to this one, Americans are seen always as being pitted against each other in accordance with their own money, class, religious, ethnic or geographic interests. A common example is the concept that the cities are consistently deprived of basic services by the farmers, the "apple knockers" who are said to "dominate" state legislatures. When it is pointed out that some one million farmers are literally driven off the land each year, the blame for this is assigned to the cities, which are said not to care about farmers. Thus the circle: The farmers, who do not have the wherewithal to make a decent life for themselves and their children, nevertheless have the power to deprive the cities of mass transportation, while the urbanites, who cannot manage to pay for street cleaners, have the muscle to drive the farmers off their land.

Examples of this sort of analysis are boundless, but whatever route the reasoner takes—be he a Marxist theoretician or a *New York Times* apologist—the only people who are never blamed for the American condition are the people who wield most of the power in the country, namely the party oligarchs.*

However their apologists in the news media and the universities contrived after the fact to remove the onus from them, the party leaders understood full well that they had blown their cover in the 1968 Democratic National Convention. They had demonstrated, before a huge television audience, that they were anything but "handmaidens of democracy," professionals attempting only to pick a winner. In Chicago's Convention Hall the oligarchs had revealed by their actions that the North and South were allies against a common threat, not ideological enemies. And most significantly they demonstrated that no person they did not trust would be permitted access to the presidency of the United States.

Party power cannot survive that exposure; it can only survive on the pretense that it does not exist. It was essential, therefore, to repair the damage, and the party oligarchy set out to do so on three fronts: 1) to "reform" the party; 2) to deplete, discourage and if necessary defeat the insurgents; 3) to replace the insurgency with a fake antiboss candidate.

The sincerity of the reform resolution that was voted in at the 1968 convention can be gauged by the fact that it was arranged by the very party leaders who nominated Hubert Humphrey and rejected a peace plank in the party platform. It was obviously spurious, for if the oligarchs had wanted to overthrow themselves they would have nominated Gene McCarthy and avoided a lot of paper work. Or, at the very least, they would have offered McCarthy the reform portfolio. Instead they gave the Commission to George McGovern,

---

* There is an absurd theory abroad in the land, most clearly enunciated by David Broder in his influential book *The Party's Over*, which holds that the political parties are now weak, fragmented and polarized; it appears that Mr. Broder would prefer that the country were organized as I have described it here—that is, as in fact it is —so long as the bosses were "responsible."

who had never uttered an insurgent word in his political life. The charade was so obvious as to be unworthy of outrage. It was, however, an important, even a vital, charade. For the oligarchy had to announce to the country—or they would not have done so—that they would cleanse themselves, that "never again" would there be a replay of 1968.

Infinitely more subtle was the effort to deflate the insurgency. The McCarthy campaign had left in its wake lots of disaffected Democrats hanging around the clubhouses angry as young bulls. The Peace Movement was still a potent force in the country, apparently immune to the advent of Richard Nixon. The expectations that McCarthy had aroused were being transplanted into the promising new soil of tax reform, ecology, Pentagon priorities. The last thing a party directorate wants is to encourage dissidents, to allow their numbers to grow, to give them issues to run on in primary contests. The problem was dealt with on two levels: the Democratic-controlled Congress offered no serious opposition to Nixon for the entire length of his term, and wherever necessary the bosses dumped elections in 1970.

COLLUSION

From the moment of Mr. Nixon's ascension, the Democratic party leadership has been living, if not always *in flagrante*, at least in separate bedrooms with the President. On nearly every major issue of the past four years—Vietnam, law and order, tax reform, inflation, ecology, military spending, the Middle East, Pakistan, press censorship, wiretapping, the space shuttle, "socialism for the rich," the ITT scandal—Democratic opposition in and out of Congress has ranged from puny to nonexistent.

"I have a deep friendship with the President," Mike Mansfield, the Senate Majority Leader, told reporters earlier this year. "Not a personal friendship—a political friendship." Mansfield had never so accurately expressed the attitude of his party. It is supported by a record of collusion so pervasive that only a political pundit could fail to notice.

A few of the more egregious examples follow.

- With senators and representatives scrambling to attend peace rallies during the October Moratorium of 1969, the Democratic leadership closed ranks with the administration and effectively took the Vietnam War "out of politics." Hubert Humphrey visited the White House and announced that Mr. Nixon was "on the right track" with his war policy; Speaker John McCormack pledged his support to Nixon; and Mansfield helped beat down an antiwar resolution sponsored by members of his own party. Thus, the Democrats informed the nation that the nation no longer cared about the war.
- In October of 1970, on the eve of the midterm elections, Nixon ordered the Justice Department to discourage citizens from bringing suits to enforce existing laws against corporate polluters. At the same time the Internal Revenue Service threatened to revoke the tax-exempt status of groups actively engaged in prosecuting such suits. The spectacle of a "law and order" President preventing people from helping to enforce the laws should have brought the Democrats down on his throat. Instead, silence. Ecology was "out of politics."
- In 1969, Joseph Barr, the under secretary of the Treasury, warned Congress of a "middle-class tax revolt" if major reforms in the tax laws were not accomplished. The Democrats wrote no legislation to eliminate "loopholes" during the course of the Nixon administration, thus taking tax reform "out of politics."
- Oil import quotas cost Americans $7 billion a year and net the oil industry in excess of $2 billion annually in profits. When a Nixon task force recommended that the quotas be dropped, the President rejected their report. Did the Democrats attack this example of "socialism for the rich"? Not a whisper. It was "out of politics."
- Under the rubric of "law and order" the Nixon administration has staged a many-pronged attack on civil liberties that has already seriously undermined basic protections of the Bill of Rights. With a few notable exceptions, the Democrats have "taken the Fifth" on these fundamental conflicts. The apologists assert that this stance is necessary in a country that has "turned to the right." Conveniently ignored, however, are

the results of the 1970 congressional elections, the last time
the country was tested on this issue. With Nixon and Agnew
basing their campaign appeals almost exclusively on "law and
order," the Republicans lost a dozen statehouses—including
six in Middle America—a number of Senate races and count-
less seats in state legislatures. Nonetheless, the repressive
tactics of the administration have remained "out of
politics."

- An opposition party could not have hoped for a better elec-
tion-year issue than the ITT scandal. Saving the Republicans
from this debacle was like squeezing the toothpaste back into
the tube. The Democrats were equal to the challenge. As
the GOP fell deeper into the muck, Mike Mansfield announced that "no case" had been made against Richard
Kleindienst, urged that his nomination for attorney general
be approved forthwith and suggested that the entire issue be
taken out of politics. Kleindienst breezed through the Democratic Senate by a vote of 61 to 19, and the ITT investigation ended.

It is a sorry record, but that is the point. The Democratic party
was not interested in raising serious issues and articulating popular
discontent. Its interest was in fatiguing the dissidents and shrinking
the base of the party. In pursuit of that goal, the party oligarchs
dumped the 1970 elections wherever insurgents or independent incumbents ran.

In Vermont, Democratic bosses campaigned openly for the Republican senator, Winston Prouty, against ex-Governor Philip Hoff,
an early McCarthy supporter. Prouty won and so did the Democratic
leaders, who were able to take a giant step toward restoring the Vermont Democracy to its traditional status as a collusive, losing patronage machine. In New Hampshire, party leaders drove out the inde-
pendents by nominating for governor a reactionary retired naval
captain—who lost. In Massachusetts the Democrats succeeded in
losing the gubernatorial contest by a landslide when the Boston Irish
voted Republican—the Wasserman test that the ward heelers were
dumping. In Connecticut the Bailey machine, faced with its first
statewide primary in the history of the state, lost the Senate race to
Joe Duffey, a McCarthy insurgent. In the general election, however,

the machine jettisoned Duffey after Bailey was "unable to dissuade" Tom Dodd from entering as an independent. As a result, the Republicans elected a senator with 42 percent of the vote.

In New York, the Democratic bosses were faced in the gubernatorial primary with the serious insurgency of Howard Samuels, who was openly threatening to smash them if elected. Since Nelson Rockefeller was then at one of his frequent "bottoms" in the polls, it was vital for the Democratic oligarchy to deny Samuels the nomination. This was accomplished with the endorsement of Arthur Goldberg by the Democratic state convention, an act that effectively splintered the New Democratic Coalition, which otherwise would have been solidly behind Samuels. Since Goldberg was a liberal with no slight credentials and was widely advertised (by the bosses) as a sure winner over Rockefeller, Samuels was deprived in the primary of united reform support. Even so, he only lost to Goldberg by a whisker and the closeness of the race proved to be a bonus for the party hierarchy, which had no intention of electing Goldberg. For Goldberg, though he owed his nomination to the party leaders, was far too independent, not to say egoistical, to be trusted with the governorship. No sooner had he been nominated, therefore, than he found himself being dumped by his old "supporters."

First, the AFL-CIO endorsed Rockefeller, on its face an astonishing act made all the more incredible by Goldberg's reputation as one of the proudest stones in the crown of Labor. The defection of organized labor from a Democratic candidate is invariably the telltale sign that the bosses are dumping, for the "movement" is umbilically related to the party and would not dare an act of menace to real party interests.

(George Meany's decision to deny McGovern the endorsement of the AFL-CIO can only be understood as an act approved—if not dictated—by the party oligarchy. McGovern's labor record in no way warrants the denial of the endorsement, which is why Meany gave no reason for the unprecedented action. Had the bosses opposed the move, Meany would never have made it, for without the Democrats, labor couldn't get a nickel out of the Congress. Significantly, Meany's action provoked no protests from the oligarchy.)

Goldberg's campaign, which ran smoothly enough in the primary, resembled the Gaza Strip once he won the nomination. His sources of money mysteriously dried up, Democrats-for-Rockefeller groups popped up everywhere, his dull manner of public speech—previously hardly noticed—was now constantly ridiculed, his style—once considered dignified—was now described as "magisterial" and "egomaniacal," his scheduling always seemed to break down; it was, in short, a hell of a mess. The result was a big victory for Rockefeller and a big victory for the Democratic bosses, who had again managed to divide and derail the insurgency movement and in the bargain do what they are best at doing in New York: delivering the state to the Republicans.

Thus, the East in 1970. Those commentators who detected a movement to the right in the liberal East had access to an easier answer if only they would see: The only real motion in the region came from Democratic organizations running away from the voters.

Outside the East the only other state where the electorate was judged by the experts to have "turned to the right" was Tennessee, where Republicans elected their first governor in history and also defeated Albert Gore, one of the more independent Democratic senators. A closer examination produces a different answer.

The Democratic bosses of Tennessee, including the late Governor Buford Ellington, not only endorsed the Republican gubernatorial candidate but also supplied him with campaign workers. And despite the assertions of liberal columnists, it was not the "rural Wallace voters" who defeated Albert Gore. Indeed, the so-called Wallace vote in central Tennessee almost reelected him. Gore was beaten in two Democratic party strongholds—Memphis, which went for Republican William Brock by 23,000 votes, exactly half of Gore's margin of defeat, and in Republican east Tennessee, where the collusive, tightly controlled Democratic organization regularly fails to contest Republican candidates in exchange for Republican votes for Democratic organization candidates in statewide primaries. If the Democratic party of Tennessee were trying to return Albert Gore to the Senate, Jonah swallowed the whale.*

---

* The Republicans, though hardly beset by "rad-libs" within their ranks, managed to get rid of the few candidates who strayed from the "law and order" line in 1970. The most conspicuous example was in New York, when Senator Charles Goodell persisted in courting the peace movement. The party, from Nixon down to Rockefeller's county committeemen, dumped Goodell by shifting money, support and endorsements to James Buckley, the Conservative candidate, who thus won the election.

In New Mexico, the Republican Old Guard ganged up on incumbent Governor David Cargo in the Senate primary, nominating Anderson Carter, a conservative,

Examples are manifold, all to the same end: The response of the Democratic party to the pervasive unrest in the country and to intra-party dissent has been to raise no issues nationally, to disappear as an opposition, to defeat wherever possible independent incumbents and insurgents, and to dump the general elections where boss-rule of the party would be endangered by victory.

CONFUSION

There remained throughout the past four years, however, the possibility that for all the efforts of the party oligarchy, the dissidents would not give up, would not be fatigued, that Mr. Nixon by his actions might throw the nation into such despair—as he did with the invasion of Cambodia—that the ground would again be fertile for a McCarthy-type insurgency, perhaps even led by McCarthy himself. To guard against this, to preempt the field, it was necessary to groom a safe "antiboss" candidate, to place no obstacles in his path, to allow him his head.

If such a candidate proved in the primaries to have only marginal support, it would be clear that all of the other tactics had worked and the party could nominate a "centrist"—that is, an obvious regular—without fear of again exposing itself as a machine. It would merely be seen, once more, as a "handmaiden of democracy," an agent of the popular will. If, on the other hand, the boss-produced "antiboss" candidate could amass strength in the country, the party could let him have the nomination, for he would be theirs whatever colors he appeared to be running under. Thus, George McGovern.

Anyone who understood this would have seen the 1972 Democratic convention for the charade it was. It did not require a Gallup Poll to indicate that there was a widespread sense among the citizenry that all was not what it appeared to be in Miami Beach. For one thing, the grass-roots delegates who were supposed to disrupt the

---

who lost to Joseph Montoya in the general election. Cargo had won two terms in the Statehouse by appealing to blacks, Chicanos and poor whites—groups never before solicited by the GOP, which had been losing elections steadily since the 1930s. In 1972, after losing another primary, Cargo announced that he was moving to Oregon because the New Mexico Republicans considered him "too independent." "I've become extremely popular with Democrats," Cargo said, "and that posed problems with Republicans."

convention and saddle McGovern with a platform he couldn't hope to win on, turned out to be a drill team, consistently voting against everything we had been told they were for—tax reform, abortion reform, gay rights, amnesty. The mass media managed to accommodate this reality to their earlier forebodings of a runaway convention by simply converting "independent grass-roots delegates" into "mature, intelligent soldiers" of a "new-breed political machine."* The acclaim lavished on the McGovern operatives for developing an organization "outside the worn-out party structure," an organization that outmaneuvered the Old Guard at its "own game," was accompanied by a sense of déjà vu for those old enough to recall the credit given the Kennedy people in the 1960 convention.

John Kennedy, who was supported by every boss extant—Daley, John Kenny of Jersey City, Charles Buckley of the Bronx, et al.—was presented in the press as leading a new machine that had shaken up the old order. Ho-hum. FDR was said to have done the same in 1932 (Mayor Curley was the "new breed"), Eisenhower in 1952 (Brownell and Dewey were the Republican "young bloods"), and Barry Goldwater in 1964 (F. Clifton White was the Gary Hart of his day). The media always treat party bosses as a collective jack-in-the-box that pops up every four years for the sole purpose of being punched by the "new machine."†

The reason such commentary receives credence is the development of "stop movements," which arise with the predictability of cost overruns in the defense industry at every political convention (except, of course, those which are convened merely to bless an incumbent President). It is always assumed—and guess who likes that?—that stop movements are conspiracies of the party bosses seeking to deny the crown to an aggressive new candidate. Since none of these stop movements has succeeded in at least forty-eight years, it should be clear by now that 1) the bosses are underachieving retards; 2) the bosses are killed off every four years but arise in order to be killed again; and 3) every candidate who comes into the convention with an unbeatable lead is an antiboss candidate.

The problem facing the Democratic bosses in the 1972 conven-

---

* For a classic example of this type of reporting, see R. W. Apple, Jr.'s column in the July 13 editions of *The New York Times*.
† No better example of such double-think can be found in modern political reporting than Max Frankel's convention analysis found in *The New York Times Week in Review*, July 16, 1972.

tion was to find a situation in which to mount a "last ditch" stand against McGovern, for without some show of resistance some people might not believe he was their enemy. The Credentials Committee provided a fine battleground.

It will be recalled that shortly before the convention opened the Credentials Committee deprived McGovern of 151 votes by rejecting the results of the "winner-take-all" California primary. As Frank Mankiewicz later noted, the convention would have been a "coronation" had McGovern been awarded the entire California delegation. Instead the conflict provided the only excitement in Miami Beach and allowed McGovern to cry robbery in the bargain.

That it was nothing more than an elaborate entertainment is proven by the fact that the people who "stole" California from McGovern gave it back to him. Thus Larry O'Brien, the party chairman, and Joe Califano, the party counsel—two longtime representatives of the oligarchy carried the California challenge to the United States Supreme Court after McGovern had won in the Circuit Court of Appeals. When they succeeded in convincing the High Court to allow the convention to decide the issue—on the brazen grounds that the party is not bound by state law—they immediately turned around and ruled that the convention could decide the question by a simple, rather than an absolute, majority. Which meant, as they well knew, that McGovern could not lose the challenge and therefore could not lose the convention. Exactly!*

---

* Shortly after this column went to press, McGovern began a tireless campaign to appease the bosses he had allegedly conquered. In New York, at the demand of the leaders he was said to have laid to waste, McGovern jettisoned his primary manager Richard Wade and installed former Mayor Robert F. Wagner to run the campaign. As a representative of the New Politics, Wagner is the quintessential sick joke. McGovern also announced plans to solicit the support of Mayor Daley and Lyndon Johnson. Around the country the Prairie Populist is following the Chinese scheme of putting out-of-state people in charge of state campaigns, thus assuring the local bosses that no McGovernite will be in a position to challenge them after the election. The candidate's courting of Humphrey, Muskie and every conceivable party hack for the vice-presidential nomination following l'affaire Eagleton should convince all but the most starry-eyed that George McGovern fully understands—even if his supporters do not—that the bosses made him and the bosses can break him.

ILLUSION

The Making of George McGovern was indeed a complicated endeavor for the oligarchy, but it is not unique in Democratic party annals. Once before the party was faced with broad antimachine sentiment in the country. Once before the party leaders had to co-opt a popular movement with a fake antiboss candidate. The year was 1896 and the candidate was William Jennings Bryan, whose "overthrow" of the oligarchy was accomplished through the will of the oligarchy. The threat was the Populist Party, which had made serious inroads into Democratic territory.

The most symbolically powerful Democratic bosses—the eastern seaboard "goldbugs," the Wall Street speculators—did not come to the 1896 convention. Bryan's nomination was hailed as a "revolution" in the party. The Populists, impressed by the "routing" of the Democratic bosses and convinced that the Bryan nomination meant that they had "taken over" the party, proceeded to invest all their hopes in the Great Commoner. After which, the Democrats dumped Bryan in the election. But Populist sentiment remained so strong that the charade required restaging four years later. Again the Democrats nominated Bryan, and again the bosses dumped the election. In 1904, these horny-handed sons of toil, who had "become" the Democratic party, nominated Judge Alton Parker, a Wall Street corporation lawyer—the antithesis of everything Populism stood for. Things were back to normal. (In 1908 the Democrats again nominated Bryan, but by then he was a reactionary and the Populist movement was dead.)

The nomination of George McGovern made things normal again for the Democratic party. If he should upset the odds-makers and win the election, the oligarchs are safe, for he is their candidate. If he loses, particularly if he is drubbed—a result the bosses seem to prefer at this point—they are perhaps even bigger winners. For if McGovern should lose badly, only Nixon and Agnew will be in better shape than the Democratic professionals, who will then be free to blame the "crazies" and the "narrow ideologues" for "destroying the party." The local Jesus Freak recruiter will have his hands full. And the message from the bosses will reverberate: You can only trust the pros to pick a winner. It will be as if 1968 never happened.

—*The Antioch Review*
Spring/Summer 1972

*   *   *

*Watergate changed everything for both parties. McGovern's devas-
tating loss surely would have put the Democratic bosses back in the
saddle for the foreseeable future, but the unraveling of the scandal
tossed all political pros, back room and front, into a herring barrel.
By 1976, the call was for the "devil least known." Thus, Jimmy
Carter.*

*Carter read the boss defense right and pulled off a brilliant coup.
The main defense against insurgency was the proliferation of primaries and state conventions. This sounds contradictory—what
could be more democratic than primaries?—but that was the point.
The Democratic leaders couldn't overtly take back the presidential
nomination; they had to make it seem as if they were doing the opposite. So the strategy: Let the people choose. However, with enough
primaries, caucuses, conventions—by 1976 some thirty-seven states
had one or another version—it was unlikely, to say the least, that any
candidate could come to the national convention with a command-
ing lead. In which event, the nomination would be brokered, and
everything would be back to normal and even better since the
"cover" was so in the tradition of democracy.*

*What the bosses couldn't figure on was Watergate; what they
didn't figure on was the media blitz that would accompany a few
early caucus and primary victories. As an "outsider," Carter was the
beneficiary of Watergate. As a "pro" who understood the news
media and the new rules, he stole a charge by picking up pluralities
in a crowded field during the opening stanzas. After that, Carter
needed one major industrial state in the North to prove that a south-
erner could win, and he found it in Pennsylvania. Once he won that
he was rounding third, and smelling that, on the eve of the Pennsylvania primary I wrote a piece for the Soho Weekly News, which will
follow.*

*Of course, the bosses could have stopped him after Pennsylvania,
and would have if they didn't know they could trust him. Carter lost
nine out of the last twelve primaries, which included a drubbing in
New York, but the leaders didn't lay a glove on him. Everything
about Carter told them he was malleable, and it was not without significance that Mayor Daley was the man who put him over the top.*

*Carter's presidency proved the bosses exactly right: He was in their
hands from start to finish. Indeed, he was so ineffectual he dumped*

himself. But the "trouble" he might have caused remained: The Dems were still open to an insurgency. If nothing changed, anybody could conceivably come out of nowhere and get himself nominated for President. What good is it to be an oligarch if you can't control the entrance to the Oval Office?

Well, now they have taken it back, grabbed it back. In an act so brazen it makes the Brink's job look like a candy store holdup, the Democratic bosses in March 1982 changed the convention rules from top to bottom, making it next to impossible for an outsider to win the nomination. It was done by the Democratic National Committee without a single spoken protest and over only a handful of "nay" votes.

Here are the highlights of the takeover:

- The "faithful delegate" rule, which bound delegates to vote for whichever candidate they were pledged to support, has been scrapped.
- Fourteen percent of the delegates to the national convention will be chosen on the basis of their office or party status and without commitment to a candidate. This hand-picked group will include up to three-fifths of all Democrats in both houses of Congress.
- Proportional representation, in which delegations are divided according to their share of the popular vote, is no longer a mandate for the state parties.
- The primary–caucus season has been cut from twenty to fifteen weeks, and bunched so that the Iowa caucus can come only eight days before the New Hampshire primary, and New Hampshire only a week before others.

So there you have it, 1984 in living color. In the colorful smoke-filled rooms of yore and lore, where once again the "pros" will be able to pick winners, just as they did in 1968.

In The Antioch Review piece, I ended up dropping a footnote: "After Goldwater's disastrous defeat, the Republican Right ceased to be trouble to the party, which is now virtually rid of its old ideological headaches." In the land of Reagan, what could have been less prophetic? But no embarrassment, what happened was Watergate. If not for Watergate, where would Reagan and the Right be today?

Where would they be had Ford not pardoned Nixon? The pardon resurrected Reagan and the Right, nearly depriving Ford of the nomination in 1976 and in the event the election. I said it better on the first guess in the Soho Weekly News. Read all about it!

HONEYMOON FOR JERRY— STOP THE PRESSES

IF WATERGATE TEACHES anything, it is that it is never too early to turn the fisheye on a President. From the moment he takes the oath he becomes, if not our natural enemy, at least our inevitable opponent. So it has been with every Chief Executive since Abraham Lincoln; is there anything in Gerald Ford's track record to indicate that he will break this hundred-year mold?

Quite the opposite. His long political career can only with charity be described as desultoriness in living color. Name a statute that would have benefited the common man, and Gerald Ford was lined up solidly against it; mention anything that would violate the Bill of Rights, or burden the poor, or smash the hopes of minorities, or harm the cities, and there was Ford hustling up votes for it in the House and on the hustings. If it appears that I exaggerate, consider that in his confirmation hearings for Vice-President, Ford could recall no issue on which he disagreed with Richard Nixon. When he finally thought of one, it turned out that he had opposed an administration proposal to divert part of the Highway Trust Fund for mass-transit development.

With our attention so long riveted on the complex saga of Watergate, it is likely that many of us have forgotten what Richard Nixon was doing to the country before the scandal broke. Was there ever an administration that so purposefully polarized the nation? Nixon and Agnew turned us against ourselves with a Law and Order orgy that pitted the good burghers of Middle America against the soft, elitist, liberal champions of the Black, Puerto Rican and Chicano. The media and the Supreme Court were under incessant attack, and before Nixon's first term was over, he had the journalists on the run and the High Court very nearly in his pocket.

The pre-Watergate litany is as long as it was once familiar: Cambodia, Laos, Kent State, the economy, the Christmas carpet-bombing, the impoundment of funds, the Southern Strategy. And in all of this medley of extemporania, Nixon could count on the faithful support of the minority leader of the House, Mr. Gerald Ford.

We are asked now to support an open-ended honeymoon for this "nice, big, easygoing guy," who has injected a "breath of fresh air" and a "Midwestern openness" into the presidency.

Is he maybe a little dumb? Well, what the hell, look where the smart guys have taken us. Does his record produce nausea? Well, gee, fella, the presidency has a way of making a person grow. Look at Harry Truman.

Since Truman is always floated as the quintessential example of the ordinary guy turning into the extraordinary President, there is nothing to do but look at him. He had some things in common with Ford. Both were party men, both cold warriors, and to the same degree: 100 percent. But Truman was smart, wily and a historian of sorts. For his time, he was a good, solid liberal in economic affairs. And yet, neither their similarities nor their differences are to the point of whether the Oval Office, like the old Yankee pinstripes, has a way of turning a journeyman into an all-star. For despite the herculean efforts of the columnists and scholars, the Truman presidency was, in its essentials, a failure and even a disgrace.

For all of his color and spunkiness, it was Truman who initiated a loyalty oath program that led inexorably to the McCarthy era; it was Truman who illegally seized the steel mills; it was Truman who went to war in Korea without congressional authorization, thus setting the stage for Vietnam; it was Truman who stacked the Supreme Court with hacks and cronies who later gave the legal imprimatur to some of the worst violations of civil liberties in history; and it was Truman who, after reluctantly recognizing the State of Israel, nearly throttled it in its crib by imposing a harsh arms embargo against it. Not to mention Hiroshima and Nagasaki.

Take away Truman—and I hope I have taken away Truman—and there is nothing left to the notion that the presidency, by itself, is capable of turning dross into gold. Indeed, a compelling case can be made *contra*, that the office turns promising men into mediocrities and worse.

Yet the satraps of the press and Congress are again busily weaving the presidency into a magic carpet, the better to sedate us against the past performance chart of Jerry Ford. That they do so in the immediate afterglow of Nixon shows how little they have learned from Watergate. Or, more likely, how little they want us to learn.

Do my eyes deceive me or are the same journalists who promised us that Richard Nixon would "grow" in the presidency now booking space in Gerald Ford's bedroom? I thought it was only yesterday that they convinced us that they had convinced themselves never to get too cozy with the Chief Executive. And yet no sooner was Tricky Dick on the Spirit of '76 than were the papers and the airwaves filled with talking pictures of that "good, decent big guy" who would "turn the country around again."

I like a nice smile as much as the next fellow. But whoever can laugh in your face can at the same time cut your throat. If that sounds rough, remember what Gerald Ford tried to do to Justice Douglas. All of which, I suppose, is a fancy way of saying that if off we must to Niagara, this time let's look at the falls.

—*Soho Weekly News*
August 15, 1974

BUT WHO'LL PARDON FORD?

WELL, THE COUNTRY boy said he didn't want a honeymoon, and now he doesn't even have a marriage. By his grotesque act on Sunday, he is locked out of our bedrooms for good, and however the deed may have damaged the rule of law, it is no small bargain that we won't have this "nice, easygoing guy" under our covers anymore. I was beginning to fwow up, as Miss Dorothy Parker once said, and as Miss Dorothy Parker also said, to her boyfriend, "fare thee well." From here on, until on the Bicentennial we retire him to Grand Rapids, Jerry Ford not only gets the fisheye, he gets the gate.

Maybe it's just my sunny disposish but I say it all works out to the good. It is true that the Nixon pardon is an abomination unto equal justice, unto simple fairness, unto the ghosts of Jefferson, Madison, Brandeis, Black, ter Horst and Warren. But what if he didn't do it? What if Ford had allowed Nixon to twist slowly, to indictment or even to conviction?

If we are to believe even partially in the polls, not to say our noses, the Republican party would have effectively beaten the Watergate rap, would have lost no more than twenty seats in the House come November. A number of statehouses, otherwise hopelessly lost to them, would have probably gone to them, including New York's. I don't care a damn for the Democrats, but I hope I care for rudimentary justice; what kind of justice would it be if the GOP survived this thing with a smile? Thumb-to-nose justice is what, and we would be back very close to where we started on the night Frank Wills found the tape on the Watergate door. Far more important that the Republicans get a measure of justice than that Nixon—who they

created, raised up and then resuscitated from the dust—take all that
there is to dish out.

It is not, when you think about it, a question of whether Nixon
has suffered enough. He is a man in flames, he suffers forever in the
knowledge that he will go down in the rathole of history. The better
he has it, the more money and encomiums he keeps, the more he is
hated by his countrymen. The day he quit he was dead, and when
you're dead you're gone. If I thought it would hurt him to dance on
the grave I'd be Gene Kelly. But you don't have to be the Luba-
vitcher Rebbe to know not to fool with the Unknown.

If Ford had held his peace, Nixon most certainly would have been
indicted. If indicted, a good 40 percent of the country would have
been with Nixon: the 20 percent who are with anything—that 20
percent who wanted to bomb North Vietnam the day we finally got
out—and another 20 percent of decent people who would have
thought we were going too far, that somehow it was wrong to put a
former President in the dock. Those who still believe that Nixon will
rise again ought to consider how easily he might have risen had we
gone all the way with him.

And in that connection, who will stand up and guarantee that he
would have been convicted? I've been around juries, on and off, for
fifteen years, and they've been good to me, but I would never—nor
would any other lawyer I've met—bet the bar tab on a verdict, not to
mention rent money. Suppose a jury acquitted Nixon? Or suppose
(more likely) a hung jury? Wouldn't that put the whole impeachment business in doubt? With Nixon already dead I'm not about to
play with the chance of one juror feeling sorry for him.

Now, thankfully, we won't have to mess with that possibility.
Ford, however inexplicably, took the nation off the hook while putting the Republican party back on the cross. In no event would he
have permitted Nixon to go to the slammer, even if there were a
judge courageous enough to put him there. So what, in practical
terms, have we lost? John Dean is in jail, to be sure; but however
much I value the People's Rat I didn't tell him to cop a plea. Nor
can I sit *shiva* over Gordon Liddy and the Cubans. As for Haldeman,
Ehrlichman, et al., I only wish I had their case. Wouldn't it be
heaven to defend Eichmann while Hitler lived by Ben-Gurion's pardon, in Tel Aviv? As to the Constitution, it survived Nixon and will
survive Ford.

Let it go. The only guy who is hurt by the events of Sunday is Mr.

Ford. And the Republican party. We have already dealt with the GOP, and it is a toast to the republic that we got Ford in the first month. He was continuously feted by the media despite that he had kept most of the Nixon Gang around, despite that he had appointed Haig to NATO, that he sounded like Hoover on the economy, that he resurrected Rocky and was as giving as a tight corset on amnesty. There is a poem goes with it, and since I obviously have Dorothy Parker on my mind, may she pardon my dust.

> For this Miss Van Horne warmed his bed
> And Scotty Reston cooled his head
> And Max Lerner and Mary McGrory
> Told a tale of Truman glory
> While Evans Novak and David Broder
> Reconditioned and tuned his motor
> And Jimmy Wechsler clipped his hair
> Why even Anthony Lewis was fair!
> They coaxed his infant nights to quiet
> And gave him roughage in his diet
> For this the pundits wrapped him warm
> That early on a Sunday morn
> He'd hear a whistle and drop his wits
> And break our hearts to clattering bits.
>
> —*Soho Weekly News*
> August 22, 1974

JIMMY CARTER ...
MY GOD!

A. J. LIEBLING led off his classic book on Earl Long with an observation as pithy as it was then indisputable.

"Southern political personalities, like sweet corn, travel badly," he wrote in *The Earl of Louisiana.* "They lose flavor with every hundred yards away from the patch. By the time they reach New York, they are like Golden Bantam that has been trucked up from Texas—stale and unprofitable."

Jimmy Carter's sorry show in the Democratic primary here made Liebling's Law smell fresh as the corn at the plantation, and if that were not enough, his "ethnic purity" line sure was. Yet Jimmy Carter lives, and if the polls are to be credited he lives very well indeed, or at least well enough to be leading the field in the Pennsylvania primary. The world has changed plenty since 1960 when Joe Liebling gave us his great essay on Southern politics. The ringing question facing a sleepless electorate is whether it has changed enough to give the barefoot boy with Bible a clear shot at the Oval Office.

I confess that I do not understand Carter's appeal. We are told, on the primitive level, that he reminds people of Jack Kennedy; primitive because it is never said that the reminder has anything to do with substantive issues. The message is that he is handsome, that he has the Kennedy aura, the glamour of semi-Camelot if not the ever-elusive real McCoy. But when did a freckle-faced middle-aged pol with liver lips turn into a sex symbol in America? He smiles, to be sure, but as has been noted, he has too many teeth. With the proper *Advertising Age* tail wind, his hair flaps, but that hair is nothing like Jack's, even if we forget that Kennedy cut his mop to look mature. As for Camelot, the most that can be said is that Carter has some of Jack's taxi squad around him; otherwise he has neither the poets nor the Harvards, not to say the Angie Dickinson Brigade.

He does resemble Kennedy in his cold war vision, which is as one with Scoop Jackson's, just as the senator from Boeing was as one with JFK. But that is not what his backers wish to emphasize; to the contrary, they and he seek to present him as a peacemaker, even as they invoke Admiral Rickover and his Trident nuclear submarines.

If he is not Kennedy, is he Eisenhower? We are told that too; the implication being that, like Ike, he is a smoothie from the sticks who is all things to all men. This line comes mainly from his enemies, who continue to believe that Eisenhower was unpopular in the country, but sometimes it comes from his legions who insist that Middle America demands a return to blandness. Is it possible, then, to be a combination of Kennedy and Eisenhower, despite that Jack ran against the "do-nothing" Eisenhower image? It is a mushy notion, but then mush is what we are told we want, after Vietnam, after Watergate, after mushy old Jerry Ford, who the last time I looked we still had.

It's a puzzlement, to borrow from Oscar Hammerstein, who if he did not create Carter would likely have been on his national committee, and may still be on it given the sainted Jimmy's connections with heaven. To be fair to his ghost, Hammerstein would have blanched at "ethnic purity"—didn't he teach us that we have to be taught to hate?—but we must assume that like all angels he reads the *Times,* and if he reads the *Times,* he reads Scotty Reston, who instructed us the other day that we ought not be brutish about Carter's "tongue-slip." Why worry that a man who ran with Lester Maddox promises never to promote the "intrusion" of blacks into the ethnic treasure that is America? I don't like the idea of transplanting black ghettos into suburbia, but I don't like it because ghettos are ghettos wherever they are. The irreducible fact is, however, that the federal government has not been doing anything like it or even thinking about doing it for more than five years. When Carter raises it, he is setting up a straw man, and if he is not doing this to appeal to racism, why then is he doing it?

He is a mountebank, and the worst kind at that; is it possible that we can take seriously a Bible-toter who claims that he has been "reborn"? The only way to understand the Carter phenomenon is by reference to his own old-time religion. He is the "Devil least known," and in a country that has known little else, this may appear as nirvana. It takes a heap of despair to turn a nation that threw out Tricky Dick into a receptacle for a piece of goods that can't be taken out into the sunlight. My prayer is that it hasn't come to that, and my real prayer is that I don't have to rely on prayer. The last time my kind went one-to-one with his kind . . . well, what's Easter Sunday for?

—*Soho Weekly News*
April 22, 1976

MAKIN' WHOOPEE

NO SOONER DID Abe Reles, that premier gossip of the first half of the twentieth century, go out the window of the Half Moon Hotel in Coney Island, than one of his old troopers in Murder, Inc., raised the wine glass with this classic: "To a great canary—who could sing, only he couldn't fly."

Comes now Elizabeth Ray, who we are told can write, only she couldn't type, who can sing, only she couldn't talk. Poor Wayne Hays. Whereas the Mob had the luxury of the Brooklyn police guarding Abie, the congressman has to suffer the FBI carrying cases of Coca-Cola to Ms. Ray's luxury flat in Arlington, Virginia. When the feds start washing informers in soft drinks, let the condemned salute.

Nor, of course, did Reles have a literary agent, let alone a mass paperback in bound galleys when he began fingering citizens who had hired him to compromise other citizens. Thus, once he met the Maker, his damage was done. But if an untoward event should interfere with Ms. Ray's witness, there will always be the Book, which however *roman*, promises to leave little to the imagination. So the Half Moon solution is out, and if the advance word on her memoir can be but half believed, so is Wayne Hays and so maybe is half the Congress.

According to sources close to *The New York Times*, Lady Ray was to the Congress what girls of easy virtue used to be referred to in my neighborhood as "train jobs," meaning that they ran from car to car. Her "novel" will depict her "heroine"—and many others of similar persuasion—as being on "total call" to members of Congress and even to their important constituents.

"Sex was the biggest game in town, it was all anybody up there thought about," Ms. Ray is quoted as saying to a friend, who told it to the *Times.*

Ah, if it were only true. Imagine if all that our legions thought about was the bedroom! Would there be war, inflation, recession, tax shelters for the rich, tax burdens for the poor, cities facing bankruptcy? Would there be crime, would there be slums? And, if we can include the Imperial Presidency—and why not, given the testimony of Judith Exner and Dorothy Schiff?—would there be anything but love sweeping the country if our Chief Executives could secure in the boudoir what they otherwise seem able only to secure in the battlefield?

We are told by none other than Woodstein that Mr. Nixon last shared connubial pleasures with Pat in 1962. If this is so, is it any wonder that he sought to stride the nation, the world? Would Watergate have been avoided had "total call" been available to San Clemente?

But alas, Freud, like Marx, is explained best by his inconsistencies. For every rumored Puritan there is a swordsman; for every impotent there is a potentate. The Archangel Woodrow was a ladykiller, which did not stop him from creating World War I. Harding, the isolationist, had a mistress in the White House. FDR, the interventionist, had Lucy Mercer and maybe Dolly Schiff. Harry Truman was faithful and we got the Bomb and Korea. Kennedy had them all and the Bay of Pigs to boot. LBJ liked to brag to reporters about Lady Bird and her skills, but however great she performed, the people of Vietnam received no benefits. Tricky Dick we have discussed, and Jerry Ford goes better unsaid, but anyway he was appointed.

So the evidence appears incontrovertible: Be they glad or sad in the sack, our leaders will do what they will do.

Does this mean that sex is irrelevant in the capital? Not a chance. What good is it to hire a pretty secretary if she can type? My Uncle Nunchik never did such a thing in the garment center. Only they shouldn't be able to write, my Uncle Nunchik knew that. And if they could sing, they shouldn't be able to fly, my cousin Lepke knew that. Even if, like Wayne Hays, he knew it a little late.

—*Soho Weekly News*
June 3, 1976

HOLLYWOOD'S
IRON LAW COMES
TO WASHINGTON

THE OLD HOLLYWOOD panjandrums had nothing on Jimmy Carter, though if they were alive today they might have a suit against him for copyright infringement. In the glory days of the great studios, the caliphs established a policy that became an iron law quicker than you could say "Harry Cohn Is a White Fang." Like its founders, the law did not fool around; it admitted of no exceptions, except when it had to, and when it had to, nobody admitted it.

And the iron law was this: Nothing Succeeds Like Failure. So if a genius lost a few million on a picture, he was immediately installed in a fancier office with a better title and a bigger budget to squander on the next project. Only after nine straight flops was he eligible to become head of the studio.

If Mr. Carter has been less insistent on quantity, he has erected higher qualitative standards than the movie moguls ever deemed possible, and there was not much they didn't deem possible. To cadge a really big job in this administration, a man has to have been intricately involved in momentous disasters; failing that, he can make it only if he can prove lack of opportunity coupled with strong and frequent endorsements of catastrophic policies.

This latter category was established to accommodate Dr. Zbigniew Brzezinski, but in the event it served also to cinch the case for Griffin Bell. Brzezinski was not quite old enough, or at least not sufficiently known, to have been credited with Vietnam during the Kennedy–Johnson era. When he ripened, he was, alas, largely blocked out of the Nixon holocaust on the grounds that there was room for only one Kissinger at a time. He managed, however, to make his name—if not its pronunciation—a metaphor for the cold war, and thus emerged early as Carter's key foreign-policy adviser, first among equals with Dean Rusk, whose qualifications go without saying, and indeed go so well that he was barred from the Cabinet as being in the nature of overkill. Even in Hollywood there were limits, though none come to mind; but be assured there were limits, if only theoretical.

As for Mr. Bell: He was a borderline case, an iffy proposition, despite his crony label, his vote to exclude Julian Bond from the Georgia Legislature, his club memberships, his humdrum judicial record, his flirtation with segregated schools. There was something missing, as if the whole were not equal to the sum of its parts. To put him across, to make him a natural for Justice, there had to be a true association with a colossal failure. Finally it surfaced, in the form of a warm, hearty endorsement for G. Harrold Carswell's nomination to the Supreme Court. Bell was now comfortably within the Brzezinski Accommodation, and the fact that he tried to hide it, and then dissembled, proved conclusively to the President-elect that he had one of the finest losers in the country, never mind the South.

Other choices were less complicated, and none was more obvious than Harold Brown for secretary of defense. As a protégé of Edward Teller, Dr. Brown was the legitimate Son of the H-bomb who grew up to be one of McNamara's bad boys in the halcyon days of the Vietnam war. At a time when certain hard-liners in the department were making fuzzy noises about bombing pauses, Brown stood up for an expansion of napalm to civilian areas. Faced with this "charge," Brown explained that he had simply "passed along" the idea, and when he said that it was no contest, Carter had his man for fair.

Cyrus Vance was a snap for secretary of state, having failed us under Johnson in the Defense Department and again under Nixon at the Paris peace tables. James Schlesinger was perfect for energy czar, since he could not even satisfy Ford at Defense and is odds-on to disillusion the conservationists. And of course, no one could match Theodore Sorensen for the CIA, what with his grounding in the Bay of Pigs.

A tidy package that bodes well for the future. The President faces several difficult challenges, particularly when openings occur on the Supreme Court. His predecessors—most notably Truman and

Nixon—have set nearly unreachable standards there, but the field is lush. In virtually every state there are judges who have been over-ruled so often that the mere mention of their names brings down the inevitable response: "And what is the second ground for reversal?" If the organized bar won't provide Mr. Carter with these candidates, I'll send him a few who'll make Carswell look like Justice Holmes.

But everybody's going to have to chip in with ideas. Congress is likely to create one hundred new federal judgeships, which is like opening all the back lots again. Can the President find enough pro-ducers to guarantee a dozen *Cleopatras* before the fiscal year is out? You can depend on it, and, like they say, hooray for Hollywood.

—*New York* magazine
January 24, 1977

TEDDY KENNEDY—
LEGAL RIGHTS
IN INQUEST

*Everybody wanted to cover the Teddy Kennedy–Mary Jo Kopechne
inquest on Martha's Vineyard, set for September 3, 1969. I wanted
to be there because I suspected there'd be no inquest. Why not? A
week earlier the judge had set ground rules that denied Kennedy the
most elemental guarantees of due process. This ruling had been universally regarded in the press as a major defeat for Kennedy, but I
smelled yakahoola. This was, after all, Massachusetts, where nobody denied the Kennedys anything, much less due process of law. I
figured it was a good shot that the judge was accommodating Teddy
by giving him perfect grounds to stop the music in the upper courts.*

*The Times had assigned Joseph Lelyveld, one of its top reporters,
to cover the story. I persuaded the editors to send me along to do the
legal analyses.*

*I arrived at the Edgartown Inn around cocktail hour on Labor
Day, two days before the scheduled inquest. One look at the bar
scene and I was sure there'd be no inquest, not at that time. The
whole damn world press was bellied up—there must have been two
hundred reporters milling about. Anytime was better than right now
for Ted Kennedy. No way he'd go into an open courtroom in front of
that crowd. His lawyers would try for an injunction in Boston, no
doubt about it.*

*Lacey Fosburgh, then a cub reporter, was on hand to assist us. I
asked her to charter a plane for Boston late in the morning; I knew*

all the commercial flights would be booked on the day after Labor Day, and as it turned out, it was no small job getting a charter.

Joe Lelyveld was understandably hesitant to leave the scene—he was expected to file a mood preview on the eve of the inquest—but I was so sure I was right it got contagious.

The next morning, in the cab on the way to the courthouse, we heard a radio bulletin. The Kennedy lawyers were moving to halt the inquest in the Supreme Judicial Court of Massachusetts. Joe sighed with relief. I laughed, thinking of all those hangover cases scrambling around trying to get nonexistent charters out of Edgartown.

While waiting for the hearing to begin, I studied Kennedy's petition. Buried deep within this lengthy document, in a manner calculated to keep the layman from understanding its import and meaning, was a remarkable demand. Kennedy was asking the Supreme Court to bar the press from the inquest! He hadn't made this demand before; indeed, he kept saying he wanted everything spread out front—he had nothing to hide. When I asked his lawyers about it, they nervously shook me off with "no comment." Jim Flug, Kennedy's legislative assistant, valiantly tried to convince me I was off on a tangent, but I knew Jim and Jim knew better. Once Kennedy asked for a secret tribunal, everything else was tangential.

But I couldn't convince Joe Lelyveld, who barely mentioned the issue in his page-one story. Since none of the other papers noticed it, the piece that follows stands alone.

FOR ALL THEIR apparent complexity, there now appears to be an almost preordained simplicity to the legal events that culminated yesterday in a court order temporarily halting the inquest here into the death of Mary Jo Kopechne. In the wake of that injunction, one ruling has emerged as the critical factor that made possible, if not inevitable, the suspension of the inquest, with which all the principals said they wanted to proceed. This was the decision August 27 by Judge James A. Boyle of the Edgartown District Court denying the request of Senator Edward M. Kennedy's lawyers to conduct the inquest according to the due process standards that prevail in criminal trials.

From the moment Judge Boyle refused to permit Mr. Kennedy's attorneys to cross-examine witnesses, introduce evidence, raise objec-

tions or remain in court throughout the proceedings, virtually all lawyers recognized that the senator could halt the inquest if he wanted
to.

It is a well-ingrained principle that restraining orders are granted
whenever there are serious legal questions concerning a proceeding
that may irreparably damage a person.

While Judge Boyle's ruling appeared to some to be a serious set-
back for the senator, from the Kennedy viewpoint it had virtues easily recognizable to experienced lawyers. For it provided Mr. Kennedy
with an eminently legitimate fallback position in the event that he
later wanted to put off the inquest.

That this fact was not lost on the Kennedy attorneys seemed apparent the other day when a source close to the senator smiled
knowingly at the suggestion of a lawyer-friend that Judge Boyle had
"played right into your hands."

A few knowledgeable lawyers wondered aloud yesterday what
might have happened had Judge Boyle granted a full-scale, due process inquest.

"If the judge granted the request for cross-examination and the
like," one said, "I don't see how Kennedy could have moved to enjoin the inquest. The only grounds left to him would have been the
publicity angle, but I believe it would have been politically impossible for him to have demanded a secret hearing if he got everything
else he asked for.

"It's also very questionable whether he'd be on firm legal ground,
since he'd be receiving a virtual trial, complete with constitutional
protections, and trials are always public."

It is entirely possible, of course, that Mr. Kennedy would have
been satisfied with a public inquest if he had been provided with
constitutional guarantees, and, indeed, his lawyers did not ask Judge
Boyle to close the hearing to the press.

But this fact was seen by some legal authorities as a two-edged
sword. They suggested that political strategy might have dictated restraint in requesting a closed hearing until the motion for a due process inquest was lost.

In support of this theory, they pointed out that Mr. Kennedy
asked for the first time yesterday that the Supreme Judicial Court in
Boston quash Judge Boyle's order permitting the press into the inquest.

The senator also said in his petition that Judge Boyle had acted "in error" in stating that he, Mr. Kennedy, would have to appear as a witness. While he did not specifically demand that he not be made to testify, he said that the original demand that he do so violated his right.

This was in apparent contradiction to his earlier statement that he would voluntarily testify.

It is thus not clear whether he will take the position that he cannot be called to the witness stand, even if he is granted his full constitutional rights and even if the inquest is held in secret.

In any event, the public impact of the senator's request for a closed hearing and also the implication that he not be called as a witness appeared to have been significantly blunted by the strategy of coupling this wish for a demand for due process.

Thus, some people here directed their criticism at what they considered Mr. Kennedy's "taking advantage" of "legal technicalities," such as the right of cross-examination. On the other hand, lawyers were beginning yesterday to question Judge Boyle's ruling rather than Senator Kennedy's objections.

For example, it seemed to some legal experts that Judge Boyle could have granted the request for a due process inquest.

They said the United States Supreme Court in June had held that cross-examination and full assistance of counsel were required in hearings held by a Louisiana labor investigating unit under circumstances rather analogous to an inquest.

Moreover, on a more pragmatic basis, the lawyers noted that a judge was always safe in granting more rights than might be required. They said that Judge Boyle's court was far from overcrowded and that it could operate if the inquest took a few extra days because of a grant of procedural rights to the senator and other witnesses.

But, of course, Judge Boyle said no, and if this gave Senator Kennedy the occasion to move for a temporary injunction, it did not altogether decide the issue for him.

By most accounts, the senator was undecided until the last minute as to whether to try to stop the inquest, apparently because he was concerned with what people might say.

Why then did he move for the injunction? And why does he now want the inquest to be a secret proceeding?

Nobody involved is answering that question, though most informed observers believed that the decision was made on the advice of Mr. Kennedy's astute lawyers.

And while no one can be sure, not a few sophisticated legal authorities have suggested that the usual reason for advising a client to avoid a public hearing is that the lawyer does not feel the client will acquit himself well on the witness stand.

—*The New York Times*
September 3, 1969

Two months later, the Supreme Judicial Court granted Kennedy's demand for a secret inquest. It was held in Edgartown in January 1970. The transcripts were not released until the spring. They showed how a judge who once appeared to be contemptuous of Kennedy's rights became a one-man civil liberties union for Teddy. The prosecutor, who could have convened a grand jury and certainly should have done so once the press was barred from the inquest, lobbed his questions like a batting practice pitcher. So nothing ever happened, and if that ain't yakahoola, what's yakahoola?

THE IRA AND CAREY

At the bar of Mrs. Ford's Skeffington Arms Hotel, Galway, in the autumn of 1965, an old fella buttonholed me.

"And did you say your name was Zion?" he asked.

"I did."

"And could you be Jewish?"

"I am."

"Ah," he said. "Ah, tell us. Tell us how you kicked the shit out of the English."

It kicked the bejesus out of me that the old guy just assumed I'd know about the great Hebrew Revolution conducted by the Jews of Palestine against the British Empire from 1944 to 1948. Few American Jews are aware there was a revolution; they think the State of Israel was created by Harry Truman and Chaim Weizmann in the back rooms of the United Nations. But I knew plenty and so was able to regale the bar with the derring-do exploits of the Stern Gang and the Irgun.

"Do you mean to say you hanged three British soldiers in Natanya?"

"And do you say you flogged Brit sergeants in Tel Aviv?"

"Are you telling us you kidnapped English officers and held 'em for ransom?"

Ah, they kept saying, ah, have another drink.

No "dual loyalty" problem at Mrs. Ford's place; I was a Jew and therefore an Israeli. Theodore Herzl never dreamt that high.

Well, I always liked the Irish. From that moment on I loved them. But not all Irishmen.

I have contempt for those who hector and lecture the girls and boyos battling to get out from under the fancy British boot that held the Island in thrall for eight centuries and continues to zap the

Northern Counties through its implanted Ulster gunmen. I've never heard a good answer to the ancient question: "What's an English soldier doing on Irish soil?" The British line, that they're only there to prevent a "bloodbath," may be acceptable to The New York Times editorial board and to those belly rolls who run the St. Patrick's Day parade. And of course to the Dublin government, which plays the English card for all the filthy lucre it's worth. But I don't buy it any more than the IRA buys it—nor any more than my old heroes in the Irgun and Stern Group bought it.

The column that follows ran in the Soho Weekly News, April 28, 1977, right after Governor Hugh Carey of New York delivered his broadside against the IRA at the Royal College of Surgeons—catch that name—in Dublin. It was immediately reprinted by most of the Irish press in America. For years, I'd been casually friendly with Huey. After this I no longer registered on his retina. L'chaim!

THE AMERICAN IRISH have come a long way since Big Bill Thompson could run for Mayor of Chicago against the King of England and win hands down. You should pardon my Jewish accent if I wonder whether maybe they haven't made too much progress, or at least their top elected officials, who appear to have nothing better to do these days than make word wars against the IRA.

On the eve of St. Patrick's Day, the Four Horsemen of the Irish–American political establishment—Kennedy, Carey, O'Neill, and Moynihan—unburdened their collective conscience with a demand that their landsmen here quit running guns and money to the provos in the Six Counties. Now Mr. Carey, in Dublin to deliver a speech to the Royal College of Surgeons, turned the event into a diatribe that made the old Gatling guns sound serene.

"If the provisionals were simply called 'the Irish killers' and the others 'the Irish Marxists,' " the governor said about the two wings of the IRA, "people would see what they stood for, and they wouldn't receive a nickel's worth of support in the United States."

But if that is all they were, it wouldn't matter a ha'penny what they were called; they'd be out of business and would have been out of business long ago. No revolutionary movement could survive as "apostles of death and violence" (Carey's compassionate description); the IRA lives because the Catholics in the North are treated like dirt under the feet of the Ulster hegemony. It is for this reason, not for "romantic" notions of unification, that arms and money are supplied by Irish Americans. The IRA never got far here with a purely political appeal to make the nation whole, just as they could get nowhere with it in the republic, not even among the majority of Catholics in the Six Counties.

Indeed, the Northern Catholics have been the most patient of people, demanding next to nothing for the most of the fifty-odd years since partition, and little more than minimal rights today. But every appeal to reason has met with the gun and the club, every effort to negotiate has been answered with deceit, discrimination, and heavier repression. The Bloody Sunday of eight years ago initiated only the latest chapter in an ugly history that dates back eight hundred years, or ever since the British Empire began its unremitting devastation of Ireland. Against this background, Mr. Carey asks rhetorical questions.

"Is the assassin the best hope for positive political change? Is the bomber to be trusted to end economic or religious persecution? Is it human rights that flows from the barrel of a gun? Just what is this mad fascination with killing and burning?"

The Black and Tans must have had a beautiful night in hell toasting this gratuitous libel, which could hardly have been equaled by the head of the Ulster Brigade. You can read the governor's broadside end to end and find not a word against the brutalities of the Ulstermen, which outweigh the excesses of the provos as Hugh Carey outweighs Stevie Cauthen. And of course, nothing whatever about the English, who have armed Ulster to the teeth and whose presence in the country makes peace and justice an impossibility.

But what has Carey and the Irish Establishment ever said or done about the tragic conditions of the people they claim to love? The Four Horsemen who signed the St. Patrick's Day Lecture have plenty of clout with the President of the United States; yet in all of Mr. Carter's morality play on human rights there is not so much as a bit part for Northern Ireland. We can exert extraordinary leverage on Great Britain, but in the face of a report from a respected, neutral international commission detailing the most egregious violations of Irishmen in English prisons, we have done nothing and Carey and his pals have kept their mouths shut. It's not on the "agenda," just as it has never been on the agenda of the United Nations, and the whole thing is so reminiscent of the Hebrew Revolution in Palestine,

1944 to 1948, that pardon me if I no longer pardon my Jewish accent.

The Zionist Establishment here and in Palestine condemned the revolutionary Irgun and Stern Group in precisely the terms used today by Carey and the Irish Republican government. American Jews were exhorted to turn their backs on the "killers and assassins" who were "madly" shooting English soldiers in the back. Nothing but disaster could come of it, we were told, even as the British army brutalized the Jews and fed arms to the Arabs.

Years later, Churchill cheerfully conceded that had it not been for the Irgun and Sternists, the British would never have left the Holy Land. Nobody knows this better than the Irish on the spot, and nobody less than the Irish of Southampton. Or as Ben Hecht put it to the Jews of Park Avenue: "The fight is between the terrorists and the terrified."

—*Soho Weekly News*
April 28, 1977

V.

SPORTS: WINNERS AND LOSERS

THE TROUBLED
WORLD OF
MIKE BURKE

In the spring of 1977, nearly six years after the Ellsberg affair, I was asked to write again for The New York Times Magazine. Martin Arnold, my old buddy from the newsroom, was appointed to a top editorial spot on the magazine, and he called me first thing. We met at Sardi's bar and Marty said, "Pick a story and go to work." And the blacklist? "It's all over," he said. "Abe Rosenthal wants you, Arthur Gelb wants you, and obviously I want you." How about Ed Klein, the new editor-in-chief of the magazine, did he want me too? "Of course."

There were a few scary moments when I wasn't sure the forthcoming Mike Burke piece would be published. I delivered it during the summer, and after it was accepted I took off for Spain. I thought it would run while I was over there, but when I got back after Labor Day, it not only hadn't appeared, it looked as if it might never go.

During my absence, a rumor circulated that Mike Burke was about to be fired by Gulf & Western, the conglomerate that owns Madison Square Garden, the Knicks, the Rangers, and so on. Somehow this rumor got to Ed Klein. Since I wasn't around, Klein asked Sam Goldaper, who covers the Knicks for the Times, to check it out. Innocent as to the ways of sportswriters and their special connections to the people they cover, Klein, when asked by Goldaper what kind of piece I'd written on Burke, told him it was "critical" of the Great Mike. Goldaper reported back that Burke could be fired imminently. So the piece was iced. You can't run a cover on a guy who might be out before the story appears.

I heard about this the night I got back from Spain, and of course I smelled a rat. I figured Burke floated the rumor about his demise in order to foreclose what he now knew was a tough piece, and that he then "confirmed" the story to his pal Goldaper. A smarmy game.

I reached him in Paris. Was he about to be canned? Maybe yes, maybe no. Had he heard anything about my piece? He'd heard, from Goldaper, that it was a "hatchet job." I said I never wrote hatchet jobs, only the truth. Now would he tell me the truth: Would the Times be embarrassed if my piece ran, in the sense that he might be gone before it appeared? Mike Burke said, "Yes, it could very well be embarrassing." I asked him, "If you were the editor, would you kill it?" He said, "Yes." I said, "Mike, it's a cover story." He said, "I wouldn't run it."

That was enough for me and it was enough for Ed Klein. If Mike Burke, one of the best self-promoters of all time, didn't want a cover story in the Times, it wasn't because it would embarrass the Times, just that it would embarrass Mike Burke.

The piece hit a gusher in the fandom of New York. Burke had enjoyed a fabulous press, despite an unrelieved history of failure. He was the Inspector Clouseau of the sports world, but you'd never know it reading the papers. I suspected his reputation couldn't survive a single exposé, that even the sportswriters would have to stifle the praise once somebody ran his record. I knew the Garden wouldn't fire him, but at least it wouldn't be the same for him again. I was right on both counts. He stayed there till his recent retirement, only nobody talked about him anymore.

It was a few days after the story ran that the New York Post, now under the rule of Rupert Murdoch, hired me to write a twice-a-week column. It suffices to say that Mike Burke sure as hell put me back in the newspaper business.

HERE WE ARE on the lip of the big sports season at the Garden, and this guy wants me to believe that Mike Burke is in trouble. Any day now, the guy says, Mike Burke is liable to be called into one of those wraparound offices atop the Gulf & Western building and told that his services as president of Madison Square Garden, president of the New York Knickerbockers, chairman of the New York Rangers, impresario of boxing, grand master of Holiday on Ice, are no longer considered to be in the best interests of Gulf & Western Industries, Inc.

The guy telling me this knows that I've been working on a piece about Mike Burke, and he's letting me in on it because he's worried that I'd be embarrassed if the piece is published just as Mike Burke is getting his walking papers. Of course, the guy adds, he is not absolutely certain that such a thing will happen; indeed, he concedes that nobody in a position to cashier Mike Burke has said a word to him. What he is getting, however, are vibrations. Not off-the-wall rumors, real vibrations.

Who is this guy saying these things about Mike Burke?

Mike Burke.

Well, I'm a big believer in vibrations, and if Mike Burke was getting them about anyone else but Mike Burke, it would be plenty good enough for me. But then, if anyone else was running Madison Square Garden, we'd all *know* he was in trouble, no vibrations necessary.

The Garden, that ultimate fantasy for every budding Rocky, has been on a downslide the past few years, owing largely to the dismal performances of its wholly owned centerpieces, the Knicks and Rangers. When Burke took over in the summer of 1973, the Knicks were World Champs and the Rangers were running a record streak of playoff seasons. In short order, both teams were nowhere. As a result, ticket sales dropped way off, and since the Garden depends on basketball and hockey to close up an annual deficit of about $4 million, it's no surprise that the arena lost money last year.

The Ali–Shavers fight promised to give the Garden a big shot in the arm, but thanks to an almost laughable failure to sign Shavers on the spot, it nearly KO'd the joint, as we'll see.

And these things are as nothing compared with the looming threat of the New Jersey Meadowlands, which will pop up with a plant as big as the Garden—thanks to a loophole in a Knicks–Nets contract that allowed the Nets to move to Jersey. In two years, the Meadowlands—only fifteen minutes from Broadway—will house rock concerts, title fights, wrestling, hockey and basketball. And then the Garden may really know loneliness.

In the ordinary course of conglomerate life, the man on top of such an elephant would be lopped off, guilty or not, and no defense allowed. But this has never been the case with Mike Burke, whose star has risen in inverse proportion to the success of his teams, beginning with the Yankees in the mid-sixties.

So why is he telling me he's in trouble?

To check his vibrations, I call around, and it turns out that there are rumors going both ways. The flack at Gulf & Western, however, scotches the thing, says there's nothing to it. And adds: "I hear you're doing a hatchet job on Mike."

I find that interesting and put it to Burke, who says he's heard the same, from a sportswriter. And adds: "I've got one foot up in the air and one foot down. I could be gone any day or I could stay, I don't know."

We're left to wonder, and knowing how well Mike Burke understands the press, I can't help but wonder whether that's not what his vibrations were about. Uncertainty is as good a way as any to kill a story, and the only thing that's certain is that we have come a long way since the first time we sat down together at Gallagher's Steak House and Mike Burke wondered why I would ever want to write about him.

It was a perfect summer night, and Burke popped the question over coffee, after a couple of hours of talk about the Yankees, the Knicks, the Rangers, the Garden, the Ringling Brothers and Barnum & Bailey Circus, the OSS, CBS, and the University of Pennsylvania football team—all of them institutions Burke has headed, or otherwise been prominently associated with, across the years. There was no fake diffidence involved; it was clear that Burke wasn't asking why, he was asking why *now*. And seemingly he had a point, for the city was not talking about Mike Burke at the moment; it was up in arms over Mets president M. Donald Grant for trading Tom Seaver to the Cincinnati Reds.

But Grant, however much in the headlines, isn't a story, he's a one-liner. "He's the guy," Murray Kempton says, "who throws you out of the all-night movie at three in the morning because you're trying to sleep."

Burke is a modern phenomenon, his success as much a product of his times as his talents. It's hard to believe he would have made it big in the good old days, when nice guys finished last. Burke is the quintessential nice guy whose teams finish last, or close to it, while he moves onward and upward. He was president of the New York Yankees from 1966 to 1972, the worst period in the team's history, save for the pre–Babe Ruth period. When the Yanks were sold, he got a piece of the team plus a fat consulting contract—and walked directly into the top spot at the Garden.

How does Mike Burke do it? *That* promises to be a story, though when he asks me why I want to write about him, I don't put it just so. It happens that at the moment I'm thinking about Herkie Lewin's face.

At a dinner party last spring, my pal Herkie Lewin is moaning and groaning with the rest of us over the grim fact that we will again face a playoff season in New York without the Knicks and Rangers. Finally the hostess, in an effort to perk us up, says: "What are you guys crying about? Think of how poor Mike Burke must feel."

All eyes turn to Lewin, the eyes have no choice. A strange sound is coming out of him, and his face is transformed into a lobster's claw. "Poor . . . Mike . . . Burke," he sputters. "You . . . have . . . the . . . nerve . . ." He starts, stops, starts, stops, ultimately goes with what he's got, a sound something like a busted muffler. And does it in a stream, like so:

Kiss of death the man's the goddamn kiss of death everything the man touches Yankees Rangers Knicks nothing too big the circus the man had the Big Top where's the Big Top now institutions fall no roots deep enough the man wipes out dynasties you have the gall to give us poor Mike Burke what are you some kind of sportswriter poor Mike Burke my———no I won't stand for it I won't have it no goddammit no.

I can't tell this story to Burke. Brash is brash, but he's sitting right next to me, matching me Perrier water to Johnnie Black, he's pleasant as can be. I can't tell him this and I can't tell him a host of others like it, such as the night Danny, the ubiquitous Sardi's bartender, began pounding his fist after hearing me talk about doing a piece on Burke.

"Mike Burke?" he says. "What do you wanna do *him* for? He's terrible, he's awful, he's the worst. What'd he ever do but take winners and turn 'em into losers? What would you want with him?"

I tell Danny to watch it, I'm liable to quote him.

"Sure quote me, you can quote me. Say Danny Fiorio said it, F-I-O-R-I-O."

Bartenders blast a lot, but never for attribution. A few nights later I check back with him, figuring he's cooled off. Does he really want me to quote him? "F-I-O-R-I-O," he says.

Since I won't tell him these stories, then how do I answer Mike

Burke on why I'm writing about him? "It seems as if there are two Mike Burkes," I say. "There is one you read about on the sports pages and hear about at Elaine's, at '21,' in the Hamptons. That one is Mike Burke the Good, the Class Guy, the Finest.

"On the other hand, there are certain bars around Broadway where if you say a nice word about Mike Burke you'd better duck."

I'm not sure he's heard any of this criticism. True, he has always been a highly visible figure, mingling with the crowds at Yankee Stadium, walking around the stands during Knick and Ranger games. But fans, as a rule, don't berate bosses face to face, unless the sportswriters are after them, and not always then. The papers have never jumped on Burke; to the contrary, he enjoys a superb press, the best in the business, a press that consistently praises him—compare the treatment of George Steinbrenner, who brought the Yankees home a winner for the first time in a dozen years—and has failed to reflect a hint of fan antipathy toward Burke. So maybe he doesn't know, who knows?

He nods gravely. "I know what you're talking about," he says. "I've heard it, I've heard it plenty. I get it at the Garden. I walk through the stands—I think it's important to do that, you have to let the fans know you care, I did it with the Yankees—and I hear it. 'Burke, you S.O.B., Burke you ruined the Yanks, you ruined the Knicks, you ruined the Rangers, Burke you b———.'"

What does he do when that happens, what does he say?

"The night Giacomin went to Detroit, [Eddie Giacomin, the immensely popular Ranger goalie, was waived to the Red Wings two years ago] I went up into the stands. I was nearly mobbed. The fans were agitated, they loved Eddie, and I understood that, he was part of the chemistry of the team. . . .

"But one guy went over the line, said he'd like to belt me one. That was too much, that got to me. I grabbed his arm. 'Okay,' I said, 'let's go outside.' His buddies were watching so he had no choice, he had to take me up on it.

"We walked around the block. I kept talking to him, I don't recall what I said, I just talked to him. After a few minutes he stopped, put his hand out, and said, 'Mike, you're all right.'"

Last year, after a Knick game, a bunch of guys hung back in the stands, drowning out another defeat in their beer. They spotted Burke on the Garden floor and began spitting obscenities at him.

"I got goddam mad," he says, his eyes showing the Irish. "I went after them, ran right up into the seats. 'Here I am, now say it again, tell me to my face.'

"For a second it was quiet, I guess they were taken aback. Then one of them laughed nervously, and then the others laughed, and one guy handed me a beer."

Well. Wow! Mike Burke did that? Mike Burke took a guy outside? He's big enough to do it, sure; at 6 feet 1 inch and 180 pounds, he's very near his playing weight of the late 1930s when he starred as halfback for the University of Pennsylvania. With his Captain Kangaroo hairdo and mod clothes, he looks at least a decade younger than his fifty-nine years. He's brave enough, that's also for sure. He was a major hero in World War II, winning a Silver Star for a cloak-and-dagger operation that preceded the Allied invasion of Salerno. Indeed, Gary Cooper played Burke (though not by name) in the movie *Cloak and Dagger*.

For all that—and as we'll see, there's more of that—the picture of Burke pulling a fan out of the stands remains wow! Mike Burke has presided over great sports ruins for more than a decade with hardly a display of pique. Whatever the provocation, he has been imperturbable, all grace. This quality, combined with an engaging personality—open, genial, *nice*—has endeared him to the press, to his employers, to everybody (it seems) but the customers. And here the irony is poignant, for few men have tried harder to please the fans.

As soon as Burke took over the Yankees, for example, he set about to remake the team's cold, ruthless image. The management during the dynasty—twenty-nine pennants, twenty world championships from 1921 through 1964—paid little attention to the amenities. Rude ushers, peremptory ticket salesmen, a security force that often performed like a Cossack farm team, dirty restrooms, lousy hot dogs, were the order of the day and night at Yankee Stadium.

Burke changed all this straightaway. He wiped the frowns off the box office guys, put Halston-hatted, Bill Blass–blazered hostesses into the stands, dressed the hot dog boys in multicolored pop art ponchos, spruced up the johns, turned the would-be Cossacks into a civilian review board, improved the food, and spent a million and change to paint the stadium inside and out.

This was pure Burke at work, the Burke of whom it was said then and said now, by friends and enemies alike, "Mike Burke is the greatest P.R. man in the world."

"Of course," said Burke then, and "of course," says Burke now, "underlying everything is a winning team." Of course, he has never had a winning team.

The Columbia Broadcasting System bought control of the Yankees at the end of the 1964 season, which turned out to be the team's last pennant until 1976. How did CBS happen to buy and why?

"We were having lunch," Burke says, "Bill Paley [chairman of the board of CBS], Frank Stanton [CBS president] and me. I was vice-president in charge of acquisitions, and as usual we were casting about for new properties. Stanton said, 'Why not the Yankees?' Paley was surprised. 'Are they for sale?' he said. And I said, 'Why don't you call your pal Dan Topping [the Yankees' president] and ask him.' A couple of weeks later, we had the Yankees.

"The funny thing is," Burke continues, "Frank Stanton didn't know a thing about baseball, and in all the years we owned the club he never went to a game. The only time he ever came out to the stadium was when we were about to paint the seats. I knew he had a fine esthetic sense, and I wanted to see if he liked the shade of blue I had chosen. He took one look at it, said 'fine,' got into his limousine and never came back."

During CBS's eight-year tenure, the Yanks finished tenth, ninth, sixth (twice), fourth (twice), and second (in 1970, but fifteen games out of first). So maybe Stanton knew what he was doing, and he wasn't the only one who stayed away. In 1972, Burke's last season at the helm, attendance dropped under the million mark for the first time since 1945. Last year, playing in the remodeled stadium that seats fifteen thousand fewer people, the team drew over two million customers.

CBS paid $13.2 million for the club and considered it a bargain. In early 1973, CBS sold it for $10 million after swallowing an operating loss of $11 million.

"The trouble was," says Burke, "we didn't go in and feel the goods. Paley trusted Topping, but Dan had let the franchise go to pot. We bought a pig in a poke."

Indeed. Although the Yankees made one of their greatest stretch runs in '64, and came within inches of winning the World Series, the dynasty was shakier than Mickey Mantle's legs. The once-great farm system was virtually empty, and the sharp trades that were the team's signature didn't happen anymore.

"The Yankees have five more years at the most under the new management," said George Weiss, the taciturn genius who built the dynasty, on the day he was forced into retirement by Topping and co-owner Del Webb. This was in November 1960. In 1965, the Yanks finished sixth, after winning five straight pennants and two world championships.

Burke became de facto boss of the team at the tail end of the '65 season when Topping—who had retained the presidency and a 10 percent piece—had clearly lost interest and was, according to Burke, "spending most of his time on his yacht." A year later, CBS bought Topping out and Burke was officially installed as president and chairman of the board of the Yankees. But his first act, in September 1965, was to hire Johnny Keane as manager, on the advice of Ralph Houk, the general manager, and a story goes with it.

Houk succeeded Casey Stengel in the Yankees dugout in 1961, after Stengel was cashiered in the purge that removed George Weiss. Houk was a huge success, winning three pennants and two World Series in three years. In 1964, he was moved up to general manager, and Yogi Berra took his place in the dugout. But Topping, not Houk, chose Berra—more to counteract the amazing New York Mets, who were winning the city's heart, if no games, under the joint tutelage of Weiss and Stengel—than because of Yogi's managerial genius. When the Yanks floundered with Berra, Houk decided to dump him in favor of Keane, whose St. Louis Cardinals were also going nowhere in August of '64.

The trouble was that both teams ended up in the World Series, and had the Yankees managed to win the final game, Houk would never have been able to get rid of Yogi. But the Cards won it, and the day after the Series, Berra was fired. The next day, Johnny Keane was the Yankee manager.

In the event, the transaction was a total disaster. Yankee fans were incensed about the bush-league treatment visited on their old hero, who was then picked up on the spot by George Weiss to assist Stengel in the Mets' dugout; and Keane turned out to be the classic case of the wrong man in the wrong place at the wrong time.

A strict disciplinarian, an old-fashioned, religious man in his late fifties, Johnny Keane inherited a hard-drinking, high-living ball club used to a light rein and confident of invincibility on the field. When Keane tried to crack down they sneered; when a series of injuries to key players destroyed their hegemony over the American League, they sulked. The result: a sixth-place finish, the first time the Yanks had ended so low since 1917.

When the Yankees won only four of their first twenty games in 1966, Mike Burke fired Keane and talked Houk into returning to the dugout. This time, however, it was Burke who didn't bother to "feel the goods."

As manager, Houk had endeared himself to the players; an upbeat type, he was forever praising them and defending them against occasional bad days. But in switching hats he became the heavy; suddenly, in contract negotiations, he was downplaying their skills, telling the same guys they weren't so hot after all. Now, back on the field, his credibility was shot. And if the team was also shot, Houk certainly had to share responsibility for *that*. He had been Topping's fair-haired boy, he knew what was happening; at the least, he was a silent co-conspirator in the destruction of the dynasty. By firing Berra and hiring Keane, he had committed overt acts that hastened the fall. Any way you looked at it, Ralph Houk was part of the problem.

In 1966, the "problem" finished last in the American League, a disaster that had not occurred since 1912. Burke gave Houk a vote of confidence, and the next year the Yankees finished ninth. In the meantime, the few class players were traded away for nobodies. By 1968, Houk was fielding a team that had less than a handful of players left from the '64 champs. But if this ended the morale problem, it exposed a new one. For it seemed that Houk, a great push-button manager (don't knock that skill without asking Billy Martin) was unable to get the maximum out of lower caliber or inexperienced ballplayers.

Burke concedes this, yet he never lost faith in Houk, and even today refuses to lay any serious blame on his manager for the failure of the Yankees. Of course, to blame Houk would be to blame Burke, and Mike Burke does not accept blame for the plight of the Yanks. Whom does he blame? He blames Dan Topping. "Because of Topping," he says, "we had to start at the bottom. There was no free agent market, you know; we couldn't go out and buy Catfish Hunter."

Which is true. It is also true that the Mets weren't in a free agent market, and as an expansion club they *really* had to start from scratch. Yet by 1969, only seven years after they began, George Weiss had a world championship flag flying over Shea Stadium. When I mention this to Burke, along with less dramatic examples of teams that moved to the top from nowheresville (Cincinnati, Oakland, Pittsburgh) he nods.

After still another desultory fourth-place finish in 1972, CBS decided to unload the Yankees. "Paley was tired of it," Burke explains. "Partly it was the image thing, we weren't winning; partly it had to do with corporate infighting—there was resentment that I was reporting directly to Paley—and partly it was the Yankee Stadium deal. Some of the executives may have seen trouble down the road on that one."

(In '72, Burke closed a deal with the Lindsay administration, where, in return for keeping the Yanks in New York, the city agreed to rebuild the stadium. Burke's leverage: a stunning offer to move to New Jersey, an offer the football Giants couldn't refuse. The Giant owners were savaged by the press and *vox populi*, while Burke was grandly praised. But there were discordant notes. The estimated cost was $24 million; at a City Council session, however, Burke refused to guarantee that or any number, would not commit CBS to pay a dime however high the figure might go. Noting that this amounted to a blank check from the city, *The New York Times* published an editorial titled "Stealing Home Plate." The editorial swiped at Burke for claiming that the deal was a "declaration of faith in the city and its future" by the Yankees. Since Burke had rarely, if ever, been criticized in the press, Paley may have seen this as the handwriting on the wall. The editorial surely was that: Yankee Stadium cost from $100–200 million.)

CBS's decision to sell turned out to be a bonanza for Burke, because Paley didn't put the team on the open market; he gave Burke the right to buy it. "Offer me a fair price and it's yours," Paley said, according to Burke, and if there is a better example of bootstrapping a boondoggle, it has yet to surface. Consider: Burke runs the Yankees for eight years, until his boss gets fed up enough to dump the team, whereupon Burke is invited to form a syndicate and get a piece of the club as a finder's fee. "Baseball," Red Smith once wrote, "is a strange world where nothing succeeds like failure."

It's not like that in television, where heads roll over a one-point drop in ratings, and no excuses. I asked Burke how long he would have lasted as, say, head of CBS News with a record comparable to that of any of his Yankee teams. He smiled, shook his head, and said, "I know what you mean."

Burke sold the team in January 1973 to a group headed by George Steinbrenner 3d, the Cleveland shipping magnate, for $10 million, which, Steinbrenner recently told me, knocked down to $8.8 million when parking concessions were taken into account.

"It's the best buy in sports today," Steinbrenner said at the time, and that one ranks with the great understatements in history. Two years earlier, for example, the Cleveland Indians went for $10.8 million, and in 1970 the Seattle Pilots were bought in a *bankruptcy* sale for $10.5 million.

It appeared at first that nothing would change under the new ownership. But three weeks into the '73 season, Steinbrenner removed Burke as president and replaced him with Gabe Paul. Publicly, the matter was handled with high diplomacy by both sides. Burke would keep his share and serve as a paid "consultant," and he and Steinbrenner, "after some rocky times," had resolved their differences on a "friendly basis." Four years later, both sides still seethe.

"When we bought the team, there was no question that I was going to run it," Burke says. "Gabe Paul was supposed to help out in the front office for a couple of years and then retire to Florida. When I announced he was joining us I *said* that—I said it was a nice way for Gabe to close out his baseball career. Obviously, George had something else in mind from the outset."

According to Burke, Steinbrenner was all over him, looking to pick a fight, looking to force him out. "It finally broke out into the open when we signed Bobby Murcer to a $100,000 contract," Burke says. "On opening day, in front of about forty people, George said to me, 'We'll see how your $100,000 ballplayer does today.' Well, Bobby struck out to end the game with the winning run on base, and George stormed into my office and said, 'There's your $100,000 ballplayer for you.' That tore it, I knew I couldn't work with him."

I wish I could report George Steinbrenner's response when I relayed Burke's version of events to him at Elaine's restaurant. But after denying the Murcer story—"Crap!"—Steinbrenner went off the record. "I don't want to get into a fight with him in the papers," he said, as if to acknowledge that you can't beat Burke in the papers. "But," he said, "go see Gabe Paul, he'll tell you what really happened."

Up at the stadium, Gabe Paul sits behind his desk looking for all the world like a mild-mannered grandpa, his liquid blue eyes smiling quizzically. "Let me tell you," he says, "Mike Burke ought to get down on his knees when George Steinbrenner's name is mentioned, he ought to thank the good Lord for George Steinbrenner."

Now why should he do any such thing?

"Mike Burke owns 5 percent of the New York Yankees [Burke told *me* he owns 10 percent], and do you know how much that cost him, thanks to George Steinbrenner? Nothing, not a plug nickel. He's the only partner who didn't have to pay for his share, and do you know what else? Mike Burke has a ten-year contract, at $25,000 a year, to be a consultant to the New York Yankees. Nobody has ever asked him to do a thing for that money. Mike Burke—I repeat—ought to get down on his hands and knees whenever George Steinbrenner's name is mentioned."

What about Burke's contention that he, Burke, brought Steinbrenner into the deal with the understanding that he, Burke, would continue to run the Yankees?

"A baldfaced lie," Gabe Paul says mildly, quizzically.

"First of all, *I* brought George in. Mike was having trouble finding a buyer and he asked me for help and I put him together with George. But more important, Mike knew from the start that after a decent interval he'd move upstairs, that I'd take over the business end and Lee MacPhail [Burke's general manager, now American League president] would run the baseball end.

"The night we signed the papers, George had to fly to Tampa, and Mike and I drove out to the airport with him. The three of us were sitting in the back of the car and we shook hands on it, we put our hands one on top of another, like football players before a game. At the airport we toasted to it and after George took off, Mike and I toasted again."

Why didn't he say anything when Burke announced he was "capping his career" and would retire in two years?

"I said plenty. 'What the hell is that supposed to mean?' I said to him. 'This isn't a question of *if,* it's a question of *when.*' Meaning when he moves upstairs and I take over. He didn't answer, just kind of shrugged and walked away.

"After that," Paul continues, "it got even more obvious that he was going to try and stick it out. It made it tough on George, George was an outsider, and Mike had the newspaper people with him. Finally, George just told him that was it, he had to go."

Did Burke say anything to him?

"That night, after the announcement, I saw him at Toots Shor's. I went over and shook hands, and Mike said, 'I feel like a man stabbed in the back with the blood running all over the floor.'

" 'You don't have any blood, Mike,' I said."

After another fourth-place finish in '73, the Steinbrenner–Paul regime began a general housecleaning. Houk was replaced by Bill Virdon, and the following year Virdon was replaced by Billy Martin. Nearly all of the CBS Yankees were sold or traded, and of course last year the team won its first pennant since 1964. How does Burke feel about this?

"You know," a sportswriter who likes Burke said to me, "Mike told me he's proud to have left the team with a strong foundation. Can you believe that? Can you?"

On July 31, 1973, three months after his ouster, Mike Burke was appointed president of Madison Square Garden Center. If this seemed strange to the average citizen, brought up on the slogan "You've Got to Be Great to Make It in New York," it was the most natural choice in the world to the Garden's owners.

"I couldn't care less about Mike's Yankee record," David N. (Jim) Judelson, the president of Gulf & Western, told me last summer, long before the rumors of corporate dissatisfaction. "I picked Mike for his chemistry, his image, his entrepreneurial skills."

But the Yankees lost $11 million under Burke. What entrepreneurial skills?

"That could have been anything," Judelson brushes it aside. "That could have been Paley's fault, who knows? And really, I couldn't care less."

Was he satisfied with Burke?

"Absolutely!"

Was Judelson aware that the fans weren't satisfied? "It's easy for fans to criticize," he says, "but they don't know the problems."

Maybe so, but only if they haven't been reading the sports pages. Every Knick fan, for example, is aware that when Burke took over following the 1973 world championship season, the team lost Willis Reed and Dave DeBusschere, that later Jerry Lucas retired, that Red Holzman was getting tired, that efforts to fill the pivot with Jabbar or Chamberlain failed, that Spencer Haywood has been plagued by injuries, that McAdoo has had trouble fitting in, that Frazier has lost a step, etc., etc. The trouble is, as the great pitcher Johnny Sain put it, "The world doesn't want to hear about labor pains, it only wants to see the baby."

In fact, I saw Judelson at Burke's suggestion in order to discuss the most famous of all Knick "labor pains," known as *l'affaire McGinnis*.

Two years ago, Burke signed George McGinnis with full knowledge that the Philadelphia 76ers had exclusive rights to the premier forward. For this "flagrant violation" of the NBA constitution, Commissioner Larry O'Brien—whom Burke had recruited for the commissionership—took away the Knicks' first-draft choice in the 1976 college draft. Since the team was coming off a bad year and would have picked high up, this penalty was the moral equivalent of capital punishment.

Typically, Burke got away virtually untouched in the press—imagine what the writers would have done to Charlie Finley or Steinbrenner or Grant?—but fan reaction was at least as harsh as the penalty. All over town Burke was cursed: "He's done it again, the incredible b——— has done it *again*."

When I question Burke about it, he is noncommittal. He doesn't defend the McGinnis deal; he implies he opposed it, but he won't say who was responsible. "Ask Jim Judelson," he says.

Judelson says: "Mike was not wholly responsible, and Mike was not half responsible. But maybe Mike was a quarter responsible, I don't know."

A few days after my conversation with Judelson, I meet Burke at the bar of the Gotham Hotel, and report to him that I have been unable to find out who was responsible for McGinnis. He nods impatiently and says, "Look, you seem only to be concerned with my sports career; I've done other things in my life, you know."

I explain that the clips are filled with background stuff on him, and so I was concentrating on areas not well known.

"Well here's something that's not known," he says. "How many people do you think were asked by Allen Dulles in 1949 to overthrow the Government of Albania?"

What?

"Yes. Dulles asked me to set up a counterrevolutionary force to overthrow the Albanian regime. It was the height of the cold war and our government wanted to see if a Soviet satellite could be freed by counterinsurgency without the use of American land or air power."

How did it work out?

"It failed. I recruited all sorts of Albanian patriots, but we finally decided, after about a year and a half, that it couldn't be done without overt American action. I wrote a long report to Dulles on it, and in 1961, when the Bay of Pigs began, I wondered why Dulles was involved. He had agreed with me in 1949, and it must have been even clearer by '61 that counterinsurgency alone couldn't work."

From the Albanian adventure, which he conducted out of Rome, Burke went to Germany in 1951 as "special adviser" to the United States High Commissioner John J. McCloy.

"Actually I was head of the CIA for the region, though I always say 'special adviser,'" Burke tells me. "I think we did an effective job, particularly in our overflights across the Soviet Union. We gathered a good deal of important information."

In 1954, Burke became executive vice-president and general manager of Ringling Brothers and Barnum & Bailey Circus. "I had to start making some money," he explains. "My family was growing [he has four children ranging in age from twenty to twenty-six, and was divorced a few years ago] and I just had to leave the CIA."

But why the circus?

"Well," Burke chuckles, "I asked the same question. The North family was very close to me—John thought of me as his younger brother—but when they wanted me to take over the circus I wondered aloud what qualifications I had."

And?

"And John Ringling North said, 'Mike, you've been training all your life to run the circus—you just don't know it.'"

In 1956, after a series of Teamster strikes against the Big Top, Burke met with James R. Hoffa. He had not been training all his life to go one-on-one with Jimmy Hoffa.

"Hoffa said to me," Burke recalls, "'Let's you and me talk business.' I asked him what business, and he said, 'Business, just you and me.' 'What about the people,' I said. 'What *people*,' he said. 'Who cares about that, I'm talking *business*.'"

In that way, says Burke, the Big Top closed down.

From the circus, Burke hooked up with CBS, shortly rising to president of CBS Europe. In 1962 he returned to New York as head of development for CBS, which led him to Yankee Stadium, where we all came in. Although where we really came in was with Mike

Burke and his future at Madison Square Garden. In pressing Burke on the source of the vibrations that were telling him his job was in jeopardy, I asked him whether the people at G & W were upset with his handling of the Muhammad Ali–Ernie Shavers fight. "Absolutely not," he said. "The fight is fine, there's been no question about that."

If they didn't question that, it's hard to imagine what they *would* question. Because the legal battle over the fight became, in the words of the U.S. Court of Appeals, "an imbroglio which bids fair to outdo the main event." And as a result of that court's ruling, the Garden was forced to sue for peace and grant a large settlement to a rival promoter or face the prospect of no fight at all. And if the fight didn't come off, Ali would have walked off with $3 million nonetheless.

The case was complex and bitter, filled with cross-allegations and factual disputes. Cut to its bare bones, it shakes down to the following:

In May, Burke signed Ali to an option contract to defend his title against Ernie Shavers at the Garden for $3 million. Teddy Brenner, the Garden matchmaker, then called Shavers' manager in Ohio and offered him a minimum guarantee of $200,000. This was apparently accepted by telegram.

However, a proposed letter of agreement sent by the Garden to Shavers differed in several respects from the terms of the telegram, which had been dictated by Brenner in the first place. A number of phone calls followed, and one sticking point became a demand by Shavers for $30,000 in front money. Brenner said he thought he could get Burke to go for $20,000, but he wasn't sure about the 30. Then, in what apparently turned out to be a critical day or two, Brenner did not get back to Shavers.

In the interim, Shavers' manager got in touch with Bob Arum, president of Top Rank, which in the past had promoted numerous Ali fights. The upshot: Shavers signed with Top Rank for $300,000, 30 grand in front. So now the Garden had an Ali option but no Shavers, and all hell broke loose.

In came the lawyers, with Top Rank moving in state court and the Garden in federal court. The State Supreme Court ruled that the Garden had no contract with Shavers, the federal court said it did. While this was happening, Ali's option, which the Garden was obligated to exercise by July 1, was running out. Now Ali got tough; he

wasn't going to mess with the thing if the fight was going to be enjoined; he'd go elsewhere and make a match. And so Burke, apparently certain of his legal grounds, guaranteed Ali the $3 million
even if the fight didn't come off.

With matters stymied in the courts, Shavers signed with the Garden. Only now he got $300,000, instead of $200,000, and he got
$25,000 more for expenses. This was okay with Top Rank, which felt
confident of *its* legal grounds.

On August 19, this confidence proved out, when the U.S. Court
of Appeals reversed the Garden's victory in the Federal District
Court and sent the case to the New York State Supreme Court for
final determination. The Court of Appeals noted that if Top Rank
succeeded in state court ". . . there will be no fight."

Since there was substantial reason to believe that Top Rank would
win there—recall, they had originally gotten a determination that
the Garden–Shavers deal was not a legal contract—the Garden was
over a barrel.

However, at an early morning meeting the next day, Burke was
curiously adamant. He reportedly told Top Rank: "I offered you
$100,000 in the beginning as a nuisance settlement, and I make the
same offer now." Theodore Herzl Friedman, Top Rank's lawyer,
walked out.

That afternoon, Alan N. Cohen, who runs the business end of the
Garden's operations, stepped in and took over the negotiations with
Top Rank.

The final settlement: Top Rank was guaranteed $300,000 against
one-third of the net proceeds, whichever was higher.

Totting it all up, the Garden's failure to immediately sign Shavers
was expensive indeed. Apart from the 300 grand to Top Rank,
Shavers ended up with an extra $125,000, and insiders say that the
Garden went for $250,000 in legal fees.

The National Broadcasting Company paid $4 million for the live
telecast, and if everything had gone smoothly, the Garden would
have come out with a profit of about $1 million.

Well, it's only money, and if past is prologue, Mike Burke won't
be fired, he'll get a raise. But even if he is let go—his Garden contract expires next August and G & W may decide not to renew, or
Burke may not want to stay, who knows?—he'll be all right, he'll
move on to something big, don't worry about it.

The jackpot question is *why*, and to answer it we must look at the world in which he operates, for in that world the question does not even arise.

Corporate conglomerates, it goes without saying, have the wherewithal to hire the best and the brightest. Yet, with few exceptions on the very highest levels, they can hardly be said to be loaded with hotshot performers. The reason: Hotshots are by nature driving, ambitious, wily, cunning, independent. They shake things up, they have little respect for the prevailing wisdom, they're outspoken, they tend to be right, and when they're right, they want the credit. Even Presidents of the United States are uncomfortable with people who question the received opinion, and this is itself such a received opinion that hardly an eyebrow was raised when Mr. Carter stocked his national security departments with men who prosecuted the Vietnam War.

Obviously, then, Burke is not unique unto the day. But he has unique qualities that made him attractive to the Garden. He's a huge favorite among the sportswriters. He's welcome all over town, all over *Europe*. He has the right friends: Felix Rohatyn, Robert Tisch, Roone Arledge, Walter Cronkite, Irwin Shaw, Paul Simon, David Merrick, Alex Cohen, John Lindsay. He goes to the right places: '21,' Elaine's, Windows on the World, the Algonquin, Broadway Joe's—and, for the common touch, the Flash Inn in Harlem, and Paul & Jimmy's on Irving Place, hard by his Gramercy Park flat. At any of these spots, or at the Garden, the stadium, the ballet, he is likely to be seen with one or another young lovely on his arm.

Summer weekends are taken at his house in Wainscott, where his neighbor is George Plimpton, and where he plays a strong third base on Willie Morris' great softball team, the Golden Nematodes. Four or five times a year, Burke travels to Ireland, to his cottage in County Galway, not far from where his grandfather was born. And rides to the hounds with the East Galway Hunt Club.

If the Garden wants chemistry, if it wants image, could it ask for anything more?

The story is told about the flack for *Cleopatra*, who flew back to Hollywood to report on his foreplay with the New York film critics.

"We're in," he said to the worried moguls. "I got to the *Times*, the *Trib*, the *News*, the *Post*, I got Winchell, I got Lyons, I got the newsweeklies, everybody's on board, we got nothing to worry about."

The moguls smiled; the submoguls cheered, laughed, clapped backs. Then, from a far corner of the board room, a voice: "Yeah. Yeah. And now if we can only get around that goddam word-of-mouth."

—*The New York Times Magazine*
October 9, 1977

HARDBALL,
HARD MONEY

I think I was the first to write in praise of George Steinbrenner, boosting him in my Soho Weekly News column soon after he bought the Yankees in 1973. Since then, I continued the kudos right smack in the face of virtually every baseball writer extant. Why? Because I'm a Yankee fan. George made the Yankees great again. In so doing, he restored my childhood and gave rich ones to my kids.

To grow up with the Yankees during the dynasty was a blessing; it allowed a child to flourish as a believer. Everything else might fail— was God dead?—but not the Yankees; the Yankees delivered. Dodger fans and other bile-filled types said that rooting for the Yanks was like rooting for General Motors. Our answer, when we deigned to answer, was that if you were in the stock market, you'd damn well root for General Motors. Baseball was for winning, and winning to the Yankee organization and fandom meant winning the World Series. Anything less was a disaster demanding immediate rectification.

Mike Burke didn't look at it that way, so we stopped going to the stadium. Did this mean we were fair-weather fans? Of course not. We were Yankee fans. We don't back losers, it's a contradiction to terms. Not baseball fans. Yankee fans.

George Steinbrenner was obviously in the great tradition of Yankee owners. I use the past tense half-advisedly and with a large prayer that it ain't so. During the World Series of 1981, George went the extra step that upset the delicate balance which had kept him tops with the fans even as he was raked over continually in the press. Things went rapidly downhill afterward, and as I write (June '82) the team is in trouble and George is really in trouble.

The Yanks can turn it around; by the time you read this, they may be in the Series. Will that necessarily turn the fans back on to Steinbrenner? Logic dictates a yes, but the June air is bad, and how do you stop something that's in the air? Well, the Great George M. is nothing if not resilient. As the kid at Shea used to say, ya gotta believe.

In any event, I'm glad I wrote the pieces that follow, which are as much an attack on the New York baseball writers—who ruthlessly savaged Steinbrenner when he was doing everything right—as they are a celebration of the once-and-future George.

———————

IT IS SAID that when they asked Babe Ruth how he felt about making more money than President Hoover, the Bambino answered, "Hell, I had a better year than he did." It is also said that Ruth never said it—for every great line there is an assassin who knows how to spell apocryphal—but revelation lies in the knowledge that nobody dreamed to ask the same question of Jacob Ruppert, who owned the Yankees and made more money on any given Sunday than the Babe made all year, forget about Herbert Hoover. Leave it to sportswriters to know where to go in their efforts to make the great metaphor for monopoly capitalism.

Now, some fifty years after Ruth earned the astonishing sum of $80,000 per, we leave it to them again, and they are having such a big time of ogling and breast-beating over the revolution in baseball salaries that they have only themselves to blame if the editorial writers and pundits are increasingly a threat to *their* monopoly. But not to worry; the other departments are simply providing a rhythm section to the sad trumpets that tell us with every box score how the greedy ballplayers with their seedy agents are destroying the Pastime.

Well, I stand with Reggie Jackson who sings "Down the riverbanks with spring," Reggie Jackson who wants to see a limousine on the way to the bankruptcy court before he takes these blues to heart. And to stand with Reggie Jackson is to stand with George M. Steinbrenner, which is good enough for me and ought to be good as gold for anyone who thinks twice about the state of the art. The great George M. has laid it in bigger than all the rest, and the only thing he worries about is winning the Series. It is all any owner should worry over, and them that do never have to worry about anything else.

If there are franchises that can't compete in the new market—either because they are in deadbeat towns where the fans don't care enough, or because the owners do not have the resources—the answer is to move to another city or sell to people with the moola. This hard but simple fact is readily understood in every business except sports, and even in some sports, notably the fight game. Does anyone suggest that Muhammad Ali has destroyed boxing because he takes down a couple of million to fight a bum in a country we can't pronounce? Do we cry for Madison Square Garden because they can't pay him enough to match him here?

I never heard anyone complain that Elton John made sixty million one year, nor that he was killing off the Beacon Theatre by demanding more than management could pay. Sinatra nets as much, perhaps more, in a week at Caesars Palace than Catfish Hunter does all summer. Nobody bitches. Book publishers stand in line to throw money at novelists with track records that make a .230 batting average look good, and if they don't like it we properly laugh and tell them to get out of the kitchen.

The which is known as competition, as supply and demand, and if I emphasize the entertainment industry it is simply to avoid the canard that "working" is different. As for that, suffice it to note that the president of General Motors was drawing 750 G's a year when he had nothing more important to do than set hookers on Ralph Nader. The critics who didn't like the Nader part said nothing about the salary, which needless to add did not include entertainment.

So why are the Met fans mad at Dave Kingman rather than at the throat of M. Donald Grant? We are told because the average working stiff can't get upset over the plight of a guy who isn't satisfied with two hundred big ones to play on the grass of big cities in summertime. But the question is not why they don't root him home, the question is why they resent him for asking. And since the same fans don't resent Elton John, Sinatra, Liz Taylor, not to say the president of GM, the answer must lie in that lovely world known as Received Opinion.

We are back, then to the sportswriters, who have delivered it to us that baseball is not a business, that a hungry ballplayer is the best ballplayer, that Branch Rickey, the lovable El Cheapo, really knew how to handle the boys of summer, that it was terrific for Jackie Robinson's character to make five grand a year, that Moose Skowron never would have hustled if George Weiss babied him with better than his hop of $28,500. And so on to the Bowery Bank where we have to watch Joe D. singing "Take Me Out to the Ball Game," which, you ought to rejoice, will never happen to Reggie Jackson.

—*Soho Weekly News*
April 14, 1977

DOWN ON THE PLANTATION WITH MEAN AND EVIL CHARLIE O.

THERE ARE CONNECTIONS between the business of journalism and the business of sports that transcend the "toy store," that lovely sobriquet Jimmy Cannon bestowed on the sports pages of newspapers. So why don't I begin with an anecdote and see if I can turn it into an analogy.

Turner Catledge, the southern gentleman who for years edited *The New York Times,* said of Nat Goldstein, the Yankee gentleman who for the same years peddled the paper as head of its circulation department, that if everyone who loved Nat Goldstein loved each other, there would be peace in the world.

You can take it from me that Turner is right; but you don't need me to tell you, if you know what a baseball looks like, that if everyone who hated Charlie Finley hated each other, there would be World War III.

When baseball writers are feeling charitable, they refer to Charlie Finley as a fascist. He runs the Oakland A's as if he owns them, which he does, but Charlie doesn't fool around. His ball club is his plantation, his players are his slaves, his managers his straw bosses. To win he'll chew 'em all up, and not only will he, he has and he does. A couple of years ago, his second baseman made a crucial error in the World Series and so Charlie fired him then and there, and his only bow to public relations was to force the poor guy to sign a paper saying he was too hurt to go on. Hurt? He was healthy as the Derby winner, and when Charlie's manager bitched, he told him, on television, that he'd let him have his freedom. Taking him at his word, the manager, Dick Williams, signed with the Yankeess, whereupon Charlie went to court and got an injunction that stopped Williams from managing New York. Outrageous, but of course Oakland won the Series that year, and then, without Williams, they won it the next year. Now they are about to win their fifth straight pennant—only the great Yankee dynasty teams did that—and this time without Catfish Hunter, the best pitcher in baseball. Charlie had refused to honor a contract clause, which would have cost him next to nothing, and so he lost the Catfish to the Yanks.

Perverse, willful, self-destructive—certainly, and right in line with what Finley did to his great left-hander, Vida Blue. Blue in his rookie year was the biggest draw since Bobby Feller, and yet Finley, who is no cheapskate, refused to give him more than fifty grand the next season. Blue skulked, held out, and had two lousy years—but he played on Charlie's terms. This year he is fine, he is great, but we will never know how great he might have been had Finley not been so adamant.

And these horror stories but scratch the surface. If ever there was a consensus in sports, it is that Charlie Finley is so mean and evil, even the rain don't fall on him.

So one afternoon in October 1974, I was in a taxicab in Washington, D.C., with Nick von Hoffman, the fine columnist who is loved by journalists as much as Finley is despised by them. And I said, Nick, supposing managing editors operated like Charlie Finley, what do you think would happen in the newsrooms?

Nick's head nearly flew off. He laughed, guffawed the way he does, infectiously, and we both broke up all the way from the airport to the Mayfair Hotel. "A revolution," Nick said, between howls, and as every journalist will spot, he did not mean the kind of revolution you'd think, given what I've said about Finley. And that is because of what I haven't said.

The other side of Charlie Finley, the thing that distinguishes him from his peers, is that all he asks of his employees is excellence. If you can hit .300, if you win twenty games, you can hold press conferences every day and denounce old Charlie to your heart's content. Call him every kind of sonofabitch in the world and he'll laugh, but only so long as you produce. Charlie Finley runs the only plantation in history with a First Amendment.

Do you have any idea how long journalists would read their bylines if they said of their editors a scintilla of the things Reggie Jackson says daily of Charlie Finley? Not only would they disappear from their paper, they'd disappear from journalism.

More fundamentally, imagine what would happen to newspapers if the only thing that counted in reporters' careers was their talent. Just that—how good they were, how right they were, how their batting averages stacked up across the year. If that were even the dominant consideration, no newspaper in the country would have the same masthead, not to say byliners.

Indeed, if that were the test in sports, Charlie Finley wouldn't be the most successful owner extant. Who knows, the football Giants might make the Super Bowl. But who needs competition when you can have teamwork? And who needs journalism when everybody knows that nobody reads?

—*Soho Weekly News*
September 18, 1975

AT PLAY IN THE FIELDS
OF STEINBRENNER

IT SAYS IN the *New York Yankees 1978 Media Guide* that Alfred Manuel "Billy" Martin (manager) "enjoys American History, with special interest in the Civil War."

Anyone with a passing interest in the history of the 1977 Yankees would likely think this a piece of heavy-handed humor, since Billy Martin last year field-marshaled one of the fiercest civil wars in the annals of baseball. But the guidebook is all facts, it doesn't kid around, and the outstanding recent fact it records is that the team survived its own clubhouse to emerge as champions of the whole world.

The Yanks had not owned this awesome title—which they once picked up in October almost as a matter of divine right—since 1962. And yet the victory was nearly overshadowed by the great battles that dominated the sports pages—and sometimes page one—all season: Billy Martin vs. Reggie Jackson; George M. Steinbrenner vs. Billy Martin; Thurman Munson vs. Reggie Jackson; Thurman Munson vs. George M. Steinbrenner; Ed Figueroa vs. Billy Martin; Lou Piniella vs. Billy Martin; Roy White vs. Billy Martin; and Ken Holtzman vs. Nearly Everybody.

But that was last year. The hot question now is this: Will the Yankees repeat? While this question is asked annually of every champion, it has a double meaning when applied to the Yanks, and even a triple meaning. Will they win again, will they fight again, will they do both again?

In an effort to dope these issues out, I spent three days and nights in Fort Lauderdale during the last week of March, hanging around the Yankee clubhouse and the bar at the Galt Ocean Mile Hotel, the "Winter Home of the World Championship New York Yankees."

Of course, three days with or without nights hardly seems long enough to figure anything out. But baseball fans come armed with arrogance. And I'm not simply a baseball fan; I am a Yankee fan, and not just a Yankee fan but a degenerate Yankee fan, and that way since age six, circa 1939. So it's not three days and nights, it's closer to forty years.

And anyway, even if not all that time, so what? In the winter I went to Cairo for four days and three nights, and on the first day a veteran journalist asked me, with a snarl: "What do you expect to learn in four days and three nights?" I said, "As much as anyone has learned in 3,500 years."

Of course, I expected more from Fort Lauderdale. In the event, I got more, although not what I expected.

First, I expected to see Sandra Dee and 400,000 kids on the beach; by the time I arrived—the Tuesday after Easter Sunday—most of the kids were back on the campus and no Sandra Dee.

Next, I expected to see George M. Steinbrenner, the principal owner of the Yankees, as soon as I got to town. But Steinbrenner was on a plane to Tampa. Steinbrenner is almost always on a plane going somewhere. The Yankee press office did not tell me he was leaving, but then the Yankee press office never knows when George is flying off. Well, I caught up with him later—in Fort Lauderdale.

Finally, I expected to spend most of my three days and nights schmoozing with the ballplayers. This was my secret reason for going down to spring training in the first place. I had a pass to the clubhouse and I stood around looking at them quite a lot, and of course I stood at the bar of the Galt Ocean Mile Hotel rubbing shoulders with some of them. But I did not exactly schmooze with the ballplayers.

The reason is that unless you are a regular sportswriter, the Yankees are suspicious of you and therefore don't like to say much more than "We're gonna be all right; my arm feels fine; I'm ready." For all I know, all ballplayers are this way with strange journalists, but I suspect the Yanks are more this way, owing to the civil war, when uncautious words—spoken even to favored reporters—got many of them into hot water.

I went over to Jim Beattie, who was sitting alone in front of his locker. Jim Beattie is a hot young pitcher. The management is high on him; it says he'll make it big someday. I told him that, and Beattie said, "Thanks."

I also said hello to Reggie Jackson, since Reggie Jackson is reputed to be an open guy and a good talker. But as soon as I told him who I was, he said: "I'm afraid of you; I won't talk to you." "But you've never met me," I said. "I'm afraid of *New York* magazine," he explained.

It seems that *New York* magazine ran something last year on Reggie Jackson that Reggie Jackson didn't like. *New York* also did a piece on George Steinbrenner, which George Steinbrenner considered a hatchet job. Reggie Jackson knew about this piece too, and told me so. But I'm a Yankee fan, I said. Reggie Jackson walked away.

If a politician did that to me, I'd drop everything and investigate him until I had enough to put him in Dannemora. But I didn't even get mad at Jackson, and when he got up to the plate the next night I screamed for him to hit it into the ocean.

On the face of it, this entire episode ought to prove that I would be the world's worst sportswriter. Instead, it indicates I'd be a pretty good one—that is, at least nothing out of the ordinary.

With few exceptions, sportswriters do not stir up trouble in the clubhouse; they go along with the party line. I never thought I'd do that, but after those few days with the Yankees, I wouldn't book it.

To appreciate how difficult it is to do it differently, one must spend some time around a ball club. Leonard Shecter used to tell me about it, but until I was there, I didn't really understand what he meant.

Shecter, who died a few years ago, was a great sportswriter for the *New York Post* in the 1950s and 1960s and a man of much wisdom and courage.

Lenny defied tradition by simply writing the truth about baseball. He told it as he saw it, following no line but his own. If a player was mean spirited, Lenny wrote it; if he was a drunk, Lenny said so; if a manager was stupid, he put it in the papers.

For five years, nobody talked to Shecter, including his fellow sportswriters.

Of course, Lenny got the best stories, and after watching the writers interview players last week it was clear why he did. Ballplayers don't have that much to say, unless they are mavericks, and mavericks don't last long in the big leagues unless they are great.

So, after Don Gullett pitched three strong innings against Minnesota, the interview around his locker went like this:

"How's the arm feel, Don?"

"Good."

"Did it bother you at all?"

"No."

"Were you satisfied with your showing?"

"I can do better, but for my first time out I was satisfied."

"Billy says he wants you to throw only ninety pitches a game; how do you feel about that?"

"I'll go along with whatever Billy wants; he's the manager."

The next morning all the New York newspapers ran this big story.

While Don Gullett is said to be less exciting than most players, the interviews generally go in that direction. Except they didn't go that way last year in the Yankee clubhouse, and even with the relative calm that has settled over the team this spring, they don't always go that way now.

Why? What happened? How did the Yankees, in their first world-championship season in fifteen years, manage to conduct open warfare in the newspapers?

I wondered about that all summer; it was so odd, bizarre. Did we suddenly have a pack of Lenny Shecters running around the Yankee lockers? Were all sportswriters playing Seymour Hersh? Here they were attacking management, the *owner*, and when had they ever done that?

When Mike Burke ran the Yankees for CBS, from 1965 to 1972, the team compiled its most dismal record since the pre-Babe Ruth era. Yet the New York writers never laid a glove on Burke—they continually *praised* him—and hardly a word was written about the blistering fan antipathy toward the management.

Then George Steinbrenner comes to town, and in five years the Yanks are on top of the world. And every day Steinbrenner is attacked in the New York papers.

For a time, I thought the difference was strictly personality; the writers liked Burke, who knew just how to butter them, and didn't like George, who seems to think butter is for putting on burns.

But while this may have something to do with it, it's not the answer. The fundamental difference is that Burke, his manager, and the team were as one. If that meant—as it surely did—that the fans had to suffer losers, so what?

The average sportswriter doesn't worry about the fans; he has to worry about the people he lives with, the people who provide him with the news, his livelihood. As long as those people stick together, the writers stick with them—and the news we get is the news they want us to get.

Steinbrenner, because he wants only to win, couldn't care less about family unity. Indeed, when I finally caught up with him in Fort Lauderdale—he showed up for a night game against the White Sox—one of the first things he told me was that he didn't want too much sweetness and light around the team.

"A schooner doesn't make many knots in a calm sea," he said. "Of course," he added, "I'm not looking for a tornado like last year."

The tornado last year had the effect of splitting Steinbrenner from the clubhouse. The writers, who live in the clubhouse and not in the owner's box, quite naturally sided with the clubhouse—and in so doing sliced George six ways to Sunday.

They did not do this to M. Donald Grant while he dismantled the Mets—until he unloaded Tom Seaver and nearly brought on a civil war in the streets. Even then, Grant didn't fare so poorly, and already they are writing about the "young, rebuilding Mets."

But Steinbrenner gets no credit in the papers—although he does fine with the fans—for building what may well be a new Yankee dynasty. Instead, he is taken to task for "buying" the championship—as if that were a crime, on a par with the felony rap he took in connection with the financing of Nixon's 1972 campaign, a transaction the writers seldom fail to recall.

The charge that the Yankees were store bought, "the best team money can buy," wouldn't bother me even if it were true. Once the free agent market for players opened, the only disgrace would have been to stay out of it, which the Mets did with results we continue to witness.

But the claim is essentially false; the Yankees were made principally on brilliant trades concocted by Steinbrenner and Gabe Paul, who this year moved from the Yankee front office to head the Cleveland Indians.

"Except for Reggie Jackson and Munson, the entire lineup in the last game of the series last year was made up of guys we traded for,"

Steinbrenner said the other night in his makeshift box overlooking first base at Fort Lauderdale Stadium.

With that, he grabbed my pen and wrote out that lineup on a piece of scrap paper, as follows:

CF	Rivers	trade
2B	Randolph	trade
C	Munson	homegrown
RF	Jackson	free agent
1B	Chambliss	trade
3B	Nettles	trade
LF	Piniella	trade
SS	Dent	trade
P	Torrez	trade

True, there were a couple of free agents not in that lineup—Catfish Hunter and Gullett. But there were others who came in trades or from the farm system: Dick Tidrow, Ed Figueroa, Ron Guidry, Paul Blair, Roy White, Sparky Lyle, Cliff Johnson.

Last winter, Steinbrenner went into the free agent market and came up with Rich Gossage and Rawly Eastwick. Together with Sparky Lyle, this could give them the greatest bull pen in baseball history.

At the ball game in Lauderdale, Steinbrenner—with his new president, Al Rosen, the old Cleveland star—raved on about how smart he was to have picked up Eastwick.

"They all bad-mouthed him, said he lost a foot off his fastball. But that's baloney. We clocked him; the kid is great. And he's an all-American boy. Right, Al?"

Al Rosen didn't look up. "He'll be an all-American boy if he wins," Rosen said.

When Eastwick got pasted, Steinbrenner got grumpy. "He's not pitching hard enough, Al. Christ, he can pitch harder than that. Why isn't he throwing smoke? He's got smoke!"

Watching Steinbrenner operate during a game lends a certain credence to another big beef tossed up against him by the press. "He sticks his nose in the dugout; he ought to let the pros handle the game," they say.

At Yankee Stadium, Steinbrenner's box looks directly into the Yankee dugout, and he's been known to get on the phone when a player is laughing while the team is losing or lazying when he shouldn't be lazying—which to George is never.

He is very tough on overweight players. "Cliff Johnson came to camp twenty-five pounds too heavy," Steinbrenner told me. "I had him doing wind sprints all day, every day. I sat right here in this box and watched him. Now he's okay, now he's down to 217."

(As if he had lost the weight himself, Steinbrenner leaned back in his chair, gave a boyish grin, and said to Rosen: "Al, we haven't been to the ice cream place for two nights. The guy's gonna miss me. I think I can use a banana split." Then to me: "My car drives itself to Baskin-Robbins; it can't help itself. And I've got Rosen hooked. You know what he likes? Get this—Al Rosen eats chocolate, peanut butter sundaes.")

With that, Steinbrenner jumped up roaring. A Yankee was called out at the plate and he didn't like the call. He pulled over one of his handful of phones and rang Lee MacPhail, the president of the American League, who was sitting in a field box.

But MacPhail didn't answer.

"He doesn't know how to open the box, damn it."

Back to the phones, and in a second a kid arrived and George gave him a key and told him to show MacPhail how to open the phone box.

"Did you like that call at home?" he asked MacPhail.

A voice came dimly through the receiver and George looked hurt.

"What do you mean I never call you when I like a decision? Look, we have films, we film every game, I'd like you to see it. And what about that call at first last inning?"

Steinbrenner is very upset about umpiring and now heads a major-league committee looking into all aspects of the problem.

"We don't pay 'em enough to start with, and we don't train 'em. They get trained at independent schools, which we have no control over. You know what they tell 'em there? They tell 'em not to take any gaff from ballplayers, and if they give any just get even with 'em next time. Can you believe that?"

I can believe anything about umps, but I told Steinbrenner that the one thing I can't believe is his assertion that he will no longer have much to do with running the team, that he'll leave it in Rosen's hands.

"I know you don't believe it, nobody does, but it's true," he said, his round face innocent as a baby's.

The trouble is, he told me the same thing last year over a drink at Elaine's, but as everyone knows, Steinbrenner was all over the team last year. And it didn't hurt the team.

For example, he pressed Martin to slot Reggie Jackson in the cleanup position, and to replace Roy White in left with Lou Piniella. Martin did not relent until August—and it worked, the team took off.

Steinbrenner took a lot of heat—in and out of the clubhouse—for signing Jackson. He paid Reggie more than any free agent had received up to that time, and this, plus Jackson's controversial nature, was the main source of the civil war. Martin was against the deal from the outset, and Thurman Munson, the team captain, was put off both by Reggie's salary and by some statements Jackson made about him. The players backed Martin and Munson, and so did most of the press. Steinbrenner, naturally, supported Reggie all the way.

Events have gloriously justified the purchase, and George is proud of it. He loves the big right fielder, who apparently can do no wrong in his eyes.

So, the other night, Reggie went up against the wall for a ball—but the ball came off the wall for a double.

"Could he have caught it, Al?" Steinbrenner asked.

"It dropped right out of his glove," Al Rosen said.

For the first time all evening, George Steinbrenner didn't answer.

—*New York* magazine
April 17, 1978

VI.

MUSIC: ONE FOR THE ROAD

OUTLASTING ROCK

"Why don't you do something easy for a change? Something non-controversial, a piece you can do fast. Do yourself a favor. Do me a favor."

That was Ed Klein's advice, delivered to me at the magazine's Christmas party in 1979, a month after my Supreme Court pieces appeared. He took the thought right out of my head, but since I knew how he hated the Court stuff, and since I never jump when an editor throws the hoop anyway, I fooled around a little.

"Uh-huh," I said, *"a kinda semi-quickie that won't have the blood running all over the floor, you mean?"*

"Well, not a quickie," he said. *"We don't do quickies. I'm talking about a good piece of reporting that won't take months to do, that you can handle nicely, easily."*

"With no trouble for anybody."

"I'm just trying to be helpful," he said.

"Let me think about it," I said.

For more than a year I'd been thinking about doing a piece on the resurgence of the pop music of the 1930s and 40s. While I was with *New York* magazine I went on the road with a show called *4 Girls 4*—Margaret Whiting, Rosemary Clooney, Helen O'Connell, Rose Marie—and was happily surprised at the great hunger for the old sounds. But one thing and another popped up, and I never got to write it. Now, maybe, I'd have the shot, and now it was an even bigger story, because everywhere you went the music I grew up on was making a comeback.

After a couple of drinks, I told Klein. *"Sounds good,"* he said, and waved a few editors over. *"Sounds good,"* they said. How long will it take to write? I said three weeks. How many words? I said 3,500. Assignment.

Eighteen months later, Father's Day, 1981, it made the paper. "Outlasting Rock," 7,200 words. Frank Sinatra on the cover for the first time in the history of the Times Magazine. Talk about blood running.

Here's how it began. I went around to record and radio executives saying "Isn't it great the way the old babies are back—Cole Porter, Rodgers and Hart, the Basie band, Mel Tormé—isn't it great?" I got back: "You're crazy, it's a fad, nostalgia, it'll pass, forget it, you're dreaming, it's dead." Not from kid executives, from people out of the Swing Era, people who loved Louis, Benny, Bing, Frank.

I got suspicious, partly because what they were saying was against the evidence, but mainly because of the way they were saying it. They were emotional: annoyed, sneering, even screaming. One guy got so upset at Elaine's one night he left the joint. Because I said isn't it great to hear Bunny Berrigan sing "I Can't Get Started" on Elaine's jukebox.

So I decided to look into the music industry. A peek up that sleaze-bag was enough to show me I had a big story on my hands. I had been asking the wrong question. I didn't need experts to tell me whether the great sounds were making a comeback—I could judge it myself. The real question was why the music disappeared. To answer it I'd have to investigate the marketing of rock-and-roll. No more quick and easy, but who cared? I was hooked, and when that happens time don't mean a thing.

I took my time, and truth to tell, much more than was necessary. I was having a ball interviewing my heroes, for one thing, and then, as often it goes, other interests intervened. I didn't deliver the piece until October and that was only the beginning of trouble.

Seven editors were waiting in Ed Klein's office when I arrived to talk about the story. I had never met with more than a couple of editors in all my years working for the magazine, and so the first thing I said was, "Who's going to read me the Miranda warnings?" It turned out to be an appropriate request: For nearly two hours they came at me as if I had committed double incest. The young editors. "Threatened," in the jargon, by my documentation that rock had been sold to the kids, these ordinarily calm, measured, even-handed editors were beside themselves. It amounted to a kind of muted primal scream.

I was more bemused than angry. I knew Ed Klein agreed with the piece, and more important I knew that he knew Abe Rosenthal and Arthur Gelb would agree. So why this squeal room? My guess is that Klein didn't like the story as written but didn't want to be the one to say it. By setting the jackals on me, however, he turned the issue in my favor by making it into a political-ideological debate.

I thought the piece needed work and had Klein simply said it I'd have done it straightaway. Instead, he opened the meeting by assuring me it was "brilliantly written." Well, no writer wants to argue with that. Now it was a matter of content, of viewpoint, and I wasn't about to let these kids dictate to me, especially since I considered them the problem—they were the victims of rock hype.

Near the end of the inquisition it came full out. Klein said that perhaps I was trying to say too much in too little space, maybe I should turn it into a two-parter. This proved too much for one of the young editors, who had been sitting with tight jaws throughout the meeting.

"I don't think the decimation of the 1930s music deserves two pieces in The New York Times Magazine," he hissed.

I got up and slowly walked over to him. And half-whispered: "I know you don't, baby, I know you don't. You don't think it deserves one piece. And that's the trouble here, you're not supposed to be the editor, you're the patient. It's your mind they've twisted. You don't have any idea what you're saying. The 'decimation' of the 1930s music, do you know what that means?"

He said, flustered, "I know who Howard Arlen is."

I almost felt sorry for the poor bastard. Howard Arlen. "That's Exhibit A," I said.

Another, a young woman, asked: "Why did you call Linda Ronstadt?"

I said, "How do you know I called her—she never returned my call?"

"Well, Linda immediately called John Rockwell [a Times rock critic] to find out what you wanted."

I said, "Then maybe Rockwell turned her off."

She said, "He wouldn't do that. But why did you call her?"

I said, "She once cut 'Little Girl Blue,' and I wanted to know why she didn't do more standards."

She said, "Oh, I know that song. It was written by Little Anthony and the Imperials."

"Exhibit B," I said.

Ed Klein was pale. Marty Arnold laughed. She said, "What's wrong?" I said, "Never mind, honey, it was Rodgers and Hart." She said, "Oh, you mean old, old standards."

With that, the war was won, but the piece was another question. Arnold said it was a snap, nothing but a rewrite, only I knew different. They wanted a new lead, and the way I write, the lead is very nearly everything; I want a piece to be seamless, and so the lead is literal—it leads into the rest of the article, usually connected to the kicker line. In this case, the "lead" ran five pages, it wasn't just a paragraph, it was an idea.

I had more research to do, as well; after all, it was nine months since I'd started and things had happened. Moreover—beyond everything—my back was up, I was mad as hell, I didn't deserve the crap they put me through. Sulk.

For a long time I couldn't look at the piece, which is not to say I stopped thinking about it. To the contrary, it was doing routines on the back of my mind. I knew I had to do it, I knew I would do it, I wanted to do it. I had spent so much time on it, talked to so many people—they'd all ask me about it every time I'd run into them—there was nothing but to do it. Only I didn't do it; I did everything else except do it.

Then one afternoon in April, I thought of an opening line: "Between the rock and the hard disco, the melody began to slip back in." I quick called Marty Arnold, who thought for an eternal second and said, "You got it." That was all I needed to get back to work. Three weeks later the piece was done, and as it turned out it was all for the better, since a real explosion had taken place in music during the interim, making it more timely than ever.

The morning after I turned the piece in, Arnold called to say it was accepted. Of course, Marty said I'd have to make a few fixes, but they'd be minor, not to worry. This time he and Klein would handle the piece, the staff was out of it, except for a line editor. There's a story that goes with it.

As soon as I knew I was definitely going to deliver, I had drinks with Gelb and Rosenthal. And told them about what happened before: the squeal room treatment in all its glory. Abe was upset. It seems that when he hired Klein, he got a commitment from him to have only two editors on a story. In the old days, before Rosenthal took charge of the Sunday magazine, every editor had a hand in the *pieces. This system promoted bureaucratic ass-covering and drove writers crazy; the result was seen every Sunday in stories boggled with inserts that stopped the run more effectively than the old Pittsburgh Steel Curtain.*

Now it was happening again, and as Abe quickly found out, mine was hardly an isolated case. So the order went out to stop it instantly. I took the order to mean—and I'm sure Abe and Arthur meant it to mean—that only two top editors would read the piece until it went over to a line editor. However, all the editors got a look at it, and once again the Young Turks moved in for the kill, this time to Marty Arnold's office.

What did they say? "All emotion," Marty told me. "Same as the last time except you weren't there." Only it didn't last two hours; Arnold simply gaveled them down and told them the piece was accepted. Period, end of sentence.

They didn't quit. The piece would run, sure, but they were determined to soften its thrust by nickel-and-diming me on every point, challenging everything from grammar to fundamentals. To this end, all hands were canvassed for critical notes, including the assistant picture editor!

When I showed up to do those "minor fixes," the line editor had the word processor lit up like a pinball machine. Nobody uses typewriters anymore, just word processors, and when an editor has a question he/she shines a yellow light on the word, sentence, or paragraph. I had so many I yelled "Tilt."

To give you an idea, in the lead sentence, "hard disco" was lit up. Why? Because all disco is hard. But underneath the quibbles there was the ultimate problem. The young editors—ever hovering around the processor, ever buttonholing me in the halls—could not accept that rock-and-roll was sold to them. Everything else might be a hype, even The New York Times, but not "their" music.

It was as if everyone born after World War II had a rock gene waiting to be activated at age nine. I said that to a bunch of them toward the end of the endless week of editing, and I think it took the steam out of them. And about time, because meanwhile they had made one more jump when they heard the piece was going on the cover.

As I've mentioned, editors always lie about the meaning of a cover—when they don't put you on it. They'll say it doesn't matter, it's in the magazine anyway, people don't really care, and so on. Of course, when you're on the cover they call excitedly to say, "Hey, you're on the cover!"

I was determined to get this piece outside; anything else would be a knockdown. The young editors looked at it from the opposite vantage point. Put it on the cover, they said, and it will look as though the Times *is endorsing the story. Exactly!*

Through Arnold and Gelb, I got it worked up to where it was a premier cover candidate. Now it had only to get the okay of Abe Rosenthal. Klein went down to see Abe and gave every argument he could muster against it—apparently to satisfy his young editors, since Ed liked the piece. Abe smiled. So we had the cover.

But what to put on it? Ed Klein asked my opinion. I said either an art cover or something with a few people—Sinatra, Basie, Lena, Bennett. Klein wanted one dominant figure, and he wanted it so much that I knew better than to bother asking why. Once an editor gets a bee like that there's no talking. So I said if it's going to be one, it has to be Frank. Klein said the piece was not about Frank, and so it would be something of a consumer fraud. I said that would be the case whomever we put out there, since the piece wasn't about any one person. But if it was to be one, it had to be Sinatra. Okay, he said. We were on for June 21, Father's Day.

Marty Arnold called a little later and said we were off until June 28. Why? They didn't have a good picture of Frank Sinatra. I got worried. Put it off and we may never make it—who knows what can happen. I told Marty he had ten minutes. If I didn't hear back that we were on for the twenty-first I'd come down to the Times, *but I'd go to the third floor, I'd see Abe and Arthur. And I'd tell them the magazine couldn't find a good picture of the most photographed figure in show business.*

Three minutes later Arnold called back. "You got it."

So this is how the story ends. I had to blackmail Frank Sinatra onto the cover of The New York Times Magazine. *It turned out to be one of the most controversial pieces ever published there.*

BETWEEN THE ROCK and the hard disco, the melody began to slip back in. A piano bar here, a big band there, a touch of Gershwin, a spot of Kern. In gay places and out-of-the-way places. Exuberant, but a little wary, like a gambler with a short bankroll. When was it, two years ago, three?

Well, look at it now.

Big bands swinging coast to coast. Jazz flourishing in the cities, waking up on the college campuses, born again in the high schools. Singers we haven't heard from in years belting out the old hay-makers, crooning the old smoothies. Piano bars, sassy and smart, popping up all over the country. Hotel dances and dancing cheek to cheek at chic parties. Kids jitterbuggin'.

And the theater. Consider the theater.

David Merrick rolls for the sky with fifty-year-old evergreens by Harry Warren and Al Dubin and turns the movie musical *42nd Street* into such a jackpot that to meet the demand—at a $50 top— he moves the show to the biggest available house on Broadway. And then it wins a Tony Award for best musical of the year.

The Duke Ellington songbook is lavishly made into *Sophisticated Ladies*, and it's instant boffo.

Lena Horne, all by herself, is selling out to audiences across all generation lines. She, too, receives a Tony.

Sugar Babies, a tribute to burlesque and the old standards of Jimmy McHugh, is a great big hit.

Ain't Misbehavin', a salute to Fats Waller, has been running for-ever. Ditto *One Mo' Time,* a celebration of black vaudeville. And *A Day in Hollywood . . . ,* featuring songs by the illustrious Richard Whiting, continues to attract large audiences.

New productions of classic musicals score on Broadway and on the road, while others wait in the wings or, like *My Fair Lady,* march majestically through the country on the way to New York.

And disc jockeys are spinning Sinatra, Ella, Bennett, Benny. A New York station switched a year ago to twenty-four hours of "the sounds that swing," and radio stations in big cities across the country are following suit—752 of them are playing big-band music, accord-ing to a list compiled by Ray Anthony, the head of Big Band 80's, an organization of bandleaders across the United States. Booming cot-tage industries are selling packages of old music to former rock sta-tions. And young rock and country singers are beginning to record 1940s tunes.

Suddenly, it appears, the Return of Style is at hand. Songs that swing or carry the torch or conjure up dinner dates and flowers. Wit,

charm, savvy, romance. Music by Rodgers, lyrics by Hart. A blue
piano, a swaggering trumpet. Frank Sinatra serving orange juice for
one. Ella Fitzgerald scatting with the Basie band. Bobby Short vainly
fighting the old ennui. Fred Astaire doing anything at all.

Style.

For nearly three decades the music has been keyed to the young,
one Hot Tuna after another Who. The only wonder was that no rock
group called itself Gresham's Law.

So a question begs about this resurgence. Is it the real thing or
simply a bash? In an effort to find out, I spent the last year talking
with people in all corners of the entertainment world. I asked: Will
the giant record companies continue to ignore the adult audience
that never went for rock-and-roll? Will radio market this audience in
a serious way? Will kids be exposed to the great songwriters and their
troubadours? To Irving Berlin, Cole Porter, Rodgers and Hart,
Schwartz and Dietz, Harold Arlen, E. Y. Harburg, Johnny Mercer,
Jimmy Van Heusen, Sammy Cahn, Burton Lane, Frank Loesser,
Jule Styne? To Tony Bennett, Mabel Mercer, Margaret Whiting,
Mel Tormé, Rosemary Clooney, Betty Carter, George Shearing, Syl-
via Syms, Anita Ellis, Woody Herman?

Will young songwriters be encouraged to write the kind of melody
and sophisticated lyrics that were the signature of 1930s and 40s
music? Can they do it? And what about the singers and musicians,
young and future? Will they tap the treasury and build on it or just
find another way to spell "new wave"?

These questions touched sensitive nerves, drawing contentious,
often fiery responses. Something was happening, and it quickly became clear that more than fortunes were involved. I felt like a cop
who happens on an accident and begins to suspect a crime. What's
everybody so upset about?

Drugs, sex, the breakdown of the family, the Vietnam War,
Watergate—from these words alone one can reconstruct a quarter
century of culture shock. Rock-and-roll music fits neatly into this
pantheon.

Everything is interconnected, of course. But in the past we had
drugs, we had sex, we had divorce, we had wars, we had scandals
and, as lagniappe, we had a Great Depression. What we didn't have
was rock-and-roll or anything else that so clearly and dramatically
delineated a generation gap.

The American popular song has undergone significant change since it came into its own as a native music around the turn of the century. But the changes were gradual, the links strong—melodically, rhythmically, lyrically. People born on the lip of World War II—even during the war—connected naturally with everything from ragtime to pop, from the waltz to the Lindy Hop.

"Bill Bailey" was written in 1902; "Alexander's Ragtime Band" in 1911; "St. Louis Blues" in 1914; "Poor Butterfly" in 1916; "For Me and My Gal" in 1917; "After You've Gone" in 1918; "There'll Be Some Changes Made" in 1920.

Kids were singing these songs and their sophisticated offspring—written by Harold Arlen & Co., played by Benny Goodman & Co., sung by Frank Sinatra & Co.—and dancing to them at high school proms as late as the mid-1950s.

Within a couple of years, the younger brothers and sisters of these kids couldn't hear that music. It was still in the air, but it was Swahili to them. They heard Bill Haley, Little Richard, Elvis Presley, Chuck Berry and, later, the Beatles, the Rolling Stones, the Jefferson Airplane, the Grateful Dead—more recently, The Clash. It didn't seem to matter if a young person was on drugs or not, if he was sexually active or not, if his parents were married or not—or even if he was fighting in Vietnam or participating in an antiwar demonstration—the music was still rock-and-roll.

While not without roots in blues, jazz, and country music, the harsh beat, the often angry—sometimes even violent—lyrics and the attendant electronic revolution served to obliterate the past to all but the cognoscenti. (There was always country-western music, of course. But it has its own history and its own evolution and wasn't really a part of the musical generation gap.)

Most people saw it—and still see it—as a grass-roots revolution, a spontaneous breakaway by teenagers and preteenagers looking for their own kind of music. The radio stations and record companies, according to this view, noticed that a giant generation was developing its own kind of music and seized the opportunity to expand their profits to unheard-of limits.

There were those who disagreed, who strongly believed that it was all a hype—an effort to sell a lower form of music to impressionable adolescents. But as the rock kept rolling, the thought seemed to have disappeared, swept away in the euphoria (or disgust) that marked the Era of the Kids. By the late 1960s, when "Never trust anybody over thirty" became the slogan of a generation, the popular-music business had decided that nobody over thirty existed. Whether grassroots or hype, it was a revolution for fair. In its wake, the great prerock treasury of American song was left for dead.

A few of the once-ubiquitous troubadours survived and even continued to wax rich. Some of the household names made occasional television specials. Others, less well-heeled, kept trucking in secondhand joints around Middle America or Europe, South America, Japan. Many simply gave up.

The superstars kept the songs going and the bucks flowing in Nevada as loss leaders for the big casinos. One wonders what would have happened to them and the music had gambling not been legal there. Bugsy Siegel wrote with a different kind of typewriter, but for inventing Las Vegas there should be a special niche for him in the Songwriters Hall of Fame.

The casinos were always attractive to performers. But, eventually, there were few alternatives. Most big-city nightclubs closed, as a result of a variety of factors: rising costs, crime in the streets, the exodus to suburbia—and the disappearance of the stars from the airwaves and the record stores.

The concert halls and arenas, once the stamping grounds of the swing bands and pop singers, became the occupied territory of rock, aided by hyperpromotion from the record conglomerates and the news media. The smaller rooms, traditionally a home for jazz groups, satellite stars and aspiring young talent, fought valiantly for a time. But with few exceptions they had gone under by the dawn of the 1970s. Rock-and-roll had become rock-and-rule.

A couple of years ago, however, rock found itself in trouble. The attributed reason was disco. When discomania died, rock was back, or so said the record companies. But the record industry is experiencing difficulties. If some of the biggest companies are showing profits again, it's largely a result of belt-tightening. The platinum album is becoming harder to attain, and double platinum is now something of a rarity (platinum is awarded to albums that sell a million units; gold, for half million). And in the first quarter of 1981, singles showed an average 10 percent decrease in sales over 1980, according to figures released by *Record World*, an industry trade publication. Many reasons are heard for this trend: inflation, recession, the end of the baby boom, bootlegging, and home taping of records. But something more fundamental may be at work.

Rock-and-roll is twenty-seven years old, which is a long run for a musical genre—the Swing Era lasted only ten years. And swing was the music of the whole nation, not just the younger set. So perhaps rock simply overstayed its welcome or, if you will, its need.

"There *is* no future in rock-and-roll, only recycled past." So said, of all people, Mick Jagger, lead singer of the Rolling Stones in an interview last summer with *Rolling Stone* magazine.

"Basically," he added, "rock-and-roll isn't protest and never was. It's *not* political. It's only—it promotes interfamilial tension. It *used* to. Now it can't even do that, because fathers don't ever get outraged with the music. . . . So rock-and-roll's *gone*, that's all, gone. . . . You can't rebel against the Rolling Stones or the Beatles."

Mick Jagger may have been overstating, but objective criteria, such as the bottom line and the lack of big-selling new groups, may support that view. Slumping record sales, depleted box-office revenues at rock concerts and a small but discernible radio trend away from rock, particularly on the AM band, are among the indicators that the rock may indeed be nearing the end of its spectacular roll.

Even so, and despite the upsurge of the old tunes, the record moguls refuse to mine the treasury of songs and songsters. There is life—and even sex—after thirty, but there is no melody. So they said and so they say. Can the record companies weather the storm by ignoring America's greatest contribution to popular culture?

A Sunday morning last winter. My fifteen-year-old daughter is having a breakfast party. A dozen kids, fourteen to eighteen. Bagels and cream cheese.

The radio is on, but they're not listening because it's not "their" music. It's Jonathan Schwartz doing what he always does on Sunday morning in New York: spinning Sinatra, Ella, Basie, Bennett, Tormé on WNEW-AM. For the last ten years, there has been Sunday morning and Jonathan Schwartz (until the station switched a year ago to twenty-four hours of music from the golden treasury).

This winter morning, Schwartz is playing a couple of song-and-dance men—two records, back to back, from separate eras. By Bing Crosby and Fred Astaire.

I order the bagel-chompers to be quiet. "Listen in," I say. "Listen and tell me who's singing."

The kids look at my daughter. But I've already warned her to stay mum. They don't know.

None of them knows Bing Crosby. None of them knows Fred Astaire.

I'm not given to apocalyptic notions. But I've got a bunch of very bright kids in my apartment, and, when they don't know the voices of Crosby and Astaire, I can't call it anything less than cultural genocide.

Who's to blame? Not the record industry, not the radio. Just ask them. They say: We give the public what the public wants.

So blame the public. Who's the public? The kids. Adults don't buy records. They say.

Frank Sinatra is the drop-dead king of the world. Translation: When Blue Eyes walks into a room, the room drops dead at his feet. And it's been true for forty years. For this reason alone it was only right that he should have been the one to discomfit the record industry by putting the lie to its claim that adults don't buy records.

There's another reason. Sinatra, despite playing to sellout crowds all over the world, has never been a megamillion record star. He had his share of gold records, but even in his halcyon days, he seldom hit No. 1 on the charts. In the rock age, his sales were generally paltry next to the big stars and not too terrific even against the lesser groups. So the industry liked to point to Sinatra as proof positive that adults don't buy records. As if in tacit agreement, the Chairman of the Board hadn't cut an album since 1975.

Last year, Sinatra made *Trilogy*, a three-disc album celebrating the past, present and future. A few weeks before the release date, I had dinner with him in New York. "You're gonna like this one, baby," he said. But he seemed a little anxious about it, and why not? He'd worked long and hard on the album at considerable cost to himself.

A lot of hopes were riding on him, particularly among singers out of the old school. If Sinatra could hit big with this one, they buzzed, maybe the record companies would wake up to what was going on in the country.

With this talk around and about, I sought out Jerry Wexler, one of the few record executives respected in the various worlds of jazz, swing pop, and rock. A former partner in Atlantic Records, Wexler is a consultant to Warner Communications, one of whose record companies would release *Trilogy*.

I said, "You must be excited about the Sinatra album."

Wexler said, "Would you like to go to the baths with me on it?"

"The baths?" I said. "I keep hearing it'll sell a half million records."

"The Messiah will have to come before we'll sell fifty thousand," Wexler said.

"Then why are you making it?"

Wexler smiled and said, "Frank Sinatra wants a monument."

So?

"So nobody has the nerve to tell him to forget it."

When the album, which retailed at $20.98, hit No. 16 on the chart published in *Billboard,* another of the industry's trade magazines, I called Wexler and asked him when I could meet the Messiah.

"It's a miracle," he said. "And since it's three records, you have to triple the number to understand how great it's doing."

I said, "I assume the record industry is going to reconsider its ways, in view of Sinatra's success."

"Look," Wexler added patiently. "That music is gone, finished. The young people won't go for it. Try and understand; it's a fact of life."

I went into the litany—the live stage, the radio, the Broadway scene, the piano bars, the depressed state of the record industry, the general marketing recognition of "gray power."

Suppose the music industry produced a new Sinatra—a young guy or girl whom kids could identify with—wouldn't he or she be the rage? Or if somebody like Billy Joel or Linda Ronstadt cut an album of old standards?

Wexler answered: "Stop dreaming."

I said, "Okay. Assuming you're right about the kids, what about the adults?"

"Adults don't buy records."

"Who's buying *Trilogy?*"

"We're at an impasse," Jerry Wexler sighed.

A year later. Sinatra's *Trilogy* has sold a half million copies and, being a three-in-one album, it's platinum plus. Moreover, his single "New York, New York" is even being played in discos around the country. And now an item appears in *The New York Times:* Linda Ronstadt is cutting an album of standards, songs made famous by Billie Holiday, Mildred Bailey, Ella Fitzgerald. The producer? Jerry Wexler.

* * *

The Reader's Digest record club is one of the most successful clubs extant. In 1965, the club produced a ten-disc album, *The Great Band Era*, and sold 1.5 million copies at $17 per. It's selling still, at about 36 bucks now, and is one of the most profitable albums ever sold. Throughout the rock age, the Digest has scored brilliantly with thick albums out of the music treasury, marketed to buyers whose average age is about fifty. One probable reason for the success of the mail-order business is that the ambiance of most record stores, with their psychedelic posters, blaring sounds, and clerks who never heard of Peggy Lee, drives adults away.

When I tell William Simon, head of the Digest's recorded music division, that the conglomerates (which own most of the major record companies) are convinced adults don't buy, he chuckles.

"Shhh," he says. "If they didn't operate on that principle, we wouldn't be in business."

Numerous record clubs are "in business" for the same reason, as are those entrepreneurs who coin money selling collections through television commercials.

The record industry has no explanation, nor can it explain why standards sell gold and platinum—even in the record stores. Unless "miracle" is an explanation.

So, Willie Nelson's *Stardust* album, a double-platinum disc containing nothing but evergreens, is a miracle. Barbra Streisand has always been a miracle. Mitch Miller's sing-along albums, which sold 20 million units in the 1960s, were miracles. The Golden-Age-of-Broadway show albums, from *My Fair Lady* to *Fiddler on the Roof,* were miracles. Hit standards by rock stars are miracles. And Frank Sinatra is a transcendent miracle.

Perhaps the record companies are finally beginning to see money in those miracles. In addition to Linda Ronstadt, Carly Simon is currently cutting a record of old torch songs, and Willie Nelson has come back with another hit album called *Somewhere Over the Rainbow.* And the growing audiences of swing bands like the Widespread Depression Orchestra cannot go unnoticed.

The question remains: Are there any young talents who can write songs in the old tradition? Some, like the early Paul McCartney, Paul Simon, Bob Dylan and Billy Joel, have shown that they can do it. "All that's needed is encouragement," says the composer Cy Coleman. "Music is a language. Songwriters are authors who have learned to express themselves musically. The disgrace of the music business is that instead of pushing people to write top quality, they push 'em to write Top Ten."

Tony Bennett and "Sold Out" signs have been synonymous for thirty years. But Bennett hasn't had a record contract with a major company since 1972, when Columbia dropped him—at the same time, he says, that they let go Duke Ellington, Leonard Bernstein and the New York Philharmonic. "We cut the tissue and left the cancer," Coleman says a Columbia executive told him, and if that's not a metaphor for the record industry, what's a metaphor?

Everywhere I went, Tony Bennett's name popped up. His open, easy style—on and offstage—belies a reputation as controversial as any in the music business. Loved and respected by his fellow troubadours, Bennett raises hackles among record executives, who call him a "fanatic" and a "troublemaker."

"I wouldn't sing the garbage they were peddling," Bennett said in a recent interview. "The record companies were forcing artists to take a dive, and I resisted. I thought the only important thing was to be trusted. And I made a stink about it. I still do. Naturally, they don't like me; I consider it a compliment. Remember, we're talking about lawyers, accountants and marketing guys; they're in charge of the business. Imagine an industry run by people who don't know anything about the product?"

Despite his complaints, Bennett is negotiating with a major record company right now. "That shows that things are beginning to change," Bennett said. "But whether I make a deal with them or not, there's a tremendous business injustice going on. The record companies have been saying for years that people like me can't sell, but we keep selling out wherever we go. To me it's twenty times harder to get people out on the town—and at least that much more expensive—than to get them to buy a record. The truth is the industry won't sell the records, not that we can't sell 'em."

Virtually all of the major artists of the prerock age are either without record contracts from major record companies or are released by small independent labels—companies with less financial backing to allow for the advertising and promotion—no matter that they appear around the world to large audiences. Peggy Lee, Mel Tormé, Billy Eckstine, Joe Williams, Frankie Laine and Margaret Whiting—the list is endless. Business injustice aside, we see the results everywhere.

How many people under thirty even know the names of these stars?

"Rock was sold the kids," Bennett said. "The name of the game is peer pressure. It started in 1954. I was there; I saw it happening. The record companies took their cue from the automotive industry: They began a program of planned obsolescence. When I came up, the idea was that when you made a record, it was supposed to last forever. Now it was the opposite. The new god was called 'turnover.' Put one rocker on and then shove in another and another. A hit in the morning, a golden oldie in the afternoon. Quality was out. It took a few years to set in, but it started in 1954."

In retrospect it's easy to see 1954 as a watershed, since that was the year Bill Haley and his Comets made "Rock Around the Clock," the record that launched the era of rock-and-roll. But among college kids, the rage was still Dixieland, and on the campuses the king was Stan Rubin of Princeton. In 1954, Rubin and his Tigertown Five staged the first college jazz concert in the history of Carnegie Hall, and it made page one of *The New York Times*.

Last year, Rubin was back in the *Times* with a big swing band that garnered a rave review from John S. Wilson, a *Times* music critic. Rubin recreates the sounds of Artie Shaw, Benny Goodman, Glenn Miller, Harry James, the Dorseys with verve, joy and muscle.

"Symphonic pop is what it is," Rubin told me one night at Manhattan's Red Blazer Too, where he plays every Wednesday night. "We use the original arrangements, and we don't fool around. Does the Philharmonic Orchestra fool around with the classics? In the same way, we're doing our best to preserve the great American swing classics."

I asked Rubin what happened after his big night at Carnegie back in 1954. He said, "We were hot tickets; we played all the campuses, society parties, the works. We did Grace Kelly's wedding in Monaco. And then the big break: We cut a record for RCA. But just before the release date, they canceled. 'Sorry, kid,' they said. 'We're going with something else; it's going to be the new music.' It was Elvis Presley and 'Heartbreak Hotel.' A perfect title. I didn't know it then, but it was the beginning of the end."

But Rubin is once again making the campus scene. And this spring, he cut four albums (at his own expense) under the rubric *Hall of Fame Hits of the Swing Era*, which he's been marketing through television advertisements. "It's moving well and we've been getting radio play," he says, "but to really make it go, we need a record company behind us."

Rubin is a good example of Tony Bennett's theory that what the music industry needs is a "genius" who will figure out a way to distribute records for independent labels.

The major companies shipped on consignment and shipped big. They gave free promotional records to the stores, which got them vital window space. They promoted to radio programmers and jockeys. They advertised. They sent groups out on tours and helped underwrite club dates. Most important, they "booted" the albums with singles, which are necessary billboards, and these singles went to the radio stations and jukeboxes.

Since the slump set in a couple of years ago, much of this promotion has been cut back. Companies recently stopped shipping on consignment and are now permitting retailers to return only one-fifth of their unsold discs. Thus stores are being discouraged from stocking the quantity of records they did a decade ago, and the young rock groups are getting a taste of what happened to the great stars of earlier days. With radio stations falling back on established rockers, Catch-22 is catching up with the new kids on the block. If you can't get radio time, you can't get the big pressings, and if you can't get pressings, you can't get radio time.

A few independent labels have been successful selling the old music—notably Concord Jazz, whose portfolio includes Rosemary Clooney, Woody Herman, George Shearing, Charlie Byrd, Dave McKenna, Marian McPartland.

Concord barely skims the available market, averaging about ten thousand sales per album. But it is setting an example that may have a serious impact: a small company servicing a discerning audience at a profit. "The main trouble with the record industry," says Bob Golden, Concord's director of artistic development, "is that the corporate structure has become larger than the sales it can generate." The inevitable result is that corporate politics has overtaken productivity, according to Golden, and the solution may well lie in decentralization. "Then record companies could focus on what they do best," he adds, "and on the audience they're trying to reach."

That solution is not necessarily limited to the kind of music that Concord produces. Already new-wave music is having difficulty making it in the mass market: Many of the groups are recording on small independent labels. Though artists generally complain about the failure of the conglomerates to promote them, it may turn out to be a healthy development for them and for music itself. The mass market—with its boom-or-bust philosophy—is certainly not synonymous with quality.

This is not to say that a decentralized record industry would have to be made up entirely of companies as small as Concord. After all, the demand may be much larger than the resources or the ambitions of such labels. Indeed, Steve Lawrence and Eydie Gormé are counting on it. They have recently found some backers to form a new company, Applause, that will press, distribute, and promote their records and those of their contemporaries. And they say that the new label has been negotiating with a roster of artists that includes Vic Damone, Peggy Lee, Sammy Davis, Jr., Shirley Bassey, Frankie Laine, Carmen McRae and Ray Charles.

Over lunch recently, Steve and Eydie explained that all these stars had a ready-made product that needed only to be sold. "The record companies have declared us dead," Lawrence said, "no matter that we pack 'em in all over the world. This new company will sell the records. The artists will produce a finished master record at their own cost—many of them have already cut them—and Applause will do the rest. Unlike the big companies, we'll pay from the first album sold—nobody's going to wait for money."

Though the big record companies haven't yet acknowledged the resurgence of the old sounds, the radio stations are starting to. In New York, the switch from soft rock a year ago at WNEW-AM, the flagship of Metromedia, was the beginning. "We died, and we went to heaven," says Jim Lowe, the station's Mr. Broadway, and the businessmen at Metromedia, smiling at advertising revenues, agree.

Since then, the WNEW format has been picked up by stations across the country, according to Jack Thayer, general manager and vice-president of WNEW, who ticked off the following cities: Los Angeles, San Francisco, Dallas, Minneapolis–St. Paul, Boston, Tampa, Seattle, Charlotte. Tony Bennett agrees: "It's taking off like gangbusters. There are three stations in Miami, Chicago, San Francisco and L.A. playing our music—three in each city."

At the same time, a cottage industry has been flourishing. Three years ago, a man named Al Ham, who was a top executive at Columbia records in the 1950s, began a new business called Music of

Your Life. Using records that he owns, borrows or buys, Ham has taped the popular songs of the last fifty years—excluding rock and country—and leased them to AM rock stations whose ratings were flagging. (The stations pay the royalties.)

When I interviewed Ham last year, he was long on optimism but short on clients. He had thirty stations signed and piles of letters from listeners, but the industry and media brushed it all off as a nostalgia trip, a fad that would soon fade. Today, Ham has more than seventy stations, from Boston to Hawaii.

Ham delivers round-the-clock programming to his clients, who require his service because their libraries are bereft of all but rock. Many former rock stations have programmers and disc jockeys who have never heard of Artie Shaw.

"No matter what I did," Ham said, "it wouldn't work if the advertisers weren't convinced. And now they are; more and more, they're recognizing the purchasing power of people over thirty-five."

The big money is no longer in the hands of teenagers, whose numbers have dropped sharply since the great post–World War II baby boom. By 1990, according to the United States Census Bureau, the teenage population will have declined by about 17 percent, or 4.6 million. Soon, in fact, they will be exceeded by the over-65 population, whose numbers will go up 20 percent by 1990 to almost 30 million.

Companies tied to consumer markets are already adjusting to these trends. But the record industry, which directed its attention almost exclusively to teenagers for two decades, seems incapable of anything more than a retrenchment.

If the radio is now reacting to the new numbers, it will not be the first time it has moved faster than the major record companies. It was the advent of the Top-40 radio format in the early 1950s that helped usher in the rock-and-roll age.

The Top-40 programmers took note of the booming, affluent teenage market, and, together with such disc jockeys as Alan Freed, made a direct hit on the kids. They were aided in no small measure by Broadcast Music Incorporated (BMI), which had been organized in 1940 with the financial backing of radio broadcasters who didn't like paying the rates demanded by the American Society of Composers, Authors and Publishers (ASCAP) for air play of its members' songs.

Since ASCAP, formed in 1914, was the only music licensing group extant, BMI began with an empty portfolio. ASCAP was, for all intents and purposes, the controller of the musical treasury, its membership a virtual Songwriters Hall of Fame.

But BMI had ownership of the radio stations, and it began by signing the young singers and songwriters whom ASCAP had ignored and encouraging disc jockeys to play their stuff and "keep the profits in the family." A 1940 BMI pamphlet distributed to the jockeys was cynically prescient: "The public selects its favorites from the music it hears and does not miss what it does not hear."

The ASCAP–BMI war has been the subject of court battles and would require volumes to do either side justice. Suffice it here to say that great bitterness remains among the older ASCAP songwriters, many of whom blame BMI for the destruction of their music.

Radio was in a panic in the early 1950s over the threat of television and began to zero in on the teenagers with a hard sell that carried a hot message to kids: Rhythm and blues, rock-and-roll, is "your music."

The timing, as it turned out, could not have been better. Kids had more money than ever before, the move to suburbia was in overdrive and family life was in a major state of flux. If parents didn't like it, so much the better. As Mick Jagger said, "The whole rebellion in rock-and-roll was about not being able to make noise at night and not being able to play that rock-and-roll so loud and boogie-woogie and not being able to use the car and all that."

Nearly all of the major record companies resisted, leaving the field to the small, independent labels. By the late 1950s the majors began to come around to "all that," and, by 1964, when the Beatles stormed America, the new world was ready for them. The older artists and their songs had largely disappeared from the record stores and the airwaves. It was a world for the children, by the children and of the children.

Nat Cole worked easy, and those who knew him said it went with his nature. Tony Bennett recalls sitting around a Las Vegas dressing room with Cole one day in 1964, a few months before he died. The King picked up the phone and called his record company, Capitol. A minute later, he slammed down the receiver and walked around the room in a quiet rage.

"What happened?" Bennett asked. Cole didn't answer for what seemed to Bennett like an eternity. Finally, he hissed: "The girl picked up and said, 'Capitol Records, Home of the Beatles.'"

"I never saw him that way," Tony Bennett said. "He just went wild. 'Home of the Beatles,' he kept saying, 'Home of the *Beatles.* What's goin' on, man, what's goin' *on?*'

"What could I say?" Bennett asked. "Nat Cole *made* Capitol. Jeez, it was terrible."

It was no longer the same Capitol, founded twenty years earlier by, among others, the great lyricist Johnny Mercer. Capitol had been bought by Electric and Musical Industries of England (now called English Music Industry, or EMI) in 1955.

On December 30, 1963, the company released its first Beatles single, "I Want to Hold Your Hand," and sold a million copies in less than three weeks. Two months later, the Beatles came to New York amidst fabulous hoopla, appeared on "The Ed Sullivan Show," and their career skyrocketed. A decade before, Elvis Presley had gained national prominence on Tommy Dorsey's television show. In view of what happened to adult music after Presley, and then after the Beatles, it's ironic that both phenomena were showcased on prime-time adult shows.

By April 1964, the Beatles had the five top singles and two top albums in the country. According to "The Book of Golden Discs," the Beatles had fifteen titles on the top one hundred at one time in 1964, and "60 percent of all discs in the U.S.A. airwaves were by the Beatles—the most amazing avalanche in disc history." (Who was the first to knock the Beatles off their No. 1 perch? Louis Armstrong with "Hello Dolly!" in May 1964, when the record companies were so sure adults didn't buy records that David Merrick, the producer of the show, had to pay $3,000 to get Armstrong's single released.)

Some people don't believe that the Beatles avalanche was a natural phenomenon, but rather was one of the greatest hypes in the annals of popular music.

Ahmet Ertegun, founder and head of Atlantic Records, a seminal figure in the industry, says that all talk about promotion and hype is nonsense. This is the general line of the establishment, but nobody puts it straighter than Ertegun.

"There's nothing we can do to make a record sell," Ertegun tells me. "The public creates the demand; we simply fill it. That's all there is to it."

In the early 1950s, Atlantic was a great jazz and pop label, but the big money rolled in later when the company signed the Rolling Stones, Sonny and Cher, and Crosby, Stills, Nash and Young, among many others. These were some of the most heavily promoted groups in history. And here is Ahmet Ertegun telling me that he can't make a record sell.

"The promotion is for their egos," Ertegun asserts. "All these tours, they don't matter, they don't sell records. The people buy the records because they want them."

I tell him what I've been hearing in my travels: that radio decided to go after the kids; that the major record companies joined in; that the catalogues of the top artists were slowly but inexorably withdrawn from the market; that the treasury of American music was denied to the children; that a lower form of music was pushed on the market and, following Gresham's law, drove out the gold; that the record industry was now barring a return of taste.

Ertegun says, "That Great Age you talk about, you know what it was? A claque of publishers and songwriters from Tin Pan Alley and Hollywood, European in origin, feeding a foreign music to the American people."

Cole Porter? European?

"He wrote in the same vein," Ertegun says.

"White Christmas"? "God Bless America"? Foreign?

"Well, consider Irving Berlin's movie *Top Hat.* About a guy at the Savoy in London. The cotton picker in Mississippi, the dockwalloper in New Orleans, the lumberjack in Washington, the gas station attendant in Houston—what did any of them have to do with that? American music was derived from the blues, there was none of that European sophistication to it. It was forced on the country, simple as that. When rhythm and blues came in, rock-and-roll, it hit a nerve; it was what the American people wanted; it was their music."

And, according to Ahmet Ertegun, better music. In *Celebrity Register,* he is quoted as saying: "I think that the rock-and-roll writers are lyrically head and heels above the Gershwins and Cole Porters for poetic content. I think Mick Jagger and Keith Richard write better lyrics than any of those old writers."

Looking at my children, their friends, and the children of my friends, I discovered something odd. In school, they take more or less the same courses we did; they read the same sort of books; they're taught the same foreign languages. After school, they play the same games we did. They even watch the same kinds of television shows—even soap operas—as their grandparents. They cheer and agonize over baseball, football, basketball, hockey, the fights. They go to the movies with us and, when we can afford it, the theater. But the music, no. The one thing we can't do together is listen to music.

Why is that? How come kids read Hemingway, Fitzgerald, Salinger, Twain and even Shakespeare—while the stereo blasts heavy metal? How is it that young adults work at similar jobs as their parents, and, when the bell rings, go to similar bars and drink the same drinks—and then drop quarters in the jukebox and shake to sounds that are unrecognizable, weird, not only to Mom and Dad, but even to their older brothers and sisters?

If the music industry is right, if the rock audience made its own market, wouldn't it be something akin to a mutation, a new breed? Yet, if so, why didn't it happen across the board? Sure, kids are different. "The kids of today" are always different. But it's a difference in degree. They still get married, have babies, go to church; and while it is true that the divorce rate is up, drugs are much more prevalent, sex is looser, it bears reiterating that there were always drugs, divorce, sex, scandal, war. Degrees. The rock is a difference in kind. And it's isolatable. It's the only thing absolutely isolatable in the good old generation gap.

A cultural convulsion of that dimension does not happen by itself. Teenagers and preteenagers do not change the world; they do not create markets; they do not destroy a music treasury.

I have to go along with Cy Coleman, who says of the music business: "They have cut out our entire past and they did it willfully; it was willfully done."

And the future?

Again Cy Coleman. "If they get behind this terrific resurgence of taste, particularly the record industry, which holds the key, we're in for a fabulous new age of music."

Stay tuned.

—*The New York Times Magazine*
June 21, 1981

David Merrick told me, a few days after this one appeared: "I know a hit when I see one. You've got the publishing equivalent of 42nd Street. If you were a box office, they wouldn't be able to get near you."

It didn't go over that way with the younger set, who flooded the editor of the letters page. These outraged music lovers mainly condemned me for my wrongheadedness, but many also attacked the

Times for allowing such rot in its pages. They were, then, as one with the young editors of the magazine. After having it all their way for at least two decades, they couldn't take one piece that went the other way. Shooting fish in the barrel gets to be a nice habit.

The letter writers were mainly quite articulate, they wrote well and with style. More literate by light-years than the music and lyrics they were so passionately defending. I could not have asked for better proof of my main point. If rock hadn't been delivered by one of the most ingenious marketing hypes in modern times—it's "your" music so by definition it can't be hyped—how explain its appeal to so many intelligent people?

The piece drew more mail than any other in the history of the magazine. A highly controversial piece seldom draws more than twenty-five to fifty letters. This one got over four hundred, not counting a hundred sent to me personally. A good 80 percent were negative, which is usual; those who like a story seldom rush to the typewriter. If they know you, they'll call or tell you about it on the street or in bistros.

I can always tell how I'm doing by when the first calls come in. If the phone starts ringing on Saturday night it's a gusher. If early Sunday morning it's terrific, if late Sunday afternoon just good. You're dead if it's quiet until Monday.

This time the phone calls started on the Wednesday before the magazine hit the streets. Only selected insiders get it that early; it's the day it's distributed to the top editors. I never got a ring on Wednesday but now I had a dozen. So I knew what David Merrick was talking about before he told me.

The piece was reprinted in a score of cities around the country and I was interviewed by a baker's dozen radio stations. It hit a nerve, for sure, and I will always be stupefied that it took twenty-seven years for somebody to write it.